CLIFF
more than a
COLLEGE

To Moli
Every blessing

Howard Mellor

G. Howard Mellor

cliff
PUBLISHING

ISBN 1 898362 35 1

British Library Cataloguing in Publication Data.
A catalogue record for this book is available
from the British Library.

**Cliff College Publishing,
Calver, Hope Valley, Derbyshire S32 3XG**

Printed by:

MOORLEY'S Print & Publishing
23 Park Rd., Ilkeston, Derbys DE7 5DA
Tel/Fax: (0115) 932 0643
using text supplied electronically

All royalties and profits from the sale of this book will go to
Cliff College.

Dedication

Arthur and Margaret

who first introduced me

to the Christian faith

and to Cliff College.

CONTENTS

List of Illustrations

Illustrations – People

Foreword

Nobody is better placed than Howard Mellor to write a book on the history of Cliff College. He is the first former student to become its Principal. His days as a student gave him a love for the College in which he later served for ten years in the capacity of Director of Evangelism and then for a further ten years as Principal. For all that time he has breathed its ethos, read its literature and taken to heart its distinctive emphases on evangelism and holiness.

In 1982 when the College celebrated the centenary of the *Joyful News* Training Home and Mission, a work which began first in Bolton, then made its headquarters in Rochdale before finding its ultimate home in Cliff College, three booklets were published about Thomas Champness, Thomas Cook and Samuel Chadwick along with a short history of the College. It is fitting that on the centenary of the work of the *Joyful News* Training Home and Mission being housed in Cliff College, a book of more substance should be written to embrace the whole lifespan of the work from its origins to the present day. *Cliff more than a College* is such a book. It will be the current, standard history of the College.

This book is thoroughly researched. Good use has been made of primary sources and all existing relevant literature. A wealth of material (biographies of former principals, minute books, articles, pamphlets and books written by former members of staff, issues of the *Joyful News* and other historical pieces) has been consulted in order to produce a coherent picture of its development. What we find in this book is a comprehensive survey. Given that all historical writings are interpretative and to some extent must reflect the subjective views of the author, there is no doubt that although Howard Mellor has written with his sympathies wholly for the College, he has striven to be as objective as possible, a task in which he has acquitted himself well.

Some of the contents of this book will be well known to those who know Cliff College and such people will revel in the fresh way the narrative is presented. The narrative includes stories about Champness, Cook and Chadwick and the way in which the College exemplified the slogan, 'Evangelise or Perish' through stirring accounts of the Cliff Trekkers. Those who have visited the College on its great Feast Days will warm to memories of the Cliff Anniversary and the Derwent Convention. Former students will be fascinated to learn of the origins and development of the Cliff Fellowship and will revisit their time at Cliff through the insights given into college life. Many will be challenged again by what is written about the demands of Christian commitment and the teaching of the College on scriptural holiness. Any readers for whom Cliff College is just a name, will catch something of the breadth of vision found in a college which has been able to change with the times, yet retain its emphasis on the central, saving truths of the gospel.

The account of the most recent developments in the College underline this ability to change and these have enabled the College to become a university validated institution offering both undergraduate and postgraduate courses. It could be argued very persuasively that without such changes, Cliff College may have faced the grim prospect of closure, a prospect which unfortunately became a reality for some Bible colleges. This should be remembered by a few Cliff supporters who have felt that Cliff has become 'too academic'. Howard Mellor, as readers of this book will discover, has always believed that in the past the College never gained from its critics the academic respect it deserved. If that is the case, the contents of this book will silence the critics. Amongst those critics were some connexional leaders and the tension between College and Connexion is dealt with sensitively in the book.

Despite all the developments, students who 'missed out' in their earlier education along with some having learning problems, may still find their place at a college which, notwithstanding the seismic changes, remains faithful to its founders' intentions – an exciting story indeed!

Space is given to new insights into areas of Cliff's work which are, perhaps, not so well known. Cliff College has always welcomed students from overseas, but not much is known in popular Cliff lore about the College's practical engagement in overseas missionary enterprise. That omission is remedied as the author traces missionary concern from the time of Chadwick to the present day work in Sierra Leone. Better known is the contribution made by the College to the development and encouragement of women's ministry. Here it is spelt out and Cliff College is seen to be in the vanguard of what has taken centre stage in the life of the church generally over the past half century. Then there is a fascinating account of the honoured place of Cliff in the rise of theological and biblical institutions. Questions are asked, also, about long accepted traditions, for example, 'Was there really a Lazarus?' in relation to the Stacksteads Revival during Chadwick's early ministry there.

Although scholarly, unlike some works of scholarship, this book is very readable and free from overmuch technical jargon. In this, it reflects the teaching tradition of the College, a tradition which is part of the reason why very many students at Cliff have found its courses so helpful.

Cliff more than a College, then, charts the progress of an institution which, in its development to becoming a university validated college, has kept in the flow of the Spirit and, to borrow a phrase used by Youth for Christ, has remained "anchored to the rock and geared to the times".

My own years at Cliff were very happy ones, working with Howard Mellor as a colleague and friend. It has been a pleasure to write this Foreword to his book, which deserves a wide readership. Those who read it will be inspired by what God has wrought over a hundred years in a place which for many has become hallowed ground.

William R Davies

Pentecost 2005

Introduction

The story of Cliff goes back over 120 years and is testimony to visionary leadership, dedicated service and creative evangelism worked out through generations of people. *Cliff more than a College* attempts to tell this intriguing story of a College and a mission all rolled into one and to highlight some of the people whose character and ministry forged its work.

It has not always been an easy history. Lack of finance has dogged the college's life, and it has never really been properly understood by its parent denomination, Methodism. It has survived because of its appeal to the people of the church in and beyond Methodism. They have been its chief support, attending the great public occasions, and being generous with their prayers and finance. Out of all of this has come a College with a fine history and a great future.

Cliff developed, from its inception, a number of key elements which I have referred to as the 'charisms' of the College. That is, the themes which form its essential nature, and they are found both in the work of the *Joyful News* Mission and at Cliff College. These are evangelism, holiness, learning, a disciplined community life and praxis. The College was born in the white-hot heat of the evangelism that Champness, Cook and Chadwick were engaged in. They taught the importance of Christian holiness for all Christian people and especially those in ministry. They were keen to teach and train people, though the learning element was of course strengthened when the mission became a college. It might be argued that the learning process only matured with the link to the University of Sheffield and the development of both undergraduate and postgraduate courses. The nature of community life today is different, of course, from the strictures of nineteenth and early twentieth century life but there remains the same commitment to hold together personal engagement with the community, regular table fellowship, prayer meetings and worship. All this is held together by praxis - the importance of putting into action the learning of the lecture room and seminar discussion. This is embodied in a mission team context which provides encouragement for students to do that which they assume they cannot, and to discover new gifts and extend their ministry. It has always been a mentoring process though that kind of language is relatively new. So these form the 'charisms' of the College.

Cliff more than a College traces the history of the College back to two streams of influence bound up in the ministry of two remarkable couples. The first stream was the desire by the congregational layman James Hilton Hulme and his wife Anne Elizabeth, to establish a college at Cliff House. He expanded the buildings but it was left to others to benefit from them. The second and most important stream was the founding of the *Joyful News* newspaper by Thomas and Eliza Champness who presided over the development of the Joyful News Mission for twenty years. It was as Champness laid down the responsibility of leadership, that Thomas Cook was appointed to lead the work and Hulme Cliff College became available.

In March 1904 the first students came to Cliff College and the work has grown and developed over an eventful one hundred years. It has been a real privilege to write this book to mark the centenary of the

College, which was celebrated on 3 March 2004. I feel all my life has been bound up with Cliff and to offer this explanation of its life and history has been a great pleasure.

I trust you will enjoy reading it.

Grace and Peace to you.

Howard Mellor

Acknowledgements

I wish to express my thankfulness to Howard Belben who accepted me as a student at Cliff College in 1967 and suggested I should candidate for the ministry; to the Methodist Home Mission Division which appointed me to be the first Director of Evangelism joining the staff in 1983; for the immense privilege of serving with a great team of evangelists and then to be appointed Principal and to lead the College through ten creative years.

I am grateful also to the staff of the College whose counsel and colleagueship I have always valued; especially Dr Bill Davies who has written the foreword and whose guidance in those early years was crucial, and to Martyn Atkins, for whom I have the utmost admiration as he presently leads the College. To those friends who supported Rosie and myself with our growing family and helped us cope with life at the centre, I am also grateful.

I am grateful to many people who have helped assemble this book: to Clive Taylor and Russ Houghton who ferreted in the archives to bring order from chaotic bundles; to those who read the script and offered comments, Shirley Alexander, Brian Hoare and Arthur Mellor. They saved me from countless errors and omissions, though I must be held responsible for any blemishes which remain. To John Moorley and his staff whose careful and detailed work has been crucial in preparing this illustrated book. To Mason Porter for his generosity which has enabled us to publish this book. To my Rosie, Beth, Lydia and Tom who encouraged and supported me. I am grateful to God for the opportunity to have served the College for twenty-one years and offer this book as testimony to its ministry in the hope that it will be an inspiration to others.

CHAPTER 1

Hulme Cliff College

L ittle did Thomas Gardom know when he bought the strip of enclosed land called 'the Cliff' in 1781, for just under twenty-eight pounds, that it would become internationally respected as a place of training and evangelism, set among the rugged hills of Derbyshire, in the scenic Hope Valley, at a point where the old Roman road from Chesterfield to Manchester crosses the River Derwent stand the villages of Curbar and Calver.

It was here, at the edge of these villages, that on 16 August 1781 Thomas bought land known as 'The Cliff'.[1] He continued to purchase land in the area and in 1790 built Cliff House. 'On a piece of freehold property in Curbar there stood a large, square, stone house, with kitchens and farm buildings built out at the side, and surrounded by 22 acres of grass land, with very few trees and only a cart track from the house to the main road.'[2]

Thomas was the eldest son of the mill owner, John Gardom who, following the success of Richard Arkwright in Cromford, had established a cotton mill by the free flowing River Derwent. In the years 1785-86, he built the original water powered mill with such care that the water wheels were considered 'the best constructed in the country'. As a result the cotton mill was able to function well beyond

1

the time that other water-powered mills had fallen into disrepair. Despite a fire in the original mill and difficulties of trade, the reconstructed mill and its wheelhouse survive today.[3] Thomas built Cliff House with similar care and lived there until his death.[4] He was buried at St Ann's Church, Baslow, and in the north aisle there is a memorial tablet which reads: 'Thomas Gardom, Cliff House, Gent. 11th January 1817, 68 years. Mary, 27th April 1832, 75 years.'

Cliff House 1790

Cliff House was put up for sale by auction during the summer of 1835, and purchased by James Hilton Hulme, a solicitor from Salford. The notice for the sale of the property ran as follows:

> Very desirable Investment in a valuable Freehold Property situated in one of the most beautiful parts of the county of Derby. By Morris and Goodier at the house of Mrs Greaves, the Rutland Arms Inn, in Bakewell, on Wednesday, 21st of August next, at four o'clock in the afternoon (unless previously disposed of by private contract, of which due notice will be given).

> An Estate in the County of Derby, most delightfully and pleasantly situated, called Cliff House, and comprising a substantial and well built Family Mansion of stone, and about 21 acres of excellent land, which surrounds the house in the form of a ring fence. The house and outbuildings are of the following description:
> House – First Floor – large dining room and drawing room, very commodious kitchen and back pantry, closet under the stairs, and a mangling room, which latter may be converted into a good sitting room. Second Floor – Four excellent bedrooms, one dressing room, china closet, servantman's bedroom over pantry, and large store room over kitchen. Third Floor – three good bedrooms. N.B. – There are excellent cellars and dairy.

> Outbuildings – One three and one four-stalled stable with lofts over them, one cowhouse with loft barn, saddlehouse, and coachhouse with rooms above them. Archway and sheds for carts, with other commodious buildings. Cliff House is 33 miles from Derby, 9 from Chesterfield, 13 from Sheffield, Buxton and Matlock, 5 from Bakewell, and 34 from Manchester, to any of which towns the roads are direct, and kept in excellent travelling condition. To gentlemen having families, and desirous of spending whole or part of their time in the country, Cliff House forms one of the most eligible residences in the county. The air is pure, remarkably dry and calculated for health; the scenery is beautifully romantic and diversified. A range of lofty rocks, forming the boundary of the extensive east moors, is

situated about a mile and a half on the east, and serves to shelter the house from the north-east winds. The river Derwent is seen winding its course through the valley on the western side, and is overhung by a rich and extensive wood on the rising hill. The front of the house has a southern aspect which is very extensive, having the beautiful grounds of Chatsworth with a view of the ducal palace from the upper rooms.

A Coach from Manchester to Nottingham and Newark passes immediately at the foot of the hill on which the house stands, and from Bakewell opportunities of travelling to almost all parts of the Kingdom are afforded by London, Manchester and other coaches.[5]

It would appear that Hulme made a pre-emptory offer,[6] and that he purchased Cliff House for £2,675 7s 0d. The earliest account of the history of the College indicates wrongly that 'Concerning the lady who owned this property, rumour is rife as to her many and various

eccentricities…she was joined in Holy Matrimony with Mr Hulme … but shortly afterwards she died, and thus the property passed into his hands.'[8]

Little is known of James Hulme. He was born to Thomas and Kitty Hulme and baptised on 28 September 1798 at St Ann's Parish Church, Manchester (still in existence and known as 'The Little Gem'). He studied law and became registered as an attorney. On 12 January 1825 he married Esther Jackson in Manchester, although it is not clear how long this marriage lasted.

James Hilton Hulme, Esq.

The Trade Directories for Manchester list James Hilton Hulme in 1828 as 'attorney, 29 or 30 Princess St; h. (home), Woodland Terrace, Broughton'. In 1832 he is listed more simply as 'attorney, house 29 Crescent, Salford'. The

1843 entry suggests a person of stature in his profession and of considerable means, 'attorney, clerk to the magistrates and commissioner for taking affidavits in the Irish Law Courts, 10 Back Piccadilly and 1 Bexley St., Salford; residences 125 Water St. and Cliff House near Bakewell, Derbyshire.' Clearly he was an able, successful person with a flourishing business, for he had two office addresses and a residence in Salford, in addition to Cliff House.[9]

In the census returns of 1851 for Cliff House, James Hilton Hulme is described as the 'head of family', aged 52, and his wife Anne Elizabeth, is aged 25, 'a beautiful and gifted lady'.[10] With her was Sarah Ellen Horton her sister (aged 23).[11] Sarah Chadwick described

Carpenter's shop etc site of the present Champness Wing

5

Hulme as 'A gentleman of stately appearance ... a sturdy non-conformist.'[12] His nephew Robert Forman Horton is reported as saying, 'My Uncle was a man of ideas; and upon his ideas he lavished his money. It is no disrespect to those who have continued his work, to say nothing which they have erected since, can equal in beauty the pigsties erected by Mr Hulme – pigsties in which no pig was ever placed, but in which I and other children used to play to our hearts content.'[13]

Farm Buildings from the Orchard (Top) Students preparing a roadway, now alongside Cliff Hall.

Hulme added to the house considerably, extending it to include rooms which became a lecture room and Principal's study when the house became a college. He made stables into offices and servants' quarters, and built or remodelled a two storey building to include a carpenter's shop, a smithy and on the first floor above, accommodation for staff and visitors. On the east side of Cliff Lane he built a Chapel for public worship, Sunday school and Bible classes.

Years later, recalling her childhood memories of Cliff, Geraldine Guinness, who married Hudson Taylor's son Howard,[14] described the property as containing 'the farm, the house, the extensive outbuildings and the little chapel'.[15] She also offers a charming recollection of the farm: 'The farmyard was entrancing, not only did the cows come for milking, morning and evening, but there were unused mushroom houses, calves-houses and unused pig-sties, as well as store rooms for the fruit and vegetables, built into a curious rambling structure at various levels, connected by winding steps, and forming the most attractive suites of little apartments to play in.'[16]

Having also furnished the house and equipped it, quite regardless of expense, Hulme proceeded to make it a centre of religious influence for the neighbourhood, and eventually for a wider area. He was a committee member of 'Calver and Stoney Middleton Mutual Improvement Society'.[17] In one of the published lectures entitled 'The Mind', James Wills of Eyam refers to the objectives of the Society. The stated assumption was that God gave people faculties of thought and intelligence which need to be exercised and improved. Wills concludes, 'Indeed we have a responsibility to do so and societies which enable that are to be encouraged and supported – they will bring self respect, self reliance, diligence and perseverance'.[18]

Out of a barn James constructed a chapel 'expending upon it much

care and money'.[19] The chapel was known as Cliff Chapel, Curbar, and it was registered with the Congregational Union of England and Wales on 13 October 1852. There is still in existence a splendid leather bound minute book especially made for the chapel, in which no minutes are recorded. The handwritten min-

Hulme's Congregational Chapel

utes of early meetings exist only on scraps of paper, and those from 1896 to 1901 are to be found in an ordinary notebook.[20]

The preacher at the opening services was Joseph Andrew, a Congregationalist lay preacher. He was presented on that occasion with a double volume book. It is inscribed in Hulme's hand: 'Presented by Mr & Mrs James Hilton Hulme, to Mr Joseph Andrew. In grateful remembrance of his kind ministrations, at the opening services of Cliff Chapel, Curbar, Derbyshire. October 1852.' The book is an interesting example of the evangelical attempt to show the efficacy of the scriptures in the face of scientific advance and the theological liberalism of the day. It contains in the one volume, *The Bible not of Man* by Gardener Spring and *The Religion of the Bible* by Thomas H. Skinner.[21]

The entry in the *Minutes* of the Congregational Union Home Missionary Society reveals Hulme's desire to have his Chapel formally adopted:

Cliff Chapel near Baslow, Derbyshire
A letter from Mr J.H. Hulme of Cliff House was read urging the claims of the district in which he resides, and where he has been chiefly the means of erecting a chapel. The Secretary stated that he had sent a schedule for answers and referred Mr Hulme to the Committee of the Derbyshire Association for a testimony and the amount of their co-operation, but as yet no decision had yet been communicated. The locality is not distant from Tydeswell and Bakewell, and the Committee deferred any determination till the judgement of the association committee be obtained.[22]

There is no further reference in the *Minutes* to Hulme, or Cliff Chapel. It would appear that the Chapel was opened before being registered, though the *Year Book* for 1853 does refer to the Chapel indicating it was established by J.H. Hulme 'at own expense'.[23]

Baptisms at Cliff Chapel were regular events. The first were those of Harriet Richardson and Benjamin Ellis on 12 October 1853, with the last recorded on 15 August 1875. There are, with the minute book, details of fifteen weddings at the chapel between 1858 and 1869. The church was registered, it seems, at the point of opening but had to be re-registered on 1 July 1857 because, as a note in the handwriting of James Hulme intriguingly says, 'The chapel was duly certified and opened on the 13th Oct 1852. Any document given by the late Mr Barker the Superintendent Registrar is mislaid, or in the possession of a person now in dementia.'[24] One can only begin to imagine what James Hulme as Recorder of Salford thought about such mismanagement!

There is the copy of a letter dated 14 July 1857 from 'JHH' (Hulme) to the Registrar in Bakewell, Mr Francis Roe, in which he made it quite clear that he wanted him to deal with the matter 'forthwith'. The letter is addressed as from the 'Town Hall, Salford', and requests his help by 'acknowledging the receipt of this communication addressed to me here where I am attending as Registrar the Sittings of the Court of ------- for the H----- of Salford and to intimate how soon we may expect to be in a position to solemnise marriages in the Chapel at Curbar.'[25] He was clearly making the unfortunate Mr Roe aware of his important legal role. Roe moved quickly to rectify the mistake or oversight of his predecessor, for the certificate was issued on the 17 July, 'posted' the following day and inserted in the *Derby and Chesterfield Reporter* (Friday 24 July, page 1 and column 3) and the *London Gazette* (Tuesday 28 July, page 2612 and column 1). Notices were posted in Bakewell, Calver and Pilsley.

Whilst there are few *Minutes* of the Chapel meetings, a note recorded on paper in 1866, in Hulme's handwriting, would suggest that the Chapel did appoint a Pastor. On 29 May of that year, 'It was resolved that the Rev Robert Jackson the recently ordained Pastor should as early as practicable pay a pastoral visit to each member of the Church'. The note, which is very difficult to read in places because of Hulme's tiny handwriting, suggests this is the first occasion that Jackson visited the members and that he had recently been appointed. 'The Deacons of the Church were requested to accompany the Pastor whenever he requires them'.[26] Hulme signed himself as 'Senior Deacon', expressing concern that visits should be made in particular 'to such of the members whose attendance on Sabbath Days, Church Meetings and week day services has become very unsatisfactory'.[27]

The Congregational Union had in 1864 received a report which promoted the employment of lay evangelists and it had published a report.[28] It is clear that the Congregationalists were actively

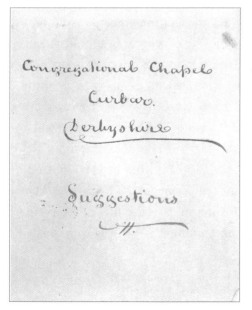

encouraging local churches to follow this pattern, which it had found to be beneficial. It is in this context that Hulme appointed Mr Jackson as pastor but with a clear mandate for evangelistic ministry. In so doing he was following the suggestion of his denomination.

Another interesting handwritten document exists which is simply entitled, *Congregational Chapel Curbar, Derbyshire, Suggestions*. It is in Hulme's handwriting but is more legible than the minute of 1866 and possibly dates from the beginnings of the Congregational Chapel in 1853. The 'Suggestions' are a series of statements and questions. The first is phrased much like a statement of evident fact with which any member of the Chapel would concur. 'On the <u>Lord's Day</u>. Let all aim conscientiously and perseveringly to avoid known hindrances to assembling with one accord at the services conducted at the chapel and especially meeting at the Lord's Table.'[29] There are questions posed for the congregation, 'Could an early morning prayer meeting be held – at what hour – and how long should it continue?'[30] There are then suggestions for the timing of services, the weekday meetings and various groups within the church such as Choir, Chapel Keeper, Male and Female Tract Distributors, then of Officers of the Chapel, who along with the Treasurer and Secretary, included 'Superintendent of Visitors to the Sick'. In the midst of the text are paragraphs which set out Hulme's view of Christian discipleship and churchmanship:

> The members of the Church resident in the respective Villages, will of course, make a point of being always present to encourage and assist others from a distance, as often as circumstances will admit. A working plan of the various services will be prepared, as soon as the agency to work such services can be ascertained. Punctuality in attending to appointments must be strictly observed and each individual undertake to provide a proper substitute in case of unavoidable absence.

> It is recommended that every deviation from the order and engagements stated on the Plan be invariably recorded, so as to check irregularity as much as possible – The necessary communications for this purpose to be made to the General Secretary.

> Saturday Evening - Let each Head of a Household establish a Domestic Prayer Meeting in his own house and let every member of the Church hold this evening sacred to individual examination and preparation for the services of the Sanctuary on the ensuing Day. Any Family or individual without a Bible or wishing to possess a superior copy of the Holy Scriptures may be assisted in procuring the same by intimating their desire to any of the Deacons of the Chapel.

The Bible Society's recent editions are remarkably cheap and superior. The Deacons will also be glad to furnish copies of the Hymn Book used in celebrating Divine Worship.

Later in the list of *Suggestions* are the following statements:

Mr and Mrs Hulme will endeavour when at Cliff House, to attend as many of the Services enumerated as they possibly can and will most cordially co-operate with the Church and Congregation in their efforts to do good.

It is considered that there is not a member of the Church who may not allow his or her name to be enrolled in the lists for visiting the sick, and Tract Distribution. Should any say, "I am not able to minister to the sick" it may be enquired – "Did you ever try?" – You know not what you can do until you try. At any rate you are able to see that the sick are not neglected, and make it your business to ask a person to visit them. There is not a single individual amongst us who may not render himself or herself useful in some form and become at least instrumental in alleviating both the temporal and spiritual necessities of others. "She hath done what she could". Which of us can hope for the like commendation from the great Searcher of Hearts?

In adopting the system of exchanging Tracts, those little messengers of mercy furnish precious opportunities of communicating consolation and encouragement to the distressed and discouraged, and both young and old may thus be blessed and made blessings.

Never let us forget the inspired declaration "he that watereth shall be watered also himself", and the Saviour's own words, "Whosoever shall give a cup of water to drink in my name, because you belong to Christ, verily I say unto you, he shall not lose his reward". We must never lose sight of the test of our discipleship to Christ. "By this shall all men know you are my disciples, if ye have love one to another". This was so manifest in the first days of Christianity that its enemies were constrained to say, "See how these Christians love one another" and we must not retrograde in these latter times, but advance and so much the more as we see "the Day" approaching – that Great Day – for which all other days were made.

Let it be our unceasing, exalted aim, to become in a pre-eminent degree, a living working Church for the Glory of Christ, each member cheerfully and assiduously performing not only the part assigned to him and her respectively, with increasing zeal, but, from time to time, with holy integrity, putting forth new and varied efforts and be ever devising liberal things so as to win souls to Jesus and attract our fellow creatures at large as we come into contact with them, to that glorious Centre, the Cross of Christ. The only true and abiding peace and rest for the soul in time and eternity.

We have often prayed that from Curbar chapel the glorious sound of Christ's Gospel might go forth, attracting all around us. Let us reiterate these prayers with redoubled zeal and energy and supplicate with holy importunity for enlarged usefulness in our individual and collective capacity for realizing our share in the Saviour's own direction – "Go ye into all the World and preach the Gospel to every creature". Yes, we cannot tell where our efforts end, like the pebble cast into the lake, one wave succeeds another in enlarged measure, till the whole is covered. So let each begin with heart and life dedication to God, and who shall limit the influence for good of the Curbar Church and its members? And we are to cheer our hearts with his own assurance, "Lo I am with you always, even unto the end of the world. Amen.[31]

It is clear that Hulme had a keen interest in the spiritual renewal of those people who lived in the immediate area of Cliff House. He was a deeply devout man who sought to use his considerable resources for missionary endeavour. His care of the Cliff Chapel, his involvement in the local Mutual Improvement Society and the establishment of the Primitive Methodist Chapel in Calver,[32] is typical of a Victorian Nonconformist philanthropist. He not only ensured the Chapel was supplied with lay preachers but was also interested in the education

Mr Hulme's Bible Class

Mrs Hulme's Bible Class

of local children and had started some form of schooling, based at least around a Sunday School and Bible Class. 'He always hoped that in some way or another the place would become a blessing in the neighbour-hood, and he tried, with a view to its future, to enlist in its favour the sympathy of his friends at a distance. He would have put the chapel and school in Trust, but that forming part of the outbuildings of the estate it could not be dealt with separately.'[33] There is a note attached to the original Conveyance document which is intended to identify the names of fields, 'I have promised to appropriate and to the erection thereon of a Congregational Chapel, Schools, Minister's House, for which purposes the same is forthwith to be conveyed by me to Trustees'.[34] It is signed and dated 8 November 1860 but the fields and the acreage are not identified and the trusteeship was not formed. Nevertheless this shows the intention Hulme had for the use of the property and the hope he had for an educational establishment as well as a church. When the property was being placed in Trust, after his death, by his wife Anne Elizabeth

Hulme, the conveyance document of 1871 referred to the 'building now used as a Congregational Chapel and School House'.[35]

Both James and Anne were determined evangelicals as the relationship between Anne Elizabeth Hulme and her gifted nephew, the scholar Robert Forman Horton, reveals. He regularly visited Cliff House as a child[36] and according to Fiddian Moulton, it was here that Horton preached his first sermons.[37] Mrs Hulme was a 'cover to cover' believer, to whom every comma in the Bible was inspired, and she was deeply distressed at all she heard about her nephew's heretical views. She repeatedly asked him to withdraw his books, denouncing him as a Unitarian, and said that her bad sight was 'a judgement on her for not resisting his teaching previously.'[38] She was a fierce critic of his liberal scholarship, and even though she 'never read her nephew's books on the Bible ... that did not prevent her from violently assailing them.'[39] She was known in the family as 'Madam' and described as a woman of 'queenly presence, (who) had a great affection for her nephew'.[40] Clearly they had a good relationship though she disapproved of his theology. Nevertheless Horton was a trustee of Hulme Cliff College and interested in its work until its sale. Intriguingly he came to preach at Cliff College during the Whitsuntide meetings of 1913 at the invitation of Samuel Chadwick.[41]

James Hulme is portrayed in all his dealings at Cliff as a charming and gracious man. A contrasting insight into the character of Hulme comes from correspondence between Hulme and fellow trustees of the Lancashire Independent College in the years 1864-1866. The Lancashire Independent College had been founded in 1816 as the Blackburn Academy to train ministers and missionaries, and in 1843 had moved to Manchester.[42] James Hulme was one of the surviving trustees of the 1843 Trust Deed and a dispute arose about the renewal

Frontice piece of Bible Handbook given by James Hulme
to Ephraim Slinn 18th March 1864

of that Deed lasting many years. The details of the dispute are held in the John Rylands Library and among the papers is a forty-three page document of the *Case for the Opinion of Counsel* by a Richard Hilditch.

Many of the original letters were sent by Hulme, but his writing is difficult to analyse, and so it was transcribed at that time by a solicitor's clerk. At the heart of the dispute, which was actually about the instalment of new Trustees, was a disagreement about the way decisions were made and Hulme's outrage that the Trustees should make fundamental decisions without his agreement and signature.[43] Hulme did not like the way a meeting was called without sufficient notice being given, and at a time it was known that he could not attend. He objected to new solicitors who had been appointed because they were Unitarians[44], and thereafter Hulme objected to every new decision that was proposed. The dispute became acrimonious, when in November 1864, Hulme claimed members of the Trust had made statements against his character and he insisted that his accuser be named.[45] Leading Congregationalists, the most eminent being the Rev John Kelly of Liverpool,[46] tried to intervene and bring reconciliation but Hulme would have no compromise.[47] A year later, on 10 November 1865, the Trustees in a letter to Hulme made it clear that they had had enough[48] and the response to Counsel's opinion being sought concludes with:

> Mr Hulme appears to stand alone, and a single trustee refusing without sufficient reason to concur in the proper action of his co-trustees will not be supported by a Court of Equity. Doubtless it would be well to have his execution of the deed, but his non execution has no effect upon the appointment of Trustees. It only leaves to him his share of the legal estate & eventually that will prove of no material importance.[49]

Nevertheless Hulme remained in contact with the Chairman of the College Committee, the Rev W. Gwyther, who conducted his funeral service. There are few references to J.H. Hulme in the Congregational records of the time.[50] The most notable comes in a description of the setting up of the early Ministers' Retirement Fund for which the secretaries are listed as Mr J.H. Hulme and the Rev D.T. Carnson of Preston. Hulme was the lay secretary from 1842 to his death.[51] Despite the dispute about the Lancashire College he does not seem to have severed links with the Congregational Union.

It may be, however, that the idea of establishing a College came to Hulme as a result of this dispute with the trustees. 'Soon he became possessed of a very strong desire to make the house a centre for training men for missionary work abroad.'[52] In the letters referring to the pastoral care of the members of the Congregational Chapel dated May 1866, there is no mention of student help or activity. Therefore it is appropriate to conclude that the idea for a College at Cliff arose between the end of the dispute in 1866 and his death in 1869.

Cliff House as extended by Hulme

The plan for Cliff to be a College occurred to Hulme as he was considering what should eventually become of Cliff House: 'While driving home from Bakewell one day, he said to his wife, "I have been thinking how I should like Cliff to be the Lord's when we have done with it;" and the feeling met with a ready response from her … His mind fixed itself with great delight at last, on the project of training lay agents for home and foreign mission work. "I have it right now! I am sure I am right now!" he said, when first naming this scheme to his wife. Shortly afterwards he sent out a circular, in which he mentioned the work he desired to see carried on at Cliff. This circular subsequently formed the foundation of the Deed under which the place is now held.'[53] D.W. Lambert follows Fiddian

Moulton in his history of Cliff indicating that 'both Mr and Mrs Hulme felt that they ought to use it (Cliff House) in some way or other for the Lord's work, and they purposed using it as an institution for the training of industrial Missionaries – men who should go into foreign countries with the love of human souls in their hearts, and with useful handicrafts at their fingertips.'[54]

Before this idea came to fruition, Hulme died suddenly at Cliff House. Anne Elizabeth Hulme indicated later, in a letter to Henry Gratton Guinness, that not long after the decision about the establishment of a College, 'he was suddenly taken ill … After my return from cottage visiting one afternoon, having left him quite well when I went out, I found him sitting in his easy-chair shivering. I was alarmed and wanted to send for the doctor, which, however, he declined … A few minutes afterwards he went upstairs, became worse, and very soon was delirious.'[55] Hulme died the following day; 'a little before five, he was absent from the body – present with the Lord.'[56] He died on 5 November 1869, aged 71, and was buried at the Harpurhey Cemetery, Manchester.[57]

In his will, James Hilton Hulme bequeathed all his personal estate to 'my dear wife Anne Elizabeth Hulme'. The estates of which he was a trustee were handed over to Frederick James Forman, a hop merchant in Derby, and William Foyster, a 'gentleman' of the city of Manchester. William Foyster was in fact a solicitor and partner in the firm of Hulme, Foyster and Foyster of Manchester. The last will and testament is dated 3 November 1869, two days before his death, with 'his mark' beside his name. A later article in the *Leeds Mission News* of 1904, reported that:

> The house he left to his widow, expressing the hope that at once her former husband's intentions might be carried out. A Trust was formed, and the house became a Training College for Foreign

Missionaries. It so happened that Dr Grattan Guinness, whilst visiting Sheffield, heard that the College might be acquired as a training institute in connection with his own work in East London. It passed into his tenancy, and during many years was used as the country training school of the Harley Street Institute.[58]

James and Anne Elizabeth had clearly lived comfortably with servants and the 1871 census lists Mrs Hulme as 'head of house' with three servants, one of whom is noted as a farmer. The wealth that James left his widow was used by her to engage in a variety of Christian work; she was involved in the missions of D.L. Moody, and in the distribution of the scriptures. Anne Elizabeth Hulme, knowing her husband's mind, determined that she would carry out his intention to form a college. 'The place was Mrs Hulme's absolutely, but she longed not only that it should be devoted to the good work as suggested, but that it should be so *during her life,* so that she might *see* the fulfilment of a desire so dear to her husband's heart. She consequently paid off a considerable mortgage which existed on the property, and very shortly after Mr Hulme's death executed a Deed of Trust, conveying it to Samuel Morley, Esq., M.P., John Crossley, Esq., M.P., and Joshua Wilson, Esq., late of Tonbridge Wells, as trustees, to see established and carried on there, an Institution for the training of "preachers, teachers, missionaries, or missionary workers, in any department, whether at home or abroad, of Christian service or philanthropy."'[59]

The title page of the conveyance establishing the trust

On 4 September 1871, Anne Elizabeth Hulme conveyed the land, which is known as the 'Curbar Estate' to a Trust, of which she remained a Trustee.[60] The purpose of the Trust was as follows:

> Towards the support of an institution to be called the 'Hulme Cliff College' and to have for its general or fundamental object or purpose the instruction or training, according to the principles and tenets of the Evangelical or non-established Christian Churches of Great Britain and

21

Ireland of pious persons (whether youths or adults) desirous from religious motives and believed to be competent or fit mentally and spiritually to become after due instruction or training lay or unordained preachers or teachers or missionaries or missionary workers in any department, whether at home or abroad, of Christian service or Christian philanthropy and such instruction or training to comprise the following subjects: the knowledge and correct use of the English language, the history and theology of the Old and New Testaments, the doctrinal faith of the Evangelical Free Churches of Great Britain as set forth in the doctrinal basis of the Evangelical Alliance and in the schedule herein, the history of missions, the art of effective preaching, instruction or training in or for any special evangelistic or philanthropic work and the daily exercise of a handycraft or of agricultural labourer or work and such. The schedule referred to above is as follows:

1   The Divine inspiration, authority and sufficiency of the Holy Scriptures.

2   The right and duty of private judgement in the interpretation of the Holy Scriptures.

3   The unity of the Godhead and the Trinity of persons therein.

4   The utter depravity of Human Nature in consequence of the fall.

5   The incarnation of the Son of God, His work of atonement for Sinners of mankind and his Mediatorial intercession and reign.

6   The justification of the Sinner by faith alone in our Lord and Saviour Jesus Christ.

7   The work of the Holy Spirit in the conversion and sanctification of the Sinner.

8   The immortality of the Soul, the resurrection of the body, the judgement of the World by our Lord Jesus Christ, with the eternal blessedness of the Righteous and the eternal punishment of the wicked.

9   The Divine institution of the Christian Ministry and the obligation and perpetuity of the ordinances of Baptism and the Lord's Supper.[61]

Mrs Hulme took advice from people running similar establishments and 'She brought over to Cliff House a German gentleman who had some expert knowledge of the kind of training

institution Mr Hulme had purposed to establish, and the whole matter was carefully considered.'[62] Her conclusion, with others who had been consulted, was that she was not able alone to establish at Cliff House the kind of institution that had been thought of, 'the idea having been to train men for indust-

Cliff House 1869   rial missionary work.'[63]

It was at this point that Anne Elizabeth was introduced to a young flamboyant preacher of noble Irish descent, Henry Grattan Guinness. It is clear from Guinness's account that he visited Cliff House sometime in the early 1870s.[64] When Anne visited their work in East London, at Harley House in Bow, 'and after seeing and hearing all about our work there she exclaimed, "Why, this is the very thing my late dear husband desired to see at Cliff!" and from that time she entertained a strong desire that we should undertake the establishment and management of the work to be carried on there.'[65] The date of her visit is uncertain but must have occurred after the establishment of the Missionary Institute in February 1873. Perhaps it was in 1873 that Mrs Hulme met Henry Grattan Guinness in London during the Moody and Sankey Revival meetings. At this time Guinness was seeking to develop further his Missionary Training Institute and so the link was made.[66] There was apparently a delay of 'a year or two'[67] which may have been caused because 'Some months elapsed after we had decided to accept the charge before Mrs Hulme (now Mrs Robertson), who was in Scotland, could remove her furniture and give possession of the place.'[68] Anne Elizabeth married the Rev David Robertson and ministered with him in Italy and England.

It was presumably Robert F. Horton, her nephew, who indicated to Fiddian Moulton that after negotiations, 'the lease became theirs in December 1875'.[69] The lease of Hulme Cliff College enabled Guinness to send men from Harley House to Cliff for part of their training. On 11 November 1880, the Trust established by Mrs Hulme was updated and the former tenants became Trustees when the names of Henry Grattan Guinness and Fanny Guinness were added. The Trust documents were further updated in 1886 and 1895. Henry and Fanny Guinness are referred to as living at 'Harley House, Bow'. It is clear that they did not purchase the College, and whilst we do not have full details, they leased the property rent free.[70]

The outstanding themes from the Hulme legacy are the sense of devotional piety, seen in the commitment to reading scripture, prayer and shared worship; an evangelical zeal to proclaim salvation, rescuing people from hell, rather than the popular evangelical view of the impending return of Christ; a social zeal borne out of a desire for the betterment of people, shown in his commitment to the Improvement Society. One absent theme is that of holiness teaching, absent too from Guinness, though very present in the Wesleyan influences, which arrived with Thomas Cook when Hulme Cliff

College became a Methodist Institution. Hulme was very concerned about 'right theology' and in the context of the rise of Liberal Protestant theology, he had a high view of divine revelation through the scriptures. In common with other Congregationalists of his day, he was concerned to train lay people for ministry and evangelism, despite his difficult experiences with the Lancashire Independent College. His desire was for an intensely practical form of training, wanting to prepare 'industrial missionaries' who would be missionary evangelists, able to deal with basic horticulture, carpentry for building houses, shoeing a horse, or keeping a cart on the road. Thus the vision that Cliff House would become a training college became a reality.

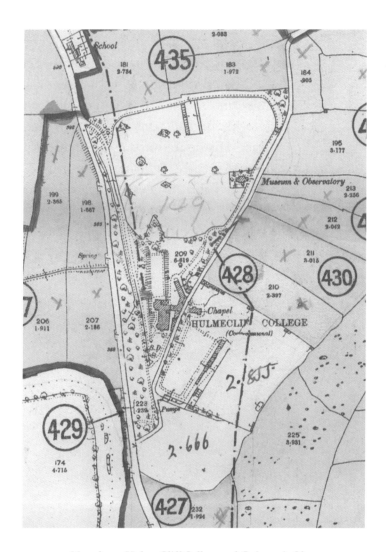

Map shows Hulme Cliff College and Guinness's Observatory

1   16 August 1781: Land known as 'The Cliff' (2 roods and 25 perches) sold by John Marples of Unstone to Thomas Gardom of Bubnell for £27 10s. 25 March 1790: Acres known as 'Derwent Side Meadow' and 25 perches of ground called the 'Crimbles' sold by Robert Lowndes of Palterton, Derbyshire to Thomas Gardom for £350. 31 March 1797: Further land sold by John Marples to Thomas Gardom for £450.

2   Sarah E. Chadwick, wife of the second Methodist Principal of Cliff College, the Rev Samuel Chadwick. *Cliff, Past and Present. The Story of how two great ventures became one* (Cliff College Archives E51, 1927). An unpublished service with hymns about the development of Cliff House and the rise of the Joyful News Mission which in 1904 moved from Rochdale to Cliff College, written and presented by Mrs Chadwick.

3   The water-wheel was removed to serve another mill in 1939, *Brief History of Calver Mill* (Sheffield: Gleeson Homes, 2000). The mill is now a series of flats and houses.

4   There is an indenture for the purchase by Thomas Gardom of a parcel of land dated 16 August 1781, which indicates he had early plans for a house. A conveyance dated 31 March 1797 to Thomas Gardom includes a dwelling house, barn, stable buildings and closed pieces or parcels of land.

5   Statement in the Cliff College Archives, with the text of the notice.

6   Joe Brice, 'The Romance of a House' in *The Cliff Witness,* Vol. 3, No.2, p.28. 'Cliff House was disposed of by private treaty' suggests that the sale never reached the auction in the Rutland Arms. Brice incorrectly has the sale of the property in 1850.

7   There is an Indenture dated 16 December 1835. 'John Gardom of Tideswell in the County of Derby … Mary Winifred Gardom, Sarah Gardom and Catherine Gardom all late of Cliff House in the Parish of Bakewell and now of Bowden in the County of Cheshire, spinsters; George Gardom of Salford in the parish of Manchester in the County of Lancashire, surgeon … Sale of the property to Hilton Hulme.'

8   W. Fiddian Moulton, *The Story of Cliff* (London: Epworth Press, 1928), p.15. This error was corrected in the second history of the College written for the golden jubilee celebrations of Cliff as a Methodist College, D.W. Lambert, *What Hath God Wrought* (Cliff College, 1954); but reiterated in a third booklet written to celebrate the Centenary of the Joyful News, A.S. Cresswell, *The Story of Cliff* (Joyful News Book room, 1983).

9   *Trade Directory,* held in the Records Office at the Salford Local History Library.

10 W. Fiddian Moulton, *The Story of Cliff*, p.15.

11 With James and Elizabeth Hulme in the 1851 census return, are Sarah Ellen Horton – sister; Elizabeth Gosdale – visitor; John Bates – servant; Robert Wright – servant; Mary Ann Martin – servant; Hannah Brooks – servant. There are no students identified at this time. Matlock Local History Library.

12 Sarah Chadwick, *Cliff Past and Present* (Cliff College Archives E51, dated 1927).

13 Lambert, p.11.

14 Hudson Taylor was a pioneer missionary who formed the China Inland Mission in 1865 and worked there with his wife Maria (Dyer). Howard and Geraldine Taylor followed him in the work of the Mission.

cont.

15 Mrs Howard Taylor, 'The Early Days of Cliff' in *Cliff Witness* Vol.1, No.5, 1937, p.92. The farm was to the east of Cliff Lane and made up of the series of buildings which are now houses, Beulah, Maranatha, Emmaus and camp toilets!

16 Mrs Howard Taylor, 'The Early Days of Cliff', p.93. These buildings have become houses, Maranatha, Beulah, and Emmaus.

17 He is listed in the notice about the Society as 'J.H. Hulme, Esq.' Others are listed but, apart from the local vicar, with no indication of their status. The Society promoted the reading of 'improving' literature and lectures for local people.

18 James Wills, *The Mind, its capabilities and Cultivation*, an address delivered on Weds 9th March 1859. Robert Leader of Sheffield published the lecture as a pamphlet in 1859.

19 *Cliff Past and Present,* p.6.

20 These books are contained in the College archives.

21 Gardener Spring, *The Bible not of Man* and Thomas H Skinner, *The Religion of the Bible* (Glasgow: William Collins, undated, but the concluding pages of the book have reviews all dated 1846), pp.334-5.

22 Meeting of May 3 1853, *Minutes of the Congregational Union Home Missionary Society No 9 (1852 – 1861)*, p.68.

23 *Year Book of the Congregational Union, 1853.*

24 J.H. Hulme, note attached to the Minute Book, Archive B12.

25 J.H. Hulme to Mr Francis Roe, Superintendent Registrar, Bakewell. The letter is his rough draft with certain sentences impossible to decipher.

26 J.H. Hulme, draft letter in his handwriting, with many alterations, being a note of the Monthly Church Meeting 29 May 1866.

27 Ibid.

28 *Minutes of the Congregational Union Home Missionary Society,* 23 Nov 1864, state: 'A conference meeting held in the Congregational Library to receive a report from the Committee of the Home Missionary Society of the results which had attended the working out of their Lay-evangelists scheme during the past three years.' The report is attached and was published on 27 December 1864 under the names of Samuel Morley (Treasurer) and James H Wilson (Secretary). The report concludes:
'That deeming this scheme of Lay Evangelistic Agency eminently adapted to meet the moral and spiritual claims of our ever-increasing population, and recording with gratitude to God the success which has attended its working, whenever it has been fairly tried during the experimental period of three years now ended, this Conference would most earnestly recommend to all the County Associations and Churches within their bounds, the adoption of a plan so simple in character, so efficient in operation and so signally blessed by the Head and Lord of the Church.'

29 J.H. Hulme, *Suggestions* dated ca 1853, p.1.

30 Ibid.

31 *Suggestions,* Cliff College Archive.

32 Richard Baggaley, *One hundred years of Methodism in Calver* (Calver Methodist Church, 1960), p.4, 'It was decided to ask Mr Hulme to preside at the Tea-Meeting'

cont.

on the opening day of the Church. They also consulted him about the documentation relating to the purchase of the property.

33 Grattan Guinness, *Hulme Cliff College, Curbar or The Story of the Third Year of the East End Training Institute* (London: S.W. Partridge & Co, 1876), p.7.

34 *Conveyance of land and property from the Estate of Thomas Gardom to James H. Hulme Esq.* dated 17 December 1835. The handwritten note is attached by a pin to the map of the property.

35 *Conveyance for the Curbar Estate situate in the county of Derby to the uses and upon the trusts therein mentioned.* 4 September 1871.

36 Albert Peel and J.A.R. Marriott *Robert Forman Horton* (London: George Allen and Unwin, 1937), p.36.

37 Fiddian Moulton, p.15.

38 Peel and Marriott, pp.161-2.

39 Peel and Marriott, p.161. Horton published *The Bible and Inspiration* in 1888, which sold widely and was a publishing success. His biographers list fifty-three other substantial works. He is described as 'Keswick with Brains' as a preacher and scholar though Peel acknowledges that his views on the Bible would not be welcome there. It seems it was this which also offended his aunt.

40 Peel and Marriott, p.161.

41 It was at these meetings that Fiddian Moulton spoke with Dr Horton and learned of the beginnings of Cliff as a College.

42 Piggin, p.291.

43 Hilditch, p.14 (still the same letter).

44 Hilditch, pp.11-12.

45 Hilditch, p.17.

46 Hilditch, p.21.

47 Hilditch, p.30.

48 Hilditch, p.41.

49 The document is signed 'Richard Hilditch, Manchester 12 March 1866' p.43.

50 There is no mention of him in either Albert Peel, *A Hundred Eminent Congregationalists1662 – 1962* or even his *Two hundred Eminent Congregationalists* (London: Charles E. Surman, 1966).

51 *Centenary of the Lancashire Congregational Union* 1806-1906.

52 *Cliff Past and Present,* p.6.

53 Guinness, *Hulme Cliff College, Curbar,* p.9.

54 D.W. Lambert, p.17, and Fiddian Moulton, p.11.

55 Guinness, *Hulme Cliff College,* p.8.

56 Guinness, *Hulme Cliff College,* p.9.

57 A card issued by the funeral director gives the details.

58 H.K., 'Cliff College', *Leeds Mission News,* No.9, September 1904 (one of the papers in Cliff College Archive E14).

59 Guinness, *Hulme Cliff College, Curbar,* p.9.

60 Sarah Chadwick, *Cliff Past and Present,* indicates this was done 'not without some opposition from members of the family', p.6.

cont.

61 Taken from the Indenture forming the Trust for Hulme Cliff College, dated 4 September 1871. The nine points are taken directly from the Doctrinal Basis of Faith of the World's Evangelical Alliance (1846), with the additional words at point 6, 'in our Lord and Saviour Jesus Christ.' See appendix 2 in Ian Randall and David Hilborn, *One Body in Christ* (Carlisle: Paternoster Press, 2001), pp.358-9.

62 *Cliff Past and Present,* p.6.

63 *Cliff Past and Present,* p.6.

64 Guinness, *Hulme Cliff College, Curbar*, p.9.

65 Guinness, *Hulme Cliff College, Curbar*, p.9.

66 Lambert, p.17 and Fiddian Moulton, p.11.

67 Guinness, *Hulme Cliff College, Curbar*, p.9.

68 Guinness, *Hulme Cliff College, Curbar*, p.12.

69 Michelle Guinness, *The Guinness Spirit* (London: Hodder and Stoughton, 1999), p.172.

70 Michelle Guinness in her first book on the Guinness family, *The Guinness Legend* (London: Hodder and Stoughton, 1990), indicated that Grattan Guinness bought Cliff Hulme College, but that was not so. Something she rectified in the later *The Guinness Spirit.*

CHAPTER 2

Henry Grattan Guinness and the Regions Beyond Mission

H enry Grattan Guinness was a big man in every sense. Tall and striking in appearance, a man of vision and big ideas, he drew others as if magnetically by his firm convictions and the enthusiasm of his devotion to God.[1] Henry was born in Ireland in 1835 and converted through the witness of his sailor brother in 1853. Having heard of the work of Captain Allen Gardener, the founder of the South American Missionary Society, Grattan Guinness might have launched into a missionary career, but ill health prevented it.[2] He began studies at the newly formed New College London, but never completed them because he was too intent on active evangelistic work.[3] On 29 July 1857, at Moorfields Tabernacle aged 22, he was ordained as an itinerant and inter-denominational evangelist. He preached to large crowds through the 1859 revival in all parts of Britain. 'In Belfast the Rev H. Grattan Guinness preached to at least 15,000 people in the open air.'[4] He was undertaking this kind of preaching at least twelve times each week in the industrial cities particularly in England.[5] While taking an enforced rest in Ilfracombe during the summer of 1860, he met Fanny Fitzgerald, and they were married in October of that year. She was a remarkable woman and pioneered the work with Grattan.

He referred to her in the following way: 'I had found a true help meet'.

The young Henry and Fanny Gratton Guinness

They threw themselves into missionary endeavour and had been greatly influenced by Hudson Taylor who in 1865 had created the China Inland Mission with the purpose of reaching those Chinese untouched by the Christian message. Henry and Fanny Guinness were the driving force for the creation of The Livingstone Inland Mission which, drawing on the experience of Hudson Taylor in China, had as its purpose the conversion of native Africans whom Henry M. Stanley's travels were revealing to Europeans.[6]

In 1866 they were in Dublin and founded a men's Bible class which they hoped would become a training home for evangelists and missionaries. To their class came Dr Hudson Taylor, and some of the students present were greatly impressed. Among them were John McCarthy and Thomas J. Barnardo who both determined to go to China. McCarthy did go, but Barnardo while training at the London Hospital was appalled at the neglect of children, and began a life committed to their care. Guinness and Barnardo (and Stephenson who began the National Children's Homes) worked together throughout their lives. They also knew later the great evangelical preacher and leader, the Rev F.B. Meyer, who became the leader of the Regions Beyond Missionary Union.

Hudson Taylor advised Henry and Fanny Guinness not to go to China but to train those who would become missionaries. In 1873 they founded the work in a house in Stepney and soon after moved into larger premises in Harley House, off the Bow Road, which became known as the Institute for Home and Foreign Missions. In a manner that reflected the policy of Thomas Champness, as we shall see in chapter three, Guinness also leased Doric Lodge, close by to Harley House in 1884 for the training of women. He separated the training of men and women, and by 1903 had trained 281 deaconesses, most of whom 'have actually gone out to the foreign field.'[7] In 1878 the Institute published a magazine called *Regions Beyond* to help with the funding and sustaining of overseas missions, and to keep their supporters in touch with the work. It was not until 1900 that the work was named the Regions Beyond Missionary Union.

Harley House,
Bow, East London

Sometime between starting the work in 1873 and 1875, 'Dr Grattan Guinness was holding some services in connection with the Young Men's Christian Association in Sheffield'.[8] It appears that this was the point of contact with Mrs Hulme, and it was then that the vision the Hulmes had for the use of their property was realised. Henry and Fanny Grattan Guinness had established the work of the Regions Beyond at Harley House but they needed an additional centre in the country where their students might gain experience in farming and at the same time have quiet for study. 'Thus Hulme Cliffe became a centre of missionary training. Students came from all over the world, many of them going to work in China under Hudson Taylor who was a frequent visitor and dear friend of the work; over fifty of them laid down their lives in the Congo;

others went out to South America, at that time an almost unheard of field. For nearly thirty years the good work continued until at the end of the century Cliff was given up and the work centred again entirely in London.'[9]

The judgement of Henry and Fanny Grattan Guinness was that this would prove a suitable extension of their work. 'We perceived that the Hulme Cliff property afforded opportunity for extension in

the right direction, that of a *country branch*. As a rule, it is not well to keep a young man studying and working in the East of London during the whole period of his training. Great advantages for practical missionary training, and for education, are counterbalanced by many disadvantages. We felt that in

Cliff House viewed from The Drive, 1875

many cases, and especially where a long course was desirable, health would be better preserved and preliminary studies pursued with more benefit amid the quiet, healthful influences of the country than amid the distractions and temptations of London life.'[10] They acknowledged the benefit of training in town evangelization for those missionaries going to India or China, yet for others, such as those going to the interior of Africa, familiarity with country life and practice in rural evangelisation is of much more importance. 'Thirty towns and villages are within easy drive of Cliff, and one of the deepest desires of the late Mr Hulme was, that North Derbyshire should itself receive benefit from the labours of the men to be trained there.'[11]

'Cliff did not actually come into our hands till December 1875. Having been so long unoccupied it required a great deal of repair, and as it was to be adapted for a very different family from that which formerly occupied it, many alterations were also needful. We could easily and profitably have laid out £1000 in these preliminary operations, and in furnishing and stocking the place ... we were obliged to go to work on the most economical scale, and attempt only the things that were absolutely needful...'[12]

The financial accounts for the 'East End Training Institute' otherwise known as Harley House, to the 1 June 1876 do not identify Hulme Cliff College as a separate item. The following amounts may refer to Hulme Cliff: 'repairs' of £324 7s 8½d and £602 1s 7½d identified as 'Furniture, Bedding, Linen, China, Cutlery, &c.'[13] Though they were also developing their work in Bow,[14] it was mainly building works which were specifically identified in the summary accounts for the year. Therefore it would seem that the Institute's investment in the newly formed Hulme Cliff College was very considerable, but they took the long-term view that it would be a good investment. 'Moreover we saw, that though the first start would be expensive, a branch of this work established at Cliff, would probably in the long-run be less expensive than any other equally important addition we could make. The house and land would be rent free, coals, living and labour all cheaper, and produce of the farm a help in housekeeping. And further, we saw in it an opportunity for adding an important element to the practical training of the students – *the care and instruction of neglected and destitute boys*. The farm would afford remunerative employment to any number of such whom we might receive, and the superintendence and training of such lads would give invaluable experience to the students.'[15]

Henry Guinness took down a 'volunteer corps' of students, consisting of carpenters, joiners, painters and glaziers, who had the skills necessary to renovate the College and prepare it for its new use. They began work to transform what at first appeared a 'lonely uninhabited house'.[16] 'They painted the outside of the house, re-hung most of the windows, eased and repaired rusty hinges and locks throughout, whitewashed the ceilings, papered rooms, and mended the floors that had been attacked by dry rot. They refloored and repaired the greenhouse, which was in ruins; repaired the roofs, and cleared the obstructed lead pipes and gutters; cleaned out the numerous stone cisterns about the premises in which quantities of sediment and debris had accumulated. They lowered the entire floor of one large barn, to convert it into a boys' dormitory; made a staircase up to it, and several windows and doors and a bath; altering and arranging the out-houses so as to adapt them for lavatories, dwelling rooms, &c.'[17]

By the end of March 1876 Mr Henry Dening, a friend of the Guinness's from Bath, who had been advised by his doctors to minister in a quieter place, said he would prefer 'one which would combine a measure of farming, with opportunities for evangelising, and a quiet residence in the country.'[18] Dening agreed to superintend the work and be the resident Principal of the newly-formed College.[19] He seems to have died the following year, for the 1876 report includes an address introducing him as 'our late Principal at Cliff.'[20] Julius Rohrbach was sent from Harley House to be the Tutor for the students and nine boys were dispatched, presumably to work in the farm and college. Altogether there were forty people in the newly formed community.[21] The students studied in the mornings (nine to one) and in the evenings, (seven to ten). The afternoons were devoted to 'working in the garden, on the farm, at carpentering and other repairs, the teaching of the boys, &c.'[22]

The 1881 census identifies Alfred Eyles as 'head of house', and he appears to have family with him, with twelve other persons recorded, of whom three are visitors, three servants and six are 'boarders'. Many of the boarders were by trade carpenters and joiners, and it may be that work was in progress at Cliff House at the time, with five carpenters, three from Scotland and two from Cornwall. Alfred Eyles

was aged 20 and young to be head of house, but he is the only one described as student missionary, and it may be that in the absence of Guinness or other tutors, he was given oversight of the college.

Guinness was a remarkable student and writer on prophetic subjects, Roman Catholicism, science and philosophy. In the *Regions Beyond* edition for November 1888 he wrote an article about the geology of the area around Cliff, another of his interests, under the title 'Hulme Cliff College and the hills around it.'[23] He received an honorary doctorate and was interested in prophecy and also astronomy. At Cliff he built an observatory in Cliff Lane, in which he placed a powerful telescope, the gift of a generous supporter of the institution. In this building, where he spent a considerable amount of time, he wrote his book, *The Approaching End of the Age*.[24]

The Observatory with its telescope c. 1880

'The Prayer Paths'
planted by Guinness

He wrote many other volumes, as did Fanny Guinness his first wife.[25] The Guinnesses encouraged their children in missionary work and Geraldine, Harry, Joy and Lucy all published missionary literature.

Mrs Guinness was indispensable to him in the management of the College. The out-buildings and gardens were planned and laid out under her superintendency including the spacious lawns, two miles of walks, and over two thousand trees planted in pairs at a cost of about £15,000. They landscaped the gardens, planting trees mentioned in the Bible which would survive in the Derbyshire weather. The trees were planted in an arboretum, on the edge of the terrace lawn and down to what are known as the 'prayer paths'. Many presently remain as mature trees in the College grounds. As a guide to the trees of the Bible Grattan Guinness used the Authorised Version which mentions thirty-seven different trees. This version was completed in 1611, long before botany became an exact science and in the translation biblical scholars chose to identify some of the trees of the Bible with familiar trees of England. Thus Amos is described as a pruner of sycamore trees, though the Hebrew word refers to a form of figs.

Others have a more exotic name. In Genesis 6:14, God commands Noah, 'Make thee an ark of gopher wood'. Gopher is very similar to the Hebrew and Greek word for cypress. Probably it was the extremely durable wood of the tall massive evergreen cypresses that, together with towering cedars and oaks, clothed the slopes of Lebanon and other mountain ranges in biblical times. There are mature cypress, cedars and oaks in the College grounds planted at that time. In Genesis 25:10, God commands Moses to build a tabernacle using shittim wood. Shittim is the Hebrew name (Isaiah 41:19) for an acacia that grows on Mt Sinai, the most common tree in the Arabian desert. It is a gnarled tree armed with spines and probably was used to form the 'crown of thorns'; our version is much less dangerous. The Holy Land is a land of palm trees, especially the date palm, but along with the mulberry, fig, olive and Judas tree they would not grow in the Derbyshire climate.

All that leaves the question about the trees of Cliff. Here is a table showing the trees of the Bible which can be found in the College grounds. Recently, and as the College's development, a landscape architect has charted all the trees in the College grounds.[26]

Trees found in the Bible.	Trees at Cliff College.
Cypress	Yes
Shittah (Acacia)	Yes, Robinia pseudoacacia
Ash	Yes
Tiel (Elm)	Yes, but only young – due to Dutch Elm Disease
Palm	
Olive	
Fig	
Cedar	Yes
Mulberries	
Sycamine/Sycomore (Sycamore)	Yes
Chestnut	Yes
Apple	Yes
Fir	Yes
Juniper	Yes
Oak	Yes
Locust-tree	Yes, another name for Robinia pseudoacacia
Judas-tree	

Henry and Fanny Guinness were fascinating figures in the missionary movement of the nineteenth century. One of the driving features of their passion for worldwide mission was their belief in the imminent return of Christ. Henry Grattan Guinness combined his theological, biblical, and scientific knowledge to establish a theory predicting when the world would end. His interest was in the interpretation of biblical apocalyptic materials found in Daniel and Revelation. In the nineteenth century there were two schools of thought, the 'historicist' and the 'futurist'. The futurist, as their designation suggests, considered that the events to which the texts refer were well in the future. The historicist however, considered the events of the texts have, for the most part already taken place, and that the final act was about to begin. This method of interpretation had been popular since well before the Reformation and Guinness rose to special prominence as an advocate. He wrote extensively about the coming of Christ, most notably in *The Approaching End of the Age: Viewed in the Light of History, Prophecy and Science* in 1878, and *Light for the Last Days* in 1887. By the time the latter book was written, the first was in its tenth edition with seventeen thousand sales.[27] There was remarkable interest in the second half of the nineteenth century in the Return of Christ. Guinness was convinced the return of Christ was imminent and published a pamphlet entitled *Fallacies of Futurism*.

He cited elaborate astronomical and mathematical calculations drawn from his considerable knowledge of astronomy and solar lunar cycles, which occupy the arguments in the first half of *The Approaching End of the Age*.[28] All this reveals a preoccupation with chronology and statistics characteristic of Victorian England, to buttress his conclusion, which was that the world would end in 1919. There is no doubt that this sense of the impending 'approaching end of the world' was one of the primary reasons for his missionary endeavour, and as such was in sharp contrast both to Hulme, and the Wesleyans who would eventually occupy Cliff College.

During the academic year the College was filled with students who were given the opportunity of gaining experience in farming, carpentry or work at the forge, as well as the evangelistic work in the many villages of the neighbourhood. In the summer the students scattered to help in Gospel missions, tent evangelism or work among seamen of the North Sea fleet. The College became a place of rest and relaxation for all the family, transformed into an attractive holiday home.[29]

After Geraldine reached seventeen, it was always her responsibility to go down to Cliff to get things ready for the guests. 'Under her direction, the classrooms became dining and drawing rooms, with ample space for the fifty or sixty visitors. Year after year the same families came, all paying their share towards household expenses, and the young people grew up in a joyous companionship

The Walk by the River Derwent immediately opposite Cliff Lane

that glowed in their memories throughout life. To parents, aunts, uncles, and other seniors, 'Cliff was their Galilee - a refuge from close, crowded, noisy, dusty, enormous London.'[30]

The summer house parties walked in the hills finding fossils, went caving, played tennis on the lawn, and rowed and swam in the flowing waters of the Derwent where there was a boat house and pier. In the evenings they had a lecture on mission in Africa, often could manage a full orchestra and occasionally spent half the night in the observatory surveying the skies.[31]

Lucy Guinness, another of the Guinness daughters, married Dr Karl Kumm who was a pioneer missionary in the Sudan.[32] Fittingly they met in Egypt when Lucy was travelling with her father, were married almost immediately in Cairo and worked tirelessly for the Sudan. Their devotion to God and each other is caught in this extract from one of Lucy's letters, 'There may come times of difficulty, pressure, hindrance, tests of faith, slow fruit and much labour, trial linked to our joy. But never can His word fail – nor He fail: 'He must reign'! In our life together, in our deepest union, in

William Rattray, Principal 1880 – 1895

our joy unspeakable, with all that it may bring; in every hour and moment...in each place – He must reign – He must reign.'[33]

William Rattray was the Principal from 1880 – 1895, running the College on behalf of Grattan Guinness. He was, 'In his cheery Scotch way, full of pleasant wit and wisdom'.[34] Before coming to Cliff he was the Head of 'the renowned Charlotte Street School' in Aberdeen.

In Kelly's *Directory* for 1887 Hulme Cliff College is noted: 'Rev H.G. Guinness, director and principal; William Rattray, resident head master.'[35] Bulmer's *Directory* of 1895 reads with a slight spelling mistake, 'On the Baslow Road, a little distance from the village, is *Hume Cliff College*, where young men are received and trained for foreign missionary work. It was erected at the sole expense of Mr Hume, and is under the auspices of the Rev H. Grattan Guinness, of East London Mission.'[36] The census of 1891 reveals the College in full swing with William Rattray (aged 69) as Tutor in Theology School and 49 students, all men, who are described as 'Boarders' and as 'students in Theology'. In addition six people are listed as servants and they undertook the tasks of Housekeeper, Cook, Parlour Maid and Man Servant. It was during

The old lecture room later to become the Common Room

this period that the gospel texts were chiselled in the stones at the side of the road leading up to Curbar Gap.[37]

Rattray taught many subjects: 'whether he was taking so-called secular subjects, or sacred, there was always an energetic earnestness that indelibly impressed the truths taught upon our minds. His words were never cold and lifeless - on the contrary, were often more like a stream of lava rushing from a long-pent-up volcano. Of course, he was seen and heard at his best in Bible expositions and theological lectures. Here he had a fine field. He lectured not only with his head, but also his soul. Cold, lifeless, speculative theology would have killed us, as far as missionary zeal was concerned; but God's truth taught by one who had been anointed to see it, who had lived it, incarnating it into his own life, and who had the gift of an anointed tongue to teach it, could not but mightily build us up.'[38]

The Lane and old entrance

Mrs Rattray died in 1889, and the couple had no children. However, *Regions Beyond* refers to a kindly woman from Scotland who nursed Rattray in his dying days.[39] She had been the 'house mother' of the college for five years, presumably since the death of his wife.

The students from the College held missions, and one such was at Dronfield Baptist Church. 'In 1892, two students from Cliffe College held a mission. God blessed their ministry with great power. Seventy people professed faith, of whom forty were baptised and received into membership. Many were young people who needed nurture and guidance. In a step of faith, one of the missioners – Rev C.J. Rendell – was appointed as the church's first Minister. This pastorate lasted until 1900, a time of great blessing and growth.'[40] Another was the Cowley Chapel at Holmsfield and the relationship between the Chapel and the College remains to this day, with students still taking services. 'The work was begun by Hulme Cliff College in 1888, when students visited the area and cottage meetings began. The present chapel was opened in 1893.'[41]

One student of the college reflected that 'Mr Rattray was a Calvinist, but so united man's free will with God's ordaining purpose, that he inspired us to plead with men as though all rested with them, and also to pray for souls and plead with God for the outpouring of His spirit as if all belonged to Him.'[42] Rattray had never himself been a missionary, which is identified in the article about him in the *Regions Beyond*, 'He never saw the heathen, he was not called to be a missionary'.[43] He died on 22 April 1895, aged 74 and was buried at All Saints Parish Church, Curbar. The eulogy on his gravestone reads:

WILLIAM RATTRAY F.E.I.S. OF HULME CLIFF COLLEGE, CURBAR

FOR FIFTEEN YEARS THE BELOVED PRINCIPAL OF HULME CLIFF COLLEGE. A MANLY MAN, A CONSISTENT CHRISTIAN, A WARM HEARTED FRIEND, A GIFTED TEACHER, FIRM, WISE, DILIGENT. HE NOT ONLY TAUGHT THE STUDENTS UNDER HIS CARE THE WORD OF KNOWLEDGE, BUT EXPOUNDED TO THEM BY LIP AND LIFE THE MEANING AND WORTH OF DUTY CONSTRAINING THEM TO LOVE AND REVERENCE IT FOR ITS OWN SAKE FOUR HUNDRED MISSIONARY STUDENTS PASSED THROUGH HIS CLASSES AND WILL LONG REGARD HIS NAME WITH GRATEFUL AFFECTION HE FINISHED HIS WORK AND LIFE TOGETHER ON APRIL 22ND 1895 AGED 74 YEARS.

HE BEING DEAD YET SPEAKETH HEB 11:4

The Rev J.F.T. Hallowes MA followed Rattray as Principal working under Grattan Guinness with guidance from colleagues at

Students of Hulme Cliff College, c. 1895

Harley House. The Regions Beyond Missionary Union refers to Principal Forbes Jackson MA as the person who oversaw the education of the students. Jackson, the senior partner, was at Harley College and from there related to Mr Hallowes and guided his teaching at Cliff. Mrs Sarah Chadwick refers to correspondence with his widow who related 'a few memories of the years spent at Cliff from 1895 to 1901'.[44] Mr Hallowes came to Cliff from Birmingham with his wife and four children who received their secondary education in Sheffield (Wesley College and the High School). She relates in a quaint way, 'There were between fifty and sixty students in residence at that time. Mr Hallowes enjoyed intercourse with these men. Many were the prayer meetings held in the College Chapel when the walls resounded with their strong young voices, and passionate prayers went up for the "Regions Beyond" for which they were being trained, and to which they ardently looked forward'.[45]

Drawing of 'The Little Gate'.
The text on the left reads:
'Cliff's sacred parting-place, from which hundreds have gone out to the ends of the earth, and from which the farewell chorus has rung out –'

He was supported by the Rev W.F. Schofield who had worked closely with Rattray. Schofield came to the College in October 1892 after being Assistant Master in the School of Lawrence Sheriff at Rugby and taught both at Cliff and Harley House. The *Minutes* for the Chapel also show that Dr Harry Guinness, the son of Henry Grattan Guinness, came frequently to teach at the College, and is described as overseeing the work. Schofield reports from London, 'The Principal, Mr Forbes Jackson, is a thoroughgoing Scotchman, and though of a very different type from dear old Mr Rattray, is doubtless an admirable man for his post. We work together most amicably...'[46]

Cliff was seen by Guinness as the place where foundation training could be given which would test the mettle of his intending young missionaries: 'Hulme Cliff College is an institution in connection with the "Regions Beyond" Missionary Union; about 30 young men here receive one year's training, and are afterwards transferred for two years at Harley House, Bow Road, London E. before entering on missionary work.'[47] Great gatherings to say "goodbye" to

47

outgoing Missionaries from Hulme Cliff College were held at the little gate below the house, opening onto Baslow Road. 'Missionary hymns were sung, and farewell prayers offered. The men were then helped into the wagonette and cheered to the echo as they drove off.'[48]

The 1899 edition of Kelly's *Directory* lists those residents as the Rev Henry Grattan Guinness DD and the Rev J.F.T. Hallowes MA (Principal, Hulme Cliff College) along with the students. Other tutors receive little mention; Julius Rohrbach is referred to as 'now working in Berlin.'[49]

There is a minute book for the Cliff Chapel, which begins on 13 December 1896 concluding on 1 September 1901. The first entry reports, 'At the service in Cliff Chapel, F.W. Schofield announced there would be a meeting in the same place on the following evening at 7 o'clock, for the purpose of forming a Christian Church.' The announcement is 'at the service' which indicates there were already some people meeting for worship but not a regular congregation. It may be that after the death of James Hulme the Congregational Chapel ceased, and during the principalship of Rattray it was not re-opened.

Those who met on 14 December were local people, 'Messrs Ephraim Slinn, George Herbert Slinn, F.W. Schofield and Mrs Martha Smith. These after due conference and prayer, each and all resolved in the name of God to own each other as members of a church, to be known as the Cliff Church, Curbar.' F.W. Schofield was asked to be the pastor and he consented. On 13 April 1897, the church meeting admitted new members, some on confession of faith, some upon application and well-known Christian conduct. Three members admitted were Mr and Mrs George Froggatt, from Calver, and Mrs Sarah Morton, of Froggatt, who are described as "old members of the Church at Cliff". This suggests that they were members of the Congregational Church begun by James Hulme. Moreover at the earlier 14 December meeting it is recorded that 'Mr Ephraim Slinn was deacon in the church at Cliff, in years gone by. It was agreed by all that he should resume his office.'

Mrs Guinness in the lounge at Cliff House

Fanny Guinness became unwell in 1892 and lived at Cliff for most of that time until her death in 1899. The whole edition of their magazine, *Regions Beyond* (Jan - Feb 1899) was given over to a celebration of her life,. She was buried at St. Ann's Parish Church, Baslow. 'For thirty years Fanny had borne a strain to which but few are equal, twelve years of motherhood, a wandering life devoted to evangel-istic labours, and eighteen years of arduous and unremitting toil, during which she combined the responsibilities, and ably executed the services of organising, financial, corresponding and editorial secretary to the East London Institute and Congo Mission.'[50] They lived a travelling existence, and their eight children were born in such varied cities as Toronto, Liverpool, Edinburgh, Bath, Dublin and Paris. Henry not only mourned her loss but felt he could not carry on the work. He attempted to ensure that his son-in-law Karl would continue their work at Cliff but when no solution could be found the lease was disposed of, and the work reverted to Harley House alone.

The Cliff Church meetings were intermittent, but the one on Sunday 11 August 1901 includes the following minute: 'F.W. Schofield stated that the main purpose of the meeting, namely, to consider what course should be taken by this church, in the event of the closing of Cliff College. F.W. Schofield indicated the events which had led towards that closing: the illness of Dr Harry Guinness last winter, his enforced absence from Harley House, the decision of the Directors of the Regions Beyond Missionary Union that all the male students should be taught during the session 1901-2 at Harley house, and the College work at Cliff should be suspended. Further he stated how these changes might affect this church: the chapel might not be available for our meetings, and he would probably be removed to Harley.'[51]

After some conversation 'It was also agreed unanimously that whether regular public meetings for Worship and Preaching could be continued or not, the membership should not be broken up. Means for keeping up communication one with another, and common action as a church were suggested and discussed, namely that a member be appointed as Secretary who could act with the Deacon, Mr E. Slinn.' George Herbert Slinn was appointed to undertake the duties of the secretary. What became of their intention to remain together is unknown but George Herbert Slinn, joined the Methodist Chapel 'around 1900', and committed himself to Methodism in many capacities.[52] F.W. Schofield taught at Harley House and after retirement went to live in Ilkley, where he lived in a house called 'Harley' and commenced 'F W Schofield's Correspondence classes' with the subtitle 'for Bible Student and Missionary candidates.'[53]

Being one of the trustees of the property, Guinness persuaded them to put the property up for sale. At first he was appalled for the initial interest came from the Jesuits. 'It became imperative to save Cliff from the clutches of Rome, the Scarlet Woman of the apocalyptic books.'[54] Henry persuaded his daughter Lucy and her husband Karl Kumm to take on Hulme Cliff College and use it for the Sudan United Mission. Reluctantly Karl agreed and their child, Karl was born in 1902, but the college was too large for their purposes. Karl was therefore relieved when the Wesleyan Methodists Henry Smart and Thomas Cook showed interest. Grattan Guinness was less enthusiastic, commenting 'the Wesleyans were not as sound in their interpretation of biblical prophecy as he might have hoped, but compared to the Jesuits they were angels of light.'[55]

Henry Grattan Guinness came from his despair to marry in 1903 the younger and beautiful Grace Russell Hurditch.[56] He was aged 67 and Grace forty years his junior with whom he had a passionate marriage. 'She gave him a new lease of life' and participated in his vigorous international ministry.[57] Grattan Guinness died in 1910 and when the news was conveyed to the World Mission Conference meeting at Edinburgh 'a wave of sorrow passed over the assembly. We all felt that the Church of Christ Militant had lost one of its great missionary leaders. To those who had known him intimately and loved him dearly there came a feeling of personal loss.'[58]

Henry and Grace Guinness

The whole development of the College was, however, to take a new direction under the influence of a figure who was never formerly a part of it. The movement of the College and its affiliation with Methodism was, in fact, to be a part of a wider Evangelistic movement founded by Thomas Champness, and to that we now turn.

Hulme Cliff College, viewed across the valley, at the end of the Guinness era

Hulme Cliff College at the end of the Guinness era

1 Broomhall, *Hudson Taylor and China's Open Century – Survivors' Pact* (London: Hodder and Stoughton and Overseas Missionary Fellowship, 1984), p.117.

2 *Life of Faith*, 20 January 1973.

3 Michelle Guinness, *The Guinness Spirit*, p.86-87.

4 Edwin Orr, *Light of the Nations* (London: Paternoster Press, 1965), p.128.

5 Orr, p.170.

6 K.S. Latourette, Vol. 5 *Africa South of the Sahara*, p.423.

7 Harry Guinness, *These Thirty Years - Special Number "Regions Beyond"* Jan and Feb 1903, p.14.

8 *Cliff Past and Present*, p.7.

9 Joe Brice, 'The Romance of a House' in *The Cliff Witness*, Vol. 3, No. 2, 1939 p.2. (note how Brice relates the way he understood, incorrectly for the most part, Guinness spelt Cliff, adding an 'e').

10 *Hulme Cliff College, Curbar*, p.11.

11 *Hulme Cliff College, Curbar*, p.11.

12 *Hulme Cliff College, Curbar*, p.14.

13 *Hulme Cliff College, Curbar*, p.113.

14 *Hulme Cliff College, Curbar*, pp.19-20, indicates, because of expanding the work at Harley House in Bow, the Institute had built new lecture rooms and other facilities costing £980 4s 0d, see p.113.

15 *Hulme Cliff College, Curbar*, p.12, words in italics are original.

16 *Hulme Cliff College, Curbar*, p.14.

17 *Hulme Cliff College, Curbar*, p.15.

18 *Hulme Cliff College, Curbar*, p.13.

19 *Hulme Cliff College, Curbar*, p.13, and *Hulme Cliff College, Curbar 1876*, p.22.

20 *Hulme Cliff College, Curbar 1876*, p. 29.

21 *Hulme Cliff College, Curbar*, p.17.

22 *Hulme Cliff College, Curbar*, p.17.

23 Grattan Guinness, 'Hulme Cliff College and the hills around it', *Regions Beyond*. November 1888, pp.337-340.

24 Sarah Chadwick, *Cliff Past and Present*, p.7.

25 Henry Grattan Guinness, *The Approaching End of the Age: Viewed in the light of history, prophecy and science* (London: Hodder and Stoughton, 1878) The original version ran to 13 editions by 1902 with American editions and published by Armstrong and Son. In 1918 a "new edition" was published edited and revised by Rev E. H. Horne (London: Morgan and Scott). It was translated into French under the title, *Latter Day Prophecies* and from French into Spanish by Eric Lund, 1884, *Can Christians fight with carnal weapons?* (New Vienna Ohio: Peace Association of Friends in America, 1870). He also wrote other volumes on prophecy relating to the Second Coming:
Light for the Last Days (London: Hodder and Stoughton, 1886) - The cover page says it is authored by Mr and Mrs Guinness. 8th impression 1934.
History Unveiling Prophecy; Time as an Interpreter (New York: F.H. Revell, 1905).

cont.

Mr and Mrs H. Grattan Guinness, *The Second Advent, Will it be before the Millennium?* with Fausett and Mr and Mrs H. Grattan Guinness (New York: J. Pott and Co, 1887).

The Divine Programme of the World's History (London: Hodder and Stoughton, 1888).

26   Information provided by Weddle Landscapes, Sheffield.

27   Both books were published by Hodder and Stoughton, the latter advertising small pamphlets, *The Divine Programme of the World's History* and *Fallacies of Futurism.*

28   Guinness had his own telescope in a specially built 'building' at Cliff College, which is now the house, 'Ataraxia'.

29   Michelle Guinness, *The Guinness Legend,* (London: Hodder and Stoughton, 1990) p.152.

30   Joy Guinness, *Mrs Howard Taylor* (London: China Inland Mission, 1949).

31   Michelle Guinness, *The Guinness Legend,* pp.152-153.

32   D. W. Lambert, 'The Story of Karl Kumm', in *Cliff Witness,* Vol. 2, No 2, p.30.

33   Ibid.

34   Lucy E. Guinness, 'Holding the Ropes at Home' in *Regions Beyond Magazine,* June 1895, p.249.

35   *Kelly's Directory* 1887 (Kingston-upon-Thames, Kelly's Directories Ltd), Matlock Local History Library.

36   Bulmer's, *History and Directory of Derbyshire,* 1895. Note the misspelling of Hulme in their text.

37   Joe Brice, 'The Romance of a House' in *The Cliff Witness,* Vol. 3, No. 2, 1939, p.29. 'Upon many of those stones are to be seen Gospel texts which were chiselled in by missionary students over sixty years ago.' The texts which remain at Curbar gap are, John 5:24 by the trough, 'Verily, verily, I say unto you, He that heareth my word, and believeth on him that sent me, hath everlasting life, and shall not come into condemnation: but is passed from death unto life.', Isaiah 1:18 'Come now, and let us reason together, saith the Lord: though your sins be as scarlet, they shall be as white as snow; though they shall be red like crimson, they shall be as wool.' and Hebrews 7:25, 'Wherefore he is able to save them to the uttermost that come unto God by him, seeing he ever liveth to make intercession for them.' I have used the Authorised Version as undoubtedly they would have used it.

38   *Regions Beyond,* June 1895, p.255.

39   *Regions Beyond,* June 1895, p.259.

40   This information comes from the small booklet prepared for the 150th anniversary of Dronfield Baptist Church.

41   Letter from Howard Belben to 'friends from Cowley Chapel', 28 April 1971. The deeds and original correspondence relating to the release of land and building of the Chapel are in the safe, Principal's Study.

42   *Regions Beyond,* June 1895, p.253.

43   *Regions Beyond,* June 1895, p.259.

44   Sarah Chadwick, *Cliff Past and Present,* p.9.

45   Ibid.

cont.

46 F.W. Schofield to Mr G.H. Slinn of Calver, 29 July 1907 (Cliff College archive BC4).

47 Kelly's *Directory,* 1899.

48 Sarah Chadwick, p.9. Note that this 'sending off' was also typical of the Wesleyan Missionaries who left Richmond College for the docks of Tilbury to catch the 'packet' to West Africa etc., Frank H. Cumbers, *Richmond College, 1843-1943* (London: Epworth Press, 1944), p.18-19.

49 Joy Guinness, p.59.

50 Lucy Guinness (ed), 'Enter Thou', *Regions Beyond* January/February 1899, chapter 3, pp39-44.

51 *Minutes,* 11 August 1901.

52 *Joyful News,* 31 March, 1960; Richard Baggaley, *One hundred years of Methodism in Calver,* p.15.

53 There exists considerable correspondence between F.W. Schofield and George Herbert Slinn who stayed in Calver as the Postmaster. It is in this correspondence that Schofield describes his continuing work of what we would call today, 'Open Learning'.

54 Michelle Guinness, *The Guinness Legend,* p.245.

55 Michelle Guinness, *The Guinness Legend,* p.246.

56 Michelle Guinness, *The Guinness Spirit* (London: Hodder and Stoughton, 1999), p.357.

57 Ibid, p.334 (d).

58 Elizabeth Pritchard, *For such a Time* (Eastbourne: Victory Press, 1973), p.49. The R.B.M.U. withdrew from Cliff in 1902, sold Harley House in 1918 and reduced its missionary endeavour though supported by significant evangelical leaders such as F.B. Meyer. It continued missionary work in Peru, North India and the Sudan until the 1970's. Increasingly co-operation was established with other missionary organisations; the R.B.M.U. does not now exist as a separate organisation.

CHAPTER 3

Thomas Champness and the Joyful News Training Home and Mission

Thomas Champness son of a printer, Charles Champness, was born on 19 July 1832 in Stratford on the edge of the Essex marshes. He had little in the way of learning early in his life, but ended his career as author, publisher, preacher, effective College Principal and Missionary leader. He sought no high position, refused payment for the successful weekly publication *Joyful News* and though troubled by long-term ill health engaged in a remarkably energetic ministry, which was summarised by a friend in this way: 'His life had six different phases. He was a missionary, a circuit minister, an evangelist, an editor, a reformer and the head of a school of prophets.'[1] Champness had a considerable influence on the Wesleyan Methodist Church in both its missionary work overseas and the evangelistic work and training in Britain. Handing over that work to form Cliff College was certainly the most important decision of his later ministry.[2] His legacy has been likened to that of William Booth who founded the Salvation Army, or Wilson Carlile who founded the Church Army, each of them working at a similar time and wanting to reach out to the ordinary person.[3]

His father, seeking employment in 1834, moved from West Ham in East London to Manchester. The family followed when he had found work and lodgings. Thomas received his few years of schooling, 'mostly at a dame school, then off to the factory from 5:30 in the morning to 7:30 at night, and this for a lad of only eight. Life was grim and strenuous in those days.'[4] Champness was an eager reader and 'devoured all he could get hold of. He read the speeches of John Bright, and sympathised with the Chartists whom he saw in Stephenson's Square digging up the paving stones with their knives during the riots.'[5]

Champness as a Local Preacher

There is a sense of pride in Champness's family history. When his wife, Eliza, wrote her tribute to the ministry of her husband, she was at pains to reveal the long history of his family.[6] The Champness family name goes back to the time of the Norman Conquest, and is found on the Roll of Honour at Battle Abbey. When he went as a Missionary to Africa, his mother, Mary, said to him, 'Boy, I don't know anything about the place where you are going, but you will never want bread to eat or a bed to sleep on, for I never turned away any poor creature from my door that I could help.'[7] Champness later said that he had on many occasions 'eaten my Mother's bread in many parts of the world'.[8]

Thomas Champness seems to have inherited from his mother 'a soft heart, and a wonderful gift of putting keen, clever sayings in a shrewd common sense way'. He said, 'I have always had a soft place in my heart for Tramps and such like, for I remember that my honoured father has had to walk from town to town seeking a place where he might earn bread for his loved ones'. It was one of his mother's sayings to her children, 'Be sure you say "Sir", when you speak to one worse dressed than yourself.'[9] It was this attitude which would endear him to rural communities.

In Manchester his father Charles had lodgings with a Methodist lady called Betty Lee. She invited him to hear the young Rev George Osborn who was to become a great influence on Champness throughout his life.[10] With this and the influence of others Charles Champness became a committed Christian.[11] This clearly affected family life, and Charles used to read and expound the Bible and pray.[12] His mother, too, read the Psalms at 9:00pm each evening. As soon as he could work Thomas became a bricklayer. Eliza Champness brought many testimonies to bear from the friends, brothers and sisters of Thomas who recorded his keenness to work, eagerness to learn and details of a deep spiritual search.[13]

Eliza described the culmination of this spiritual search: 'At last after months of seeking, he found the light. A simple hearted but devout chapel keeper was used for his deliverance, when he bluntly said to him, 'Thomas, the Bible says, "Ye shall find Me when ye seek Me with your whole heart". Thus as he earnestly sought he found that Christ was really and truly his Saviour.' Although no date is given, there was no doubt of his conversion.[14] Soon, as was the custom, the new convert was taken right into the fellowship and set to work.

At first, owing to Champness's youth and lack of education there was little encouragement from the Superintendent who made it clear that the Local Preachers of that circuit were 'a very superior class of men'.[15] Thomas was perceived simply as an ill-educated bricklayer. Refusing to be discouraged and wishing to practise the art of public speaking, he borrowed a chair and started to preach on a piece of waste ground. The young preacher soon attracted neighbours and passers-by. The Preachers' Meeting heard of this, and despite the earlier views of the Superintendent, in March 1855 he was given a 'note' as a local preacher. He progressed rapidly, as the *Minute Book* of the Oxford Circuit of the Wesleyan Methodist Church, Manchester indicates, and in March 1856 he was received on full plan.

Thomas Champness, the young missionary

Things continued to move quickly for Thomas. The following year he was presented to the Spring Ministerial Synod as a candidate for the Ministry. Before this he would have had to gain the backing of his circuit and would have faced questions at the December Quarterly Meeting. In July 1857 the Connexional Committee examined him and asked, as they did every candidate, the extent of his offer. Would it be for the Home work or for the Overseas work? Apparently Champness replied, 'I offer for the world'. The President of the Conference, the Rev Robert Young, asked him, 'Will you go to Africa?' 'Yes, if you send me', he replied. The President then posed the following question, 'Will you go to Sierra Leone? Before you answer, let me tell you that Sierra Leone is the white man's grave. In front of the Freetown Chapel there is a row of graves on each side of the walk, and a young missionary lies in each grave; some of them lived only a few months. Will you go?' Apparently, 'With the greatest calmness imaginable he courageously replied: "Yes, if you send me".'[16] By this time George Osborn, instrumental in his father's conversion, was a Secretary for the Wesleyan Methodist Missionary Society. Not surprisingly, Eliza Champness, in retrospect, saw the hand of Osborn in the immediate appointment of Thomas for the mission field. He was accepted in July and on the

7 September 1857 in the *Circuit Minute Book* it is recorded that because he had been accepted as a missionary to Sierra Leone, his name should be 'dropped off our Plan'.[17]

Normally, accepted candidates for the Wesleyan ministry who offered for the overseas work trained at Richmond College, London. Champness left the family home on 15 September 1857 for London to be the guest of the now influential George Osborn. He was invited to preach at the prestigious Bayswater Methodist Church. Champness left for Plymouth on the 20 September, with Osborn who, on 23 September 1857, was to ordain him and another missionary (at the Devonport chapel) before heading out for West Africa. 'With no college training, with next to no experience, he was sent to one of the largest missionary circuits in Methodism with a membership of nearly four thousand, and with difficult circumstances awaiting him, of which, by-the-by, he seems to have known nothing when he set out.'[18] Thomas Champness, apparently, had no fear. 'He was young, robust, and enthusiastic; the fire of youth was in his blood; life was all before him, and he was ready for anything in the service of his Lord and King'.[19] He stayed in Sierra Leone until 1860 'having out-lived or out-stayed all who greeted him when he first set foot in Sierra Leone.'[20] His co-worker and friend, the Rev Robert Dillon, wrote of him at the end of that period, 'The three years of his ministry in the colony greatly endeared him to the African people. His

Sierra Leone

winsome personality and free social nature gained him troops of friends.'[21] He returned from West Africa in 1860, and in March 1861 records in his journal:

Since the last entry in this journal many events have taken place. My health broke down completely, and I was absolutely compelled to leave Sierra Leone, or leave my bones in that inhospitable country. Much as I had suffered, it was hard work leaving, perhaps never to return. I embarked on board the *Athenian* (Captain Lowrie), 21st April, 1860; and after a pleasant voyage landed at Liverpool on the 12th of May.

Reached home the same evening, and was received as one from the dead by my dear friends. In a few days I left for London to see the Secretaries. Was exceedingly well-received, put up at Mr Osborn's; the day after was taken sick with bronchitis and strong fever. Was very ill for some time, was kindly nursed by Mrs Osborn and family. Stayed in London six weeks; taken ill again, returned home. Went to the Isle of Man with father and the Somersets. Came home and went to Conference; stayed with Mr Osborn again, and enjoyed it very much.

After Conference went to spend a few days with my friend Dillon at Salcombe; thence to see my new friend Mitchell at Buckfastleigh, Devon. There I met with the young lady who is now my wife; the Lord bless our union! From this place to the home of Miss A.'s friends, to ask permission; then to London for a day or two, and then home. I put some time in at Manchester and the neighbourhood. On the 6th October received a letter from Mr Osborn asking me to return to West Africa. I replied in the affirmative at once, and after three days set off for Devon to ask my dear Mary to accompany me; she at once left for home. I brought her to Leicester[22], and then went on to Manchester. Spent a fortnight getting ready, and then to South Grange, the home of Mary, where I stayed another fortnight. We were married at the Parish Church, Bishop's Itchington (there being no possibility of having the knot tied at a Methodist chapel), 14th November 1860.

Left for London, saw the Secretaries and a few friends; in two days left for Manchester. Spent the next six days among my friends and on 24th November we sailed for Lagos. We reached our destination December 21st, stayed a few days at Lagos, and then to Abbeokuta in the Gold Coast District.

Since we arrived we have had much sickness to contend with, but have been cheered by the divine presence and blessing. In consequence of sickness I have not preached often, but have now begun to take my regular work.'[23]

The couple enjoyed the work but they both had bouts of illness.[24] It appears that Thomas made few entries into his Journal during this time and Eliza Champness had to rely on surviving letters to his parents. Mary Champness was a fine missionary, rapidly gaining a knowledge of the language, and had already begun a good work among the women and girls. Suddenly she became ill. 'To her husband's great grief, she was stricken down with what proved to be a mortal sickness, for after three weeks of great suffering she passed away on 23 September 1862. The sorrow of that time is too sacred for us to unveil.'[25]

This must have been a most terrible bereavement for Thomas. His wife was a 'beautiful Christian', well-informed, cultured, and accomplished. She had been engaged as a governess in families where her work had been appreciated, and she had grown in Christian faith and maturity. As a girl she was friendly and attractive. One of her school friends described her: 'I remember Mary Archer perfectly - her appearance, her quick movements, and her expressive face. She had a very bright nature, a very clear musical voice, and her features readily expressed any emotion present in her mind. She was naturally independent, but was always ready to give help to any who needed it, and it was always given in the kindest manner. Her ideals were high, and her life agreed with them. I should think she would develop the highest characteristics of a noble woman. Her influence on those around her must have been good. These are recollections of close on sixty years ago, but are as vivid today as they were then.'[26]

In the report to the Wesleyan Methodist Conference from 'The Gold Coast District' the description of the work at Abbeokuta focuses on the loss of Mary Champness. The opportunity, however, was not missed to promote the needs of missions. 'Many have been our trials this year, but the greatest of them was the death of Mrs Champness. She was pre-eminently fitted for the work she was called to. The females here have lost a kind and judicious friend, who felt for them as a sister, and would doubtless have done much towards elevating them in the social scale. A wide field of labour lies before those who will enter it. The Egba women need much labour specially addressed to them. If the women of England could see what are everyday sights to us, they would not hesitate, but would offer themselves, or the means of sending others, to the rescue. Satan counts more women than men among his worshippers. It is painful to see women and girls offering gifts to him who tempted and overthrew Eve, bringing sin, pain, and death to our fair world. May the removal of Mrs Champness be the means of awakening many of her countrywomen to see their own share of the responsibilities and the privileges of mission work!'[27]

Champness recounted her death in his journal and added 'I mean to give myself more fully to the Lord; to study the Word of God more and to work harder. Lord, help me to do this, for Jesus sake.'[28] He was bitterly lonely, could not bear to be at home and did not write again in his journal until the following March, 1863. He became increasing unwell and was ordered to return home by doctors in May 1863.

The return to England brought Champness before the public in a quite unexpected way. It was the Jubilee Year of the Wesleyan Foreign Missionary Society, and large meetings were to be held all over Britain. In common with many Missionary Societies at the time, the Wesleyan Methodist Missionary Society held its London meetings to publicise its work in the Exeter Hall on the Strand. The meetings for the Wesleyan Methodists were held on 2 May 1864 with the Right Hon. Joseph Napier in the Chair. The penultimate resolution of that day was 'That the thanks of the Society be presented to ... for their very acceptable Pulpit-services on the same occasion'.[29] Altogether twenty-five people are named with the Rev Thomas Champness last in the list, it would appear, in order of seniority.

George Osborn, President of Wesleyan Conference 1864

Dr George Osborn was Missionary Secretary and the President of the Conference for that year. He had always taken a great interest in Thomas Champness, and admired his commitment to the difficult situation in West Africa and Sierra Leone in particular. Dr Osborn invited him to be his assistant for his presidential year.

Because Champness's health had not been good he agreed to remain on the English stations for a year before returning for a third term to West Africa. From September 1864 he was stationed at Kineton in Oxfordshire, a country circuit suitable for his recuperation and the family home of his late wife, Mary. Part of the arrangement for preaching in this single minister country circuit was to offer a Sunday a quarter to the adjacent Banbury Circuit. Champness was entertained for lunch in the home of a local preacher and their daughter, Eliza Mary Kilby. Eliza describes the beginning of their relationship: 'One thing led to another, acquaintance ripened into friendliness, and in the spring of 1865, when I was about to pay a visit to some London friends, it was perhaps not surprising that Mr Champness should ask for my address, intimating that he had business which would shortly take him to town, and that he would like to be allowed to call and see me.'[30]

Champness did call and they attended a chapel meeting together led by the young minister Luke H. Wiseman. The next day Eliza records a romantic outing, during which she and Thomas went up to London on an old Thames steamboat called *Matrimony*, and after which Thomas asked Eliza to marry him.[31] They were married in Banbury during August 1865, with a honeymoon on the Isle of Wight. Champness had not succeeded in persuading the Missionary Committee that his health was robust enough to return to Africa, and he was instead appointed to the Banbury Circuit, staying there for two years. It was standard for Methodist ministers to move every two or three years. His ministry between 1864 and 1882 reveals that pattern.[32]

Throughout this period his health broke down, and particularly at Oxford Place, Leeds the congregation urged him to do less work. In the summer of 1872 he had a complete breakdown, and because of the help of 'Leeds friends' Thomas and Eliza were able to rent a small house in Banbury where he rested for a year. In fact, he could not face the worship of the Methodists, and attended the Quaker Meeting Rooms which 'attracted him, and in their quiet meetings for worship he communed with the Source of strength and grew refreshed'.[33] It took six months for his health to return and he was then stationed to a quiet circuit in Guernsey. They were years of great joy as well as considerable sadness. Whilst the time at Guernsey was restorative for Thomas, two of his children died in an epidemic of whooping cough during March 1874. He was deeply distressed by this and wrote in his diary for the following day, 'Was ill; thought I too should die.'[34] The following summer the family moved with their three surviving children to Louth. We have an insight into the typical Sunday for Champness from his own journal:

> A lively time at the seven o'clock prayer meeting. I think they were pleased to see me. I met a class at 9.15, and preached at 10.30; congregation rather thin, many families away on holidays; preached from 'The Barrel of Meal'. At 2p.m. I talked a bit in the Sunday School on 'Thou, child, shalt be called the prophet of the Highest'; 2.30, met two classes; 6p.m., service, better congregation; preached with liberty from 'The Christian Race'. Administered the Lord's Supper to a large number of communicants.[35]

Following three years in Louth, Champness moved to the prestigious City Road Methodist Church in London, at that time self-consciously promoting itself as the 'home of Methodism'. During this time he preached on Home Mission deputations, and in Ireland worked with Ira Sankey.[36] He also published his first volume of sermons, *New Coins from Old Gold*. The book was dedicated to his father through whom he had 'first learned that the gold of the land is good'.[37]

The Wesleyan Methodist Church had taken the decision to establish a Missioner in every District. The Rev Alex McAuley was instrumental in establishing this Connexional scheme of District Missioners and in 1879 Champness was appointed to the Newcastle-upon-Tyne District. His patron in this move was the merchant T.H. Bainbridge who owned a store in Newcastle. Here Champness had a free hand to encourage mission work and engage in evangelism, with the resources of Bainbridge to help him.[38] Eliza Champness had evident pleasure[39] in using extracts from his journal for this period. Champness had a fruitful ministry among the miners of Durham and Northumberland.

It was in Newcastle that he began the process of training young men for evangelism: 'As time went on, it was impressed on Mr Champness' mind that from many a village congregation there might be gathered together ardent and enthusiastic young men, who, when duly instructed and trained, could be well employed as Evangelists to the country places, as helpers, and extra workers with the ordained ministers of the circuit. He found such men eager to learn, hungry for a better knowledge of the Bible and the doctrines of the Christian religion, and he gathered some of these together in the early hours of the dark winter mornings in his own study, into a Theological Class, which was to some, the first step on the ladder of learning how to preach.'[40] This activity was the genesis of the type of work which would lead to the training begun in Bolton, and ultimately to the Joyful News Mission.

In May 1882, Champness was approached by the Foreign Missionary Secretaries to return to West Africa as General

Superintendent and Chairman of the Lagos and Gold Coast Districts. Eliza Champness reports the incident in some detail, and it is clear that she stood in his way, fearing for his health. Curiously, though returning to the mission field was his first desire, had he done so, he would almost certainly, not have begun the work for which he is most famous.

The Manse,
Bradford Road, Bolton

He was willing, and even eager to go; but, 'in obedience to some mysterious impression, his wife could not feel able to let him go alone. She knew, as no one else could know, how far that eager missionary's spirit soared above the body's powers, and though she struggled against it, in spite of herself she felt directed into declaring that, if he went, she must go too. This was said to be impossible, and, after a time of intense trial to both, he decided that it was the divine pleasure he should remain in English work.'[41]

The difficulty of her decision is revealed in the comment, 'God was working out His own programme, and, looking back on that terribly trying episode, I can see how it was that, even after wrestling prayer and tears, I could not assent to his going alone to the deadly West Coast'.[42]

In 1882 Champness and his family moved to Bradford Road, Bolton. During the Autumn of that same year, a Connexional Committee was contemplating the production of a halfpenny paper, which was intended to tell in simple and popular words the story of revival in Methodist circuits and Home Mission stations.[43] It would appear that Champness had been at Bolton as District Missionary for only three months when he received a letter from the President, the Rev Charles Garrett, suggesting he should become the editor of the newspaper. So it was that at the age of fifty, he was approached to undertake work which would engage all his powers for another twenty years. Both Eliza and Thomas became the editors of the successful *Joyful News* newspaper .

Through the newspaper, the *Joyful News*, there had come to them an awareness of the needs of village Methodism. If only young men could be trained and sent out to work in a simple but wholehearted way, what might be done! This idea came to Thomas and Eliza Champness as they had their early morning time of prayer together. Out of this came the 'Joyful News Mission'. They had made a donation with the first year's profits to the 'Wesleyan Methodist Worn-Out Ministers' Fund' and they decided the following year to 'try what could be done with men that were not worn out'.[44] The work began by taking two young men into the manse at Bolton, sharing the home life, studying and doing evangelistic work in the slums and the villages round about. Champness caught the vision, which much later was to become Cliff College. He proposed that such lay training was something that Methodism ought to do, and described his part as 'just doing something in a small way until Methodism is ready to undertake something of a scale worthy of itself.'[45] Champness proposed that the space for such training should be provided by the Connexion in one of the colleges which were not full. 'Birmingham would be the best of the Colleges for such an enterprise.'[46] It was in 1885 that Champness became a member of the Legal Hundred, the inner and ruling body of one hundred ordained Wesleyans. This suggests that the Wesleyan Methodists had recognised the importance of his work and its growing influence.

By the end of 1885 Champness had ten men in training in his home in Bolton, and four out in the work. That work grew phenomenally and by 1889 there were no fewer than eighty-nine evangelists, eighteen of them working overseas.[47] For a time from June 1885 they moved to the larger house at 118 Manchester Road, Bolton.[48]

The first Joyful News Caravan

On 14 May 1886, Champness and Josiah Mee, to whom he looked for guidance, went to the dedication and opening service of the first Gospel Mission Van in Selby, built at a cost of £100 by a Mr Carr of the York Wesley circuit.[49] Carr had encouraged people in the area to contribute to the cost, and the *Joyful News* indicated that 'friends'[50] contributed, which Sarah Chadwick translates as being 'supported mostly by Quaker ladies in the city of York'.[51] Champness was greatly taken with the horse-drawn gospel caravan and on the return journey remarked, 'We must have one of that sort.'[52]

Champness saw the opportunities which could be afforded by caravans, enabling evangelists to tour the countryside preaching and distributing good literature. In typical fashion he let it be known in the *Joyful News* with an illustration on the front page and a

71

description of the likely work based on the ministry of Mr Carr's Gospel Van. 'The Editor of the "Joyful News" would like to realise the dream of our artist, and be found either in person, or through one of his Evangelists, preaching from the platform of a Mission Car. He feels that we ought to have one for the use of our own men, but it costs something like one hundred pounds to build and furnish it. Are there any of our friends who will find us the money?'[53]

A family had an old horse drawn caravan on the coast of Kent, which they had used for holidays, and offered it for sale to Champness for £20.[54] A farmer at Tarporley, Cheshire, had a horse which was past farm work but equal to pulling a van along the road. Someone else sent a set of harness. Champness sent a student called

One of the larger 'Gospel cars'

David Pilgrim, the son of a Norfolk farmer, to take the horse and return with the caravan. Josiah Mee, friend and supporter of Champness, recounts the details of the journey seeing in it the guidance and protection of God. David Pilgrim collected the horse, secured the van, and drove steadily back, singing and preaching all the way in town and village, and at last arrived safe in Rochdale. The whole trip for man and horse had cost the *Joyful News* fund something under two pounds.[55] The gift of the caravan to be a Gospel Car was the first event of what would become a hallmark of the *Joyful News* Mission, where evangelists moved around the country, preaching and distributing literature. In the 9 September issue of the *Joyful News* there is a reference to 'Mr A Brittain with the "Joyful News" Caravan in Kent' in the list of *Joyful News* Evangelists.[56] The work developed quickly, would later involve Thomas Cook as Connexional evangelist and eventually lead to the ministry of the 'trekkers'.

In 1886 Champness was appointed to the Rochdale (Wesley) Circuit after 'A terrible calamity had befallen the circuit. It was a time of deepest distress and anxiety'.[57] There were altogether twenty-five young men in training for mission work and therefore it was important to find a home big enough. The former Superintendent's house was insufficient in size, but a suitable large house was secured by the circuit steward at the expense of the *Joyful News* and they moved to Cambridge House.

When the appointment to Rochdale was agreed the first step was to find a house, for the ordinary minister's manse was no use at all. Near to the chapel was a large empty house; it had been untenanted

Cambridge House, Rochdale

for years and was gladly offered to us at a low rental, if we would put it in order for ourselves. On the snowy morning when we went to view it, our feet sank in the dust on its floors, we counted eighteen broken windows, while an old and useless stove in the kitchen, and dingy dirty papers on the walls, told us there would be some money to be spent on it – yet, it had possibilities, and a huge room at the top of the house would make a fine dormitory for the brethren.

They moved in August of 1886, and the motto worked in brick on the outside, which declared 'Labour is a delight', was fully proved true as they got rid of the dirt, and made the place habitable. 'The men worked hard. While 'Owd Mo' was scrubbing the tiles in the entry he made a discovery, and called out – 'Here, missis, here's some writin' o' some mak' in some furrin' language, I think'. There was a Latin inscription in the tiles, which meant 'Peace to all who pass over'. It was with a great sense of peace, hope, and faith in God, that they began residence in Rochdale at Cambridge House which became the headquarters of the Joyful News Mission.'[58] They had a *Joyful News Convention* in September 1886, though Eliza remarked that it would be 'the first and last of its kind, as such a gathering though delightful enough was too costly to be repeated'.[59]

Joyful News Evangelists in their Caravan

Champness had not been to theological college, and yet he had acquired many skills as a preacher, evangelist and leader. These skills he shared with the students who came to the *Joyful News Home* in a kind of seminar environment, which became known as 'The Grindstone'. 'It is at the Grindstone that the native wit and spiritual genius of Champness flashes out most strikingly. The Grindstone was the class, held often at 7:00am when Champness met his young men and helped them to sharpen their wits by talking together over their work as preachers.'[60] Some of these classes were recorded week by week in the *Joyful News* to help to encourage other would-be preachers who did not have the benefit of Champness's teaching. They were full of wise, practical advice and a call for courageous service.

Champness was committed to the work in the rural areas and in the summer of 1886 when the work of the *Joyful News* moved to Rochdale, he was invited to speak to the Wesleyan Methodist Conference. It was at this Conference that Thomas Cook and Thomas Waugh were ordained, both being Connexional Evangelists, and the West London Mission was formed and led by Hugh Price Hughes and Mark Guy Pearse. Champness affirmed this work but indicated he felt called to the rural church:

> 'I rejoice greatly that you are trying to save London, and I pray God to bless every one of you; but my work is in Village Methodism, and it shall always be so. You must remember that there is a stream of human life always running out of the villages into London and our other great towns, and if you would make that stream pure, you must go right to the source of it ... I want ... to carry the gospel to the man who wears the smock-frock ... I shall put all I have in it, in the hope that the blessing of God will be upon it to the healing of the villages.'[61] The speech, for which he had no notes, was later published as a book, written up from memory by a hearer. In it he showed his distrust of the Established Church; 'in some places the poor man knows that if he sends his boy to the Methodist Sunday school, there is no place for him at the parish day school, and his little girl is told that she must not expect to have a prize or to go to the gala if she dares to go to the Methodist chapel.'[62] To effect change in the rural work would take additional people to minister and mission. He proposed to the Conference a scheme showing that his evangelists were not as expensive as an ordained minister: 'these men will cost £200 a year each less than a minister' and the church could not afford to increase the numbers of ministers.[63]

He indicated he already had evangelists in circuits who were undertaking excellent work, and whether preachers or not they could minister in the villages 'like angelic ferrets.'[64] Champness proposed that the Methodist Church appoint evangelists across rural

Methodism on what he would later call, 'Joyful News Lines'. The Conference listened politely and though during the following years it relieved Champness of the Superintendency of the Rochdale Wesley Circuit, the 'help' given to Champness was largely warm praise of his efforts rather than the strategic change he had suggested. One might comment that the same state of affairs remains today!

Thomas and Eliza Champness (centre) with Rev J. & Mrs Todhunter (left)
with students outside Castleton Hall, June 1897

The young men were lodged in Cambridge House, and the minister's house which was a circuit property Champness took over and used as a Book Depot. The Rev Theophilus Woolmer, who was the Connexional Book Steward, encouraged Champness by all means in his power. It was Woolmer who sent him the wire blind with lettering, which appeared in the window of the book depot and announced the existence of the *Joyful News and Wesleyan Book Depot*.[65] The depot became the busy hub of the expanding printing business which provided finances for the training and employment of the evangelists, and in 1893-4 donated £1000.[66] Champness was full of ideas and enterprise in the early 1890s, 'There is always something new on the way – if only a halfpenny tract.'[67]

In 1887, the Home Mission Committee honoured the work of Champness in its *Report* to the Conference. 'The Committee has put on record by formal resolution its appreciation of the work of the Rev Thomas Champness in the gathering, training and employment of Lay Evangelists, and believes that here may be found an agency which will prove to be given of God for this pioneer work, as well as for the revival, and in the future even the sustaining of some portion at least of our village work which is now feeble and inefficient.'[68]

One thing which contemporary readers will find surprising is that Champness smoked a pipe for many years, and declared to his friend, William Wakinson, that no-one enjoyed the weed more than he did.[69] 'It is significant that he never smoked when he was missioning because he was conscious that his efficiency would be impaired. But he sought compensation for his abstinence when he was at home on a Friday and Saturday. He blazed away at his "baccy" with an energy that suggested the exhaust pipe of a motor lorry. When he secured Castleton Hall and his young disciples gathered around what he termed his "grindstone", he could not (dis)allow them to smoke if he did so himself. Therefore he finally renounced the habit.'[70]

Champness had a love of foreign missions, being himself a returned missionary and reluctantly, because of the determination of Eliza, declined to return to West Africa. He had the responsibilities of the Rochdale Wesley Circuit and the growing number of students and evangelists under the *Joyful News* banner. In 1887 the President of the Conference visited Champness and saw the sheer volume and value of his work. Champness was offered an assistant from the 'list of reserve'.[71] This gave him the opportunity, not for rest, but to enlarge the work. 'The thought of the perishing heathen, and the feeling that he ought to take some steps to meet the lack of workers on the mission field, pressed upon him day and night.'[72] By the end of three years at Wesley, Champness was able to take his entire stipend from the *Joyful News* and the Book Depot.

At the celebration of the first five years of publishing the *Joyful News* in 1888, Champness asked readers to 'honour the "Joyful News" birthday, Feb 22nd, by making it a day of special prayer that God will lay his hand on fifty men whom he will choose, and call them to this work for Him…of godly, earnest and fully devoted Evangelists to One Hundred.'[73] There had been five years of successful publishing and four years where increasingly the task of training had become a priority. Champness indicated the extent of the work undertaken, and listed fifty-five evangelists including a Sister Fervent, in southern Spain, and Mr Garstang in the Bookroom. They had trained altogether sixty-eight *Joyful News* Evangelists during that time.[74] They made this fifth anniversary the occasion to publicise in the *Joyful News* their decision to respond to an invitation to send missionaries overseas. The first two missionaries, Simpson and Edlin, sailed for India on the 19 April.[75] In 1889 Champness was relieved of the itinerant ministry and the Superintendency of the Rochdale Circuit (offered in 1887). At that time he employed 89 evangelists with 18 working as missionaries and 20 of the men were in the home.[76]

REV. THOMAS CHAMPNESS,
EDITOR OF "JOYFUL NEWS" AND "BANNER OF HOPE."

Thomas Champness as the Joyful News readers
saw him

Eliza states that 'The charm and freedom of the itinerant life are all right for an ordinary family, but the Joyful News Evangelistic household would be a difficult affair to move about every three years, and it was felt that a Home more permanent must be set up.' They began to look around for a big house, with not too high a rent, and strangely enough a property became available. They had noticed, on the outskirts of Rochdale, an 'old, queer-shaped, picturesque place'.[77]

It seemed an impossible dream but Mr James Duckworth, an MP who tenanted the house, purchased a property and was about to move. A thorough inspection of the house indicated it was suitable and offered at a moderate rent. They determined to take Castleton Hall on a lease for ten years, and, after adaptation, renovation, and decoration, were able to move into a home which was much more suitable for the accommodation of men for training and rest.

Castleton Hall, Rochdale

The announcement of the move was made in the *Joyful News* in August 1889 under the heading of 'Our New Home, Castleton Hall Rochdale,' 'with a large lawn in front, stands this commodious and picturesque structure.'[78] Intriguingly this announcement gives an insight to the limitations they found in Cambridge House. At Castleton Hall, 'there are two large and lofty rooms, in which we can sleep twenty men without any difficulty. Besides this there is a kitchen garden more than an acre in extent, which will not only produce the things we need but will secure for the men a proper amount of outdoor exercise … hitherto the men have had to sleep two to a bed, but we have purchased iron beds enough for every man to have a bed for himself.'[79]

Champness and the Joyful News Flag

The formal opening of Castleton Hall as the *Joyful News* Home was on 17 September 1889. The preachers were all the key people in Methodism, and Champness supporters: Charles Garrett, Hugh Price Hughes, Henry Smart, Josiah Mee, Nehemiah Curnock, Henry Rattenbury, H. Scholefield, and J. Todhunter who had been a tutor with Champness since the move to Rochdale. The Rev Charles Garrett hoisted a flag, with the words, "JOYFUL NEWS" HOME, in red letters. The assembled host gave three cheers for the 'Queen, for Charles Garrett, for the Forward Movement, and for Mr and Mrs Champness.'[80] The extensive grounds at Castleton Hall needed continuing attention and it was there that 'Manual' was started, a custom which continues to this day.[81] At the new Home they could have fifty men in residence with some of them remaining for only three months.

When he took Castleton Hall, Champness set about the development of the movement on a large scale. He published a book setting out his plans under the title, *Shall Methodism Attack the World on 'Joyful News' Lines?*[82] Chadwick refers to the booklet in his Cliff College Report in 1930:

The plan was a kind of mixture of the China Inland Mission and the Church Army, with suggestions borrowed from D.L. Moody and General Booth. There were seven lines on which the work was organised:

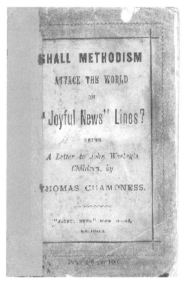

Champness's manifesto for mission

1. They were to be the Ally and not the rival of existing Agencies.

2. To use our own Sons ourselves instead of letting other Agencies have them.

3. To hold out no premium to unworthy motives, because no salary shall be given.

4. To send into the Foreign Field only those who have proved themselves equal to it by the work they have done in England, and the economical way they have lived.

5. To secure none but Effective Men, because they are obliged to retire if, after a fair trial, they are not successful.

6. To pass into the Ranks of the Ministry those who have proved themselves fit to do the Work.

7. To depend upon the Unsolicited Gifts of God's People, so as not to interfere with Subscriptions and Collections for Connexional Purposes.[83]

With these seven aims Champness proposed that Methodism should have two or three of his Evangelists in every Circuit and on every Foreign Mission Station. The conditions were spartan, the pay meagre, and the administration autocratic. No one had a salary or even a fixed allowance. The Evangelists' needs were provided for, and an account of every penny had to be given when application was made for further supplies. Nevertheless there was no lack of men and women willing to train and work with Champness. Some were sent into the work with only twenty weeks training, but they overflowed with enthusiasm, initiative and godliness. Methodism never really took to the scheme, though many Circuits welcomed the work of the Evangelists. Champness received criticism for his vision. In a private diary, he wrote, 'I am feeling very much the conduct of the ministers. I have to smart for this effort we are making to train men to do the work which some ministers cannot do and will not do. But the work of God must be done, and if I can raise up men to do it, I shall, whatever it costs me ... I have a joy set before *me*, and I shall win it – the joy of seeing the work well done, and in the villages of England and Africa hundreds of men doing the work of God on *Joyful News* Lines.'[84] On the foreign field there were difficulties which led Champness to the conclusion that there, in the work of the Methodist Church, the plan was not workable. For twenty years *Joyful News* evangelism was worked on the lines laid down by Champness.[85]

Eliza Mary Champness

Champness relied on Eliza throughout their marriage as the person who in effect ran the institution at Cambridge House and then Castleton Hall, and particularly as sub-editor for the *Joyful News*. Together they dealt with the issues that confronted them, and though they had willing helpers and wise people around them, Thomas referred to their daily conversations of the issues as a 'committee of two'.[86] They also had the practice of praying each morning at 'the beginning of the day – sometimes very early in the morning – with a cup of tea together, and a brief season of prayer.'[87] It was undoubtedly this bonding and prayer which became the real power in the *Joyful News* movement as a whole.

Joyful News Evangelist
Mr Darvil

Joyful News Evangelist
Mr Walter Bradford

Champness had a very charming way of raising money. He would indicate that he himself, or he and Eliza considered that a particular venture was now the new way ahead, and it could be achieved if someone would send a particular sum of money, finding the caravan and horse, sending missionaries to India, or increasing the number of students. The *Methodist Recorder* carried a story indicating that 'Mr Champness refuses to beg'[88] but he was a good businessman, sharing his needs openly in the *Joyful News* and at every opportunity. He printed envelopes when he was at Cambridge House with a small drawing of the house and the caption, 'Mr Champness says that if every Methodist took a copy of the "Joyful News" weekly, he would keep a Hundred Evangelists'.[89] As already noted earlier the newspaper and the profits from the sale of books were the key elements in funding the development of the Home and the Mission. The *Methodist Recorder* commented on this, 'Very often the Mission is in straits for money. It must have collapsed long ago but for the help which has come from the *Joyful News* and the Book Depot.'[90] The Rev H.T. Smart called the *Joyful News* 'a good milch cow, and if all who love the villages will only help to feed her, she will produce enough to enable the Editor to do great things for the men in smock frocks',[91] therefore 'Push the Joyful News'.

People gave to the work as they heard of the missions and the work of the evangelists. Week by week these, normally small gifts of a few shillings or pounds, were individually noted in the *Joyful News*. Champness was also in touch with some businessmen in different parts of the country; thus the Bainbridge family in Newcastle continued to support the work through to its arrival at Cliff.

In her brief history of the work Eliza indicates that people gave because they trusted Champness, as well as believing in his work. 'And right well and heartily has the wealth of well-to-do Methodists

Joyful News Evangelist
Mr Williams

Joyful News Evangelist
Mr Hamilton

been entrusted to the man who, as they could plainly see, was ready to spend it for the extension of Methodism in the villages, and the practical training of those who should carry the message of salvation through the land. The charm of a great purpose has been the means of evoking sympathy, prayers, and help, from the first day until now.'[92]

Things were not always easy and in 1895, when income was at a very low ebb he was prepared to take immediate and significant action, though it was painful to do it.[93] The *Joyful News* carried the grim tidings under the title 'Dismissal of Sixty Joyful News Agents.' 'We have been troubled by the fact that the Joyful News Mission had not been supported as it formerly was. And this has been accompanied by a decline in our Book business; consequently we have not been able to give as largely as we have been used to.'[94] Unusually the English is clumsy in this report, which suggests there is real emotion in the statement. The report went on to say that, 'Accordingly we have sent a circular to most (about 60) of our workers saying they must not consider us any longer responsible for their support.'[95] However as a result the income increased and the Champnesses made every effort to reduce expenditure.[96]

Champness was a campaigner and used the *Joyful News* to gather support for his views about temperance and his proposal to the Methodist Conference that no-one engaged in the 'liquor trade' should be appointed to an office within the Church at any level.[97] Week after week he promoted this view. As chapter 4 indicates graphically he regularly spoke against the evils of drink. Indeed as he passed over the editorship of the newspaper to Chadwick, the assumption is that the forces ranged against these crusaders of the gospel are 'Strong drink and Sin'.[98]

Joyful News Evangelist
Mr Thomas Dyer

From the late 1880s, when he and his wife formed an alliance with Mr Clegg, they had maintained a home for training female evangelists, first of all in Halifax and then at Rugby and finally at Wellington. The lease for that home in Wellington had been closed when Miss Winter retired and the home was disposed of. They paid great tribute to the work of Miss Winter. 'We cannot be too thankful for the good work done by Miss Winter in the Home for Women Workers at Wellington. She has succeeded in a remarkable way in teaching and training our workers to understand the Word of God, while their help in visiting the cottages of the working people, as well as the lodging house at Wellington, and in the villages of that Circuit, is of great value.'[99] There would be a gap of sixty-three years before women were welcomed as students at Cliff College.

The final years for Champness were not easy. He was seventy and had not been in the best of health. During the autumn of 1902 an outbreak of smallpox caused not only illness among those training, but forced a reduction in their work and the closure of the Home. 'Still, when we think that only one of the men had to be removed to the Hospital, we are grateful to God. Our medical man said it was a miracle that we had only one case.'[100]

The lease of Castleton Hall was to expire in 1903 and in their report to the Conference, Thomas and Eliza asked to retire. 'The force of years makes us less fit for the strenuous duties we have hitherto attempted, and we must retire into the background. We indulge in the hope that Methodism will not allow our work to drop. We should like to retain our Foreign Mission workers in our own hands, but the villages should be cared for, and young Local Preachers trained for Service ... we are grateful to God and to the Wesleyan Conference for allowing us to work on the lines of the "Joyful News" Mission, and we speak with affection and appreciation,

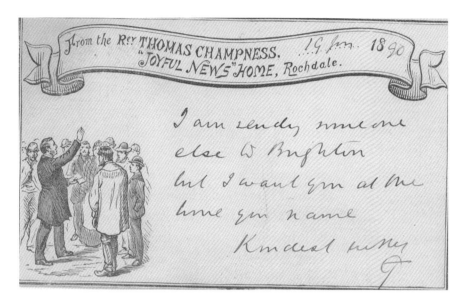

Champness lost no
opportunity to
promote the work

not only of those who have given the money, but those who have trusted us with a free hand. We also speak with delight and esteem of the men and women who have toiled for our Mission at home and abroad.'[101] As they laid down the responsibilities of the *Training Home and Mission* in the summer of 1903, Thomas and Eliza had in the employ of the Mission thirty-five men and thirteen women.

Champness was also against the Education Act of 1902, with a hatred which is described as 'unquenchable'.[102] The Act had the effect of requiring all ratepayers to be responsible for the maintenance of religious teaching in day schools throughout the country. Normally this teaching would be delivered by the Church of England Parish Priest and Champness, who was fiercely Nonconformist, objected to this. When in retirement as a super-numerary, he went to Leicester gaol as a Passive Resister because he refused to pay what he regarded as an infamous sectarian rate.'[103]

Thomas died in Lutterworth in 1905 where he was buried in the Methodist churchyard. In a rather quaint requirement he was buried head first towards the chapel wall, just at a point where he and Eliza sat in the congregation, so he would be as close to her in death as in life. She took geat delight in the opening of the 'Champness Wing' at Cliff and her writing continued. In March 1909 the *Joyful News* announced with sadness that, 'The mother of the *Joyful News* movement is gone'.[104] The articles were written by Josiah Mee and Henry T. Smart, who had worked with them from the beginning, and both Thomas Cook and Samuel Chadwick. Cook wrote, 'What Mrs Booth was to the Salvation Army, Mrs Champness was to the *Joyful News* Mission ... Her entire consecration to the work, her extraordinary gifts and energy, her ability in the management of affairs, her keen insight into human character and her wise counsel are the things for which she will be remembered.'[105] Thomas and Eliza Champness together laid the foundations for the ministry and mission which still continues at Cliff College.

Thomas Champness towards the
end of his life

1 William Wakinshaw, 'Men Who made Cliff, 1. Thomas Champness', in *Cliff Witness*, Vol. 1, No 6, p.104.

2 It is at this point that many projects fail, because the founders are not able or willing to hand over responsibility and step down leaving 'their project' under the supervision of another. A tragic example would be the Luton Industrial College, envisioned and led successfully by the Rev William Gowland, but he was unable to face withdrawal and wanted to retain an office in the building when his successor was appointed. Inevitably the work has now ceased.

3 Joe Brice, *The Crowd for Christ* (London: Hodder and Stoughton, 1934), pp.11-23.

4 Archive item E19 which we have not been able to identify as an article in the *Joyful News* or *Cliff Witness.*

5 E19 p.2 (hand written notes by Samuel Chadwick).

6 Eliza M. Champness, *The Life Story of Thomas Champness* (London: Charles Kelly, 1907). Their friend and supporter Josiah Mee also finds this interesting in his *Thomas Champness as I Knew Him* (London: Kelly, 1906) pp.99-100.

7 Sarah Chadwick, *Cliff, Past and Present*, p.1.

8 Sarah Chadwick, *Cliff, Past and Present*, p.1.

9 Sarah Chadwick, *Cliff, Past and Present*, p.1.

10 George Osborn became the Secretary for the Wesleyan Methodist Missionary Society, and President of the Wesleyan Methodist Conference. He helped Champness at a number of crucial times in his ministry, not least when Champness returned from West Africa.

11 Eliza Champness, *The Life*, p.6.

12 Eliza Champness, *The Life*, p.27.

13 Eliza Champness, *The Life*, pp.17-34.

14 Archive E19, p.2.

15 Eliza Champness, *The Life*, p.35.

16 Taken from a letter from the Rev Richard Harper, who was also present in the interview as a candidate and reported to Mrs Champness in a letter 18 November 1905 and printed in *The Life*, pp.43–44.

17 Eliza Champness, *The Life*, p.41.

18 Eliza Champness, *The Life*, p.45.

19 Eliza Champness, *The Life*, p.45.

20 Eliza Champness, *The Life*, p.97.

21 Eliza Champness, *The Life*, p.97.

22 It would appear that Mary Archer lived in or near Kineton where Mr Archer was a circuit steward. Thomas Champness returned there in 1864.

23 Eliza Champness, *The Life*, pp.99-100.

24 Eliza Champness, *The Life*, pp.104, 107 and 112.

25 Eliza Champness, *The Life*, p.114.

26 Eliza Champness, *The Life*, p.114.

27 *Report of the Wesleyan Methodist Missionary Society 1863*, p.123.

28 Eliza Champness, *The Life*, p.114.

29 *The Report of the Wesleyan Methodist Missionary Society for the year ending 1864*, pp. v – vi.

30 Eliza Champness, *The Life*, p.127.

cont.

31 Eliza Champness, *The Life,* p.128.
32 1864 Kineton; 1865-7 Banbury; 1867-70 Otley; 1870-72 Leeds (Oxford Place); 1872-3 Banbury for a year's rest; 1873-74 St Peter Port, Guernsey; 1874-77 Louth; 1877-79 London City Road circuit with responsibilities at St John's Square; 1879-82 Newcastle-on-Tyne.
33 Eliza Champness, *The Life,* p.161.
34 Eliza Champness, *The Life,* p.168.
35 Eliza Champness, *The Life,* p.172.
36 Eliza Champness, *The Life,* pp.187-8.
37 This is indicated in the dedication at the front of the book after the title page. We do not have a first edition, 1878 but a fourth edition published by the Joyful News Book Room.
38 T.H. Bainbridge was a patron of many societies, including the Children's Home begun by the Rev Bowman Stephenson, and in time was to become involved with Cliff College.
39 Eliza Champness, *The Life,* pp.190–208.
40 Eliza Champness, *The Story of the Joyful News Mission* (Rochdale: Joyful News Publishing, 1899), p.2.
41 Vallance Cook, *The Life*, p.209.
42 Vallance Cook, *The Life*, p.210.
43 *Methodist Recorder*, Winter 1894, p.49.
44 *Methodist Recorder,* Winter 1894, p.50.
45 Chadwick in 'Thomas Champness' E19, p.5.
46 *Joyful News,* 9 April 1885
47 Chadwick in same paper in E19, p.5.
48 Eliza Champness*, The Life,* p.223.
49 *Joyful News,* 27 May 1886.
50 Ibid.
51 Sarah Chadwick p.12.
52 Josiah Mee, *Champness*, p.63.
53 *Joyful News,* 1 July 1886.
54 Eliza Champness, *The Story*, reveals that the money came in two donations, one by a Bolton lady and the other by a London friend, p.6.
55 Josiah Mee, *Champness,* pp.64-6.
56 *Joyful News,* 9 September 1886.
57 H.K., in the *Methodist Recorder* (Winter Ed. 1894), p.50. Eliza reveals that the minister in question absconded with the savings of his people, resulting in their financial ruin, p.227.
58 Eliza Champness, *The Story*, p.7.
59 Eliza Champness, *The Life,* p.236.
60 Chadwick, 'The Wit and Wisdom of Thomas Champness' E19, p.5.
61 Eliza Champness, *The Life,* p.234, part of the statement by Champness to the Conference which was published later that same year as *Old Salt in a New Cruse.*
62 Ibid, p.230.
63 Ibid, p.231.

cont.

64 H.K., *Methodist Recorder* (Winter, 1894), p.50.
65 Eliza Champness, *The Life*, p.245.
66 H.K., *Methodist Recorder* (Winter, 1894), p.53. Champness expected to pay an evangelist £50 per annum.
67 H.K., *Methodist Recorder* (Winter, 1894), p.53.
68 *Report of the Wesleyan Home Mission Fund,* 1887.
69 William Wakinshaw, 'Men Who made Cliff, 1. Thomas Champness', p.105.
70 William Wakinshaw, 'Men Who made Cliff, 1. Thomas Champness', p.105. I have added the prefix in parenthesis because without a double negative the sentence and the point made do not make sense.
71 Eliza Champness, *The Life,* p.242.
72 Eliza Champness, *The Life,* p.242.
73 *Joyful News*, 16 February 1888, p.1.
74 Ibid.
75 There is no explanation given for this change of plan. It is possible that the Champnesses decided, despite his connection with the region, not to send a Joyful News Missionary to West Africa, where so many Europeans had died.
76 Eliza Champness, *The Life,* p.244.
77 H.T. Smart, *Thomas Champness as I knew Him,* p.81.
78 *Joyful News,* 1 August 1889.
79 *Joyful News,* 1 August 1889.
80 *Joyful News,* 26 September 1889.
81 Joe Wood (ed), 'Under Thomas Champness at Rochdale', in *The Cliff Witness,* Vol. 2, No 6, 1938, p.93.
82 I assume this was published by Champness from the Joyful News Book Room shortly after his move to Castleton Hall in 1889. We do not have a copy in our archive.
83 Joe Brice, *The Crowd for Christ*, (London: Hodder and Stoughton, 1934), p.37 where his list is set out slightly differently but covers the same points, though in a different order.
84 Eliza Champness, *The Life*, pp.241-2.
85 *Cliff College Report 1930,* p.16-18.
86 Eliza Champness, *The Life,* p.249.
87 Eliza Champness, *The Life,* pp.217-8.
88 *Methodist Recorder,* Winter edition 1894, p.54.
89 Taken from a used envelope dated 3 October 1888, in the College archive, section C.
90 *Methodist Recorder,* Winter edition 1894, p.54.
91 *Joyful News*, 9 September 1886.
92 Eliza Champness, *The Story*, p.2.
93 Eliza Champness, *The Life,* p.261.
94 *Joyful News,* 11 July 1895.
95 Ibid.
96 The *Joyful News* for 8 August records income £131 13s 6½d and an expenditure of £21 1s 8d. This continued for some months, though eventually as they took on more evangelists, income hardly met expenditure.

cont.

91

97   *Joyful News,* 10 August 1899.
98   *Joyful News,* 7 September 1905.
99   *Report of the Wesleyan Home Mission Fund, 1903.*
100 *Report of the Wesleyan Home Mission Fund, 1903.*
101 Ibid.
102 William Wakinshaw, 'Men Who made Cliff, 1. Thomas Champness', p.105.
103 William Wakinshaw, 'Men Who made Cliff, 1. Thomas Champness', p.105.
104 *Joyful News,* 11 March, 1909.
105 Ibid.

CHAPTER 4

The Joyful News

Thomas and Eliza Champness had been at Bolton, he as District Missionary, for only three months in the autumn of 1882, when he received a letter which would transform his ministry. It was from the President of the Wesleyan Conference, the Rev Charles Garrett. Champness noted in his diary, 'Nov 10th – Letter from the President respecting a new paper, and asking me to go over and see him. Find they want me to edit!!!'[1]

Eliza Champness refers to the fact that there was only one Methodist paper at the time, 'and, in the nature of things, the cause of evangelism could only find infrequent place in its pages'.[2] They wanted the newspaper, if produced, to be like the *War Cry* which General Booth had begun three years before and which was devoted to evangelism.[3] Carlile then followed Champness within years publishing the *Church Army Gazette*.[4]

Champness declared his willingness to accept the editorship on two conditions: that he would receive no salary and that he should have a free hand and full editorial responsibility.[5]

Eliza Champness indicates that the President and his committee were ready to grant the second condition, but the first staggered them! No salary? No, not a penny. Thomas would not be their paid servant. Apparently Garrett was authorised to offer £600 with which to commence the new paper.[6] It would appear that the committee had looked for other ways of producing the paper and considered three options – the Wesleyan Book Room, the *Methodist Recorder* (then a quarterly magazine), and an independent printer, but no one would take it on. 'Nov 25th – Heard again from President respecting the paper, and determined that I go in for it.' In his Journal for the 27 November he noted, 'Have letters from Woolmer[7], the President, and one signed by Dr Osborn, though written by Woolmer. Shall have to take the paper. God bless me in it, and help me never to write one bitter word!!!' For a week or two the negotiations were carried on with the other possible publishers, but a satisfactory solution could not be found, and therefore the President and Dr Osborn pressed the matter on Champness. 'Dec 2nd – Letter from G Osborn. I have to do the work of editing the paper. May it be a converting agency!'

Having decided to take the project on, Champness began to search for a sub-editor and printer. The former was necessary because he was to continue as the District Missionary in the Bolton District, and clearly the publication of a weekly newspaper would be time consuming. There was difficulty in finding both.[8] In typical fashion Thomas and Eliza mobilised their energies in two ways; they turned to prayer and invited Josiah Mee to join them, whilst at the same time 'he ventilated it (the needs for the paper) in his letters and thus enlisted the prayers and sympathy of his friends.'[9] This dual approach, of prayer and publicising the need, was typical of the way Champness tried to solve problems.

Eliza's account is compelling: 'Conversing together very early one morning about this time, we found ourselves again at the usual theme, the newspaper that could not be produced, and my husband said: "You see I am not rich; if I had even a little capital, it would be different. However I am not worrying; if the Lord wants us to do it, He will make it possible." And as we prayed the way was suddenly made so plain to us that we neither of us ever doubted that it was from the Lord. A small legacy from my father, the interest of which had been a sort of "reserve fund" in our limited resources, was placed at the disposal of the new venture, and together we praised God and resolved to go on in His strength. My husband accepted my co-operation with great joy, and it was characteristic of him that he lost no time. "We will begin at once," he said, "and you shall be my sub-editor."[10] It is not surprising that Eliza took on this task. She was clearly a woman of considerable literary ability. Her account of the life and work of Champness is outstanding and compares very favourably with the biography by Josiah Mee. She is described as 'intellectually one of the strongest and most vigorous women in Britain'.[11] Thomas related to his wife with deference and respect, first in not going to West Africa, and then when, with evident enthusiasm, he appointed her to the post of sub-editor. There were some senior Methodists though who had 'doubts about the propriety of a woman editor'.[12] From February 1893, the title page

Josiah Mee

of the newspaper declared the editors to be Thomas and Eliza Mary Champness.

Many of the printers were asking too much for undertaking the work of printing the paper, but Josiah Mee knew of a young printer in Bacup, Mr W.J. Tyne, who calculated that the project was feasible.

Mee had been impressed by his business dealings and his general experience of printing including the *Bacup Times*.[13] Tyne was willing to invest a few hundred pounds in the plant necessary for this project,[14] and Champness remarked to him, 'Mr Tyne, we will make you the best-known printer in Methodism, sir.'[15]

The question of the name for the newspaper had not been resolved. In a morning prayer meeting around the kitchen table, Thomas, Eliza and Josiah Mee were conscious of this need when Josiah quoted familiar lines from an Isaac Watt's hymn, 'The joyful news of sins forgiven, of hell subdued, and peace with heaven.'[16] Champness seized on the name. 'That will do Josiah. We'll call it *Joyful News*'.[17] In smaller print underneath the name they inserted 'of sins forgiven, of hell subdued and peace with heaven'.

On 22 January he recorded in his Journal, 'Settled to go on with the paper. The Lord of hosts is with us, and in His name we will set up our banners!'[18] It is astonishing that only one month later the first issue of the paper was published and the volume of work is hinted at in Eliza's comment 'What care and pains were ours in preparation for that day!'[19] The first edition made the policy clear:

WHAT WE WANT
  News of Recent Revivals
  Stories of Remarkable conversions
  Answers to Prayer
  Illustrations of providence

WHAT WE DO NOT WANT
  Politics
  Controversy
  Connexional Finance

JOYFUL NEWS,

A Journal devoted to Recording and Spreading the Glad Tidings of Salvation.

EDITED BY REV. THOMAS CHAMPNESS.

No. 1.   Registered for Transmission Abroad.   THURSDAY, FEBRUARY 22, 1883.   Price ONE HALFPENNY.

FIRST WORDS.

We begin our task in the spirit of thankfulness. This enterprise comes to the front in a time of peace and increase, and it is our work, as it will be our joy, to tell of the kindling and spreading of the holy flame of Revival. Why should there not be a spiritual awakening all over the country? and why should not the Methodist people be the widest awake of all? The years that are past can tell enough of hours wasted in sleep or idleness, while the plough has been left in the unfinished furrow, and the precious grain, which might have been "seed for the sower and bread for the eater," has been devoured by the fowls of the air. Thank God, there are already the signs of a glorious season. The fields, it not in every place "white unto the harvest," are green with promise for the reaper, whose sickle, it may be, has wellnigh rusted on the nail for want of the brave and industrious hand to wield it. "He that soweth and he that reapeth" shall "rejoice together." It is so, even now, in part, and we confidently look for an abundant harvest of souls to be ingathered to the Lord's garner. It is with the hope of encouraging all kinds of "labourers for the harvest," and of fostering revival ideas, that we have taken our place among the religious agencies of the day. Will not our readers pray that we may have the desire of our hearts, in spreading the intelligence of a general outpouring of the Holy Spirit? It will be our delight to chronicle both work and results, at home and abroad, and in every way that lies in our power to push the frontier line of

our King's territory farther and still further, till He comes Himself to take possession of the kingdom promised to Him by the Father.

As we wish to set our contributors an example of brevity, it only remains for us to say, in the words of Boaz, "The Lord be with you;" and we shall be glad if the toilers in the Lord's field reply, "The Lord bless thee."

HINTS TO THOSE WHO WRITE FOR THIS PAPER.

1.—Be Interesting.
2.—Never Use Two Words when One will do.
3.—Do not Exaggerate.
4.—Write on One Side of the Paper Only.
5.—If You are not an Educated Person do not Worry About Grammar or Spelling; we will Make it all Right.
6.—Sign your Name, and send it to Rev. T. Champness, 80, Bradford Street, Bolton.

What we want.
News of recent Revivals.
Stories of Remarkable Conversions.
Answers to Prayer.
Illustrations of Providence.

What we do not want.
Politics.
Controversy.
Confessional Finance.

How to be charitable, and at the same time help the circulation of "Joyful News."

Buy sixpence worth of this number, and give them to a hungry boy to sell. He will hand his bread, and put good reading into the hands of some who would not have seen our paper.

BIRMINGHAM.

The Rev. T. COOK

Begins a MISSION in ISLINGTON CHAPEL, ON SUNDAY, MARCH 4th.

METHODISTS OF BIRMINGHAM Rally round him, and expect that hundreds will be converted the first week.

Any one wishing to advertise Services can have a Special Edition of the Paper from 100 upwards, with their Advertisement put in the above space. For terms apply to the Printer,

W. J. TYNE, Bacup, Manchester.

TELL IT OUT.

"My soul shall make her boast in the Lord, the humble shall hear thereof and be glad. Oh, magnify the Lord with me, and let us exalt his name together." When David wrote these words he had been having a good time, and he was determined to let folks know it. Friends, if the Lord blesses your soul, "make your boast in the Lord." Perhaps it may cheer up some "humble" one, who is tempted to look on the dark side. Preachers, if God has not His seal on your work, and sinners are being saved under your preaching, don't let a false shame keep you silent. "Magnify the Lord with me," sang David. It is a snare of the devil which says—"Oh, I don't like to boast of my own success." Dear friend, it is not your success. Don't be over modest, nor at all backward in saying

"Praise the Lord!" It is His work. Only Jesus can save precious souls; and when the news of sins forgiven reaches the penitent at your Sunday night prayer meeting, it is not your doing, but

"The Spirit answers to the blood
And tells him he is born of God."

Glory for ever to Jesus; "let us exalt His name together."

ELIZA M. CHAMPNESS.

SERMON

By the Rev. CHARLES GARRETT, President of the Conference, AT THE LAST SERVICE IN OLDHAM STREET CHAPEL, MANCHESTER.

Thursday, February 1, 1883.

TRANSCRIBED FROM SHORTHAND NOTES TAKEN BY WRIGHT A. SHORELTON, REPORTER FOR "MANCHESTER GUARDIAN."

"The Lord our God be with us as He was with our fathers. Let Him not leave us nor forsake us." 1st Kings viii. 57.

My text, as you know, is from the prayer that Solomon offered at the consecration of the Temple—the most sublime prayer, I suppose, that was ever offered from human lips. It was marked by deep reverence, and great humility, and it everywhere recognises man's absolute dependence upon God. My text may be regarded as almost a summary of this prayer; and it has struck me as being specially applicable to the peculiar circumstances under which we are met to-night. "The Lord our God be with us as He was with our fathers; let Him not leave us nor forsake us." You will see that there is, first, a grateful recognition of God's presence with the fathers. When Solomon uttered these words he, of course, referred to the fathers of the Jewish nation. And who can denist that God was with them? An almost unbroken series of miracles proclaimed His presence. I wish to apply the words to our Methodist fathers, and an almost—may I not say a quite?—

unbroken series of moral miracles demonstrated His presence with them. Let us look at them for a while, that we may be humbled, and stimulated, and so led to copy their example, that we may be prepared to carry out and complete the work which they began. One of the great defects of the present generation of Methodists is their want of acquaintance with their Methodist forefathers. There are, I fear, a large number of our young Methodists growing up to whom the names of, say, John Nelson, and Mrs. Hester Ann Rogers have no charm. This ought not so to be, and if to-night, in the few words that I shall speak, I can only persuade the young people who are listening to me to go home and study the glorious biographies which we possess, I am quite sure that our meeting will not have been in vain.

Let us look then, I repeat, for a moment or two at our Methodist forefathers, and we shall see that "there were giants in those days." Mine is a very rough sketch of them—and I must therefore be very imperfect; but

LOOK FIRST AT THEIR FAITH.
They were men "strong in faith, giving glory to God." The late George Dawson said that what the world wanted was a church for doubters. I thank God the Methodist church has never been able to supply that want. Ours is a church for "believers." For "believers suffering," it may be; for "believers fighting," it may be; for "believers working," it may be, but not for believers doubting. Their faith was simple, and strong. What God said, they believed, because God said it, and they did not want any man, or any set of men, to endorse the words of Jehovah. To them God was God, and the devil was the devil, and sin was sin, and pardon was pardon, and hell was hell, and heaven was heaven. Hence when they went out they had a creed, and they could say, "We believe, and therefore speak." And that is one secret of their success. When a preacher is in the pulpit, there is a sympathy between you and him which enables you at once to discover

JEHOVAH—NISSI!   JEHOVAH—JIREH!

The Rev. Charles Garrett, President of the Wesleyan Conference, Preaching the Last Sermon in Oldham-street Chapel, Manchester, Thursday, 1st February, 1883.
(Drawn and Engraved by J. Spence, Market Street, Manchester.)

Issue No. 1 of the Joyful News

They made some policy decisions which would make the *Joyful News* into the most progressive Methodist newspaper of the time.[20] They determined to have an illustration on the front page and the first issue depicted the final services at the Oldham Street Chapel, Manchester, where the President Charles Garrett was the preacher.[21] The picture showed the full congregation and Garrett in the pulpit. Eliza reports, 'The picture was crude and ill-executed; it cost us a lot of money, and much trouble and anxiety, for we were totally ignorant of the business as to procuring illustrations; but it was a triumph in its way, for it adorned (!) one of the first halfpenny religious papers in the world, and absolutely the first illustrated Methodist paper in this country.'[22] The sermon preached at the final service of the chapel before the building of the Manchester and Salford Mission, was printed in full.[23] The text was 1 Kings 8:57, 'The Lord our God be with us as he was with our fathers. Let him not leave us nor forsake us'. Appropriate too, for Thomas and Eliza and a small company of their friends had invested great energy and risked much in the launch of the paper.

They had also decided to make the *Joyful News* into a campaigning newspaper, taking a lead in encouraging evangelism and mission. This was not simply a vehicle reporting news. They wanted to initiate that news by encouraging Christian people to be engaged in the ministry of evangelism. 'The paper became a new kind of tract, and was bought for distribution.'[24] Part of this strategy was to secure regular articles from leading Methodist writers including Hugh Price Hughes, Mark Guy Pearse, Josiah Mee and the younger Thomas Cook, but the bulk of the material came from *Joyful News*' many supporters. It was to be a people's paper and the editors deliberately invited ordinary people from every corner of Methodism to send in articles and comments about the work of the church, under the heading 'Missions and Revivals'. They enlisted people to write reports, 'Hundreds of letters, with copies of the early issues, were sent out to enlist the help of those who could write or "report" and very soon the Methodist people responded joyfully to our appeal for news from all quarters.'[25]

The key to Champness's fresh style is identified in a series of articles published as 'The Young Preacher's Guide'. Champness bears witness that next to the Bible itself, no writer influenced him more than Bunyan. Chadwick, reflecting on the ability of Champness to communicate easily with working people, commented, 'The man who has mastered from Bunyan will be in touch with the common people as few men can be...'[26]

Champness clearly read widely and valued the works of George Herbert, John Ruskin, and John Richard Green's *Short History of the English People*. He also paid tribute to the Baptist preacher C.H. Spurgeon. He sought to emulate their ability to describe and to capture the imagination of the reader. 'With such a background we are not surprised that Champness reveals wisdom as well as wit in all his writings. There is moreover a depth of spiritual understanding, a deep heart experience of the things of God, and withal a tender appreciation of the problems and trials of human life. He knew and understood the common people. No wonder they heard him gladly and treasured his printed words.'[27]

Within less than a month after its first issue, the sales reached 30,000 and Champness records in his journal, '*Te Deum Laudamus!*'[28] People used the paper for evangelistic purposes, and the young Samuel Chadwick sold five hundred copies of the first issue. A man was converted, and in telling the story 'SC' wrote his first article for the *Joyful News*. In response Champness, in a way that was more prophetic than he could know, wrote to Chadwick, 'There is money in your ink-pot, if you care to take it out.'[29] Champness was creative about increasing the circulation, and in July 1884 he launched a scheme in which he offered 'a suitable present' to anyone who could distribute the paper to fifty subscribers for six months.[30] Champness was hoping for one thousand 'boys and girls' to assist in this task. Prizes of up to a value of five shillings were distributed the following February.[31] This was a significant task and it was not repeated. By the end of the 1880s the circulation was 50,000 per week.[32]

REPENTANCE JUNCTION.

The impact of the *Joyful News* was such that it was imitated in a number of places. One unusual result was *La Bonne Nouvelle* published by Mr H.W. Gibson of St Cloud, Paris within six months of Champness's first edition. It began as a result of a mission at St Cloud,[33] and Gibson arranged for it to be printed and distributed as an evangelistic and nurturing paper on *Joyful News* lines. Champness promoted *La Bonne Nouvelle* by suggesting that young people learning French may find it helpful, for they 'will get good and holy ideas while they improve their knowledge of the language.'[34]

At the end of the first year he was in a position to send a donation to the 'Wesleyan Methodist Worn-out Ministers' Fund'. There is some question about the amount – 'HK' in the *Methodist Recorder* says £200,[35] and Eliza £100.[36] However the *Report of the Worn-Out*

EVANGELISTIC SERVICES

Are now being held in the

WESLEYAN CHAPEL.

Thus saith the Lord:

"CONSIDER YOUR WAYS."

The above represents No. 12 of "JOYFUL NEWS" series of Placards, and is intended for the announcement of Special Services. The size is 30 by 40, printed in red and black, and may be had at 3s. per dozen, from Rev. T. CHAMPNESS, 118, Manchester Road, Bolton; or W. J. TYNE "JOYFUL NEWS" Office, Bacup.

Wesleyan Methodist Ministers' and Ministers' Widows' Auxiliary Fund, to give it its full title, for the year 1883, simply indicates among other donations from Methodist organisations, 'and £50 from the Proprietors of *Joyful News*.'[37] Two further donations are recorded. For the year 1884 there was, '£100 from the Proprietors of the *Joyful News*, being double the amount in previous years.'[38] The third donation is for the year beginning 1885 and is again '£100 from the proprietors of *Joyful News*, per the Rev Thomas Champness.'[39] These are significant donations, as £100 was equivalent to £5,000 today.

Regularly there were pleas for people to increase the circulation and discounts for bulk buys so that people could make a small profit towards their own local work. Champness decided that the employment of the evangelists would rest with him and the paper would enable him to fund the project; therefore, 'Push the Joyful News'.[40]

Tyne's imprint from a Joyful News Almanac 1899 which shows the relocated address

PRINTED AND PUBLISHED FOR THOMAS AND ELIZA MARY CHAMPNESS BY W. J. TYNE & Co. LTD., EDGELEY PRINTING WORKS, STOCKPORT; P
PRICE ONE HALFPENNY.

W.J. Tyne - a picture from the Joyful News 1917

As the circulation grew Champness became concerned that the printing press remained at Bacup, where there were only twenty-four trains daily, and urged Tyne to go to Manchester. In February 1890, his printing press was moved to Edgeley Printing Works in Stockport, where 'hundreds of trains passed through daily'.[41] The paper was printed there until the 11 July 1940 edition, and after that in Chesterfield by Wilfred Edmunds.[42] 'W.J. Tyne was a shrewd businessman, sensitive and shy. He seldom advertised, and lived, worked, sacrificed, and uprooted his home – all for the sake of *Joyful News*. His business did well and he sported a new De Dion Bouton car, one of the most reliable cars of its day, when few could afford such luxuries.'[43]

In addition to his role with the *Joyful News* Champness was also a prolific writer of books, tracts, an entrepreneur both in publishing and in the development of a missionary organisation. It would appear that George Osborn had adduced, early in Champness's ministry, that he was a man of unusual gifts and coveted these for the overseas Church. Champness threw himself into the work of the *Joyful News* and in those early years was District Missioner, Newspaper publisher, and he also developed the training of young men from his home.

In September 1883 he advertised, 'Anyone wishing to LOCALISE THIS PAPER could have the last Column on the fourth page, and this, with the one on either side, TO BE PUBLISHED WEEKLY or MONTHLY for 16s. extra.'[44] Clearly he saw the possibility of the newspaper making a link with local communities and this successfully increased the circulation.

At this time a series of different items was published, all with the same intention of encouraging people in their Christian devotion and desire for evangelism. The first of these was a *Joyful News Almanac* for 1884, containing a 'Portrait of the Editor; a Temperance picture with a scripture text for every day of the year; and other useful information – price one halfpenny.'[45] These Almanacs sold extremely well and were published during Thomas's editorship until 1904. One famous and widely sold Almanac for 1894 has an illustration of the Revs. Samuel Chadwick and Dinsdale Young.[46] Early in 1884 he published 'Joyful News Tracts' at the incredibly low price of 1s 6d for 1000.[47] The illustrations on the front page of the *Joyful News* aroused considerable interest, and he consequently advertised, 'Cartoon Tracts' which also sold extremely well.[48]

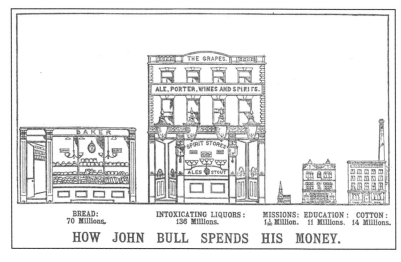

HOW JOHN BULL SPENDS HIS MONEY.

Although Champness haad indicated in the first edition that he did not want either 'controversy' or 'politics', he was not afraid of using the *Joyful News* as a campaigning publication. The first occasion was in the summer of 1888 when he published a leading article under his own name entitled, 'The Parasite Ecclesiastic.'[49] In this article he is very critical of ordained colleagues, referring to them as 'Mistletoe Ministers' who do not work hard, and lead a parasitic life in circuits, indicating that they move on when their batch of sermons is preached. At the Conference meeting in July 1888 exception was taken to the article, which was read out from the platform to cries of 'Shame'.[50] Thomas was unrepentant, writing the following week in the *Joyful News*: 'None of those who cried 'Shame' when the article was read in the Conference denied the truth of it. The existence of parasites was neither doubted nor denied; but we are told that we ought to have spoken to the Conference rather than to the people.'[51]

He also used the *Joyful News* as a campaigning newspaper to gain the support of the Temperance Movements. From the beginning of the paper there are stories of converted drunkards who had changed their ways, and a hymn in honour of the blue ribbon.[52] From 1 January 1886 he launched and published *The Banner of Hope,* an illustrated monthly magazine depicting on the cover a flag flying in the breeze with the words, 'For God, our Country and the Children'.[53] The halfpenny illustrated monthly magazine was advertised as being 'interesting and practical, and will contain Temperance Stories and Recitations, and Songs, besides Articles written by men and women who are pledged to oppose the drinking customs of our country. We hope the Band of Hope and Temperance Societies will subscribe in great numbers, and that our new venture will become a great success.'[54]   Thomas announced that his brother Henry Champness would be the 'Travelling Agent' for this and all other *Joyful News* publications.

Most powerful weapons in promoting the Temperance Movements were the regular graphic illustrations which showed the way drink drove families to poverty and ruin, in contrast to the prosperity of the publican and the 'liquor trade'.   This was sometimes also

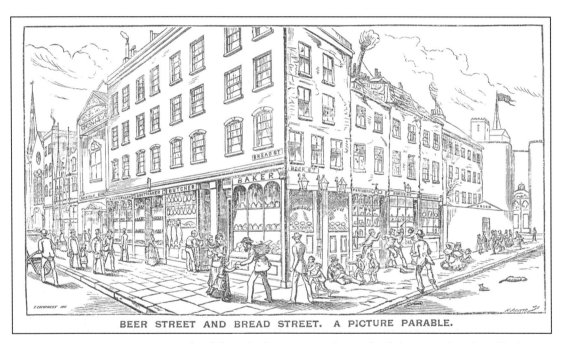

BEER STREET AND BREAD STREET.   A PICTURE PARABLE.

compared with missionary needs and giving, as in the Christmas issue for December 1895 where John Bull is depicted carving the Christmas Pudding.   A huge portion goes to the brewer and the tiniest slither to a missionary.   The caption reads: 'I am sorry for you Missionary, but you see our Drink Bill is so heavy that we cannot spare you more than I have given you.   Drink, £138,000,000; Foreign

Missions, £1,050,000.' This was a recurring theme throughout the Champness period.

One article, not written by Champness but expressing his view entirely, put the matter very starkly: 'Total abstinence is a subject which must engage the attention of all who are engaged in Christian work. The time is hastening when all Real Christians will be total abstainers.'[55] From 1897 he spoke annually at the Methodist Conference about the 'terrible havoc caused by drink among our people' declaring it to be 'inexpedient that manufacturers of strong drink shall be elected as office bearers in the Wesleyan Methodist Church.'[56] The matter was not settled and after the Conference of 1899 he published the 'Champness Resolution'. This resolution stated, 'That in view of the sorrow and sin caused by the drinking habits of the people, the Conference thinks it in the highest degree undesirable that any person directly engaged in the Liquor Traffic should be nominated for office in the Wesleyan Methodist Church'.[57] He publicised his statement on postcards and it featured regularly in the *Joyful News*, especially as the time for the Conference drew near. The campaign was successful and seventy Circuit Memorials supporting the motion were sent to the Conference of 1903. However the resolution failed, and therefore he urged his readers in August 1903 to send postcards supporting the motion and published their names in the *Joyful News* week by week.[58] By the following year he had over 13,000 responses, gathered the support of Rank, Holden, Chadwick and Collier and his argument won the day though with a different wording.[59] He was ecstatic: 'The excitement of the occasion, following, as it did, on trying experiences, was almost too much for him. Those who were with him recollect how he very nearly fainted; but he wrote to me very joyfully, and with a glad heart I joined him in praise to God.'[60] Champness and his supporters saw the campaign against the 'liquor trade' as a gospel imperative and gave great energy to it through the pages of the *Joyful News*.

By the mid-1920s there was a significant reduction in the major articles and illustrations about Temperance in the *Joyful News*. In fact in the issues from 27 September 1926 to 28 August 1927 there is not one article urging temperance. In contrast, during the period February 1904 to February 1905, when Champness was basking in the success of his campaign, there were no fewer than seventeen major articles and many minor ones.[61] Typical of the early years of Chadwick's editorship is the period September 1911 to August 1912 when there are seven.[62] Temperance then became a subject considered once a year normally in mid-November, close to what was called 'Temperance Sunday'. An urgent campaign was relaunched in the autumn of 1931 when the Free Churches were lobbying Parliament about the licensing Laws. Dr S.W. Hughes wrote fiery articles condemning 'moderate drinkers, and urging all churches to become centres of the Temperance movement'. The consumption of alcohol since the War, he noted, was the same as the National Debt, £7,000,000,000.[63]

Around 1895 the *Joyful News* began to lose its creative illustrations and dynamic articles. The graphics became smaller and less complex, presumably cheaper to produce. There are old graphics reproduced, many of them about the drink trade.[64] Adverts for the Southport Convention, Bovril and Robin's starch competed on the front page.[65] The main articles are fictional stories meant to encourage devotion to Christ. Gone from the front page are the outspoken articles and the major issues about overseas missions, though Champness does bemoan from time to time the lack of interest in foreign mission, e.g. 'Why is there not more ... Enthusiasm ... for Foreign Missions?'[66]

Gone too is the enlightening correspondence from *Joyful News* missionaries.

It is not surprising that in 1905, at the age of seventy-three, an announcement appeared in the *Joyful News*, 'To the Subscribers to *Joyful News*', Thomas and Eliza acknowledge 'we are growing older than we were, and the alertness we once had is no longer ours'.[67] Champness had handed the paper to Smart and Cook and they in turn invited Chadwick to join them.[68] 'The Rev H.T. Smart, Thomas Cook and Samuel Chadwick will, at the end of this month, become the owners of "Joyful News".' Champness had retired to Lutterworth as a supernumerary Minister but he was still preaching 'seven times a week'.[69] Chadwick who had edited the quarterly magazine *Experience* from 1890 and started *The East End* when in Shoreditch, did have some journalistic experience. However, because of his work in Leeds he could not undertake the responsibility of editor without help. He turned to Miss Annie Douglas who had lived with the Chadwicks when she was teaching at the Leeds Girls High School, and had subsequently taken a post teaching in one of the Cambridge colleges.[70] Annie Douglas agreed to give up her post and moved to live with the Chadwicks. She moved with them to Cliff Park in 1907 and then to the Principal's House living with them until Chadwick's death. He relied on her organisational skill and at Cliff she was 'Lecturer and General Superintendent, as well as being responsible week by week for *Joyful News*'.[71]

The front page of 7 September 1905 edition has a now famous illustration depicting the hand-over of the editorship of the *Joyful News*, in the form of crusader knights who are laying siege to a fortress and handing over the standard of the *Joyful News*. Champness hands the standard to Chadwick, with Cook and H.T. Smart looking on with countless warriors in the background. The

Fortress carries the words, 'Strong Drink and Sin' against which they persevere.[72]

Chadwick wrote of Champness after his death later that autumn, 'He had a vivid, virile, and versatile pen. Folks read what he wrote. They had to. He was a Warrior as well as a Great Heart. He was a fearless tilter at men and things. He was an offence to parasites, and he gloried in the assaults upon the strongholds of drink and gambling, lust and mammon. There was never an editor like him.'[73] The announcement by the new team was very complementary of the work of the Champnesses, and the newspaper heading, 'Founded by Thomas and Eliza Mary Champness' remained for decades.

Immediately there was a renewed layout and push for an increased readership. Chadwick enlisted Ernest Hasseldine to make the drawings for the front page, which had been so very innovative in the early editions. Chadwick also suggested that churches could purchase bulk copies and encourage poor people in their neighbourhood to sell copies of the *Joyful News*, buying at a discount and keeping the profits.[74] These were ideas which seem to have sprung from the extensive work he undertook among the poor in Leeds. In that respect the *Joyful News* was in effect an early version of *The Big Issue*. He also made sure that the festivals of Christmas and Easter were appropriately marked in the *Joyful News*. Previously

Joyful News – the fore-runner of The Big Issue?

they had been passed over. The new format was successful financially and 'the income through the medium of the Joyful News had considerably increased.'[75]

Josiah Mee had supported Thomas and Eliza from the beginning; 'he prayed it into existence'[76] and had offered advice from his experience of being a printer, gained prior to his ordination as a Minister.[77] From 1883 until his sudden death, he regularly made a contribution and continued to give Chadwick welcome advice when he became the editor. His last contribution was an almost finished appreciation of the ministry of Samuel Chadwick in the week he became the President of the Conference in July 1918.[78]

In any generation the circulation of a newspaper is an important issue and one which every editor needs to consider. In the spring of 1914 Chadwick spent time promoting the newspaper and announced in March that the circulation was up 5,000.[79] From January 1917 the heading proclaimed that this was not only the *Joyful News* but included the *Methodist Chronicle*.[80] There is neither editorial comment nor any recognition of this in the summaries that were later written by Crowlesmith, but presumably it showed the difficulty of publishing during the War, when many papers and magazines ceased publication. During this period the cost of paper rose in price from 1s per ton to £1 per ton, a twenty-fold increase. The First World War complicated Chadwick's strategy to increase the circulation and he had to increase the price to one penny.[81] Chadwick returned to this theme in the issue of 10 March 1921 where he made a call for the 'Joyful News Campaign to Double the Circulation'. He made the link, as did Champness before him, between sales of the Joyful News and the funds to train more evangelists. 'The Joyful News has always been a revival paper, Cliff College has always been a revival Institution.' He contrasts the country's need for 'Regeneration' as against the post-World War I desire for 'Reconstruction'. Chadwick challenges readers to double the circulation to 100,000 indicating that if this happens he could support 100 evangelists.[82] The 24 March 1921 issue indicated the circulation had risen by 5,000 and in July that circulation was up by 33%, though Chadwick very carefully never gave actual figures.

J.W. Crowlesmith whose pen name was 'Metholay', a regular contributor to Joyful News

Throughout this time there were advertisements which brought in funding. On the 24 May 1923 there was one for 'Whist Drives' and many scandalised people wrote to him, 'too many for the editor to reply to'. He promised he would never let it happen again, the inference being that the advertisement had slipped in by permission of the printer rather than a policy of the editor.[83]

The *Joyful News* was very positive about the proposals which led to the Union of the Wesleyan, Primitive and United Methodists in 1932. As early as 1922 the paper carried an account of the discussion of this issue at the Methodist Conference, Carver Street, Sheffield. Chadwick described the discussion, and concluded the article, 'Yours in the fellowship of our Lord's Prayer that His People may be One as He and the Father are One.'[84] In contrast to some evangelical leaders Chadwick supported the Union and wrote in September 1932, 'We are all of one mind in our rejoicing over the United Methodist Church, and pray with one heart and one faith that the year may abound in grace, power and glory, to the salvation and sanctification of the Redeemed.'[85] There is no doubt that he used the

Norman Dunning with his student production team

combining of the churches to plead for additional resources for evangelism. Through the winter of 1927-28 there were a number of articles calling for more evangelists, for ministers to be more evangelistic and for the Church as a whole to see membership as a process of discipleship, not merely counting numbers. The articles reached a climax in early January 1928 when 'Metholay', the pen name of J.W. Crowlesmith, suggested a target of 50,000 new members with Norman Dunning the following week hoping for that many converts.[86] The essentials of Wesleyan devotion and theology were brought to the readers by printing Wesley's 'Portrait of a Methodist' as a contribution to discussions about the priorities of the new church.[87]

In his 'Layman's Diary' Crowlesmith indicated how he had been involved as a supporter of the *Joyful News* from the very beginning with Champness and in 1910 joined Chadwick, Cook and Smart as the 'Joyful News Cabinet' who directed its progress. Cook died in 1912, and Smart in 1914, leaving Chadwick and Crowlesmith between them to pilot the *Joyful News* until 1932. Miss Douglas was an able sub-editor, and tutors Dunning, Lambert and Brice wrote an increasing number of articles during the 1920s.[88] There were, at this time, tough decisions to be made about the viability of the project and moral decisions about advertising. One advertiser approached Crowlesmith who declined the offer even though it would have been very financially advantageous.[89] The company was not identified, but the reader is left to understand it was involved with tobacco or alcohol.

Following Chadwick's death the editorship of the newspaper was passed on to W.H. Heap who had for many years been a correspondent, and also probationary Minister with Chadwick at Leeds.[90] Mrs Chadwick conferred her part ownership of the *Joyful News* to the College and the following Spring a private limited company was established.[91] It was at this time that we have the first published use in the *Joyful News* of the motto 'Christ for All - All for Christ'.[92]

Under the editorship of Heap the paper began to look beyond the internal issues of the Church whilst still remaining true to the charisms which had become essential to the paper. John Crowlesmith, under his own name, wrote a series of articles exploring

W.H. Heap

the practical and moral issues regarding running a business on Christian lines. This was then published as a book, *Christianity in Business Life*.[93] There was a weekly column 'The Tasks and Triumphs of World Methodism' which encouraged people to look outward towards mission. Throughout the 1930s, there remained the key topics of personal evangelism, evangelistic ministry, holiness, Bible study, prayer, personal devotion and Temperance, and occasionally a discussion of the Lord's Day Observance.

Heap had an insatiable appetite for world and community issues. It was under his editorship that the *Joyful News* looked at international concerns in a way which was unprecedented and unrepeated. He continuously kept his readers abreast of topical issues across the world, and this, at a time when the political, economic and military situation was in ferment. Indeed, before the end of the decade, war would again engulf the world on three continents. Typical of his writing were his 'Notes of the Week' which during the month of November 1933 covered the following diverse topics: 'The Tangled Skein of Politics'; 'The German Danger'; 'The World Economic Catastrophe'; 'Palestine, its progress and Troubles'; 'Rural Education'; 'Death on the Roads'; 'Our National Government'; 'Religion in Germany and Russia'; 'The Herring Fishery'; 'The Social Consequences of Gambling'; 'The New

Session of Parliament'; 'The Italian Enigma'; 'Treatment of the Unemployed'; 'Fascism'; 'Disarmament', and 'Honesty in Politics'. In contrast to this breadth of understanding and comment, the general evangelical movement was sinking deep into a piety which was blinkered to the intellectual and political issues of the day. James Packer admits that evangelicals of this period had a poor image, and were viewed with good reason as espousing 'archaic theology, spiritual conceit, ecclesiastical isolationism, social unconcern, pessimism about the world and the church, and old fashioned life-style and cultural philistinism.'[94]

It is of course the case that the central elements of Cliff's evangelical theology continued to be promoted in the paper. Broadbelt in his columns made much in March 1934 of the publication of Chadwick's new book *The Gospel of the Cross*[95] along with other books by Samuel Chadwick and Joe Brice. In that same month Broadbelt also opened the 'Joyful News Book Depot' at Cliff College[96] with a range of evangelical titles by Chadwick, Brice; the stories of a London ministry by the Anglican, Hugh Redwood; and exposition by the Baptist, Graham Scroggie.

John Broadbelt's wife, Lilian, died on Christmas Day 1935 and 'JAB', as he was affectionately known by friends and colleagues, did not contribute to the *Joyful News* until 13 February when he explored the theme of death and comfort for the bereaved. It remains a very sensitive piece of writing. By Easter his writing had regained its full confidence and forward planning.

At this time the College decided to publish a magazine designed to keep in touch with the growing number of past students. The first issue of the *Cliff Witness* was January 1937 edited by D.W. Lambert and supported whole-heartedly by Broadbelt. In the first issue Lambert identified its main purpose as, 'an attempt to answer a long-

JANUARY, 1937　　　　　　　　　　　　　Vol. I　No. 1

The Cliff Witness

THE MAGAZINE OF CLIFF COLLEGE AND ITS FELLOWSHIP

felt need. From time to time students of Cliff have expressed their desire to have a magazine of their own. Also old Cliff men, members of the Cliff Fellowship, have felt the need of some such link.'[97] Broadbelt expressed the hope that the magazine would be 'a spearhead of special use to preachers, evangelists, mission band workers, and to all who feel called to a fellowship of prayer and service for revival'.[98] The magazine ran successfully, often with articles which looked back to the days of Champness and Chadwick. In the eighteen issues Cook is mentioned four times, but the emphasis was on Chadwick with 14 of the 18 issues featuring his writing or an article about his ministry. So there grew up in the College the impression that Chadwick was the great entrepreneur, overshadowing both his predecessors and successor.[99] The *Cliff Witness* ceased publication at the outbreak of War in 1939 though, as we shall see, the title re-emerged in January 1964.

In the summer of 1939 W.H. Heap, who had edited the *Joyful News* in the midst of a very active ministry, superannuated, that is retired. However he continued as editor of the *Joyful News* and immediately his powers of journalism and understanding of the world situation were put to the test. In response to the declaration of war, Heap made pertinent comment with short articles entitled, 'Why Does God Permit War?'; 'On the Use of Force'; 'Hitler's Intention'; 'A Provincial London'; 'Rumours'; 'Give Us News'; 'The Navy in Time of War'; 'Care for the Troops', and 'Read your Bible'.[100] Similarly 'JAB' published a careful article entitled 'War and a Christian view' followed by four further articles exploring faith in wartime.[101]

Interestingly the slogan on the title page, which under Heap (influenced undoubtedly by Broadbelt) had been 'Evangelise or Perish', became in September 1939 'Prayer Changes things'. The following Spring the *Joyful News* reduced its pages to four.

In September 1940 the *Joyful News* celebrated its 3001st edition and 'Metholay' commented on the remarkable survival of the paper during a period when the *Methodist Times* had been taken over by the *Methodist Recorder*, and *The Wesleyan*, supported by those against Methodist Union, had failed. In rather quaint terms he made the point, 'Both of these ventures after expenditure of much capital and literary ability passed to the mortuary of defeated hopes and dead schemes. During the same period in the world of undenominational weeklies a large number were launched, flickered and fell.'[102] In the same article Crowlesmith paid tribute to the editors, Champness, Chadwick and Heap who had been forthright in their comments; 'no journal can even be useful if it is edited in the temper of a tame rabbit!'[103]

During the winter of 1939 – 1940 many articles were about the evils of dancing and card playing and the decisions of Conference about these matters. It is sadly typical that when faced with a huge challenge to faith and life, such as that afforded by World War II, institutions often focus on marginal issues. During the first two years of World War II there was considerable talk of a renewed 'Forward Movement' and preparation for this as soon as peace would appear. In the third year it faded away to be replaced in the fourth year with talk about how to rebuild the war-damaged chapels.[104]

The Rev Maurice Barnett, an ex-Cliff student who became the Superintendent of the Westminster Central Hall, wrote about the 'Christian Commando Campaigns',[105] a rather dramatic title for an evangelistic mission. The article did not indicate the locations of the campaign, except that it lasted for ten days and had been 'in factory, licensed clubs and luncheon clubs, in military camps and in the open air.' The Methodist Conference of 1939 called for the renewal of the 'Forward Movement', which had been so effective at the turn of the century with Hugh Price Hughes and others. Colin Roberts, who was General Secretary of the Home Mission Department, gave leadership to the shape of this 'aggressive and adventurous evangelism'.[106] His concern was that a fluid social order, 'being melted still more in the furnace of war ... if there is to be any advance towards a Christian order of society, there will need to be more Christians, millions more.'[107] The slogan for the work was 'New Men for a New World', and the pattern of risky evangelism set in the workplaces and alongside leisure pursuits fitted in well with the ethos of the *Joyful News*. There were regular short stories and a number of major articles.[108]

The *Cliff Choruses*, which had been so popular since their publication in 1934, gained renewed popularity in the post war period and a new edition was published in 1946, this time with 117 popular choruses and containing the tune 'Crimond'.[109] The new edition of *Cliff Choruses* was so popular that by November 1954 two hundred copies of the music and 3,500 of the words were being sold each week. They were seen as having 'catchy tunes' and used in the open air where, 'passers-by...stop for a moment or two and then go off again obviously humming the catchy tune they had just heard.'[110]

The *Cliff College Choruses* came into being at the request of many churches for a permanent record of the songs used by Cliff evangelists on their missions. They were first edited by the Rev Tom Jones in 1934 and were so successful that a second volume of choruses edited by the Rev J.H. Stringer was published later.[111] A further edition of *Cliff College Choruses* edited by the Rev Joe Brice was printed, with 114 choruses.[112] *Cliff College Choruses No.4* edited by J.H. Stringer was published as a 'new enlarged edition' in 1946 and quickly became the standard version. The rise of the 'Cliff Youth Fellowship' and the success of the youth camp sealed the success of these choruses.[113] This post-war version of *Cliff Choruses* quickly became used in every part of the world with regular sales to Australia, Canada, Panama, West Indies, South Africa, Malaya, USA, West Africa and Singapore. The latter had a standing

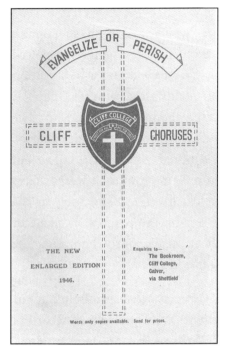

order for 220 music copies and 5,000 copies of the words per annum! The choruses were widely used in Church services and fellowship groups for all ages well into the 1960s, when the *Youth Praise* series began an avalanche of music publishing which continues to this day. *Cliff Choruses* are still used in a surprising number of churches but normally by older groups. Three or four times a year the College has a request for replacement copies in letters which indicate, 'our copies are rather dog-eared'. As recently as November 2003 an order was received from Singapore for a music copy and 1,000 words copies.

Circulation difficulties began to affect the *Joyful News* in the post-war period, with the exception of 1954 when Billy Graham visited the College. In May 1956 the editor, then J.H. Broadbelt, indicated difficulties with the viability of the project and drew attention to an urgent need to increase the circulation by 3,000, but it only increased by 300.[114] His friend the Rev Maldwyn Edwards wrote a regular column 'Window on the Street', containing comment on current affairs. However this was not as wide-ranging or as incisive as were the articles of W.H. Heap. Some of the articles make very strange reading today. For many years there was a Women's Column entitled 'Monday Afternoon', always written by the same man, the Rev William J. May. In contrast there are a number of perceptive articles, some by J.H. Stringer who had been a tutor at Cliff and eventually joined the staff of the recently formed London Bible College. His article 'Fundamentalists: An Apologia' is a robust defence of evangelical theology, a warning against being marginalized in theological discussion, and counsel to scholars not to neglect the spiritual life.[115]

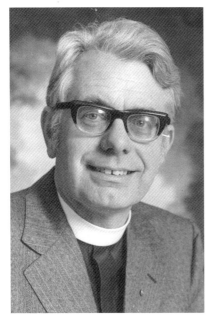

Amos Cresswell

In early 1957 Broadbelt indicated in writing to the Chair of the Directors, W.E. Sangster, that he would resign as editor of the *Joyful News* from the 31 August 1957. 'Apart from osteo-arthritis, diabetes and old age, I am very well'.[116] Eagles followed as editor when Broadbelt retired and immediately endeavoured to increase the circulation. The following year it had increased to 9,000, but it still needed to be 10,000 to break even.[117]

Amos Cresswell, then New Testament Tutor, took over editorship of the paper in September 1961. He persuaded the Board to change the name and with a flourish, in January 1962, *Advance* was launched. Cresswell brought a new look to the paper with contemporary graphics and lively reporting. One wag was heard to say, 'The only thing that has Advanced is the price!' The decline of the paper could not be halted, however, and the sheer effort involved, at a time when the College was hoping to establish different subjects in the curriculum, meant that in December 1963 the publication ceased.

ADVANCE

INCORPORATING

JOYFUL NEWS

No. 54 (4108) REGISTERED AT G.P.O AS A NEWSPAPER THURSDAY, JANUARY 10, 1963 FOURPENCE

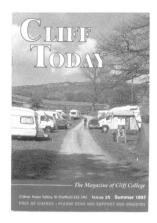

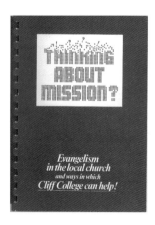

The College then looked to a former title for inspiration as a way to keep in touch with supporters. From January 1964 the *Cliff Witness* was published, at first bi-monthly and then quarterly. In September 1990 this was replaced by *Cliff Today*, which allowed for longer articles as well as information about the work of the College. Neither of these magazines was attempting to comment about the whole church, but on the work of the College. At their best they included articles which made perceptive comments on the Church's mission and ministry.

In 1984 the College decided to embark on publishing tracts and materials for use in evangelism, under the label Cliff College Publishing. With the help of John Moorley, formerly a Cliff evangelist and then Managing Director of Moorley's Print and Publishing Ltd, it became possible to print tracts at reasonable prices. This was followed by booklets to support the developing mission strategy, *Thinking About Mission*, which after five years became *Together in Mission*. Cliff Publishing also produced a series of booklets, *Alive in the Spirit*, and *Preparing for a Mission*. When the Rev Philip Clarke joined the staff he produced a series of excellent booklets prompting people to think about mission, *Being a Mission Church, Jesus at Tesco, The Hedgehog Scenario,* and *Overflow.* The relatively good reception of this material gave the College the courage to launch a series of books such as *The Art Of Evangelism* by Billy Abraham and *Overhearing the Gospel* by Fred Craddock. Cliff Publishing also added two of the Chadwick titles, *The Path of Prayer* and *The Way to Pentecost, and* Arthur Wood's excellent book on Wesley, *The Burning Heart.* A new Academic Series was launched in 1997 and the first title was *Our Doctrines* written by Kenneth Cracknell, a discussion of the function of Methodist theology, 'our doctrines', in relation to

decisions made by the Methodist Conference. The next two came from conferences of the British and Irish Association of Mission Studies, *An Invitation to God's Future*, with among others Jurgan Moltmann; and *Mission and Spirituality*, containing a paper by David Hay and remarkable pieces from Africa, by Robert Kaggwa and Laurenti Magesa. New volumes in the same series and other publications are under preparation, so the work of publishing, begun as a newspaper, continues.

1   Vallance Cook, *The Life,* p.211.
2   Eliza Champness, *The Life,* p.212.
3   Joe Brice, *The Crowd for Christ* (London: Hodder and Stoughton, 1934), p.26.
4   Joe Brice, *The Crowd for Christ* (London: Hodder and Stoughton, 1934), p.32.
5   In *The Story*, Eliza Champness reports that the response was actually rather blunt. 'Promptly Mr Champness replied – 'I will be the Editor on two conditions. 1st, I must have a free hand. 2nd, I will take no salary whatever.' p.2.
6   H.K., *Methodist Recorder*, 1894, p.49.
7   The Rev Theophilus Woolmer was connexional secretary of the Wesleyan Book Room London.
8   Eliza Champness, *The Life,* p.213.
9   Eliza Champness, *The Life,* p.214. The legacy was in the form of two small cottages, and the rental supplemented their meagre income. Joe Brice, *The Crowd for Christ* (London: Hodder and Stoughton, 1934), p.26.
10 Eliza Champness, *The Life,* p.214.
11 H.K. in *The Methodist Recorder,* 1894, p.52.
12 Dr Ernest Rattenbury writing about his father's response to Eliza as editor, *Joyful News,* 12 May 1932. The Rattenburys formed an influential dynasty in Wesleyan Methodism.
13 Kenneth F. Bowden, 'William John Tyne, A Man of God', in *The Cliff Witness*, Spring 1983.
14 Ibid.
15 Josiah Mee, *Thomas Champness*, p.53. Mee also notes that Bacup was an 'out-of-the-way place for the issue of a new and widely-circulating paper; but Mr Champness observed, 'Great movements have sprung from many little places besides Bethlehem.'
16 The first line of the hymn is 'Join all the glorious names of wisdom, love and power', which is 78 in *Hymns and Psalms* and the lines appear in verse 3.
17 Thomas D Meadley, *Kindled by a Spark*, Cliff College 1983, p.24.

cont.

18 Eliza Champness, *The Life*, p.215.

19 Eliza Champness, *The Life*, p.215.

20 The *Joyful News* carried illustrations on the front page when typically daily newspapers had the 'Personal Columns' and religious periodicals had various advertisements. None had text and major illustrations.

21 Chadwick referred to it years later, 'The first half-penny picture paper was a novelty.' *Joyful News,* 13 December 1928.

22 Eliza Champness, *The Life,* p.215.

23 *The Cliff Witness,* Spring 1983.

24 *Joyful News,* 13 December 1928.

25 Eliza Champness, *The Life*, p.217.

26 Chadwick, 'The wit and wisdom of Thomas Champness', in E19 pp.1-2.

27 Chadwick, 'The wit and wisdom', E19 p.3.

28 Joe Brice, *The Crowd for Christ* (London: Hodder and Stoughton, 1934), p.29.

29 Joe Brice, *The Crowd for Christ* (London: Hodder and Stoughton, 1934), p.30.

30 *Joyful News,* 10 July 1884. The large advertisement appeared on the back page for the following two weeks also.

31 *Joyful News*, 25 February 1885. There were three prizes distributed.

32 Kenneth Bowden, 'William John Tyne'.

33 *Joyful News,* 7 June 1883.

34 *Joyful News,* 12 July 1883. See also a reference to *La Bonne Nouvelle*, 6 September 1883.

35 H.K., p.52.

36 Eliza Champness, p.217.

37 'Report of the Worn-Out Wesleyan Methodist Ministers' and Ministers' Widows' Auxiliary Fund' p.2, in *Wesleyan Methodist Reports 1884* (London: Wesleyan Methodist Conference, 1884).

38 'Report of the Worn-Out Wesleyan Methodist Ministers' and Ministers' Widows' Auxiliary Fund' p.1, in *Wesleyan Methodist Reports 1885* (London: Wesleyan Methodist Conference, 1885).

39 'Report of the Worn-Out Wesleyan Methodist Ministers' and Ministers' Widows' Auxiliary Fund' p.2, in *Wesleyan Methodist Reports 1886* (London: Wesleyan Methodist Conference, 1886).

40 *Joyful News,* 9 September 1886.

41 Kenneth Bowden, 'William John Tyne'.

42 Ibid, and *Joyful News,* 11 July 1940.

43 Kenneth Bowden, 'William John Tyne'.

44 *Joyful News,* 27 September 1883. There is no record of the benefits of this and the idea is not repeated. The Methodist Recorder, in recent years, regularly had the same idea and with the same purpose of the newspaper extending its distribution.

45 *Joyful News,* 22 November 1883. There are two copies of the *Almanac* in the College Archives, for 1896 and 1899.

46 *Joyful News,* 9 November 1893.

47 *Joyful News,* 6 March 1884.

48 *Joyful News,* 19 February 1885.

cont.

49 *Joyful News,* 19 July 1888.

50 Eliza Champness, *The Life,* p.240.

51 *Joyful News,* 26 July 1888.

52 *Joyful News,* 3 May 1883. The Blue Ribbon movement was very active in Wesleyan Methodism and people wore a metal badge or brooch of a tied blue ribbon. There was also Staffordshire pottery to celebrate the movement.

53 *Joyful News,* 10 December 1885. The College Archives have only one bound copy of *The Banner of Hope,* for the year 1908, which by then was edited by Josiah Mee.

54 Ibid.

55 *Joyful News,* 25 July 1889, in an article entitled 'Temperance' by H. Britten.

56 Eliza Champness, *The Life,* p.264.

57 Eliza Champness, *The Life,* p.267.

58 *Joyful News,* 20 August 1903.

59 Eliza Champness, *The Life,* pp.270-1. Arthur Rank was treasurer of the Home Mission Department, Holden a Connexional Secretary, and Collier a celebrated preacher at the Manchester Mission.

60 Ibid.

61 14, 28 April; 5, 26 May; 2, 16 June; 21 July; 4, 11 August; 22, 29 September; 6 October; 17, 24 November; 1, 8 December and the 19 January.

62 9, 16, 30 November; 11 January; 8, 15 February and the 7 March.

63 *Joyful News,* 12 and 19 November 1931.

64 *Joyful News,* 14 and 28 April 1895.

65 *Joyful News,* 2 June 1904.

66 *Joyful News,* 9 June 1904.

67 *Joyful News,* 31 August 1905.

68 D.W. Lambert, *The Testament of Samuel Chadwick* (London: Epworth Press, 1957), p.57.

69 *Joyful News,* 31 August 1905.

70 *Joyful News,* 20 October 1932.

71 Lambert, *Testament,* p.58. After Samuel's death she moved with Sarah Chadwick to the 'White House' at Stanton Ford and died on 3 November 1942.

72 The illustration was first used in the *Joyful News,* 7 September 1905.

73 *Joyful News,* 10 November 1905.

74 *Joyful News,* 21 September 1905.

75 Minutes of the Committee of Management, 2 June 1910.

76 *Joyful News,* 11 July 1918.

77 Lambert, *Testament,* p.56.

78 *Joyful News,* 18 July 1918.

79 *Joyful News,* 14 March 1914.

80 *Joyful News,* 4 January 1917.

81 *Joyful News,* 13 September 1917.

82 *Joyful News,* 10 March 1921.

83 *Joyful News,* 1 June 1923.

84 *Joyful News,* 23 August 1922.

85 *Joyful News,* 1 September 1932.

cont.

86 *Joyful News,* 5 and 12 January 1928.
87 *Joyful News,* 8 January 1930.
88 *Joyful News,* 31 March 1932.
89 *Joyful News,* 20 October 1932.
90 *Joyful News,* 25 February 1943.
91 Minutes of the Cliff College Committee, 7 March 1933. The Directors were Crowlesmith and Broadbelt representing the College, each party owning a hundred £1 shares. If either party were to sell then they should first be offered to the other member of the Company.
92 *Joyful News*, 27 October 1932.
93 Crowlesmith, *Christianity in Business Life* (Rochdale: Joyful News Bookroom, 1933).
94 James Packer, 'Taking Stock in Theology', in John King (ed), *Evangelicals Today* (London: Lutterworth, 1973), pp.15-16.
95 *Joyful News,* 14 March 1934.
96 *Joyful News,* 28 March 1934.
97 *The Cliff Witness,* Vol. 1, No.1, p.1.
98 Ibid.
99 Fourteen issues had a major article by or about Chadwick, or one of his sermons. In the 18 issues, there was only one article about Cook and three sermons by him.
100 *Joyful News,* 14 September 1939.
101 *Joyful News,* 26 October 1939.
102 *Joyful News,* 5 September 1940.
103 Ibid.
104 *Joyful News,* 2 September 1943.
105 *Joyful News,* 11 November 1943.
106 Colin Roberts (ed), *These Christian Commando Campaigns* (London: Epworth Press, 1945), p.7.
107 Ibid.
108 *Joyful News,* 11 November 1943, 13 April 1944, 4 July 1944, 13 July 1944, 27 March 1947.
109 *Joyful News,* 25 September 1952.
110 *Joyful News,* 4 November 1954.
111 Both Vol.1, Nos.1-77, and Vol.2 Nos.78-152, were published by Cliff College.
112 This Vol.3 was undated, published at the Whit Anniversary in 1939 and promoted in the *Cliff Witness,* July/August 1939, p.57. It had 94 choruses but a second edition Vol.3 included a supplement making 114 in all.
113 They were originally printed in Hull by Vandyck Press, but the firm ceased to operate so Cliff College bought the plates and printed it locally in Chesterfield, by Wilfred Edmunds Ltd.
114 *Joyful News,* 10 May 1956.
115 *Joyful News,* 1 November 1956.
116 *Joyful News,* 14 February 1957.
117 *Joyful News,* 7 August 1958.

CHAPTER 5

'Try Women'

The story of the rise of evangelistic and missionary endeavour in the nineteenth century seems to be dominated by male figures. It could therefore be assumed that women were not involved. However, many women were in fact noted as significant leaders and preachers in the missionary, evangelistic and holiness movements of this time. Their apparent absence may be because the ministry of women evangelists is largely centred on relationships and 'particular features that go with a female evangelism; narrative form, relationality, domestic or small scale settings and an eschewing of power motifs in proclamation',[1] mean that their contribution has not been fully recognised.

From the very beginning of the *Joyful News*, Eliza was involved in editing alongside Thomas. The paper made reference to women who preached and in March 1885 the lead article was entitled 'Try Women'. Written by the Superintendent of the Southport Circuit, The Rev W.H. Tindall, the article advanced the need for women workers, 'My special reason for writing is... that you seem to be short of men now for the special work in the villages. Why Not Try Women?'[2] Although the main argument was utilitarian, rather than theological, the article was a radical departure for the policy makers of the Wesleyan Methodist Church. The ministry of women was controversial throughout the nineteenth century. There was reluctant acceptance and downright opposition, as well as some enthusiastic appreciation.

The comprehensive biographical study of leaders of the missionary movement, *Mission Legacies*, identifies 78 people who gave a significant lead as missionaries, theologians, strategists and administrators, with a relative absence of women.[3] The period of history covered begins with the Baptist missionary William Carey in the late eighteenth century and continues until the late twentieth century. Of those identified, only six are women: Helen Montgomery (1861-1934) and Lucy Peabody (1861-1949) who promoted the ministry of women's missionary organisations among Baptists of the United States; Ruth Rouse (1872-1956), 'missionary, evangelist, and pioneer in reaching students in countless universities and colleges around the world';[4] Florence Allshorn (1888-1950) was a missionary in Uganda who, on returning home to England, trained missionaries and founded the St. Julian Community in Sussex;[5] Ida Scudder (1870-1960) who pioneered health care for women in India, developing hospitals, clinics, training systems for health workers and a programme of rural health care and community development,[6] and Charlotte (Lottie) Moon (1840-1912) who was a missionary in Tengchow, China, where she ministered for almost forty years. Her death from malnutrition, refusing food so that colleagues and the children in their care could eat, immortalised her work, and in telling her story the Southern Baptists raised considerable funds for mission.[7]

Even where a book is written to celebrate the ministry of women such as Lavinia Byrne's book about women's spiritual writings, few are involved in evangelism or preaching. She has biographical notes on 92 women of whom 36 were writing or ministering in the second half of the nineteenth century. Of these, only six were preachers: Hatty Baker, the first woman to be a pastor of a Congregational church;[8] Catherine Booth, who preached within the Salvation Army; Evangeline Booth, her daughter, who became the worldwide General of the Salvation Army in 1934,[9] and Elizabeth Comstock, a Quaker in the United States of whom Abraham Lincoln wrote 'Give Mrs Comstock access to all hospitals, and to all inmates with whom she desires to hold religious services.'[10] Of those listed, the person who most closely matches the work of the Joyful News Female Evangelists was Sarah Grubb (d.1842); 'she preached in markets and in the streets for fifty-two years'.[11] Rebecca Jackson too was, 'a visionary and Shaker eldress who preached sixty-nine sermons in the summer of 1834 on a preaching tour of Philadelphia'.[12] Presumably it was not unusual for her to preach but this tour was an extension of her normal preaching ministry. Many other women are mentioned who undertook substantial ministries but are not mentioned as preachers or evangelists. We should note however the work of Isabella Gilmore (1842–1923) who was asked by the Bishop of Winchester to 'reshape the Anglican Deaconess Order. This had been founded in 1862 as an Order parallel to male clergy, to consist of independent women working in parishes, who would be answerable only to the bishop.'[13] This work was primarily fulfilling a pastoral role in the parish.

However, there are studies which give substantial evidence of both the spirituality and the nature of the ministry of nonconformist women in this period. The most recent published research on women's ministry in the nineteenth century is *Constrained by Zeal*, by Linda Wilson.[14] Wilson argues against the view that women preachers were so associated with cottage-based religion that they disappeared as the cottage industry was undermined in the industrial revolution at the beginning of the nineteenth century.[15] What Linda

Wilson has achieved is to identify the considerable number of women who had a noted ministry in the nonconformist denominations, through studying obituaries of a carefully selected sample from the Baptist, Congregational, Primitive Methodist and Wesleyan Methodist Churches.[16] Only one of these 244 women is described as a 'preacher', the Primitive Methodist Sarah Starbuck, 'a consistent member of the Primitive Methodist society at Holbeach, Lincolnshire, leading a class, supporting missions, and occasionally preaching'.[17]

Others are identified as being involved in evangelistic endeavour such as tract distribution, rather similar to the activity of James and Ann Elizabeth Hulme. Eleanor Esling, a Baptist in Diss, was active, 'teaching poor children, and visiting cottages to distribute tracts.'[18] The Congregationalist, Mrs Wigner, was 'running Bible classes, "winning souls" and being a peacemaker between individuals.'[19] Another Congregationalist, Mrs Dickson, felt it was her 'obligation to convert the young men who worked for her husband and lived in her house in Bure, near Lancaster.'[20] Similarly Olive Helmore, also a Congregationalist, was 'an active evangelist amongst the poor in her home village of Emsworth, near Havant.'[21] Some others are noted for speaking about the faith, and some did lead Bible classes and Sunday schools. One such was the Congregationalist Lydia Pitman who 'taught a Bible class, and her lessons were comparable to good sermons.'[22]

A few women were involved in particular forms of church leadership. Elizabeth Marsden, who died in 1853, was both a missionary in Armenia and a deaconess in Leeds. A Cong-regationalist trained by her father 'in her knowledge of scripture',[23] she was a remarkable woman. 'She married a (Baptist) pastor, and although she was busy with church and charitable work, as well as looking after a young family, she still found time for literary work. For a time she edited the *Christian Ladies Magazine*, and she also produced tracts and prepared the first volume of her father's memoirs. Sadly she died at an early age'.[24]

Many are recorded as involved in lay work in the church. The Wesleyan, Charlotte Mason, 'led a class...for several years. She was also an active visitor of the sick, and participant in prayer meetings'.[25] However, most reflections on the ministry of women are typified by comments such as, 'she was active in a variety of good works';[26] 'she was involved in a range of activities including the support of foreign missionaries, and the establishment of a female prayer meeting. She also in due course became the Sunday school superintendent.'[27] The main focus of ministry for women was assumed by both men and women to be within the confines of the home, and therefore many were involved in teaching children and developing Sunday schools, sharing with other women and forming women's devotional meetings, caring for friends and neighbours and setting in place systems for the care of the poor. However, towards the end of the nineteenth century, as women began to see their potential abilities, and to live longer through and beyond child bearing,[28] there were distinct developments for women's ministry. 'Once empowered, women's evangelising activities constantly break out of these domestic limits. The prayer group turns into a revival meeting, with women as organizers, and then as preachers. Benevolent societies turn into women's home and foreign mission societies with their own budgets, their own leadership in women's hands.'[29]

When it comes to the influence of holiness teaching, we find that women were particularly influential in the holiness movements both in the United States and in England. Phoebe Palmer (1807-74) is called the 'Mother of the Holiness movement'. She developed and popularised a theology that included an emphasis on total surrender to God, bringing full cleansing from sin.[30] Hannah Pearsall Smith (1832-1911) and her husband, Robert, became popular speakers in the holiness movement, and in the mid 1870s they were instrumental in the beginnings of the Keswick movement. They had espoused a very optimistic theology, which believed one could by obedient surrender obtain holiness of life. Typical of this teaching is Hannah's book *The Christian's Secret of a Happy Life* published in 1875.[31]

There are 'invisible' women in the sense that they were supporting their husbands. We have already seen that for Thomas Champness the professional gifts of Eliza were crucial; similarly with Henry Grattan Guinness and Fanny, who in effect managed the missionary organisation while he was away preaching and teaching around the world. In the initial years of the China Inland Mission, Maria Dyer was critically influential with her husband Hudson Taylor, in formulating the policy to appoint young single women as Missionaries. It was widely believed in Protestant missions that the presence of a wife would reduce the risk of sexual temptation. However the 'untended deaths and agonies of women and children were a heavy price to pay for masculine frailty'. [32]

Hudson Taylor, a friend of Henry Grattan Guinness, was prepared to challenge the established view if he had evidence of God at work in a particular way or place.[33] He departed significantly, in a number of ways, from the established protocols of missionary organisations. His policy in relation to single women as missionaries arose from experience. In 1865 he founded the 'China Inland Mission', and the following year sailed for China with a party of fifteen including eight single women, at a time when there were only thirteen single women missionaries in the whole of China. In recruiting 'working men' as well as others, Hudson Taylor was adopting a quite different practice from that of other Missions. But in encouraging *young* unmarried women to go too, he was showing a conspicuous disregard for precedent.

Chinese women were difficult to make contact with, and were confined with bound feet to the family courtyards. 'In Ningbo he had seen how effective women missionaries could be. Maria herself had been so fluent and at ease in Chinese homes that she was always in demand.'[34] Hudson Taylor understood that to reach the Chinese women then 'Christian women must go to them, beyond the walls of institutions. And if women in inland China were to hear, missionary women must face the hazards ... Quiet work in Chinese homes could be as effective as overt evangelism among men.'[35] A colleague of his, William Burns, had emphasised the value of a biblical Order of female lay evangelists and the 'need of women to work among Chinese women whose secluded lives made them inaccessible to men.'[36] The China Inland Mission focussed from the outset on the need for women who would minister in their own right. 'The younger they were, the sooner they would be fluent in Chinese.'[37]

The change in the place and ministry of women can be monitored by their increasing presence at major missionary conferences. In 1860 there was a Missionary Conference in Liverpool without a single women present.[38] In 1874-83 the Church Missionary Society sent sixteen single women as missionaries, and in the period 1883-93 they sent one hundred and ninety-two.

The recognition of the ministry of women came early in the Methodist movement. Wesley always encouraged those women who had an 'extraordinary call'.[39] His overriding desire to spread the gospel gave rise to a pragmatism in which Wesley was keen to deploy all methods in the interests of gospel proclamation. To Alice

Cambridge he wrote, 'Give them (men) all honour and obey them in all things, as far as conscience permits. But it will not permit you to be silent when God commands you to speak; yet I would have you give as little offence as possible; and therefore I would advise you not to speak at any place where a preacher is speaking near you at the same time, lest you should draw away his hearers. Also avoid the first appearances of pride and magnifying yourself.'[40] However, following Wesley's death there was a move to exclude women from the pulpit. The Irish Conference in 1802 agreed, 'it is contrary both to scripture and to prudence that women should preach or should exhort in public'.[41] The following year the British Methodist Conference dealt with Question 19 on its Agenda, 'Should women be permitted to preach among us?' They gave the answer: 'We are of the opinion that in general they ought not. But if any woman among us think that she has an extraordinary call...she should address her own sex and those only...under the following regulations: They shall not preach in the circuit where they reside until they have obtained the approbation of the Superintendent and a Quarterly Meeting. Before they go into any other circuit to preach, they shall have a written invitation from the Superintendent of such a circuit and a recommendatory note from the Superintendent of their own circuit.'[42]

The accepted view of Methodist historians has been that after this Conference decision, the number of women preachers reduced considerably with one or two notable exceptions such as Mary Taft. A typical conclusion is, 'The women preachers were driven from the community which had inspired them'.[43] This view of the place of women preachers in nineteenth century Methodism is now changing, partially as a result of the research of John Lenton,[44] and a recent paper from the Rev David East, who has shown that despite the official view of Wesleyan Methodism, there was at local level a number of continuing women preachers whose existence was disguised by stratagems such as a * on the plan.[45] David East highlights the ministry of one female lay preacher, Sarah Mallet, who preached in the South Norfolk area and he also emphasises the crucial leadership roles played by women. Certainly the situation in Ireland was difficult for women preachers who were confined to preaching to female congregations. This led to some curious practices. In the 1830s the male followers of Anne Lutton were reduced to dressing in women's clothing in an attempt to hear her preach![46] Throughout the nineteenth century there was increasing though not consistent opportunity for women's participation: 'Through the network of voluntary societies and organisations which clustered around the religious denominations, many women were given the opportunity to engage in social and administrative work in their communities. The domestic sphere widened to take in Sunday schools, foreign and domestic evangelistic missions, temperance, educational, Bible and tract societies. The various reports indicate the areas in which it was felt women could be particularly successful – teaching, sponsorship, promotion and persuasion.'[47]

Within the British Methodist Church, John Lenton has established beyond doubt that not only did women continue to preach after the 1803 decision, but that they were welcomed in their own and other circuits.[48] 'Of the 25 women who were preaching in Wesleyanism in 1803, very few stopped or left as a result of the Conference regulations.'[49] Rather than the ministry of women preachers dying out as a result of the 1803 regulation there were, in terms of early nineteenth century Christianity, a significant number of new women preachers. Lenton lists twenty-four women preachers, some of whom preached with considerable success, such as the two friends Charlotte Berger (1791-1877) and Mrs Harriett Webster (c.1780-1863) who 'opened several preaching rooms in Essex and began to preach further afield, e.g. Hertford, Waltham Abbey, Poplar, Maidstone, Saffron Waldron and even Newmarket. By 1822 the *Bury Gazette* could describe "Two famous female preachers preaching...at the Wesleyan Chapel at Diss ... Several hundreds could not gain admission".[50] Clearly most of the women preachers did not gain such notoriety. They spoke in circuits to mixed congregations, like Mrs Jane Treffy (1769-1829) when there was no other preacher available.[51] Moreover from 1860 there was a renewed sense of call by women to preach,[52] and Lenton lists a total of sixty-eight names not including the Joyful News Evangelists or Deaconesses.[53] From the mid-1880s there was a significant increase in the number of female evangelists, not least because of the inclusion by Champness of women in this work.[54] Lenton is convinced that there were many 'hidden' women preachers because Superintendents, even late in the century, did not wish to incur the wrath of the Conference.[55] As well as the increase of women preachers through the ministry of the Joyful News Mission, the *Joyful News* also lists women preachers who are not Joyful News Evangelists, and twenty are mentioned in the period February 1887 to April 1888. This upsurge in female preaching is mirrored in the work of missionaries and mission organisations. There was another very significant change in 1910, when the Conference repealed the 1803 decision. 'Where, however, a woman preacher possesses these exceptional gifts, and gives evidence of having received a Divine Call to the work of preaching, liberty should be given her for the exercise of her gifts. But in all such cases the preaching of women shall be subject to the following conditions:

1. They shall not preach where they reside until they have obtained the approbation of the Superintendent and Quarterly Meeting.

2. Before they go into any other Circuit to preach they shall have a written invitation from the Superintendent of that Circuit, and a

recommendatory note from the Superintendent of their own circuit.

N.B. So far as possible the preaching of Women shall be restricted to neighbourhoods in which there is no opposition to such preaching.[56]

From 1910 onwards there are many more women preachers, and the 1934 *Local Preachers Who's Who* lists nine hundred and forty-five women, mostly coming on the plan after this date, of whom sixteen are Wesleyans from before 1910. Lenton concludes his paper with the assertion that 'there were far more women preaching in Wesleyan Methodism after 1803 than we had dreamed. The total number I have found so far is 252, and the rate I have been discovering them in the *Joyful News* means that the true figure must be at least three times that number. Their contribution should not be overlooked. The movement for the ordination of women could not have begun without the progress made in the nineteenth and early 20th centuries.'[57]

The significant Methodist thinkers in the development of evangelistic ministry in the nineteenth century knew one another, preached together and sought the counsel of each other. Stephenson, Champness, Cook and Guinness it would seem, worked with each other and were all keen to engage women in the work of the gospel. Thomas Bowman Stephenson appointed 'our deaconess, Miss Entwistle' in his work at Bolton.[58] He had been inspired in developing this appointment by a visit to Germany to the Kaiserwerth centre for deaconesses in 1871. The Children's Home, which he founded in 1869, had an Order of the Sisters of the Children, which grew in number and eventually included training, probation, ordination and a special uniform.[59] In the period which followed the founding of the *Joyful News* Training Home and

Mission, Hugh and Katherine Price Hughes were also recruiting 'Sisters of the People' to engage in the pastoral and evangelistic work of the West London Mission.[60]

It is with regard to this historical context that we now come to the work of Thomas Champness and his influence on the training and ministry of women evangelists. From 1879-1882 Champness was a District Missioner in the Newcastle District where he used both men and women as colleagues in the work. Among the women, the most notable was Miss Parsons.[61] As the *Joyful News* Mission developed he became convinced of the need for female evangelists.

On his travels through Britain, Champness was moved by the need for a special work, which godly women could do in the villages and small towns. 'Their ministry was just the kind of thing needed in scattered hamlets, where lonely Methodists were seldom visited by the ministers. At the same time he found godly servant-maids and factory lasses, and others, who were longing for openings into Christian service, but who could never hope to find an outlet in the city Sisterhoods, where women of gentle birth and better education were preferred.'[62] The strategy employed by Eliza and Thomas Champness was both clever and effective. They needed to educate their readers prior to the appointment of female workers, but they were clearly determined not to wait for public opinion, rather to lead it. In their newspaper they included stories of the effective ministry of women. One of the first was in April 1883, when under the title 'Honourable women' they reported 'news from St Bart's, West Indies'. Here there was a shortage of local preachers and therefore no-one to take the services, 'Well how were they to manage for the Sunday services? The women came forward; THEY undertook the work ... So for about two years these noble women have kept the society together ... I think they have shown themselves true sisters of the loving Mary, the fragrance of whose deeds fills the church for ever; of the same stamp and rank as those brave women who laboured together with St. Paul, and verily in heaven they shall reap of their abundant labours a blessed and plentiful harvest. Oh that those splendid congregations in England, which have been deprived of the ministrations of the Word of Life, would, from their fullness, impart it to those who know what it is for there to be a 'famine of hearing of the word of God' at any rate from the lips of a regular preacher.'[63]

In May 1883 a short article was published, written by 'E.A.' and entitled 'How a young woman began to work for Jesus'. It was on the front-page and described the response she had made, 'About three years ago, after attending a Home Missionary meeting, and hearing there of the great work to be done in Liverpool'. She then established a cottage meeting and went from door to door inviting her neighbours. The purpose of the article was to encourage women to become involved in evangelism, 'If we only have a Saviour's love shed abroad in our hearts, and, losing sight of self, we ask him to use us, He will do so.'[64] From the 23 August 1883 Agnes Threlfall became a regular contributor to the *Joyful News* writing of the joy of bringing someone to faith in Christ.

In his article, 'Try Women' mentioned earlier, W.H. Tindall, wrote, in March 1885: 'My special reason for writing is…that you seem to be short of men now for the special work in the villages. Why Not Try Women? Is there any reason against doing so? There were some regulations passed more than eighty years ago on the subject of women preachers; none since, that I am aware of'. Tindall does not explicitly suggest women preachers, but states 'Suppose you had a list of really suitable women for the work, could they not be sent two-by-two, never alone, to help in our villages.' He ends the plea with the following comment, 'The extravagancies of the

Salvation Army should be avoided, but certainly the Army has shown what women can do in winning souls ... Ladies have recently been speaking to mixed audiences in City Road Chapel and elsewhere.'[65]

The *Joyful News* followed this with a series of articles throughout March 1885 concentrating on the effective ministry of women. It would seem to have been the intention of Eliza and Thomas to try to influence the debate within the Wesleyan Methodist Church, which was about to review the decision taken in 1803. The 19 March edition ran a story, 'Our Sisters at work - Glorious times at Ainsdale'. This included Champness's testimony to the important work of women, and details of the effectiveness of their work. Clearly his conclusion was, as Wesley had decided, that if God was using women, then the church should be training them. 'Thank God he has visited Ainsdale and many souls are now rejoicing in the blessed experiences of saving grace. Miss Tindall opened the Mission on Sunday, March 1st, with a service for the Young, and has conducted each service since. Men and women, deep dyed in sin, have turned to the Lord and found salvation ... this is the second week of the Mission, but the throng is greater; each service crowded. We cannot close it; we must go on till all these seeking, hungry souls are satisfied in Jesus.'[66]

Other places copied the impetus created by this article in *Joyful News* promoting women's ministry. A story appeared that same month from Boddington in the Banbury Circuit, entitled 'Trying Mr Tindall's recipe': 'A new departure was taken here on Thursday evening, when we did the thing advocated in the *Joyful News* No. 107, viz., a lady from Grimsbury occupied the pulpit. The experiment exceeded our expectations for not withstanding that some say that a woman's place is in the home, the result of Miss Lake's labour here shows that as one said the other day, women can do what men cannot.'[67] H.T. Smart also wrote an article commending an unnamed lady involved in evangelism among mill workers, especially those abusing alcohol, entitled 'What a lady is doing for some Lancashire Working Men'.[68]

The reason for highlighting the issue in March is made clear to the *Joyful News* readers in August; the Wesleyan Methodist Conference had discussed the contentious issue of women preaching. It is in Eliza Champness's column (it is signed the Rev Thomas Champness when he writes it himself) that reference is made to the Conference debate which decided not to 'relax the Rule on this subject.' She then sets out the 1803 decision in full and goes on to challenge it: 'We are inclined to think that the majority of people are wishful that every one should be allowed to preach, if only God has showed that in the exercise of his sovereignty He has given both grace and talent to the speaker, be it man or woman.' It could not be put more clearly. The Champnesses wanted, and fully intended, to employ female evangelists. They certainly could see the importance of women's ministry in the late nineteenth century. Women could, with ease, enter homes, speak with other women, visit the sick and families, as well as have a more public preaching ministry.

They had to wait for three years but in March 1888 a front page article appeared in the *Joyful News* announcing the '"Joyful News" Female Evangelists' Home'. Under the names of both Thomas and Eliza, the announcement reveals they had made an arrangement with a Mr George Clegg who had already begun training female evangelists. They were in effect adopting his work as part of the *Joyful News Mission*. George Clegg had, in Halifax, a home which:

> he has furnished as a training and resting place for the devoted young women whose names have been in our columns from week to week this winter. We feel very glad to welcome Mr Clegg and his workers as a new branch of our service, and we wish them as much joy as it is

possible for them to have under their new name. Miss Cook is to remain the Superintendent, a very remarkable and successful evangelist.

We trust that godly, intelligent, and suitable young women will be moved by the Holy Spirit to enter on this constantly widening field of Christian usefulness ... It has now become a recognised principle that we should employ our own daughters, no less than our own sons in evangelistic toil.

They also referred to the work of Hugh Price Hughes in London, where 'young ladies who, realising the great spiritual destitution of the people, have given themselves up to visiting and ministering to the sick and needy, under the care of Mr Peter Thompson in the East and Mr Hughes in the West End. In many places these women are holding Missions, and their winning words are being blessed by God to the conversion of many souls. Miss Wilson, of Carlisle, is also earnestly engaged in most successful mission work, and has been wonderfully blessed this winter... Altogether the outlook for the employment of godly women, suitably trained and cared for, is most encouraging; and it is therefore with joy that we hail the Halifax "Joyful News" Home as part of our organisation.'[69] The Home was run on "Joyful News" lines,[70] with George Clegg and W.H. Greenwood, also of Halifax, as the bursar.[71]

Although Champness had just taken on this work of training female evangelists for Britain, the same article indicates they were also looking at a further expansion for the ministry of women with the possibility of 'Joyful News Female Missionaries'. 'The more we study the needs of the heathen in foreign lands, the more we are led to see that there is a great work to be done by Englishwomen who are willing to live among the people, not so much as school teachers, but as Evangelists... We earnestly ask all those who so constantly help us by prayer, to join us now in seeking the Divine direction in this matter; and we are sure God will open our way if He wants us to do the work.'[72]

The article concluded that 'We live in days of blessed progress, and we predict that in a few years, by God's good hand upon His church for good, there will be a large army of devoted men and women, acting as evangelists under control, and yet not pressed into one mould, but allowed to grow according to their individuality, to bring glory to God, and good to the world.'[73]

This statement was made under the joint names of Thomas and Eliza, a strategy they often employed when they felt the issue was important or there was real possibility of opposition. The same week, prayer was requested for the following female evangelists, eight of them; Wilson, Taylor, Dodd, Mitchell, Theobald, Greenwood, Cook (in charge of the Home) and Moore.[74] This new phase of ministry was most successful, and within the short space of a year there were eleven *Joyful News* Female Evangelists as well as eighty in the list of 'Joyful News Evangelists', of whom thirteen were overseas…most were out missioning though thirteen were 'resting' or 'training'.[75]

It would appear that the Home for Female Evangelists moved to larger premises, at The Home, Kingsley Place, Halifax, but the information is overshadowed by the move of the *Joyful News* Home to Castleton Hall. Kingsley Place was 'where they received training, and to which they could return for intervals of rest. In all about fifty-two young women came into the ranks, most of whom did splendid service. Mr Champness controlled their appointments, corresponded with them, and occasionally gave an hour or two for a lecture as he was on his journeys.'[76] At what was described as 'Mr Clegg's Home in Halifax' there were in 1893 twenty-four women with Miss Cook now as 'Principal'. Of these only two were 'resting', whilst all the others were at work around the country.

There are in existence detailed testimonies from Mary Jane Smith, and Mary Ann Dixon, two of the *Joyful News* Female Evangelists. Mary Ann Dixon had been converted through the ministry of Moody and Sankey in their 1883 London mission. At the age of 30 she enrolled with Champness and the *Joyful News* Mission, training in Rugby from September 1894. Her grandson, Brian Hills, has undertaken research from the *Joyful News* and he has been able to ascertain exactly where she was and what she was doing every week for the period September 1894 to April 1897.[77] She trained for twenty weeks and then in common with other women there was a pattern of work, further training, and resting at the *Joyful News Home* in Rugby

Mary Ann Dixon

and her family home. 'The general pattern was always five to six months working, then six to eight weeks 'resting''[78]. This suggested pattern comes from information on Mary Ann Dixon; the diary of Mary Jane Smith suggests longer placements, but this information alone may be too narrow a foundation for us to have confidence that this pattern relates to all *Joyful News* Female Evangelists.

Mary Ann Dixon was assigned to the North Walsham and Cromer Circuits from February to July 1895, Hitchin and Stevenage from October to March 1896. Unusually, without a break, she was posted to Whitehaven, and after a six-week rest, to Oakham in Rutland in November 1896 for three months. Her entries in the *Joyful News* come abruptly to an end in

April 1897. She had been assigned to Ryton-on-Tyne though she never arrived. Mary had met a devout Methodist post-man, Frank Hills, in December 1895 in the chapel at Walkern near Stevenage. It would appear they decided to marry.[79] Brian Hills notes that 'there were no tributes or 'goodbyes' in later issues of the *Joyful News*, perhaps they felt she had let the side down by abandoning the cause, for the charms of a humble postman!'[80]

Mary Jane Smith's experience was not dissimilar, though we only know what her diary reveals. She was converted on 30 January 1889 following a meeting led by two Joyful News Evangelists in the village of Frolesworth, Leicestershire. She moved to live at Milnrow, near Rochdale, where she was involved in the Wesleyan Church and received training from May to the August 1892. During that time she attended classes with Joseph Todhunter, Mr and Mrs Champness and David Hill, a missionary from China on furlough and staying with Champnesses.

She was influenced by the holiness teaching of Champness and others and on 19 May she claimed 'the blessing of entire cleansing'. Her entry for that day is, 'I this morning claim the blessing of entire cleansing. According to the light I have I believe that the blood of Jesus Christ cleanseth (me) from (all) sin and by simple faith I claim the blessing now. Lord help me to trust thy every word. "The day is past and over, all thanks to thee, oh Lord" for thy cleansing power. This has been a day of quiet trust; no outburst of sudden joy but a sweet peace has filled my heart and as temptations have presented themselves to me I have cried, Lord cleanse me now. Let thy blood go on cleansing, keeping clean. I bless thee God for the experience of this day.'[81]

Life for Mary Jane was not austere, partially because she was 'billeted' with a kindly woman and family, but also because of a variety of cultural visits. In her second week at Milnrow she was taken down a coal mine to see its workings. Later she attended Castleton Hall to see the Champnesses, but finding them out played croquet with Miss Champness, Messrs Brown and Whittome... 'I do thank God for the joys of serving him and for his many mercies to me.'[82] On 1 July she had a day out at Southport with Mrs Champness and others, though it would appear the main reason was to visit the Holiness Convention. The relationship between the Convention and the *Joyful News* was very close. It would be expected that Mrs Champness was welcomed as a special guest but despite being a student, Mary's diary records, 'Took our seats on the platform, Mr Chadwick was the speaker and very practical he was.'[83] She appears from her diary to have been introduced to many people, including 'Miss Cook, Mr Clegg and several of his Evangelists.' In August she had three days in Blackpool and particularly enjoyed a steamer around Morecambe Bay.[84]

The *Diary* reveals a passion for people to know the certainty of the faith she had. The 12 July 1892 was an Election Day and Mary Jane records the event, 'What earnestness on the part of the voters. What excitement. Oh that they were half as anxious to make that other "calling and election sure". This a question that affects eternity, the other that he may be a Member (of Parliament) for a few years. Oh Lord, make me earnest about perishing souls.'[85]

12th This has been the election day. What earnestness on the part of the voters. What excitement. Oh that they were half as anxious to make that other "calling & election sure." This is a question that affects eternity the other that he may be member for a few years. Oh Lord make me earnest about perishing souls.

On 16 August she received a 'call to be in readiness to go to the Devon and Dorset Mission', and she arrived three days later in Budleigh Salterton. After only one month there she received a letter from 'Mr C. telling me to go on to Collingbourne, Wilts. to conduct a fortnight's mission...I believe the Lord will use me in the conversion of many souls and make me a blessing to others.'[86] Mary Jane shared the mission meetings with others and she sang, preached and made the call for response. Like all fervent evangelists she was keen for commitment: 'I spoke on "What do you do with Jesus", had a good time some under deep conviction but none to come out. May God work mightily in the heart of the people.'[87] There were converts and at the end of the mission she met the new class meeting which eight had joined. She confidently expected others to follow.[88] The believers had been 'quickened' and there were three converts. She returned to the Dorset and Devon Mission but this time to the neighbouring village of Colaton Raleigh. One other mission is recorded in her *Diary* for February 1893, with little comment except that she preached to congregations of two hundred and there were a number of converts, 'This has been a glorious Mission, 19 have professed to find peace and 24 Pledges have been taken. God Bless and Keep them.'[89]

> 21st Praise the Lord for the blessings of our my.
> First Sunday in Devon. In the morning Mr Rigall
> preached at the Chapel. After dinner Mr Rigall
> Mrs Gibbs & I drove over to Newton Poppleford
> took the portable Harmonium & I played Mrs Gibbs
> & Mr Rigall spoke, we took Tea with Mrs Wheaton
> & on entering her room the first Photo I saw
> was W. N. she commenced talking of him & asked
> if I knew him, We had two open airs & I played
> the Harmonium such a congregation of children
> & grown up people we then went into the
> open air room & had thirty children & a few
> adults I gave the address may the Lord bless
> the seed sown & save Newton Poppleford.

Her work consisted mainly of leading Bible studies, the Class and Band Meetings in the church and much pastoral care. She visited homes where the families did not attend the church, especially those who were poor, and almost every day she led and spoke at cottage services. She also often visited the landed gentry, 'taking tea', singing songs or solos, and playing the piano or harmonium. Clearly Mary Jane was a talented woman with an ability to mix comfortably with all kinds of people and the *Diary* suggests they took her to their hearts.

Mary Jane did encounter some hostility. With a Miss Salmon she travelled on the train to Colyford where she was working, and 'a clergymen of the Church of England came and got in our carriage and was exceedingly polite. I believe he thought Miss Salmon a

Sister of the Church but when he found that we were dissenters he said the church ought to do the work and not us.'[90] This was an untypical response to Mary Jane who like Mary Ann Dixon found people kind, welcoming and attentive to their testimony.

From there she went immediately to Chard and a Mission in a Baptist Chapel, again with some converts, though her *Diary* ends abruptly on the 24 February 1893 without a summary of this mission. The Diary finished at this point but her work as a *Joyful News* Evangelist continued until May 1895 and her last appointment was in Taunton.[91] It was in the summer of 1895 that Champness had to reduce the number of evangelistic staff by sixty and Mary Jane Smith was an early casualty.

In April of 1893 an article headed 'Our New Home', reported that the training of the women has moved from Halifax to a new home based at 'Joyful News Home', Rugby. 'Please pray that our daughter who is at the head of the Home, may be strong for the work. She is young to have so great a responsibility.'[92] The expansion of the work did lead to a crisis of funding, which, typically, Champness confidently laid before the *Joyful News* readers. 'Then we shall need FUNDS if we are to go on. We have begun this enterprise not because we have plenty of money, but because there is a great and pressing need for hundreds of women workers... Again we say, pray for the Home for Village Sisters at Rugby'.[93]

Even when in July 1895 the Champnesses had to dismiss sixty 'Joyful News Agents' they still retained thirty-two of whom eight were women and twenty-two 'are with Mr Clegg.'[94] The solvency of the project was in question at other times. In the *Diary* of Mary Jane Smith, she records on 22 July 1892, 'We are in great financial straits. Mr C. has given us notice. May God open up the way.'[95] In fact Mary

Jackie Waterman

Jane made no effort to leave, though on 25 July she was concerned, 'Much troubled about the work this morning but the Lord is ever nigh to comfort.'[96] In the late 1890s the number of *Joyful News* Evangelists settled to just over fifty. In February 1900 there were fifty-four including twelve single women and four married women. Additionally they had in training eleven Local Preachers at Rochdale and six, presumably women, at Rugby.[97]

On the day Cliff College opened, 3 March 1904, Champness listed in the *Joyful News*, ten Joyful News Evangelists of whom four were women. In addition there were three missionary couples supported by the *Joyful News* Mission. Most of the male evangelists became Cliff College Evangelists working with the Home Mission Gospel Cars under the direction of Thomas Cook. None who continued with Cook were women.[98] Within two years the only single female listed in the newspaper as a Joyful News Evangelist was Miss Coles and 2 July 1907 was the last entry shown for her. After this date the '*Joyful News*' evangelistic staff listed were Moses Welsby with the three missionary couples until July 1908 when Eliza Champness announced that the overseas work was closed.[99] The College had to wait until 1969 for the next female Cliff College Evangelist who was Jackie Waterman.

This retrograde step within the ministry of Cliff College is parallelled in other parts of evangelicalism. In a fascinating study on the evangelical movement in Ulster in the nineteenth century, Hempton and Hill indicate how women 'achieved a temporary position of influence in the early stages of the evangelical revival which was not sustained into the nineteenth century when male ministers, trustees and administrators regained full control.'[100] They go on to show that the ministry of women was diverted through the 19th century into the development of women's ministry for and by women. A 'vast array of voluntary religious associations had opened up new opportunities for female endeavour which did not encroach on the activities of men.'[101] This would lead later to the marginalisation of women as leaders of the missionary movements.

The development and power of the women's movement can be charted by their presence at major conferences on mission. In 1860 in Liverpool there was a Missionary Conference with no women present but in 1888 the 'Centenary Conference' in London was attended by 1600 men and, significantly, 345 women. In 1893 the first Women's Congress of Missions was held in Chicago, and the year of the Edinburgh Conference coincided with the Jubilee of Women's Societies.

'When they celebrated the Jubilee of the American Women's Missionary Societies... in 1910, there were 44 Women's Societies in the US (quite apart from at least seven from Britain and others from Germany); between them they were supporting 1,948 American single women overseas. They had mobilised 2 million American women in support, giving an average perhaps of only 4 cents each per week, or $2 per year, but that added up to more than $4 million.'[102] Quite remarkable leaders arose such as Helen Montgomery and Lucy Peabody, who displayed tremendous skill and vision in organisation. They had sent many women as missionaries and educated the churches about mission, selling 50,000 study books annually. Montgomery commented, 'The women's missionary movement made more demands on the brains of their adherents than any other missionary movement before or since.'[103]

The hard fought leadership of women's societies which grew up in the nineteenth century by women was undermined in the period 1910-1930. 'Women's societies progressively merged with denominational or general missions. This extraordinary resource and mobilisation was lost. Initially these experienced women leaders were given places on joint boards, but as they retired they were replaced by men. Yet the women of the Islamic and Hindu worlds can only be reached by missionary _women!_ It has recently been suggested that, because of the more rigid structure of the denominational missions with their emphasis on ordained men, women tended towards 'faith' missions where they could be more liberated.'[104]

Women's absence from student life at Cliff and their presence only as maids and kitchen staff, has not been a proud part of Cliff's history. The earliest suggestion that there might be female students came in an article, written rather out of character by Chadwick during December 1929. This took the form of an editor's letter entitled, 'Women Students and Cliff College'.[105] He wrote of the need to embrace new ideas and states that he was willing to do so. Following the sudden death of Fiddian Moulton, the substantial house 'Cliff Park' had become available from the beginning of the Spring Term until the summer of 1930, and Chadwick considered the possibility of using it to provide accommodation for a growing number of female enquirers.[106] 'Since term began we have had enquiries, and several times in recent years we have received several women who wanted to come as students for a short term as guests. We propose to open the door, and give them the opportunity. We can take eight or ten women students for the next two terms. If it is in the heart of any to come, let them write to me for particulars, and we will tell them all we can about Cliff College and what we will attempt to do for them. If there is no response, we shall be content to go on as we are, thankful for the opportunity to have made the offer.'[107]   It would have been a courageous woman who in fact followed up this ambivalent offer, since Chadwick made it clear later in the article that even in the face of applications from women both at home and abroad, given the heritage of the *Joyful News Mission,* he had been against the idea from the beginning. 'Neither Mr Cook nor I ever entertained the idea of opening the College to women; Cliff is a men's College; it has always been a men's College, and we saw no reason why it should be anything else.'[108]   He referred to the Women's branch of the Joyful News at Rugby and George Clegg's Home in Halifax, 'but a separate organisation for Women's Evangelists is a different proposition.'[109] Not surprisingly no women became students in the spring of 1929. The College archive does not stretch back to any correspondence with prospective students, but it is assumed that no one took up the offer.

The CLIFF WITNESS for friends of Cliff

| VOLUME 3 | MARCH 1966 | NUMBER 2 |

WOMEN STUDENTS FOR CLIFF

The Cliff Committee has decided, after careful thought and prayer, that we should become a mixed college from September, 1966. We want to share some men hear the call to the ministry at Cliff, so some women may find here a vocation for such full-time service as the Deaconess Order, which is short of Lincoln and Grimsby District in 1952, and served Cliff for years as an inspiring lecturer and an active member of the community. This distinguished

The issue of women and Cliff was not raised again in publications about the College until the arrival of Howard Belben as Principal in the autumn of 1965. His first report as Principal to the Cliff College General Committee, of which we only have a summary, covers many aspects for the possible development of the College and its courses, including 'Cliff and women'.[110] At the Policy Committee the following January the 'proposal to admit women students was accepted in principle.'[111] The single line of text in the *Minute*, 'It was unanimously decided that women students be admitted from September 1966', does not do justice to the widely held view among the Cliff Men's Fellowship that this would be a retrograde step.[112] One student commented to the Sheffield Telegraph, 'If we have girls here it would prove too big a temptation I am sure. We are very isolated up here and if you have men and women together all the time it would be very distracting.'[113] That was not the considered view of the staff and the decision was boldly promoted in the *Cliff Witness*

issued immediately after the Committee with the headline, 'Women Students for Cliff'.[114] Howard Belben had argued for what was seen by many people as a dramatic change to the College, and he advanced seven arguments as sound reasons for the change. However he prefaced them all by indicating that the Cliff Committee decided, 'after careful thought and prayer'.[115] The reasons were that: women play a full part in the life of the Church as Lay Leaders; women as well as men are looking for the training offered by the College; men and women work as colleagues in Christian ministry, so they should train together; women and men attend the short courses offered by

Miss Mary Lambert

Cliff and why not the full-time course; women may hear a call to fulltime ministry, for instance, in the Deaconess Order; almost all

The Rev Kathleen Bowe

Mrs Susanne Garnett

Further Education is co-educational, and 'there is room for more students'.[116] A cohort of fifteen female students arrived at the College in September 1967[117] and the place of women has been significant since that time. For many years now the proportions of men to women have been about fifty-fifty with the pendulum swinging no more than sixty-forty either way.

In a strange contrast to this reticence to admit women, Cook had from the beginning appointed women as tutors. Miss Lilian Hovey came from Sheffield to teach English and elocution. She was the first laywoman to attend the Wesleyan Methodist Conference and was clearly influential. Chadwick brought Miss Annie Douglas to Cliff. She had taught in Leeds and on the Cliff staff taught 'Biblical Geography'; also she was the effective editor of the *Joyful News* throughout Chadwick's time. Annie Douglas lived with the Chadwicks both at Cliff Park and in Cliff House. In many ways the arrangement was a curious one but she was a support to both Sarah and Samuel Chadwick.

The first full-time female Tutor of the contemporary era was Mary Lambert who came in September 1968 to teach Church History, the second-year Bible study, and to share in the teaching of English and Evangelism. Mary was also to take charge of the new Conference Centre when it was opened.[118] This she undertook with great enthusiasm and the College promoted a bi-monthly conference from the very beginning. Her workload, the pastoral care of female students and the conference business proved too much, and she became ill early in 1970 and returned home to Somerset. It was with great joy that many years later Dr William Davies invited Mary to rejoin the staff for a year as 'President's Assistant' during the time he was President of the Methodist Conference. Mary took on his teaching load of Theology and Church History while he was absent.[119] It was for her a second opportunity to be a Cliff Tutor, and she served with great distinction.

The longest serving female Tutor has been the Rev Kathleen Bowe who came to the College in 1984 as Old Testament Tutor and stayed until 1993. She also taught Pastoral Studies and led the music of the College for many years. Kathleen had been teaching before candidating for the ministry, and at Bristol gained a love of Hebrew and the Old Testament. She continued the great heritage of Old Testament scholarship within the College and was an excellent Tutor and teacher. In the Summer of 2000 the College appointed Mrs Susanne Garnett as a lay tutor. Susanne had considerable experience in teaching social studies and politics, and had worked extensively with aid organisations. Susanne engaged enthusiastically with the students, challenged the College about fair trade issues, edited *Cliff Today* and developed her teaching area. In 2001 she became leader of the part-time courses and Director of the Open Learning Centre helping to develop the work of the College. She returned to overseas development work in the summer of 2003.

Mrs Michelle Shaw

The list of full-time female teaching staff is not a long one, but there have been many extremely good part-time tutors, not least Lilian Hovey, Annie Douglas, Doris Hallam, many of the Tutor's wives, and presently, Ann Hodgson and Jane Carter teaching English and giving English Support (part-time), along with Michelle Shaw as Pastoral Studies Tutor (half-time). Clearly there is a balance of women and men on the governing structures and for many years the College has been well served by female evangelists. A future challenge for the College however will be to rectify what could be seen as a significant weakness in the overall make-up of the full-time tutorial staff. What is revealed by this study is the importance of women's ministry and the vital role the College has played in the training of women for mission and ministry.

1   Alison White, 'Bearers of an Idle Tale: Women as Evangelists in the Christian Tradition', *Anvil Vol. 13 No1*, 1996 p.21.

2   *Joyful News,* March 1885.

3   Gerald H. Anderson, et al (eds.), *Mission Legacies* (Maryknoll, New York: Orbis, 1994).

4   Anderson, *Mission Legacies,* p.93.

5   Anderson, *Mission Legacies,* pp.110-116.

6   Anderson, *Mission Legacies,* pp.307-315.

7   Anderson, *Mission Legacies,* pp.205-215.

8   Lavinia Byrne, *The Hidden Tradition, Women's spiritual writings rediscovered* (London: SPCK 1991), p.185.

9   Byrne, p.186.

10 Byrne, p.187.

11 Byrne, p.189.

12 Byrne, p.190.

13 Byrne, pp.188-9.

14 Linda Wilson, *Constrained by Zeal, Female Spirituality amongst Nonconformists 1825 – 1875* (Carlisle: Paternoster Press, 2000).

15 Deborah Valenze, *Prophetic Sons and Daughters: Female Preaching and Popular Religion in Industrial England* (Princeton, New Jersey, 1985).

16 Wilson, See her Appendix pp. 228 – 274 which gives a list of all the women whose obituaries appeared in the official newspapers of these denominations. That is, they were women of noted spirituality and ministry, however that had been exercised. The number of women listed is 63 Baptist, 60 Congregational, 61 Primitive Methodist, and 60 Wesleyan Methodist. Valenze wanted to have a fair sample across the denominations, but there are in fact many more Primitive and Wesleyan obituaries of women published in this period. The contrast can be observed in the research published by Michael Watts (*The Dissenters,* Vol. 2 (Oxford, 1995), pp. 48-80, who analysed conversion in dissenters of the early part of the nineteenth century. He found 670 obituaries mentioning conversion, of which only 55 were Baptist and thirteen Congregational. The remainder was Primitive and Wesleyan Methodist.

17 Wilson, p.262.

18 Wilson, p.233.

19 Wilson, p.252.

20 Wilson, p.244.

21 Wilson, p.245.

22 Wilson, p.249.

23 Wilson, p.240.

24 Wilson, pp. 240-1.

25 Wilson, p.270.

26 Wilson, p.242, regarding Agnes Campbell.

27 Wilson, p.236 regarding Mrs Millard.

28 So many of the obituaries used by Wilson have the tragedy of women dying young from disease or child bearing.

cont.

29 R.R. Ruether, *Sexism and God-Talk* (London: SCM, 1983), p.198.

30 Thomas Oden (ed), *Phoebe Palmer: Selected Writings* (New York: Paulist Press, 1988).

31 Hannah Pearsall Smith, *The Christian's Secret of a Happy Life* (Westwood, New Jersey: Fleming H. Revell, 1952).

32 Deborah Kirkwood, 'Protestant Missionary Women; Wives and Spinsters', in *Women and Missions: Past and Present,* ed. Bowie, Kirkwood and Ardener (Providence, RI and Oxford: Berg 1993), p.26.

33 Normally the missionary women were married, but as early as 1825 Robert Morrison wrote to the London Missionary Society suggesting the need for, 'some unmarried ladies of experience and education…with the design of teaching English and the principles of our holy religion to pagan girls.' *Dictionary of Evangelical Biography,* p.774. Even the influential Rufus Anderson, contemporary of Henry Venn, counselled missionary societies in 1836 that despite being urged to send out unmarried females, 'unmarried females should rarely be sent on missions.' Rufus Anderson, 'An Introductory essay on the Marriage of Missionaries' in *To Advance the Gospel: Selections from the writings of Rufus Anderson*, Pierce Beaver (ed.) (Grand Rapids: Eerdmans 1967), p.213.

34 Broomhall, Vol. 4, *Survivors Pact,* p.47.

35 A.J. Broomhall, *Hudson Taylor and China's Open Century* Vol. 3 *If I had a thousand Lives* (London: Hodder and Stoughton and The Overseas Missionary Fellowship 1982), p.407.

36 Broomhall, Vol. 4, *Survivors Pact,* p.48.

37 Broomhall, Vol. 4, *Survivors Pact,* pp.47-48.

38 Griffiths, p.14.

39 Paul W. Chilcote, *John Wesley and the Women Preachers of Early Methodism* (Metuchen, New Jersey: Scarecrow Press, 1991) p.254.

40 C.H. Crookshank, *History of Methodism in Ireland,* 3 Vols. (London: 1885-9), Vol. 2, p.31.

41 *Minutes of the Methodist Conferences in Ireland,* Vol.1, 1744-1819, p.152.

42 *Minutes of the Conference 1803* pp.188-9.

43 Christine L. Krueger, *The Readers Repentance, Women Preachers, Women Writers and Nineteenth Century Social Discourse* (Chicago: University of Chicago Press, 1992), p.81. See also Dorothy Graham, 'Women Local preachers' in *Workaday Preachers,* ed Batty and Milburn (London: Epworth, 1995) pp.165f; Earl Kent Brown, *Women of Mr Wesley's Methodism* (Edwin Mellen Press, 1983) and Janet Burge, 'Impudent Women', in *PWHS* Vol. 21, pp.93-101.

44 John Lenton, *Labouring for the Lord, Women preachers in Wesleyan Methodism 1802-1932. A Revisionist View*.

45 David East, *Early Methodist Preachers,* unpublished lecture given 26 March 2003, at the Wesley Centre, Oxford; part of the Westminster Institute, Oxford Brookes University.

46 E. Thomas, *Irish Methodist Reminiscences: Memorials from the Life and Labour of the late Reverend S. Nicholson* (London: 1889), p.10, quoted by Hempton and Hill, p.134.

cont.

47 Hempton and Hill, p.138.
48 John Lenton, *Labouring for the Lord, Women preachers in Wesleyan Methodism 1802-1932. A Revisionist View.*
49 Lenton, p.3.
50 Lenton, p.4.
51 Richard Teffry Jr., *Memoirs of Mrs Jane Teffry* (London: 1830), pp.64-69.
52 Lenton, point 3, p.2.
53 Lenton, Appendix 3, p.15.
54 Lenton, point 6, p.2.
55 Lenton, p.8. See also Dorothy Graham, who concurs with this citing examples of Primitive and Wesleyan Preaching Plans where women are indicated by initials so as to hide the appointment of women preachers to take services, 'Women Local Preachers', p.185.
56 *Agenda of the Pastoral Session of the Wesleyan Methodist of Conference 1910,* p.69.
57 Lenton, p.13.
58 Lenton, p.10.
59 W. Bradfield, *The Life of the Revd Thomas Bowman Stephenson* (London: C.H. Kelly, 1913).
60 P.S. Bagwell, *Outcast London, A Christian Response* (London: Epworth Press, 1987), pp.24f. At an even later time this was followed by 'Lady Workers' in the East End Mission and other of the Missions at the turn of the 20th Century.
61 Lenton, p.10.
62 Champness, *The Life,* p.258.
63 *Joyful News,* 12 April 1883. The capitals are in the original article.
64 *Joyful News,* 3 May 1883.
65 *Joyful News,* 5 March 1885.
66 *Joyful News,* 19 March 1885. There is also an account of a mission conducted by Miss Tindall at Dumbarton, 16 June 1885; and in Bootle, 22 Oct 1885.
67 *Joyful News,* 26 March 1885.
68 Ibid.
69 *Joyful News,* 29 March 1888. The home is situated at 24 Gladstone Road, Halifax.
70 *Joyful News,* 29 March 1888.
71 *Joyful News,* 29 March and see also 12 April 1888.
72 Ibid.
73 Ibid.
74 Ibid.
75 *Joyful News,* 7 February 1889.
76 Eliza Champness, *The Life*, p.258-9.
77 Brian M. Hills, *Mary Ann Hills (nee Dixon) 1864-1946* (unpublished, 2004) p.2.
78 Ibid, p.3.
79 Ibid, pp.3-4.
80 Ibid, p.4.
81 Mary Jane Smith, *Diary,* 19 May 1892, Cliff College Archive.
82 Mary Jane Smith, *Diary*, 27 May 1892.

cont.

83 Mary Jane Smith, *Diary*, 1 July 1892.
84 Mary Jane Smith, *Diary*, 6–9 August 1892.
85 Mary Jane Smith, *Diary*, 12 July 1892.
86 Mary Jane Smith, *Diary*, 21 September 1892.
87 Mary Jane Smith, *Diary*, 25 September 1892.
88 Mary Jane Smith, *Diary*, 20 October 1892.
89 Mary Jane Smith, *Diary*, 10 February 1893.
90 *Joyful News,* 9 January 1893.
91 *Joyful News,* 23 May 1895.
92 *Joyful News,* 20 April 1893.
93 Ibid.
94 *Joyful News,* 11 July 1895. Champness had to cut his endeavour severely due to shortage of funds from both his publishing business and the gift income. He was both realistic and had faith for the future. 'We have been troubled by the fact that the Joyful News Mission had not been supported as it formerly was. And this has been accompanied by a decline in our Book business; consequently we have not been able to give as largely as we have been used to.' Note the clumsy English here. 'Accordingly we have sent a circular to most (about 60) of our workers saying they must not consider us any longer responsible for their support. There are 32 JNE of whom 17 are overseas. There are 4 single women and four married in the 32. In addition there are four evangelists in two caravans. Three training and two resting from overseas. 20 are with Mr Clegg and two of the 'Out and Out' caravans are resting. As will be seen by the list, we have still a number of men at work, as well as those in charge of the Caravans, whom we shall try to keep. The men and women in the Foreign work also must be supported…we believe that this trial will be for our good, and we will not repine or worry, believing that adversity is among the good things promised to the children of the King of Heaven.'
95 Mary Jane Smith, *Diary*, 22 July 1892.
96 Mary Jane Smith, *Diary*, 25 July 1892.
97 *Joyful News,* February 1900.
98 *Joyful News,* 3 March 1904.
99 *Joyful News,* 16 July 1908, a letter from Eliza indicates that this work is now closed.
100 David Hempton and Myrtle Hill, '"Born to Serve": women and evangelical religion' in *Evangelical Protestantism in Ulster Society, 1740-1890* (London: Routledge, 1992), p.130.
101 Ibid.
102 Griffiths, p.15.
103 Ruth Tucker, *Guardians of the Great Commission* (Grand Rapids: Zondervan, 1988), p.41.
104 Griffiths, p.22, referring to a suggestion by Ruth Tucker in *Priscilla Papers 1996*. His italics and underline.
105 *Joyful News,* 5 December 1929.
106 Ibid, 'we have a house on our hands, and the question arose as to what use we should make of it.'
107 Ibid.

cont.

108 Ibid.
109 Ibid.
110 *Minutes of the Cliff College General Committee,* 14 October 1965.
111 *Minutes of the Cliff College Management Committee,* 27 January 1966.
112 *Minutes of the Cliff College General Committee,* 10 March 1966.
113 *Evening Telegraph, Sheffield*, 11 March 1966.
114 *The Cliff Witness,* March 1966.
115 Ibid.
116 Ibid.
117 *The Cliff Witness,* January 1967.
118 *The Cliff Witness,* August 1968.
119 *The Cliff Witness,* Autumn 1987.

CHAPTER 6

Joyful News Missionaries

Despite his decision not to return to West Africa Thomas Champness maintained a keen interest in overseas missions. As the 'Joyful News Home and Mission' developed, Champness became committed to supporting and sending missionaries abroad. It was this aspect of his work which would become most controversial.

From the beginning of the *Joyful News* Champness invited prayer for missions. Within weeks of the publication of the paper, he gave a call to prayer for the Central China Mission Band, with a special reference to the work of the pioneer Wesleyan missionary the Rev David Hill.[1]

Although the main themes promoted in the *Joyful News* were evangelism in Britain, the urge to temperance and a call to holiness, there is throughout the publication a significant minor theme of overseas missions. In all these aspects of work Thomas was constantly looking for workers. Typical is the call in the *Joyful News* 'for the Lord's service in the Wesleyan Methodist Missionary Society, Wanted Immediately. Strong men like Joshua who will not be ashamed to take their stand and say in the presence of the people.'[2]

He supported the Missionary Societies' Public Meetings at the Exeter Hall on the Strand in London.[3] The Exeter Hall had been built in 1832, with a main hall seating 3,500. The great Victorian evangelical societies met there in the spring every year, at what were generally known as the 'May meetings'. Champness had addressed the Wesleyan Missionary Society Centenary celebration at the Exeter Hall on his return from West Africa. Many of the meetings were held in the presence of parliamentarians and even Prince Albert.[4]

David Hill

The *Joyful News* gave a prominent position to an advertisement for the meetings in 1884 with the invitation, 'Let all Methodists pray for a Baptism of the Holy Ghost on all who speak or listen'.[5] Eliza attended the 'Great Missionary Meeting' sending back by telegraph an account of the meeting and the speakers.[6] A number of short articles began to appear such as one entitled, 'Good News from Central China'[7] indicating that at Wuchang there had been conversions as a result of the ministry of David Hill.[8] A letter was published from Calcutta about the missions in India. This included assurances of British soldiers and sailors being converted and also, 'the signs of progress are more numerous in the native part of our work'.[9] There is also an extended article about the work among the British Army in Secunderabad, India, where a large class meeting of forty-eight members has 'a lady in charge of it'.[10] In the second year of publication of the paper, when a pattern of news and editorial articles had begun to emerge, there were many short articles about overseas missions. Most focussed on news of revivals or extensions of the evangelistic work and come from South Africa,[11] from the Hindustani Circuit in Lucknow,[12] Bangalore,[13] Lombardy,[14] South Africa,[15] Le Havre,[16] Cape of Good Hope,[17] the Bangalore Tamil Circuit,[18] Japan,[19]

Montreal,[20] Cairo,[21] South Ceylon District,[22] Benares, India where a Miss Bush addressed the 2nd Lincolnshire Regiment,[23] and from Bellary, India, with the Bedfordshire Regiment.[24] This reveals an irregular pattern but built, for the reader, an overview of the immense need for courageous missionary enterprise.

The actual Foreign Mission work began as the idea of a Wesleyan Missionary, the Rev Owen Watkins, who 'employed a young Kaffir in South Africa at the expense of Mr Champness.'[25] Eliza Champness observes that, 'in this way...the Mission of *Joyful News* had quietly begun'.[26] It may have begun quietly but Champness saw the possibilities for promoting and extending this new missionary endeavour. In advertising the *Almanac* for 1885 there is a 'Portrait of Hans Aapjee, Our African Missionary', which was the first indication of *Joyful News* missionaries.[27]

Champness was determined to press the need for missionary endeavour partly to advertise the *Almanac* and also to bring home to its readers the possibilities for the *Joyful News Mission*. In December he published a portrait of a "Joyful News" Native Missionary in Africa.[28] He knew well the power of images and used the portrait of Hans Aapjee to drive home his desire to send missionaries abroad. Earlier in the year, news of Hans Aapjee, who was described as a 'Joyful News Missionary in South Africa'[29], was launched upon the readers of the *Joyful News*. The writing of the Rev Owen Watkins had set the platform for the establishment of such a mission. Watkins wrote, 'I got back from Hans Aajpee's station yesterday morning. We had a very pleasant and profitable time there. The people came out in crowds, three miles from the station, to meet me, and sang me into the town. I baptized one hundred and eighty-three adults and children, and administered the Sacrament of the Lord's Supper to one hundred and sixty three members'.[30] This report about

Hans is given with enthusiasm and the determination that there should be more *Joyful News* missionaries.

It would appear that Champness 'adopted' as foreign workers people who were in touch with him and to whom he probably gave monetary as well as prayer support. He retained contact with them by letter and editions of the *Joyful News*. Such a person is identified in a letter from Robert Simpson in Barcelona.[31] Simpson is not introduced as a minister, and may have been a tourist or businessman. He had visited a church at El Clot near Barcelona and found there, 'your "Joyful News" Bible woman at work.'[32] Sister Fervent was a Roman Catholic lay woman who had found Christ and was somehow in contact with the *Joyful News*.[33] She was regularly included in the list of *Joyful News* Evangelists. There is no evidence that either Thomas or Eliza met Sister Fervent, but he seems to have supplied her with Bibles and tracts for distribution.

The whole matter of missionary involvement was brought into sharp focus by a joint article from Thomas and Eliza Champness in February 1887. The title of the article on the front page was, 'Shall "Joyful News" have a Mission In Africa?'[34] Champness indicated he had evangelists who would be willing to go. 'We don't see why we should not have a Layman's Mission working on Methodist lines.'[35] They explained that they had experience of mission in Africa and the decision, whether or not this should begin, relied on 'someone offering us a passage for our first "Joyful News" African Evangelist.'[36] Within a month they had begun to consider and work out the strategy for such deployment. 'We have concluded to send out two men to South Africa, but we are not in a hurry. We are not yet sure where to locate them, and shall not move further till we see our way more clearly. We have as much money promised as will make it right to begin as soon as we know where to send them. Let our friends pray for light. We may not send the men out for months, but it is settled that we shall have a "Joyful News" African Mission, and we have no doubt but that the God who has so signally helped us already, will do so more and more.'[37] Their first thought had been to send men to West Africa but, because of the high incidence of illness and death, they decided to think again. It would appear that whilst Champness was willing to place himself in danger, he was not willing to require that of others. He explained this to his readers: 'We shrink from sending the men to Western Africa on account of the unhealthiness of the climate ... Let our friends pray on.'[38]

In April of that same year he established his main aim and commissioned the first missionary: 'We have a theory about Evangelists abroad as well as at home ... we must have cheap labour, and we must have our own sons in the gospel who are prepared to go and preach the gospel to every creature, and that without salary, only receiving the actual cost of maintenance. We shall give each man we send out a couple of suits of everything, sending him out others as he may need them, and giving him only such money as he is compelled to spend. Mr David Pilgrim is the first man we have selected. He is a godly and earnest man, who has the get-on-ableness which a man needs who goes among barbarous and heathen people.'[39] David Pilgrim was clearly a resourceful and reliable *Joyful News* Evangelist who, as noted in chapter three, was entrusted with collecting the first Gospel van.

It was only after the publication of the decision to expand the work to include missionary endeavour that Champness had contact with the Wesleyan Methodist Missionary Society. He was a man of independent mind and had, through the newspaper and his supporters, the resources to embark on such ventures. Thomas and Eliza had an interview with the Rev John Kilner, one of the secretaries of the Wesleyan Missionary Society.[40] Kilner had become interested himself in the proposed scheme and written to one of the Chairmen of the Districts in South Africa, offering him the services of two *Joyful News* men. 'We expect to hear in a month ... We shall hope to send the brethren Pilgrim and Chisnall in October ... We shall need money for passage and outfit ... we shall be glad to hear from anyone who can give us counsel in this matter.'[41] Pilgrim[42] and Chisnall were chosen to go to the Zulu Mission.[43] They sailed on the 'Trojan' for South Africa, 'the first, but please God, not the last of our missionary band.'[44] Arriving at Durban, they travelled to Ladysmith, and then on to Maritzburg in Natal.[45]

Champness was entreated to send a *Joyful News* Missionary to West Africa but since he knew well the perils, he asked for prayer.[46] Though he appears to have made the decision to send one person, he was also requested to send people to China, 'We should like to send Mr David Hill one or two men.'[47] In fact the next placed *Joyful News* Missionaries were Simpson and Edlin (who had originally been selected for West Africa), and they were sent to India.[48] He remained ambivalent about West Africa, where Eliza did not want Thomas to return.

Champness was a prolific strategist at this period of his life. The income from the *Joyful News* had enabled the training of both men and women as evangelists, the sending of male missionaries, the development of publishing books, tracts, simple Bible study and nurture materials. The work of publishing was funding evangelism, which in turn gave a profile for prayerful and financial support for the work as a whole.

During 1887-8, Champness sent out missionaries and contemplated further expansion using not only men but also women in this work: 'The more we study the needs of the heathen in foreign

Alice Lord

lands, the more we are led to see that there is a great work to be done by Englishwomen who are willing to live among the people, not so much as school teachers, but as Evangelists ... We earnestly ask all those who so constantly help us by prayer, to join us now in seeking the Divine direction in this matter; and we are sure God will open our way if He wants us to do the work ... We live in days of blessed progress, and we predict that in a few years, by God's good hand upon His church for good, there will be a large army of devoted men and women, acting as evangelists under control, and yet not pressed into one mould, but allowed to grow according to their individuality, to bring glory to God, and good to the world.'[49]

The first female *Joyful News* missionary was Alice Lord who came from Bagslate, Rochdale. Champness had worked in the circuit and invited Alice to offer for the overseas work which she did in 1887. 'Miss Lord volunteered for foreign service in a strange land 7,000 miles away, as one of his first J.N.E.'s. She gave farewell addresses to very large gatherings at Bagslate and Lanehead, and sailed in September, 1888, to Ceylon. After some years ministering with great acceptance she married and after revisiting home and conducting a service in the Chapel, accompanied by her Cingalese servant boy, she died in Ceylon, leaving one child, now in Bagslate.'[50]

Champness had begun a creative and innovative movement and it was a sad moment when, due to jealousy or actual difference of policy, he was faced with opposition. In May 1888 it became clear in the preparation for the Conference in July, that the Mission House was running into debt. Champness with his new idea was an easy target and 'During the conversation, which was a very interesting one, a minister of great frankness and openness of character, said that the "Joyful News" movement, with which he sympathised, was partly to blame. The speaker argued that the money sent to us was so much the less sent to the Mission House.'[51]

Joyful News missionaries to China – E.C. Cooper is seated on the left.

Champness refuted the argument that he or his missionary activity was to blame by indicating that the Missionary Society's debt for the previous year stood at £16,000, and the income to the *Joyful News* Home and Mission amounted to £5,640 1s 9½d across a four year period. He also pointed out, 'let it be borne in mind, also, that of this amount, £1,028 8s 1½d has been sent to us in payment for the services of the men from the places where they have laboured.'

He continued to make his desires known through the paper, proposing that one hundred lay evangelists be sent abroad.[52] There was an inflow of money from his readers and at the same time 'men from the ranks of *Joyful News* evangelists offered themselves for service abroad.'[53]

The work was growing very quickly, and by 1889 he had eighteen *Joyful News* Missionaries and three 'native agents', one in Spain, one in India, and one in China.[54]

Champness's *Joyful News* articles persuaded the Conference to appoint a 'Special Committee to consider the whole question of the provision and employment of Lay Agents at home and abroad'.[55] This was reported in the *Joyful News* which indicated the committee would meet in December and also challenged them to consider the following questions:

1. Shall there be a list of authorised Lay Workers, and shall such men as are on that list only be recognised?

2. Shall we make provision for the Agents thus authorised when they are sick, or become worn out, and how shall the funds needed for such provision be raised?

3. Would it be well to set apart one of the Colleges for this kind of Agency?

4. Shall we use in our Foreign work a large number of men who cannot become Ministers, and if so, will they be allowed to marry?[56]

The following week an article by Eliza Champness entered a theological debate about the nature of the missionary task. Two Anglicans, Sir W.W. Hunter and Canon Taylor, had criticised the work of Protestant Christian Missions, especially Indian Missions. Hunter advocated the 'Pauline Method' which although not clearly stated, related to the concept of mission as dialogue. It is clear from the article that Hunter was not happy with evangelism among the Hindus particularly, preferring what he called 'dialogue', in the sense of sharing different spiritual journeys. Eliza appears to be irenic, 'Far wiser it is to consider calmly the statements they make, and search carefully into the reasons which have made men, who are reputed wise, doubt the success of the work which they no less than ourselves, hold to be for the good of the world and humanity. If there is any fallacy in their reasoning, wise lovers of mission work will point it out without loss of temper, and in the spirit of Christian love.'[57]

However, she defended preaching evangelism commenting, 'If Paul had stood up to-day in Benares, in Kandy, in Shanghai, or in Calcutta, and had said some of the words recorded of him in the Bible, would the "Pauline Method" have won the affections and secured the reverent adhesion of the cultured Hindoo or Chinese idolater?'[58] She then referred to the 'True Pauline Method', and the proclamation of the gospel of the Cross, and concluded, 'Let these criticisms only cause us to examine ourselves as to our being true followers of Paul, as he followed Christ...only a strong stimulus to renewed and more vigorous effort to bring the world to Christ.'[59]

Through the autumn there are short articles about missionaries and in December 1888 a leading article, 'Native Agency versus "Joyful News" Evangelists'.[60] The Champnesses had been criticised for not using indigenous missionaries and wasting the *Joyful News* monies sending people. Champness indicated he was in favour of 'native agents' and that he paid twenty pounds 'towards the support of a Bible-woman in Spain' and more recently, to Daveethu, a convert in Secunderabad. However he made plain the immensity of the task which he felt could not be met by converts alone. Two of his missionaries, Simpson and Edlin, had a circuit with 3,788 villages in India and with them are, 'one European Minister, a Native Minister and two or three Catechists. What are these among so many?'[61] Undaunted by the criticism and because of the need, he was committed to sending *Joyful News* missionaries; 'we shall go on, so long as the Lord of the harvest sends us men, and the Methodist people give us the money!'[62]

Champness was keen to ensure that evangelism was a priority in the training and ministry of his own and other missionaries. In an article entitled, 'Are we wasting our Missionary Income',he was very critical of the Mission House, for spending so much money on training people to take University degrees when the need, as he saw it, was for evangelists.[63]

His own experience in West Africa, along with his early impressions of the mission work by *Joyful News* missionaries, led him to support criticism by the Rev Hugh Price Hughes of the missionaries in India. This included the Wesleyan Methodists. The criticism came in two articles printed in the *Methodist Times* in the Spring of 1890 entitled 'A New Missionary Policy of India'.[64] Hughes alleged that ordained missionaries of all denominations lived a luxurious life-style among the upper class Brahmin society.[65] 'The result is, that men who left the London docks with the simplest ideas of life and duty, full of lofty purposes of self denial and devotion, have scarcely trodden on Indian soil a twelvemonth before they find themselves settled down to a mode and fashion of living from which a year ago they would have shrunk back in dismay.'[66] Hughes indicated that some missionaries were embarrassed by the salaries provided and in the Mysore District had returned some of their wage.[67] Nevertheless many lived in comparative luxury: 'The missionary in India with £300 a-year and his bungalow ... is able, with ease and comfort, to mix in Anglo-Indian society in a style which he could not possibly do on less than £1,000 a-year in England.'[68]

The Missionary Society, after initial enquiry, established a sub-committee of senior Methodists who met over four full days from 27 to 30 May 1890. Eventually *The Missionary Controversy, Discussion, Evidence and Report 1890* was published on the 14 July in that same year and records all the articles, minutes and reports in full, similar to Hansard and covering 388 pages. The unanimous finding of the sub-committee was a "complete exoneration of the Indian missionaries of our society."[69]

Champness was called to the sub-committee and the work of the *Joyful News* Missionaries came under scrutiny. The situation in India was defended by two ministers who had been sent by the 'brethren in India' to rebut the criticisms. One of them, the Rev George Patterson, indicated that he had nothing but admiration for Hughes and, 'I should like also to make a similar remark, with reference to another equally honoured and equally loved member of this committee – I refer to Mr Champness. Mr Champness has all his life been an earnest missionary, and he is now developing an organisation which, we trust, will be a very valuable and almost indispensable auxiliary to the work of this Society in India and elsewhere. We in India have always regarded Mr Champness' work with hopefulness. We have received the men he has sent us with cordiality and affection, and have assisted them as far as it lay in our power.'[70] The information laid before the sub-committee indicated that the stipend for a married couple without children ranged between £230 and £250 depending on the region in which they were placed and for single missionaries, £125 – 150.[71] Champness made it clear in his first submission that he had no wish to criticise others but that he had experience, at that time, of some single missionaries and one married pair. 'He had discovered that two or three unmarried men living together might live in great comfort in India at a cost of £50 a year each – and that he was prepared to prove in so far as figures could prove anything. He knew from his own observation that those men lived as well as young men in this country lived...and better.'[72] He had later to offer an explanation to a detailed interrogation of his financial support of the *Joyful News* missionaries. His assessment was that it cost '£50 a year each'[73] and he submitted the accounts for his evangelists at Mysore.[74] His experience of only one married couple in Ceylon was that 'They do not cost me quite £100 a year.'[75] As a result of this experience Champness suggested that the stipend should be no more than £80 for a single missionary.[76] Despite some of his pointed writing, he did not like antagonism and controversy and when he was fiercely attacked in the committee, found this deeply hurtful.[77]

The sub-committee had discovered that one of his *Joyful News* Missionaries, Mr Grant, had become 'disconnected from the "Joyful News" Mission in November, 1889.'[78] An extended letter from Grant in Madras was produced and read to the sub-committee, 'to illustrate this point – that the financial limit imposed by Mr Champness on these men may sometimes work to their detriment, and that one of Mr Champness' men believes that the financial limit *has* worked to his detriment.' It is clear from the detailed questioning that Champness kept a close eye on missionaries even when they were thousands of miles away. He revealed eventually that, 'Mr Grant wrote to me very sharply, and I began to feel that I had made a mistake in sending him out.'[79] Champness was obviously relieved when he left.[80] It is also revealed that Champness gave another of his married missionaries, Mr Maynard, a month's notice to quit, 'I think Mr Maynard was ambitious to be a leader out there. I was not prepared to indulge his views ... so I told him I did not intend to make him an officer, and that he would very soon increase his expense.'[81] The heart of the criticism of Champness was summarised by one of his questioners, Mr Brunyate:

> Mr Champness has said that he paid his men their charges, and that they got what they desired. But all this evidence goes to show that whether

there be a limit written down on paper or not, there is a limit written down in Mr Champness' own mind, and that limit seems to be £50 per year, and as soon as this limit is passed his men are dismissed.

Mr Champness: I deny that in *toto*.[82]

It is unfortunate for Champness that the record of his *Joyful News* missionaries in India was not wholly good. His interrogators in summarising the predicament, state pointedly, 'The point I wish to emphasise is that out of the seven men Mr Champness has employed in India, one has died under painful circumstances, and two have either been dismissed by Mr Champness or have had to break away because of the financial limit.'[83] His responses were seen to be very weak and the point against considerable reductions in pay for missionaries had been made.

In Champness's support there was a wise comment from the Chairman of the Mysore District, the Rev J. Hudson. This gave a high commendation of the character and work of the *Joyful News* evangelists. 'At the inauguration of a scheme as this, enthusiasm makes men willing to undergo more self-denial than they will when the novelty has worn away...while I think Mr Champness is too sanguine with respect to the financial part of this scheme, I have faith in it, and think it well worth a trial.' Despite his illness and depression following the four days of the inquiry, Champness continued to send evangelists overseas on 'Joyful News lines' and they were to work in India, Ceylon, China, Africa, and the South Sea Islands.

Eliza reveals in her book an open letter to Methodists written by Thomas to be published after his death. He indicated that after the Missionary Controversy he wished to send many more lay evangelists to work abroad but was restricted from doing so. He admitted that he could have withdrawn from the Wesleyan Missionary Society, gained funding from doing so and appointed many more people. He chose to stay within 'the Church I love' and though his letter reveals the pain he felt, he looked forward to a time when missionary endeavour would find greater support.[84]

Cover of Hymn sheet for Valedictory Service

On the 14 October 1890 there was a valedictory service for three missionaries who included William Argent and Ernest Cooper who were 'designated for China'. In what was a tragic mistake, Argent was brutally murdered in June the following year. William Argent had been sent by David Hill to Wusueh in Central China and from there on the steamer to Hankow. On the final day, 'the cry of "fire" caused Mr Argent and Mr Green, of the Chinese Custom's service, to leave the steamer-office for the scene of the fire. This fire turned out to be the burning of Mr Boden's house, which had been assaulted by a riotous mob, who had been incensed and maddened by rumours that a man had been seen carrying off four infants for the Roman Catholic Foundling Home in Kiukiang, thirty miles away, and that he was conveying them there with a view to cutting out their eyes for "foreign Medicine". It is said that a man really was carrying four infants in a basket, and that he was taken to a local official, but that this local official, finding that the plaintiffs refused to give their names to the charge, declined to have anything to do with the case. The man carrying the basket was then roughly handled by the crowd, now collected, and one of the infants was killed. Seeing this the mob, more infuriated than ever, cried, "Let us attack the Missionaries' houses." They soon broke the doors in. There were three women and four children who escaped through an outhouse, were physically attacked by the mob, saved by native Chinese and hidden by a Sub-Prefect of the district. Mr Argent came while all this was going on, and came no doubt to see what help he could render. He reached the door of the Wusueh chapel; the crowd, seeing a foreigner, first began to beat him in a shoemaker's shop. The master of the shop turned them out into the street, saying he would not allow this in his store. Then, almost at once, a heavy blow from a carrying pole came crash upon the head of our dear brother, splitting open his skull. Of course he fell; then, as though that were not enough, the murderous crowd pounded his head on the stone pavement; but it was soon over. His spirit was with the Lord in Paradise.'[85] David Hill, in his comments about the death of Argent indicated that the interior of China was experiencing a time of political instability.[86]

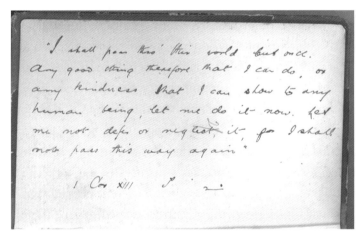

William Argent's writing inside the cover of his Daily Light

Argent was a renowned *Joyful News* evangelist, being a gracious man and in his devotional book *Daily Light* he inscribed a verse which typified his life's purpose. In the College archives there are three folders of weekly correspondence between Champness and the missionaries in China. Two contain letters from Champness to Argent, Tollerton, Hudson and Ernest Cooper. The letters run from 1888 until 1899, and the replies contained in one volume are taken from the *Joyful News* in which they were regularly published. Space does not allow a detailed survey but they indicate the level of pastoral support from Champness and the mission, are a primary source for research into mission practice in the late nineteenth century, and social commentary about missionaries who deliberately chose native dress and lived side by side with Chinese in the interior. Champness wrote weekly to all his missionaries, sometimes individually by hand but mainly a typed circular letter with news of the *Joyful News* Mission. He engaged in a dialogue in this correspondence and almost every week indicated a passage he was studying and urged his missionaries to send their comments to aid his reflections.

Joyful News Missionaries in China
(back l-r) W. Argent, E.C. Cooper;
(front l-r) A.C. Tollerton, S.J. Hudson

Champness's work in training Missionary Evangelists was similar to Hudson Taylor's, though there is no evidence they met. The Wesleyan Methodist Missionary Society sought to set up the apparatus of a colonial Church. They built stone churches which looked every bit like those found in English towns, and established hospitals and schools, dependent on the British Missionary compound. However Champness's *Joyful News* Missionaries, like Rowland Allen at the turn of the century, and Vincent Donovan many years later, sought to bring the gospel by empowering local people and supporting their growth – rather than by bringing the complex, financially draining structures of the empire. My conclusion is that whilst Rowland Allen's motives were missiological, Champness simply wanted more workers from limited resources. For him more evangelists meant a greater number of people evangelised.

Despite any misgivings Champness had about the Wesleyan Missionary Society following the Missionary Controversies, he continued to send missionaries. In 1893, ten years after the launch of the *Joyful News*, he had one hundred and twelve in the list of *Joyful News* Evangelists, including twenty-one missionaries.[87] The progress was tempered by setbacks. That same year came the sad news of missionaries who had died: 'the brave and ardent James Edlin, the industrious and seraphic Alfred Tollerton, the gentle yet heroic William Argent, the gallant and godly David Pilgrim, and earnest, devout William Trebilcock.'[88] The first anniversary of William Argent's death was used for launching the "Argent Memorial Fund" for the Joyful News China Mission.

Champnesse was committed to the missionary effort and when, sadly, things were difficult financially and he had to dismiss sixty *Joyful News* agents he retained all the seventeen who were working overseas.[89] 'The men and women in the Foreign work also must be supported ... we believe that this trial will be for our good, and we will not repine or worry, believing that adversity is among the good things promised to the children of the King of Heaven.'[90] Even when he handed over the rest of the work to Thomas Cook he retained all the remaining *Joyful News* missionaries. There were three couples, Adkin, Chisnall and Pearson, as foreign missionaries, six among a total of ten evangelists.[91]

In July 1908 Eliza Champness wrote a letter to the *Joyful News:* 'When the Joyful News Mission was handed over to Rev Thomas Cook five years ago, it was understood that the few remaining Foreign Missionary Evangelists should be directed by Mr Champness, and that he should be responsible for their support until some better arrangement could be made.' She indicated that the remaining missionaries, Mr and Mrs George Pearson working in New Ireland, were to be supported by the Australian Wesleyan Missionary Society, and Mr and Mrs Chisnall working in Pondoland were to join the staff of the Native Training College there. She made it clear that she would continue writing to them but would not in future raise funds for the 'foreign workers,' and thanked the readers of the *Joyful News* for their support, 'from the first day until now'.[92]

So ended a remarkable chapter of the work of the *Joyful News Mission*, which was inaugurated, defended, underwritten and visited by Thomas and Eliza Champness. Few Colleges have repeated this work of lay evangelists being sent to the mission field. Cliff tutors and indeed evangelists and students have preached, lectured and visited many parts of the world but it is a pale shadow of this great vision, one which because of the Missionary Controversy was never really fulfilled.[93] Today third year students have a long placement and they have in recent years visited Poland, Kenya, Guyana, Brazil, the Philippines and Ireland. This scheme has had a profound effect on the students involved as their written and spoken reflections reveal. The College has also established work with European Churches and since 1998 has had a European Evangelism Enabler, a post presently held by Eva Walker. The most dramatic development in recent years has been the establishment of the International Learning Centre, led by the Rev Richard Jackson. The project is run in partnership with the World Church Office of the Methodist Church and in the summer of 2004 came to the end of the first cycle of a two-year part-time course for one hundred students in Sierra Leone. As Sierra Leone emerged from twenty years of war, the church grew significantly and this programme was established to train the ministers and lay leaders of this vibrant and growing church. It is envisaged that the College will offer the programme of study again, for West Africa. It is the intention to gift the course to that part of West Africa and in future years move to another region. How apt that after one hundred and twenty years Thomas and Eliza's vision for the work in West Africa has been reawakened in this training project. Over the years the work of involvement with overseas missions has changed but new opportunities are before the College as a result of this International Learning Centre.

1   *Joyful News,* 12 July 1883.
2   *Joyful News,* 20 March 1884.
3   Champness attended in 1887, *Joyful News,* 14 April 1887.
4   Ian Bradley, *The Call to Seriousness* (London: Jonathan Cape, 1976), pp.140-141.
5   *Joyful News,* 24 April 1884.
6   *Joyful News,* 8 May 1884.
7   *Joyful News,* 28 February 1884.
8   *Joyful News,* 28 February 1884.
9   *Joyful News,* 13 March 1884.
10 *Joyful News,* 12 June 1884.
11 *Joyful News,* 12 June 1884.
12 *Joyful News,* 19 June 1884.
13 *Joyful News,* 3 July and 4 December 1884.
14 *Joyful News,* 10 July 1884.
15 *Joyful News,* 17 July 1884.
16 *Joyful News,* 31 July 1884.
17 *Joyful News,* 7 August 1884.
18 *Joyful News,* 14 August 1884.
19 *Joyful News,* 6 November 1884.
20 *Joyful News,* 13 November 1884.
21 *Joyful News,* 27 November 1884.
22 *Joyful News,* 8 January 1885.
23 *Joyful News,* 29 January 1885.
24 *Joyful News,* 5 February 1885.
25 Eliza, *The Life,* p.218. Also see *Joyful News,* 10 September 1885, a letter from the '*Joyful News* Missionary Hans Aapjee' by Owen Watkins.
26 Ibid.
27 *Joyful News,* 6 November 1884.
28 *Joyful News,* 18 December 1884.
29 *Joyful News,* 17 July 1884.
30 Ibid.
31 *Joyful News,* 27 January 1887. El Clot was then a village outside Barcelona. Now it is part of the city and is named as a station on the underground network.
32 Ibid.
33 *Joyful News,* 27 January 1887.

cont.

34 *Joyful News,* 24 February 1887.
35 Ibid.
36 Ibid.
37 *Joyful News,* 10 March 1887.
38 *Joyful News,* 2 June 1887.
39 *Joyful News,* 28 April 1887.
40 *Joyful News,* 21 July 1887.
41 *Joyful News,* 21 July 1887.
42 *Journal* of David Pilgrim, 1888 to 1891. It is an intermittent journal of his work in South Africa among the Zulu people, working for farmers and preaching to the native workers. He arrived in December 1887. Pilgrim died on 29 November 1891 and his obituary is in the *Joyful News,* 11 February 1892.
43 *Joyful News,* 14 and 28 October 1887.
44 *Joyful News,* 10 November 1887.
45 *Joyful News,* 12 January 1888.
46 *Joyful News,* 15 December 1887.
47 *Joyful News,* 5 January 1888.
48 *Joyful News,* 19 April 1888.
49 *Joyful News,* 29 March 1888.
50 Coupe, Howarth and Taylor (eds), *Bagslate Wesleyan Chapel Centenary Souvenir* (Bagslate: Bagslate Chapel, 1910), p.59.
51 *Joyful News,* 24 May 1888.
52 *Joyful News,* 26 July 1888.
53 Eliza, *The Life,* p.243.
54 Eliza, *The Life,* p.243.
55 *Minutes of the Methodist Conference 1888,* p.241.
56 *Joyful News,* 11 October 1888.
57 *Joyful News,* 18 October 1888.
58 *Joyful News,* 18 October 1888.
59 Ibid.
60 *Joyful News,* 20 December 1888.
61 *Joyful News,* 20 December 1888.
62 Ibid.
63 *Joyful News,* 28 February 1889.
64 Hugh Price Hughes, 'A New Methodist Policy for India', which formed two articles in *The Methodist Times,* 11 and 18 April 1890.
65 *The Missionary Controversy: Discussion, Evidence and Report, 1890* (London: Wesleyan Methodist Bookroom, 1890), p.5. This book is a word for word record of the discussion and questioning, similar to a *Hansard* or Parliamentary inquiry, and includes the whole of the articles published in the *Methodist Times.*
66 *The Missionary Controversy,* p.5.
67 *The Missionary Controversy,* p.7.
68 *The Missionary Controversy,* p.6.
69 *The Missionary Controversy,* p.369.
70 *The Missionary Controversy,* p.43.

cont.

71 *The Missionary Controversy,* p.26-27. Couples received £14 per child, and the stipend included costs for servants. The Stipend in the British Conference in 1890 was £180, see p.72.

72 *The Missionary Controversy,* p.71.

73 *The Missionary Controversy,* p.181.

74 *The Missionary Controversy,* 'Appendix C', pp.351-353.

75 *The Missionary Controversy,* p.192.

76 *The Missionary Controversy,* p.71.

77 Eliza, *The Life,* p.252-3, where she reveals the pain the Controversy caused Thomas and his illness following the sub-committee.

78 *The Missionary Controversy,* p.186.

79 *The Missionary Controversy,* p.188.

80 *The Missionary Controversy,* p.183, 'Mr Grant went out on Nov. 14, 1888, and left about June or July, 1889.'

81 *The Missionary Controversy,* p.187.

82 *The Missionary Controversy,* p.187.

83 *The Missionary Controversy,* p.188.

84 Eliza, *The Life,* pp.254-5. She indicates that since 1906 'foreign missions were being conducted on broader lines' and that what Champness had hoped for had come to pass in a 'great revival of missionary zeal', p.256.

85 Letter from the Rev David Hill, 8 June 1891, and included in a tribute to William Argent and Alfred Tollerton, both *Joyful News* Missionaries who died in China at this time, in Eliza Champness, *Faithful Unto Death* (Rochdale: Joyful News Depot, 1891), pp.35-37.

86 David Hill in Eliza Champness, *Faithful Unto Death,* p.38.

87 *Joyful News*, 23 February 1893. The missionaries were listed in the following way: Adkin in Arsikere, Mysore, India; Berkin in Tehngan, China; Bond in Ibadan, West Africa; Chisnall in Pondoland, South Africa; C.S. Champness, Dempsey, Entwisle, Tatchell, and Geear, in China; Ernest Cooper in Lung Ping, Central China; Fryer in Kwang Chi, Central China; Harris in Bangalore, India; Hudson in Kwang Chi, Central China; Overs in Lagos, West Africa; Pell in Hanchwan, China; Shaw in Hankow, China; Mr and Mrs Simpson and Mr Swann in Chitaldrug, Mysore, India. Mr and Mrs Braithwaite were resting at the Joyful News Home.

87 *Joyful News,* 11 May 1893.

89 *Joyful News,* 11 July 1895.

90 Ibid.

91 *Joyful News,* 10 March 1904.

92 *Joyful News,* 16 July 1908.

93 We should note most of the Principals of the College have regularly toured overseas. Originally these tours would take a year or so but today the relative ease of travel allows trips of two weeks or so. Thomas Cook travelled to South Africa and New Zealand – Australia; Chadwick toured South Africa and had regular visits to the US. Norman Dunning managed a two-year tour of the world. More recently our visits have been for periods of ten days or a fortnight.

CHAPTER 7

Rise of the Colleges

The churches of the Congregational or Independent tradition were enthusiastic about
training, and as a result academies and colleges were numerous. It
was from within this tradition that James Hulme had the vision for
Cliff House to become an Independent College. The first
Congregational institution was Homerton College, founded in 1730,
and following 1789 there was an explosion of Congregational and
Independent Colleges (see Table 1, p.187). The Lancashire
Independent College, Manchester, with which Hulme was
controversially connected was one such college.[1] It is clear that
among Congregationalists the concept of small and quite
independently run colleges was well understood. Hulme's vision that
Cliff House might become a college for the training of 'industrial
missionaries' was therefore quite in keeping with his tradition.

Nonconformist colleges in the early nineteenth century had a
received tradition, which came from two main strands. The first was
among the dissenting academies which were created in the wake of
the Great Ejectment in 1662, following the publication of the Prayer
Book and the Act of Uniformity. On St Bartholomew's Day 1662
upwards of two thousand clergy of Puritan persuasion who refused to
conform to the *Book of Common Prayer* and Episcopal ordination had
been ejected from their livings. The second significant strand came
as a by-product of the Eighteenth Century revival. Through the
patronage of the Countess of Huntingdon, Trevecka College was

Didsbury College

founded for the training of Evangelical Anglican clergy who held 'Methodist tenets' during the Wesleyan Revival.[2] Opened in 1768, clergy from other Churches benefited from the training at Trevecca, because the Countess did not have a narrow view of denominationalism, and that model was one followed by many evangelical colleges through the 'missionary century'.

The variety of institutions can be assessed from a study of the provision of missionary training among the Protestant denominations in the period to 1860. At a time when the Particular Baptists had four training colleges, the General Baptists three (though only one at any one time), Wesleyan Methodists two, the Church of England eleven (though the number varied) and the Congregational and Undenominational Churches sponsored nineteen colleges. There was no shortage of places to study.[3] This significant expansion of provision for ministerial and missionary training is the context within which Cliff Hulme College was eventually formed.

James and Anne Elizabeth Hulme were committed evangelicals and the theological basis of Hulme Cliff College was written into the Trust Document to direct that the teaching of the College would be evangelical.

Table 1.

Congregational and Undenominational

Theological Training Institutions.[4]

c. 1780-1860

College	Date Founded	Significant Principals
Homerton College, London (united with Highbury and Coward to form New College, London (1850)	1730	John Pye Smith (1806-50)
Western Academy, Devon (Axminster from 1752, Exeter from 1828, Plymouth from 1846)	1752	J Small (1795-27) G Payne (f. 1827) R Alliott (f. 1850?)
Newport Pagnell Evangelical Instit-ution, Bucks (undenominational – students transferred to Cheshunt, 1850)	1782	W Bull (1782-1814) T P Bull (1814-41)
Gosport Academy and Missionary Seminary, Hants (closed 1825)	1789	D Bogue (1789-1825)
Cheshunt College, Herts (Countess of Huntingdon's Connection 1768-1792, moved to Cambridge 1905)	1792	J Harris (1839-50)
Rotherham Academy, Yorks	1795	E Williams (1795-1813) J Bennett (1813-28) C Perrot (1829-34) W H Stowell (1834-50) F J Falding (c. 1852)
Hackney Academy, London (at first undenominational, 1887 moved to Hampstead)	1803	G Collison (f. 1803)
Glasgow Theological Academy	1811	R Wardlaw (1811-53) G Ewing (1811-39)
Blackburn Academy, Lancs (Independent College Manchester from 1843)	1816	J Fletcher (1817-22) G Payne (f. 1822)
Language Institution in aid of the Propagation of Christianity, or the Oriental Missionary Academy, Holburn, London (closed 1831)	1824	R Morrison H Townley F Johnson

Highbury College, London (previously Hoxton Academy 1778-1826)	1826	E Henderson (1830-49)
Hoxton Mission College, London (closed 1830)	1826	E Henderson (1826-30)
Turvey and Ongar Academy (from Turvey, Beds to Ongar, Essex 1838, closed 1844)	1829	R Cecil (1829-44)
Coward College, London (previously Wymondley College)	1833	T W Jenkyn
Airedale College, Yorks (Idle Academy to 1831)	1834	W Scott (1833-56)
Brecon Independent College, Brecknockshire	1838	H Griffiths (f. 1838)
Spring Hill College, Birmingham	1838	F Watts T R Barker
Bedford Missionary College, Beds (transferred 1866 to Cotton End)	1840	J Jukes (1840-66) W Alliott (1840-66)
Cotton End Academy, Beds (closed 1874)	1840	J Frost (1840-74)

Though colleges as we understand them are a relatively modern phenomenon, the desire for and the process of education for Christian ministry is not new. Clement of Alexandria (ca 150-215) gives some very mature reflections when explaining his teaching method for Christian leaders:

Education is a word used in many different senses. There is education in the sense of the one who is being led and instructed; there is that of the one who leads and gives

Headingley College

instruction; and thirdly, there is education in the sense of the guidance itself; and finally the things that are taught, such as precepts. The education that God gives is the imparting of the truth that will guide us correctly to the contemplation of God, and a description of holy deeds that endure forever.[5]

It is not the purpose of this book to chart the history of education for mission and ministry. It is sufficient to highlight three distinct models which all unite in the training of what became known in the twentieth century as the Bible Colleges. In the early church the method of preparation for ministry was an apprenticeship model, one of catechesis and nurture where the process of learning focussed around the handing on of the tradition and the scriptures as part of the process of discipleship. This survived until the fifth century and the development of the monasteries.

Handsworth College

As early as 388 Augustine recognized dangers in the lack of education of the clergy and saw an urgent need for an educated elite. Benedict of Nursia (c. 480-550) established what he called 'the first school for service to the Lord', for his monks, mostly laymen at Monte Casino, Italy. He believed that idleness was the enemy of the soul, and indeed the 'Rule' set out that a monk had three tasks: spiritual exercises including community worship and private devotion, manual labour and study. Those living under this rule held all things in common, and took a vow of obedience and commitment to community. The monastic schools became the main seats of learning and they were among the first to establish libraries. Most if not all the colleges combined patterns of devotion including community and private prayers, manual labour, study and missionary endeavour. Benedict's Rule became the basis for most monastic schools and affected the ethos of the nineteenth century missionary and evangelistic schools and colleges.

The third model of training emerged as a result of the Renaissance and during the Reformation when education for all priests and ministers was valued more highly and given greater status. In response to this need the Protestant Reformers also called for education and most of them founded schools. Martin Luther, for instance, published a treatise in 1524, *To the Councilmen of All Cities in Germany that they Establish and Maintain Christian Schools*. There was recognition that Clergy should be given both a general education and theological and pastoral studies. Gradually the training of clergy moved to specialised colleges known as Seminaries in the United States, Academies in continental Europe and Theological Colleges in Britain. There were a considerable number of colleges founded in the second half of the nineteenth century with an acceleration in the third quarter of the century at the same time Champness was training both men and women.[6]

Wesley House, Cambridge

The desire for an educated and missionary clergy was not confined to Europe. Bishop Juan De Zumarraga, the energetic leader of the newly formed Diocese of Mexico, founded the *Colegio Santa Cruz en Tlateloclo* in 1536 with the purpose of training indigenous clergy and expanding the missionary effort.[7] This was seen as one of his finest achievements. Though Zumarraga had high hopes for this college they were not fulfilled due to the 'insurmountable difficulty of celibacy'. In a manner not dissimilar to the Victorian philanthropists he established schools, hospitals, churches and convents. He also encouraged the development of agriculture, local crafts and simple industries.

Another example of theological training comes from India at the Serampore College founded by William Carey and his colleagues, Marshman and Ward, in 1819. The College was founded for the instruction of Asiatic, Christian and Other Youth, in Eastern Literature and European Science.[8] The College did not immediately achieve all they had hoped because there was not in India at that time an adequate substructure of education. However the desire for Christian denominations to establish colleges and universities to train Christian leadership as envisaged at Serampore College contributed significantly not only to the development of education in India but also to the development of missionary education in the 19th century. The emergence of the missionary movement and the explosion of both denominational and non-denominational colleges following the impetus resulting from William Carey's *Enquiry*[9] meant that within a period of fifty years the vision of Zumarraga, expounded three hundred years earlier, was being replicated all around the world and especially so in Europe and North America.

The Methodist commitment to education began well. John Wesley was devoted to education and the *Minutes* of the first Methodist Conference opened with the questions, 'What to Teach?' and 'How to Teach?'[10] Wesley spent considerable time on overseeing the establishment of the school at Kingswood in Bristol.[11] Despite this, the training of clergy became controversial: 'In the stormy history of English Methodism, the issue of ministerial training produced one of the loudest thunderclaps'.[12] It was not surprising, given the schisms of Methodism after Wesley's death and the vitriolic pamphlets which were produced, that many Methodists argued that the strength of the emerging church resided in its body of lay preachers. Early in the nineteenth century the powerful figure of Jabez Bunting, though avowedly committed to Wesleyanism, showed his ambivalence to theological education. He wrote, 'I am no friend of Colleges or Academies: but I do think that some regular, systematic plan ought to be adopted with respect to the young Preachers, during their four years of probation, which, without interrupting their pulpit labours, would make them more accurately and thoroughly acquainted with Divinity as a science, and qualify them for more extensive and permanent usefulness.'[13] Other streams of Methodism, apart from the Wesleyans, were suspicious of the theological education of ministers, fearing they would lose the 'common touch', though each Methodist stream eventually opened colleges.[14]

However the mood changed when in 1806 Adam Clarke raised the matter in a more positive light at the Methodist Conference in Leeds: 'We want some kind of seminary for educating workmen for the vineyard of our God, as need not be ashamed. We need without delay to get such a place established, either at Bristol or London.'[15] It was not until 30 years later in 1835, almost one hundred years after Wesley's conversion, that the first Methodist college to train ministers was opened at Hoxton.[16]

Richmond College

The Wesleyan Centenary Fund, which was organized in 1838, included the aim of developing theological training. Until Champness started the training for the Joyful News Missionaries, theological education in Wesleyan Methodism was solely for ministers. In 1844 a college was opened in Didsbury, Manchester, and the following year, 'the Richmond branch of the Wesleyan Theological Institution' was founded at the top of Richmond Hill, Surrey. Even at that point the word 'college' was regarded

Hartley Victoria College

with suspicion.[17]

All these developments in training had an impact on the nineteenth century missionary colleges which sought to emulate the discipline of the monastery, the practical training of the early church and learning from the academy. This can be illustrated by the way Grattan Guinness deliberately approached his work. The principles are documented for us in his report of the *East End Training Institute* for the year 1876-7, in a section entitled 'Training and Testing'.[18] He identified a process of rigorous testing: the *physical health* by evangelistic work and manual labour; the *mental powers* through 'six to nine hours a day of close study'; their *grace*, 'by giving them hard and humble work to do...if a man objects to or slurs these lowly tasks, as beneath his dignity or as disagreeable to his tastes, we question at once whether he possesses the grace, good sense, and self denial needful for a Missionary'; their *spiritual power* in which they give evidence of a 'zeal and love for souls, if they succeed in turning many to righteousness, there can be little doubt they are calculated to be useful Missionaries at home or abroad.'[19]

The elements of training are set out succinctly for us under three headings:

PRACTICAL TRAINING in various useful arts, including medicine, agriculture, gardening, carpentering, printing, navigation, swimming, shoemaking, tailoring, &c., and in habits of activity, order, and industry by dispensing in measure with servants, and requiring some amount of daily attention to domestic affairs.

INTELLECTUAL TRAINING, by cultivating habits of continuous attention and application, and by furnishing the mind with needed information. In addition to Biblical and theological instruction, the studies pursued embrace the routine of an English education, together with Greek and Hebrew, medical and scientific knowledge, and, where needed, modern languages.

EVANGELISTIC TRAINING, by exercising each in school work, street preaching, house-to-house visitation, personal dealing with inquirers, and public preaching in the open air and in buildings. [20]

When Thomas Champness, who of course had never attended a Theological College, developed the *Joyful News* Training Home and Mission, his motives were merely the development of workers for the task of evangelism, rather than the love of learning. However what he developed in training his Evangelists had many echoes of the testing and training used by Grattan Guinness. Champness originally hoped that the Methodist Church would use one of its existing colleges to train evangelists. When it became clear this would not happen he moved to Castleton Hall and the idea of the Training Home became celebrated in Methodism. There is no evidence that he had an understanding of the history of theological and missionary learning, but he placed the *Joyful News* Mission with its missionary aim and combination of learning, community prayer and work, with the practice of ministry, firmly in the monastic model. It was at Castleton Hall that the pattern of training, which has been the hallmark of Cliff, was established. It is characterised by praxis, the interface between the academic learning, and practical experience of mission and ministry. This was something which Chadwick would later deliberately emulate both with the College timetable and the 'Methodist Friars'.

It is a great tribute to Champness that he had the wisdom to gift the project to the Home Mission Department of the Wesleyan Methodist Church when he retired. There was risk involved in doing that. The Church might not undertake the task with the same ability or dedication he had shown, or it might refuse to train evangelists just as it had rejected his ideas about missionaries. However Champness handed over the task of training evangelists and Thomas Cook was appointed by the Conference. Champness greatly admired what Cook had achieved in the first year and on the only occasion he came to Cliff College he commented, 'I feel like a duck, that has hatched a swan'.

Cliff Lane and Joyful News entrance

1 Piggin, p.291.
2 Henry D. Rack, *Reasonable Enthusiast, John Wesley and the Rise of Methodism* (London: Epworth Press, 1989), p.453. Though Wesley was very critical of the Calvinist teaching which eventually prevailed there.
3 Piggin, *Making Evangelical Missionaries*, Appendix 4, pp.290-293.
4 Table formed from information in Piggin, *Making Evangelical Missionaries* pp.291-292.
5 K.B. Cully, *Basic Writings in Christian Education* (Philadelphia: Westminster, 1960) pp.34-42.
6 Theological Colleges and Bible Colleges presently offering courses are listed in, Heather Wraight (ed), UK Christian Handbook 2002/3 (London: Christian Research, 2001), pp.458-466.
7 A. McCormack 'Zumarraga (Cumarraga), Juan De' in *Concise Dictionary of the Christian World Mission* (London: Lutterworth Press, 1971), p.681.
8 A. Christopher Smith, 'William Carey, Protestant Pioneer of the Modern Era', in Gerald H. Anderson, *Mission Legacies* (Maryknoll: Orbis Books, 1994), p.251. 'Asiatic' refers to the children of European fathers and Indian mothers.
9 William Carey, *An Enquiry into the Obligations of Christians to use means for the Conversion of the Heathens in which the Religious state of the Different Nations of the World, the Success of former undertakings, and the Practicability of Further Undertakings are Considered* (May 1792).
10 *Minutes of the Wesleyan Conference* (1862), i, I.
11 F.C. Pritchard, 'Education' in (ed) Davies, George and Rupp, *A History of the Methodist Church in Great Britain Vol.3* (London: Epworth, 1983), pp.279-281.
12 Stuart Piggin, *Making Evangelical Missionaries, 1789-1858* (Sydney: The Sutton Courtney Press, 1984), p.204.
13 T.P. Bunting, *The Life of Jabez Bunting, D.D.* (London, 1859), p.259. Though he became the President of the Hoxton Theological Institution when it opened in 1835.
14 F.C. Pritchard, *A History of the Methodist Church,* p.292.
15 W. Bardsley Brash, *The Story of our Colleges 1835-1935: A Centenary Record of Ministerial Training in the Methodist Church* (London: Epworth Press, 1935), p.26.
16 F.H. Cumbers (ed), *Richmond College*, p.11.
17 F.C. Pritchard, *A History of the Methodist Church,* p.287.
18 H. Grattan Guinness, *Story of the Third Year of the East End Institute* (London: S.W. Partridge, 1877), pp.65-70.
19 Ibid, pp.66-67.
20 H. Grattan Guinness, *Story of the Third Year of the East End Institute* (London: S.W. Partridge, 1877), pp.65-70.

CHAPTER 8

Thomas Cook

Thomas Cook holds a unique position in the Wesleyan Methodist ministry. He never attended college and from his acceptance as a candidate in 1882 he had only two appointments, as Connexional Evangelist from 1882 and then as first Principal of Cliff in 1903 until his untimely death in 1912.

Cook was born on 20 August 1859 in the northern town of Middlesbrough where his father was involved in the iron works.[1] His mother was a member of the Wesleyan Methodist Church and guided the young Thomas Cook in his early spiritual growth. His father made no profession of faith until he was in his fifties.[2] When Thomas was 16 years old he was engaged as a pupil teacher by the Middlesbrough School Board, which suggests he had a capacity for learning and speaking which had been noticed by others.[3] In the same year of 1875 the Middlesbrough Circuit

Thomas Cook

held a special series of services and during that time he responded to the invitation to follow Christ. 'There was neither excitement nor sentiment about my brother's conversion. There were no tears; not even a tremor of a limb. But there was conviction and an enlightened determination.'[4] The influence of his mother was strong for, as she was ill at the time, 'he went straight from the chapel to her room and without waiting for any enquiry announced the glad fact – *"Mother, I have given myself to Jesus tonight".*[5]

Thomas was a fine cricketer and a particularly fierce bowler. He regularly claimed three wickets with successive balls. Although he loved the game he decided to lay it down, and instead took up regular open air preaching. Another young man, Albing Toft, was converted about the same time and Albing made a 'good strong open-air stand. It had the appearance of a box with a step attached. It was painted green and letters of brass were screwed on the front indicative of their purpose – "STAND UP FOR JESUS".'[6] These youthful preachers took the box out each evening to a 'strategic corner and in youthful, burning tones, told of all that God had done for them, and they created a deep impression on people. 'They were mere boys, but they had a story to tell. God had forgiven them, Christ had received them and the Holy Spirit had assured them.'[7]

Cook was received as a preacher in the South Bank circuit but also preached around the Northeast towns in not only the Wesleyan, but also Primitive, Wesleyan Reform and Salvation Army services. During his time as a local preacher he came into contact with Joshua Dawson of Weardale. Dawson was a preacher of Full Salvation on the lines of Wesley, Fletcher and the Early Methodist preachers.[8]

Holiness was to be a particular theme of Cook's life and preaching, and both Smart and Vallance Cook indicate that the contact with

Joshua Dawson was particularly instrumental in both his understanding and early experience of holiness. Cook yearned for that perfect love, and he determined, cost what it might, he would not only be saved, but he would be saved to the uttermost.

> Having already tasted of the grace and power of God, all his instincts and conceptions of the divine nature told him that behind such words and promises there was actuality and fact. It was not a shadowy ideal, now looming and now lost, but an experience that harmonized with all that he knew and believed of God. He felt that the Thrice-Holy One, who had said, "Ye shall be holy; for I am holy," would make the provision and do the work that was beyond the power of unaided mortal. So he asked, and sought, and strove, and – he'd found!... by a simple effort of faith, deliverance came, the last enemy was cast out, sin's stain was cleansed away, and great peace filled his soul.[9]

So in December 1878 the Middlesbrough Circuit received Thomas as a fully accredited local preacher. Indeed he was welcomed in pulpits around the region and in 1879 held his first mission at Espland Hill, near Appleby.[10] According to Smart he preached in Newcastle to as many as 4,000 people at once. About this time Cook had a remarkable dream. 'He dreamt that he was standing by a lake that was crowded with fish, and that he was casting in the nets, and enclosing a great multitude of fish, while a voice said to him, "I will make you a fisher of men"'.[11]

Thomas Cook was a day-school teacher and he had opportunity to attend Westminster Training College. However the conviction came that he should enter full time ministry and in the autumn of 1880 he was nominated in his circuit as a candidate for the ministry. This was approved unanimously. Henry Smart makes great play of the fact that because Cook preached on Perfect Love in his trial service and made an appeal, he was eventually turned down by the 'July'

Connexional Candidates Committee in the following summer.[12] In fact, Smart does acknowledges that 'It so happened that the number of candidates was that year in excess of the demand, and for this reason chiefly, his offer was not accepted, and the July Committee did not recommend him to the Conference.'[13]

In November 1880 the Rev Joseph Bush, who was the Chairman of the Halifax and Bradford District, offered Cook the post of lay evangelist and so began a flourishing ministry in the District.[14] On some occasions the numbers attending the meetings were so great that Cook had to appoint a policeman to keep order.[15] The Report of the District Home Mission Sub-Committee presented to the Halifax and Bradford District Committee indicates, 'Mr Cook's labours were remarkably owned of God. The Churches were quickened, believers were sanctified, and many sinners were converted to God. During the first six months it was found, on careful inquiry, that 2,000 persons above fifteen years of age, and a large number of younger people, had been helped in the inquiry-rooms; and, taking the whole of the first year it is quite within the mark to say that 3,000 persons professed to find peace with God. Of these, over 1,000 adults were reported by the superintendent ministers of their respective Circuits as having begun to meet in class. Three hundred joined junior Society classes, and large numbers became connected with other Churches.' [16]

Cook was a candidate for the Wesleyan Ministry for the second time in late 1881,[17] now aged twenty-two. The church had the wisdom to accept him at the Conference of 1882 as a Minister on Trial, and appointed him immediately to the new post of Connexional Evangelist. The *Minutes* of the Conference simply record, 'Thomas Cook, who shall act under the direction of the Home Missionary Committee'.[18] The General Secretary of the Home

Mission Department had become aware of Cook's work and wrote to him prior to the Conference, 'I should like you to come under my care during next year, and intend to ask that this course may be taken in your appointment. While you are favoured with evangelistic success, such as you record, I think that you should continue to go from place to place. The Lord has dealt tenderly and bountifully with you, and as long as you keep humble and prayerful, He will honour you.'[19]

In the November 1882 magazine of the *Methodist Recorder* Dr Bowden wrote of the appointment and a new initiative, 'a departure carefully considered and adopted by the Conference of 1880, but delayed until the providence of God gave the right man to do the work of a Connexional Evangelist. Such a man has been given this year in Thomas Cook, and an important movement of aggressive work has been begun, which we hope will greatly extend.' [20]

> ...A little while ago we were in serious danger from tame, pretty preaching. Sermonettes were laid upon the Bible by some men, and read without apparent feeling, or any attempt at direct appeal. If an earnest spirit of evangelism gets abroad, such preaching will either be 'killed or cured'. This, in itself, would be a Connexional blessing of no little worth. It is bad enough to listen to a pretty little essay, when the man has made it during the week, and it is fitted in some sense to the people who hear it; but it is very much worse when the weak discourse was written ten years ago, and is far removed from the sympathies of both the reader and the hearer... If an aggressive spirit prevails, and men preach the Word to save souls from death, there will be no place found for the small, cold, travelling essay, or for the man who carries it about with him. District missionaries have been for some years at work, and a missionary for the Connexion is the healthy development of that kind of service. The Methodist preachers were originally a band of evangelists moving to and fro, and waking up the parishes of the land. John Wesley gave them this rule;

'You have nothing to do but to save souls.' He intended them to be an auxiliary force to the parochial clergy... Districts, Circuits, and preachers can become dormant and stagnant as surely as clergy and parishes... The preachers and class-leaders can keep the round of their classes and pulpits with conscientious regularity, and yet be half-asleep. The evangelist may be wanted today for the Circuit, as surely as a hundred and twenty years ago the Methodist preacher was needed for the parish. Both circuits and preachers will be healthier, brighter, and more useful for a break in their routine, and for the presence of the man who has 'nothing to do but to save souls'.... The spirit of aggression on the ungodliness and sin around us must be maintained in its vigour, or very soon the Church will not be able to hold its own. This Connexional evangelism is not only the expression of an aggressive spirit, but it will awaken and foster that spirit, and will thus increase not only the members in Society, but also the general vigour and strength of the Society, and thus prevent the 'scattering' which is inevitable, unless we continue to 'gather'. Methodism has had a time of chapel building and financial enterprise; we want now a time of chapel filling and good spiritual work, a revival in every Society.[21]

Cook's ministry was remarkable. It is reported that in his first year as Connexional Evangelist he saw nearly six thousand people 'seeking salvation.'[22] This was unusual ministry even for the late nineteenth century, and often there were over a thousand seekers in a mission and two or three hundred seekers in the enquiry rooms at once.[23] Today we would think of these scenes as akin to a revival. With the great Central Hall preacher, Gregory Mantle, he founded 'Out and Out', which was both a network and periodical, to encourage Methodist members to be involved in evangelism and this ministry was not confined to Britain, but he was also successful in his evangelistic tours in Australia, Ceylon and South Africa.[24]

Some people suggested that he be sent directly to this appointment because 'a College training would spoil him'. Watkinson, who candidated with him, refuted this 'delusion', pointing out that Thomas Waugh, who joined Cook after his theological training at Headingley, was equally successful as an evangelist and teacher of Holiness.[25] Indeed Watkinson refers to Josiah Pearson, a Methodist leader of the time, who commented on Cook's ministry, 'He spoke of the evangelist as little more than a stripling, slenderly equipped it might be from a human standpoint but filled with the Spirit and mightily owned of God as a winner of souls.'[26] The appointment of Cook as Connexional Evangelist was quickly followed by that of the Rev Thomas Waugh, and by the Rev Edward Davidson.

It was through his friendship with Joshua Dawson that Cook met Dawson's fourth daughter, Mary Anne. They married on 28 June 1888. In October 1889 a daughter, Grace, was born but in the following February 1890 Mary Anne was taken seriously ill while visiting her father and died.[27] Grace spent her teenage years at Cliff and married Mr Percy Groves.

Cook's ministry was quite outstanding even when placed in the context of a revival in the East Lancashire and West Yorkshire area. He is reputed often to have preached to weeknight congregations of two thousand.[28] His preaching was inspirational as reported in 1889 when he conducted a ten-day mission in the large Wesleyan Methodist Church in Helston, Cornwall. 'Large congregations assemble nightly, many of the visitors coming from miles away. On Sunday night the place was densely packed, both in the gallery and below, with extra seats in the aisle until it was considered judicious not to accommodate any more. Holiness Meetings have been well attended. The enquiry rooms present a lively feature, large numbers of both sexes finding their way there at the after meetings. Requests for prayer also form a prominent feature of the services.'[29]

There was at this time a large, granite built Wesleyan Methodist Church in St Ives where the sanctuary seated more than one thousand. Thomas Cook held a mission in this church in 1890 and the evening before its commencement he called a meeting of the trustees and requested they make a doorway through a four-foot granite wall into another room. His powers of persuasion were considerable because these Cornish fishermen created the door through a four-foot wall that night. Until its closure there was a brass plaque beside the door on which was written:

> This doorway was made one Saturday night at the urgent request of the Reverend Thomas Cook, Connexional Evangelist. He believed that the minister's vestry, which was to have been used as an enquiry room during the mission he was about to commence, was not large enough to accommodate all those who would be seeking Christ. So great was his faith that he was able to persuade the Trustees of this Church to have this doorway made during the night. His faith was justified, for beginning the next day, seven hundred men and women passed through this doorway in the course of the ten days of the mission. [30]

Thomas Cook was not only a persuasive preacher in England but also overseas. In 1886 he ministered in Norway, at the invitation of the small Norwegian Methodist Church.[31] In 1892 he toured South Africa from April to November visiting all the main centres and preaching at 220 services. Cook was distressed by the 'prejudice he found existing at that time on the part of the Europeans against the natives'.[32] In Durban he took the considerable risk of holding a service for black South Africans in what was known as the 'European Church', 'his belief being that since so much blessing had been received there would be no opposition on the part of the Whites to the Zulus coming to their church'.[33]   Once again we see Cook's determination, and in taking the service in this way he also made a significant point about the injustice he saw. Like Chadwick in Leeds and Wesley before him, Cook did not have a social policy regarding injustice, but believed that if sufficient people were converted, then change would come. Smart summarises the issue well when among the reflections on this tour he remarks, 'We would fain hope that the prejudice we have just named has abated ... but we wish to say that as far as we can judge the future of South Africa depends upon the success the Churches may have in wiping out racial prejudices and feuds, and in welding together in one compact body the heterogeneous elements that form the population of South Africa'.[34]

Cook was a widower for four years and then married Jessie Foster of Markenfield Hall, near Ripon on 10 January 1894. Just after their marriage the couple left for a tour to Australia. Little is known about Jessie though she organised the housekeeping of the College when Thomas was Principal. Thomas and Jessie embarked in February 1894 on what was to be his most successful overseas tour. They had a great 'send off' at the Exeter Hall in London with 2,500 people present to pray God's blessing on their ministry. Many people there were associated with the 'Out and Out' ministry and publication, but the congregation of this filled hall was a great tribute to his ministry.[35] They arrived in Western Australia and starting at Albany, they began a tour of all the major cities through Western and South Australia, Victoria, Tasmania, New South Wales and Queensland. Thomas and Jessie also visited New Zealand and on his return journey, remained in Ceylon to preach. He was invited to preach in all the leading churches and often colleges and conferences. However, he was not at home in the official setting of the Church courts. Smart indicates that in Sydney, Cook was invited to preach the 'official sermon' and remarks, 'Mr Cook had no great sermons, but he had many useful ones'.[36] Cook was an evangelist at heart and a preacher of Holiness. His practice was to lead the whole of the meeting, so there was no break in continuity, and then to invite enquirers, at the end of the sermon, to go through to an 'after-meeting' where men counselled men and women the women enquirers. Each worker was 'adorned with a rosette, the aim being to prevent undesirable workers from entering the room.'[37]

Normally after the sermon there was a time for quiet, and so Cook's method of the 'after meeting' was considered dramatically different. Jessie Cook participated fully in this ministry and hundreds responded. The New Zealand Conference in the Pastoral Letter to the British Conference gave thanks for 'this time of refreshing of a special character'.[38] Thomas may have had difficulty in speaking in the official courts of the Church but as an evangelist his mission was unparalleled and he considered it a time of revival, thus the title of his book, *Days of God's Right Arm*. There is an interesting insight into the leisure time of Thomas Cook. He was a conchologist, a collector of shells. Throughout this tour he gathered interesting specimens to add to those from South Africa all of which were exhibited and labelled in the museum at Cliff.[39] Thomas and Jessie Cook returned to England in December 1895 and for a further eight years Cook continued as a Connexional Evangelist. Following the retirement of Champness and at his suggestion, Thomas Cook was invited to take over the work of the 'Joyful News Training Home and Mission'. Cook had always been associated with Champness and though he had not regularly taught the students, the ministry of Cook was often advertised and reported in the *Joyful News*.

The first task for Cook in his new appointment was to find a new home for the work since the lease had expired at Castleton Hall. The Home Mission Committee had expressed the view, 'That the Home

shall, if possible, be located in a country district in which the services of the residents may be made available as Local Preachers or Exhorters for as large a number of villages as possible.'[40] With the help of the Rev H.T. Smart, an old friend and now the Chairman of the Sheffield District, Cook heard about the availability of what had previously been called 'Hulme Cliff College'.

The buildings at the beginning of Cook's Principalship

Therefore to the work of Cliff came, with the exception of the *Joyful News* Missionaries, the Champness legacy of the Training Home and the *Joyful News* Evangelists. This was joined by the Gospel Car work and the evangelists associated with them. The *Joyful News* Evangelists came under Cook's direction and they became known as lay agents working mainly in the rural circuits of Methodism. There were fifty-eight such evangelists in the country, and the establishment of Cliff College meant that in all future

appointments 'no man shall go into the work until he has received some measure of training.'[41]

The College therefore became the head-quarters of the Gospel Car Mission in the summer of 1904. Their ministry was very effective and with the accustomed Victorian fascination with numbers they proudly

James Wood Memorial Car no. 17 in 1906

declared: 'Last year these men conducted 8,403 services. They reported that 7,211 persons decided for Christ at their meetings, and that they had sold £1,919 4s. 11d. worth of books.'[42] The fifty-eight

'The men are their own servants'

trained evangelists were at work in the rural and most needy circuits of the Connexion, and in addition to this there were the thirty-six 'highly competent travelling evangelists' in charge of thirty Gospel Cars; these were still the horse drawn type caravan, working in every part of the country.[43]

The College was ideal for the purpose and the 'Joyful News Training Home and Mission' was relocated to Cliff College. There was accommodation for sixty students in dormitories and the style of community life which had grown up at Castleton Hall continued. 'The men are their own servants; they scrub the floors, clean the windows, make the beds, and keep the whole place in the most perfect order.'[44] Cook encouraged the students to participate in sports, enjoy the fresh air, manual exercise, and beautiful surroundings. The medical doctor in Baslow complained that the students did not give him enough to do. 'You feed them too well, Mr Cook, to make them profitable to doctors.'[45]

From the very beginnings of Cliff College, as evidenced in an article written after only six months, it was apparent that the students

came with differing purposes. Some were avowedly preparing for the ministry; others were in training for lay agencies, either in circuits or in connection with the Gospel Cars; others were Local Preachers, 'who often at great sacrifice of time and money, are glad to avail themselves of the opportunity thus afforded for self-improvement, and especially for improvement in the art and practice of preaching.'[46] The student community changed consider-ably each new term, which lasted ten weeks. In the early years, some students came for the whole year, but most came for one or two terms.

Cook had considerable experience, but like Champness he had not benefited from the opportunity of a college education. He was a passionate evangelist and expected every man to be a winner of souls. If they failed he challenged their faith, and suggested that 'they might by all means win some'. He gathered a well-qualified group of tutors while he committed himself to the consideration of the wider policy of the College. He appointed Mr C.E. Oxenborow Rush, BA, Tutor in General Subjects; the Rev Samuel Chadwick (p/t), Lecturer on the study of the English Bible; the Rev Alfred Bingham (p/t), Tutor in Homiletics; the Rev John Grimshaw (p/t), Tutor in Theology; the Rev Marmaduke Riggall (p/t), Tutor in Theology; Mr Peter Williams, BA, Assistant Tutor; Mr John J. Studley, Student-Tutor; Miss Lilian Hovey (p/t), Lecturer on Elocution; and Mr S.W. Thompsom BA. Even though many were part-time, this was an impressive group of tutorial staff. He also invited visiting speakers, and Grattan Guinness came to the College on one occasion in 1905. John Newbould, a student that year recalls, 'He created a wonderful impression on us all. He gave us a lecture on "Japan and her wonderful possibilities". He said he thought Japan had a very great future.'[47]

The purchase price of Cliff College, including the renovations and furnishing, had reached a total of £12,500. The whole of this amount had been sent with the exception of £750. The needs of the College seem small in comparison to today's £1.5m turnover but it would be significant even then. Cook needed more than £60 each week (£3,000 at today's prices) to cover 'fifty men to board, lodge, and educate, and more than sixty others to maintain who are working in the rural circuits of Methodism.'[48]

From the beginning he became inundated with applicants. Almost immediately Cook had a vision for an enlarged College because the College was not only full of students, but applications steadily increased. 'We have received one hundred and twenty applications from men who wish to come for training next autumn. We cannot possibly accommodate more than fifty men, so that seventy of these will have to be refused. There is demand for a place twice the size of Cliff College.'[49]

Cook therefore brought to the College Committee in October 1905 a proposal for the enlargement of the College. The Committee was initially unwilling to proceed and counselled delay, because they thought that though the purchase and renovation costs had been met, the further costs of an extension would be considerable. The story behind this incident was told in glowing terms by Cook's biographer, Henry T. Smart:

> His committee counselled delay, but consented to his going on with
> the enlargement if he first secured the cost. In the following week he

inserted a notice in *Joyful News* to the effect that he needed a thousand pounds for this purpose, and that if any one was led to send him the amount he should conclude it was the will of God that the project should be carried out. The day after this intimation appeared, he chanced to go to Manchester on his Master's business, and it was his hap to meet a friend at the station who does not belong to the Methodist Church, but who had often succoured him. The friend asked about Cliff College: was it full? Had he any difficulty getting students? He replied it was overfull, and that he had to turn away many eligible candidates. 'Why not enlarge it?' said the friend. 'Because I have not the money,' was his answer. A slight pause followed, and then the friend said, 'I have a thousand pounds of the Lord's money in the bank; I will give it you.' He asked, 'Have you seen *Joyful News* this week?' The lady said she had not. Mr Cook then told her of his appeal, and she closed the incident by saying, 'I am glad to have a share in the work; this interview is evidently of God; I will send you a cheque for the amount in the morning.'[50]

Mrs Champness laid the foundation stone for the new wing on 21 June 1906

At the following meeting on 1 February 1906 Cook was able to report, 'that a lady had promised £1,000 towards the extension of Cliff College on condition that the work be proceeded with without delay. Other gentlemen had promised an additional £1,500, which brought the amount promised to £2,500.' There is a little confusion in the sources about this finance. According to the student John Newbould, the person at the station was Mr Frank Crossley, and the reported conversation is then identical to Smart's version.[51] Crossley was a Primitive Methodist layman, making Crossley's Oil Engines and one of the leaders who began the Star Hall in Manchester.[52] The death of Thomas Champness in the autumn of 1905 also gave impetus to the fund raising, and a new wing to be called the Thomas Champness Memorial Wing was built. Cook's faith was undimmed by the scale of his vision and with enthusiasm he wrote, 'We believe, with Mr Spurgeon, that so long as institutions of this sort are doing good work the money will be forthcoming. When funds are not available it is time to consider whether the work is any longer needed. At present we have every reason to thank God and take courage.'[53]

Mrs Champness laid the foundation stone for the new wing on 21 June 1906 and the building was opened by Mrs Henry J. Pope on Easter Monday, 1 April 1907. The project took immense faith and vision, but Cook was able to house up to one hundred men in the new wing, which was two to a room, some of which are quite small. 'With this increased accommodation we shall be able to pass a hundred and fifty men annually through the Institution, giving each man the benefit of six months training.'[54]

In this building project Cook achieved far more than he had declared to the College Committee. Not only was the Champness Wing erected but he also doubled the Dining Room in size, extended the original Congregational Chapel across Cliff Lane, and built Cliff Park as a house for the incoming tutor, Samuel Chadwick. He also had to provide a new water supply, with a reservoir at the top of the rose garden, covered with six-foot long flagstones.

During his ministry as a Connexional Evangelist Cook had learned the art of fundraising among Christian people. He informed the readers of the Cliff College *Report* that he needed an extra £500 to avoid debt and then added, 'We believe we are doing the sort of work the Methodist people wish done, and that they will not allow the work to suffer for lack of funds.'[55]

Cook's Chapel

Cliff College only functioned partially as a College in the session October 1906 – March 1907, though there were fourteen students listed. They seem to have received some tuition, engaged in mission in the area and assisted in the running of the College. It took remarkable faith in the project to reduce training drastically during what would have been the College's second full year. However Cook's faith was rewarded for in the summer term of 1907 there were 77 students. The reports to the Methodist Conference of 1907 were entitled 'Cliff College, Gospel Cars and Circuit Evangelists', which indicates the breadth and complexity of the work Cook was involved in. He was extending the College, building accomodation, appointing staff and appointing, mentoring, and financing the Circuit Evangelists and Gospel Car Evangelists. It was in this 'sabbatical' year for the College that Cook persuaded the Connexion to appoint another fulltime Ministerial Tutor, and the College Committee 'recommended that the Home Mission Committee should ask the Conference in its Representative Session to sanction the appointment of an additional Minister … who shall assist the Rev Thomas Cook with special reference to the Biblical and Theological training of the students.'[56] The Committee further recommended the appointment of the Rev Samuel Chadwick as from the Conference of 1907.[57] Cook had a high regard for Chadwick and commented that he would 'add greatly to the efficiency of our staff, and will be of incalculable benefit to the men.'[58]

We can identify, seated from the left, the Rev Samuel Chadwick, the Rev Thomas Cook, Mrs Jessie Cook,
Miss Lilian Hovey, the Rev Marmaduke Riggall
and standing in the middle, Cecil E. Oxenborrow Rush

Cook was a father figure in the College, and he took great care of the staff and students besides being visionary about the future needs of the institution. From the beginning of his work Cook was keen to show the success of the College in terms of student development and outcomes. 'More than a hundred men have been in training, of whom twenty-five have been qualified for evangelistic work. Twenty-seven have been recommended by the District Synods as suitable candidates for the ministry, and the remaining fifty have returned to their homes and secular vocations, greatly helped in their work as Local Preachers by what we have been able to do for them.'[59]

A mug shows the College prior to 1905. (Note the mis-spelt Cliff)

This kind of statement occurred annually as though an apologetic for the continuing work of the College as a lay training institution.

In the summer of 1906 the work of the Gospel Cars was undermined by 'some of the best men trained at Cliff College, and employed on the Gospel Cars' being attracted to work in the Methodist Church in Canada.[60] The committee expressed delight that 'Cliff College is able in this way to contribute so largely to the success of Methodist work in the Dominion' but also suggested 'that caution must be exercised in relation to these arrangements with Colonial Conferences'.[61] At the same time the Committee saw the increased demand for evangelists as justification of the building plans which were in hand. The evangelistic work was a very significant part of the ministry of Cliff. 'More than eight thousand persons have professed a decision for Christ in services ... they have sold books to the value of £2,500. Hundreds of Temperance pledges ... we have twenty-nine vans constantly at work, manned by thirty-five Evangelists. In addition to these we have working under our auspices upwards of forty other Evangelists in the rural circuits of Methodism.'[62]

However, as early as May 1907 Thomas Cook reported to the College Management Committee that 'the Cars were not in as great demand as formerly, and that it had been necessary to reduce the amount charged to Districts and Circuits ... the novelty had somewhat worn out...the cost of removing vans from place to place

deterred some, but the chief reason was that Evangelists could now be obtained at a cheaper rate.'[63]   The policy adopted was to reduce the number of Gospel Cars when they needed renovation, or could be sold. Four were sold in 1909 bringing the number available to fifteen.[64]

Despite the reduction of Gospel Cars there was no sign of abatement in the evangelistic fervour which characterised the College. Open air meetings on Baslow village green, at that time a rendezvous for trippers during the summer, and meetings in lodging houses for men at Stoney Middleton, were the sphere of organised and enthusiastic evangelistic work every Sunday.[65] Most of the students were preaching in the villages each Sunday along with the open-air services and most weeks, 'there is the joy of the harvest.'[66]

Gospel Car parked on the drive at Cliff

The stance of teaching at the College reflected Cook's evangelistic ministry: 'At Cliff College definite doctrines are held and taught. We hold by the doctrines of grace and teach ruin, redemption and regeneration in the old-fashioned way.'[67] Cook had chosen his staff wisely; Rush was an excellent Director of Studies and Chadwick was

Thomas Cook and Samuel Chadwick at the Conference 1907

inspirational. 'Mr Chadwick's lectures on Bible study have been greatly appreciated by the men. Some of them have been heard to say, that if they got nothing else at the College it was worth all the sacrifice and effort they had made to be allowed to attend these classes. We cannot bestow the soul-saving gift, but we can enrich it by suggesting ways and methods which we have learned by observation and experience'. [68]

During 5-15 July 1907 the first Summer School was held.[69] Not only was the College full, but many slept in cottage homes in the adjacent villages, and even with this help, some had to be refused. The syllabus contained special lectures on Bible study, Christian Evidences, Sermon Construction, Theology, Practical Evangelism and many kindred subjects. 'This development is full of great possibilities for the spiritual welfare and influence of Methodism. It was decided not only to continue the movement but also to extend it as much as possible.'[70]

This was the beginning of the public ministry of the College which would become so very significant. In addition to the Summer Schools recruiting Local Preachers in the main, Thomas and Jessie Cook welcomed, from 1909, visitors from all parts of the United Kingdom to 'enjoy the quiet, rural beauty for which the district is famous. By this means nearly £400 was raised towards the upkeep of the place. Apart from the financial benefit to the College, this arrangement has afforded opportunity for pleasant social intercourse between Christian people of all ranks of life, and has often led to greatly enriched lives and service. Some of these summer visitors have become the best supporters of the work.'[71]

*Ready for Manual
pre-1924*

The Summer Schools grew in size and influence. In 1911 there was a 'fine audience of over 100 men – rather younger on the whole than those who came last year – and the teaching was appreciated.'[72] The Cooks also welcomed guests in the summer and were excellent hosts. They had discovered what Guinness knew and Broadbelt would find out, that 'A holiday at such a centre is something more than a holiday, for even during that season it is impossible to be insensible to the general influence of the place, and many a subscription to the work of Cliff College has come as a result of the interest awakened in those who have had a holiday season there.[73]

With the new wing in full use the College could receive more students, and in the first full year, 1907-8, there were altogether one hundred and fifty men, with eighty resident normally, staying for an average period of six months. Cook summarised the students' purpose for coming:

> Our men are mostly sons of the poor, such as come from the factory and plough. The majority of them have no intention of seeking service for which there is monetary remuneration. They come

The first students

seeking better equipment for the service of God and the church, and return afterwards to the circuits and secular employment.

Some come avowedly as candidates for the Ministry. The educational test is so constantly rising that those who have had but slender educational advantages have little chance of being accepted for the Ministry apart from such help as we can give. They come to us bent on making the most of their opportunity, and it is remarkable how many have given proof of their call and fitness for the work. Our estimate is that 40 men who have been trained at Cliff College are accepted annually for the Ministry at home or abroad.

There is no more important part of the work than the training of evangelists. It is not sufficient that men who do this work should be zealous; special training is necessary, or their hearers will be repelled by their incompetence and ignorance...But our chief work is to raise the status of the Local Preachers of Methodism by starting young men on the right lines of study, giving them new samples of knowledge and inspiring them with loftier ideals.

Our aim is not only to instruct, but to inspire. [74]

Fifty-seven Cliff College men were employed as lay agents or evangelists in the circuits of Methodism. Many were doing ministerial work where it was impossible to maintain the number of ministers in a Circuit. After seven years of Cook's leadership the College had become a viable institution: 'The total annual expenditure, which included the cost of Evangelists working in the Circuits and on the Gospel Cars, was about £5,000. Towards this expenditure the students have contributed £900; the summer school realised £250; annual subscriptions £900; Gospel Cars £100; collections where Missions have been held by Cliff College Evangelists £800, summer visitors £450, Home Mission grant £500; Local Preachers Connexional Committee £100. The other £1000 was raised chiefly in small sums which came through the *Joyful News* and £500 at the Anniversary. Once again we have the satisfaction to report that the income for the year will meet expenditure.'[75]

The death of Thomas Cook on 21 September 1912 was quite unexpected; Chadwick had returned to circuit work in the Yorkshire Coalfields. Athough Cook had been ill for some time he had been expected to recover. However, for two years he had ministered under conditions of physical weakness and considerable pain. On his way to a private Nursing Home in West London he had a meeting with Chadwick, Smart and Crowlesmith about the *Joyful News*. 'Mr Cook was in the chair, as usual, and, though he was in pain and could not help showing it, yet how cheerful and hopeful he was.'[76] They then drove Cook to the Home and he waved them goodbye saying, 'It will not be for long. I'll be back at Cliff soon!'[77] Whilst undergoing

The Rev W. Fiddian Moulton

surgery he became ill and died. He was only fifty-two.[78]

The College Management Committee met on the 27 September to 'take into consideration the urgent arrangements rendered necessary by the lamented death of the Revd Thomas Cook.'[79] The Rev Joseph Shrimpton had been appointed as a tutor to succeed Chadwick to teach Theology and Homiletics and was living in Cliff Park. Though Samuel Chadwick had moved to the South Yorkshire Coalfields he was given the charge of the 'discipline, finance and management' of the evangelistic work including the Gospel cars.[80] Shrimpton took the pastoral oversight of the College and the Rev W. Fiddian Moulton consented to increase his tutorial work. A weekly staff meeting was called for to include Chadwick, Shrimpton and Moulton. Kirkup and Rush were to manage the College.[81]

'The committee desires to express its profound sorrow upon the death of the Revd Thomas Cook, the first Principal of Cliff College and to record its high appreciation of the great service which he has rendered to the Church of God during his ministry of thirty years. Not only was Mr Cook one of the most highly gifted and successful evangelists of our Church, but his name will always be associated with the establishment of Cliff College for the training of lay workers, the success of which has been largely due to his wise direction, business aptitude and devoted labours. By his winsome character and fervent zeal for the salvation of men, he deeply influenced the students who came under his care, whilst his sincerity of purpose, singleness of aim and able management of the Institution won for

Cliff College the confidence and support of all ranks of the Methodist people. The Committee gives thanks to Almighty God for the saintly character and useful life of His servant, and desires to convey to Mrs Cook and the members of the family the assurance of its sympathy and prayers.'[82]

The legacy of Cook to the College was measured in the student outcomes and in 1912 the *Report to the Home Mission Fund* summarised the numbers and destinations of students: 'During the last seven years 725 students have passed through the College; 119 of these have been accepted for the Home Ministry, 79 are in Canada, 62 in the United States, 42 in Australia, 10 in South Africa and other parts of the world, 61 are Lay Agents and Evangelists in this country, while 352 have gone back to their circuits as Local Preachers.'[83]

Jessie Cook remained to manage the College through the year until the August of 1913. The Committee was especially indebted to Mrs Cook. 'With heroic faith and courage she has administered the domestic side of College life, and consented to stay for the usual visitors in the month of August.'[84]

A Memorial Wing was built in memory of Mr Cook, which provided many of the things he had hoped for in the new Champness wing, but had to be left out of the scheme when the costs were revised down. Spontaneity, affection, and gratitude marked the Memorial Fund appeal. Gifts came from converts of Mr Cook's earlier ministry in every part of the world. Chadwick, reflecting on the year, summarised, 'Upon all our work there has been the good hand of God. Special need has been met by special grace, for which we give special praise.'[85]

The Thomas Cook window in the College

Chadwick's comments about Cook and his Principalship of the College are heartfelt, and are typical of the flowing prose he used so readily in many of his articles. 'It is impossible to estimate the service he rendered as its first Principal. He gave himself to it without reserve. He had an exalted idea of its mission, unbounded faith in its possibilities, and an unwavering confidence in its work. He inspired the students with lofty ideals of holiness and a consuming passion for the salvation of souls.'[86]

There are in the College archives two bound copies of a hand-written student magazine called the *Cliff Collegian*, each covering a term in the session 1912-13.[87] H.J. Ivens was the editor of the mag-azine though helped by other able students who included Leslie Weatherhead. As editor, Ivens wrote an article entitled 'The Influence of the late Rev Thomas Cook'. In it, and as a new student who arrived after Cook's death he wrote, 'It is only by noting the affection and reverence in which old students always speak of him that we can form some estimate of the love and regard he must have taken in them.'[88] He asked the question, 'What was the secret of the influence of Thomas Cook? It was simply that he took Jesus Christ as his companion. Wherever he was, there God was. Mr Cook never left God out of anything. The greatest spiritual enterprises and the household accounts were alike, submitted to the Master.'[89]

What was the secret of the wonderful results in his preaching? In this regard he is not uncritical of Cook: 'We are told that (like Moody and other men of God who have been mightily blessed) he was not a brilliant orator. The secret of his conversions (numbered in thousands all round the world) was that Mr Cook emptied himself of all but God. God made him His mouthpiece…there was nothing in Mr Cook to prevent the Spirit of God working, nothing in him to stop the flow of reviving grace.' [90]

There is also an *Appreciation* by a continuing student. 'We little thought as we bade him "Goodbye" on that Monday morning a few weeks ago that it would be the last time we should see him alive. His cheery "Good Morning", his genial handshake and his buoyant spirits all betokened an early return to the place he loved. But such was not to be.' [91]

The student, Robertson, finishes his tribute with these words, 'Brethren, this is holy ground. The fact that Thomas Cook trod it has made it sacred and given it hallowed associations and memories. In these rooms he prayed; for this College he schemed, toiled, and planned, sacrificed and interceded, and we enter into the fruits of his labour'.[92]

The Committee of Management for the College considered the ministerial staffing of the College. The recommendation was for a Principal and Resident Tutor, the latter to be the Rev W. Fiddian Moulton. Remarkably the sub-committee made no definite nomination about the Principal but suggested that 'the qualifications necessary' for the post were met by either the Rev S. Chadwick or the Rev J.W. Allcock. [93] In the end the Committee on that day unanimously recommended Chadwick and Moulton for the two posts.[94] Chadwick was to lead the College for the next twenty years and influence its future long beyond that.

The Thomas Cook window in the College

1   Henry T. Smart, *Thomas Cook's Early Ministry* (London: Charles Kelly 1892). The Cook family evidently moved 'to the country' for three years where they attended the local Parish Church. Clearly Smart is relieved they returned to Middlesbrough where they could again be under the influence of Methodist preachers. See pp.8–12.

2   Arthur Skevington Wood, *On Fire for God*, (Sheffield: Cliff College 1983).

3   Vallance Cook, *Thomas Cook Evangelist – Saint* (London: Charles Kelly, 1913) p.27.

4   Vallance Cook, p.28.

5   Vallance Cook, p.29. The italics are the author's.

6   Vallance Cook, p.35.

7   Vallance Cook, p.35.

8   Vallance Cook, p.44.

9   Vallance Cook, p.45-6.

10   Smart, *Early Ministry*, p.32.

11   Smart, *Early Ministry*, p.33.

12   Smart, *Early Ministry*, pp.43-8, *The Life*, pp.43-4.

13   Smart, *Early Ministry*, p.47. William Wakinshaw agrees with this view, that the conference had previously accepted too many candidates; in 1880 only 50 were accepted and in 1881 no candidates were accepted. 'Men Who made Cliff, 2. Thomas Cook' in *Cliff Witness*, Vol.2, No.1, p.8.

14   Smart, *Early Ministry*, p.49.

15   Smart, *Early Ministry*, p.62, and in one instance he paid the constable half-a-crown and instructed him to remain in the porch during the service.

16   Smart, *Early Ministry*, p.67-8.

17   Smart, *Early Ministry*, p.69.

18   Minutes of the Wesleyan Methodist Conference 1882.

19   Smart, *Early Ministry*, p.72.

20   Smart, *Early Ministry*, pp.72-74.

21   Ibid.

22   Joe Brice, *The Crowd for Christ*, (London: Hodder and Stoughton, 1934), p.50.

23   Ibid.

24   Thomas Cook, *Days of God's Right Hand, Our Mission Tour in Australia and Ceylon* (London: Charles Kelly, 1896), where he tells of a remarkable evangelistic tour in which ten thousand people responded to appeals he made.

25   William Wakinshaw, 'Men Who made Cliff, 2. Thomas Cook' in *Cliff Witness*, Vol.2, No.1, p.9.

26   William Wakinshaw, 'Men Who made Cliff, 2. Thomas Cook' in *Cliff Witness*, Vol.2, No.1, p.8.

27   Henry T. Smart, *The Life of Thomas Cook, Evangelist* (London: Charles Kelly, 1913), p.90. However see Vallance Cook who indicates they were only married for 13 months, p.44.

28   Joe Brice, *The Crowd for Christ*, (London: Hodder and Stoughton, 1934), p.24.

29   *Cornish Telegraph*, Thursday 18 April 1889.

cont.

30 Wesleyan Methodist Church in St Ives known locally as 'the Wesley'. The congregation united with the congregation at Bedford Road in 1993. 'The inner door from the chapel into the schoolroom was made at the special request of Rev Thomas Cook (circa 1890) he wanted to make a convenient passage into the enquiry room'. A hand written note - Thomas Shaw Collection Truro Museum. The building still exists and has multi-function use as a community centre and hostel.

31 Smart, *The Life,* pp.95-98.
32 Smart, *The Life*, p.124.
33 Smart, *The Life*, p.119.
34 Smart, *The Life*, p.124.
35 Thomas Cook, *Days of God's Right Hand* (London: Charles H. Kelly, 1896), pp.11-15.
36 Smart, *The Life*, p.144.
37 Cook, *Days of God's Right Hand,* p.215.
38 Vallance Cook, pp.250-2.
39 Smart, *The Life*, p.243.
40 *Minutes of the Home Mission Committee,* 23 April 1903.
41 H.K., 'Cliff College,' *Leeds Mission News*, No 9, September 1904, p.3.
42 H.K., p.3.
43 H.K., p.3.
44 H.K., p.2.
45 H.K., p.2.
46 H.K., p.2.
47 John Newbould, *The Roots and Early Growth of Cliff College* (Unpublished archive paper), p.13.
48 *Reports of the Wesleyan Home Mission Fund,* 1905, p.125.
49 *Reports of the Wesleyan Home Mission Fund,* 1905, p.125.
50 H.T. Smart, *The Life of Thomas Cook, Evangelist* (London: Charles H. Kelly), 1913, pp.216-7.
51 John Newbould, *The Roots and early Growth of Cliff College* (Unpublished paper, Archives), pp.67-9.
52 Ian Randall, 'The Pentecostal League of Prayer: A British holiness Movement', in *Wesley Theological Journal,* Spring 1998, p.190.
53 *Reports of the Wesleyan Home Mission Fund,* 1906, p.126.
54 *Reports of the Wesleyan Home Mission Fund,* 1907, p.107.
55 *Reports of the Wesleyan Home Mission Fund,* 1907, p.108.
56 Minutes of the Committee of Management, 1 February 1906.
57 Ibid.
58 *Reports of the Wesleyan Home Mission Fund,* 1907, p.108.
59 *Reports of the Wesleyan Home Mission Fund,* 1905, p.124.
60 Minutes of the Committee of Management, 6 November 1906.
61 Ibid.
62 *Reports of the Wesleyan Home Mission Fund,* 1906, p.126.
63 Minutes of the Committee of Management, 30 May 1907.

cont.

64 Minutes of the Committee of Management, 29 April 1909. There would seem to be a difference of ten Gospel Cars between 1906 and 1907. Presumably these ten were not fit for sale and discarded.

65 *Report of the Wesleyan Home Mission Fund*, p.118.

66 Ibid.

67 *Report of the Wesleyan Home Mission Fund,* 1907, p.108.

68 *Report of the Wesleyan Home Mission Fund,* 1908, p.105.

69 *Report of the Wesleyan Home Mission Fund,* 1908, p.105.

70 Minutes of the Committee of Management, 8 December 1908.

71 *Report of the Wesleyan Home Mission Fund,* 1910, p.111.

72 *Report of the Wesleyan Home Mission Fund,* 1912, p.70.

73 Ibid.

74 *Report of the Wesleyan Home Mission Fund,* 1908, pp.104-5.

75 *Report of the Home Mission Fund*, 1912, p.70.

76 *Joyful News,* 31 March 1932.

77 Ibid.

78 Vallance Cook p.30, Thomas was outlived by his mother to whom a pastoral letter was sent from the Middlesbrough Circuit where she lived.

79 Minutes of the Committee of Management, 27 September 1912.

80 Minutes of the Committee of Management, 27 September 1912.

81 Ibid.

82 Minutes of the Committee of Management, 27 September 1912.

83 *Report of the Home Mission Fund,* 1912, p.69.

84 Minutes of the Committee of Management, 9 June 1913.

85 *Report of the Home Mission Fund,* 1913, p.58.

86 *Report of the Home Mission Fund,* 1913, p.57.

87 There are two bound copies of the *Cliff Collegian*, each covering a term in the session 1912-13. It is a student hand-written magazine. Cliff College Archives, E 63.

88 *Cliff Collegian, October 1912,* pp.21-23.

89 Ibid.

90 *Cliff Collegian*, pp.22-3.

91 J.G. Robertson, 'An Appreciation of Thomas Cook', in *The Cliff Collegian,* October 1912, pp.24a-d.

92 *Cliff Collegian*, p.24c.

93 Minutes of the Committee of Management, 4 April 1913. The name of Allcock has a line through, with the mark of 'stet' beside it. Clearly there was some debate about the appointment.

94 Ibid.

CHAPTER 9

Unless The Lord Builds the House

The Cliff College estate was purchased from the Trustees of Hulme Cliff College, originally established by Anne Elizabeth Hulme on the wishes of her husband and following his death in 1869. The Rev Henry T. Smart was presiding over a meeting in the Bakewell circuit when he heard of the availability of Hulme Cliff College, recently vacated by the Regions Beyond Missionary Union.[1] Smart contacted Cook and together they visited the College and prayed in what is now the Common Room, covenanting to do whatever God's will was. They became convinced this was the place for the work to continue.[2]

The Lecture Room in Cook's day (later the Common Room) – where Smart and Cook prayed.

Immediately prior to the Conference of 1903, the Home Mission Committee met and received the following report: 'The Secretary stated that, acting on the resolutions of April 23rd, 1903, preliminary negotiations had been entered into by the Rev Thomas Cook, with the Trustees of Cliff College, Calver, near Sheffield, with a view, either to the transfer of the property to Methodist Trustees, subject to existing Trusts, or its purchase absolutely, to be held in Trust for the Home Mission Committee.'[3] A very significant group was gathered for the sub-committee, which then in large part became the College Committee. The sub-committee, which had met at Camborne on the 23 July 1903, consisted of senior ministers and lay people, the Rev Dr H.J. Pope in the Chair, the Revs Thomas Cook, Henry T. Smart, Thomas Champness, Simpson Johnson; Messrs Thomas Walker, S.M. Johnson, John Crowlesmith, William Walker, Moses Atkinson, with Mr T.H. Bainbridge and Mr Joseph Rank, attending at their request.

Two options were before the sub-committee, one which offered a form of lease, and the preferred option, 'That the property should be purchased absolutely for the sum of £7,500, subject to an order being obtained from the Charity Commissioners authorizing a scheme to that effect.'[4] To make the purchase possible the Committee resolved to appropriate £1,500 of the income of the year 1902-3 towards the cost of renovation and furnishing, and £2,000 from the Twentieth Century Section of the Home Mission Fund, towards the cost of purchase. The remaining portion of the money was advanced as a loan from the Funds of the Home Mission Committee.[5]

College Common Room

With the agreement of the Trustees, Cook approached the Charity Commissioners, who sent an official on a cold, wet, foggy day, who after walking on muddy roads from the railway station, commented, 'Oh, well, then leave it at that. It is all the place is worth on such a day as this'.[6] The property was then purchased absolutely for the sum of £7,500. Dr Pope and the Rev Thomas Cook had been given powers to act on their behalf. The price was agreed, though it took the whole of the autumn of 1903 for the solicitors to contact all the surviving Trustees, who being missionaries, were scattered across Europe, Africa, India and America. The Deed was signed on the 31 December 1903.

The *Joyful News* announced the 'Opening of Cliff College', in March 1904. Eliza Champness was present but Thomas, who was often ill at this time, was not able to be there. His work is honoured, 'who though not able to be present, was one in loving sympathy and delight in the consummation of his own desires for the future of his work.' Dr Harry Guinness was there to represent the Guinness family and former Trustees. Samuel Chadwick, who would become so associated with the College, was also present.

In her brief article Eliza described the College with its 'lecture room for fifty men … restful bed chambers … only in one or two instances did I see rooms containing more than two beds and these

were proportionally larger than usual … then down a winding stair to the large bath chamber, with six baths, and the spacious "day lavatory" with its ample provision for the ablutions of fifty men'[7].

There is an article about the College written in the summer of 1904 for the *Leeds Mission News*, presumably at the request of Chadwick. It is the only description of the College at that time and gives us the best clue as to the estate and

Cliff College viewed across the Derwent. The observatory is partially obscured by Cliff Park (c. 1907)

231

buildings, as Cook received them from the trustees. 'The place is much more than an ordinary dwelling house. Since the days of Mr Hulme it has grown. Wings and outlying buildings have been erected. An observatory has been built, the white dome of which is a landmark for miles. The observatory is fitted up with a great reflector telescope, a transit telescope, with two sidereal clocks. The room below the dome is used as a Museum and contains Mr Cook's magnificent collection of shells, and around the walls hang missionary trophies gathered on Evangelistic tours. The laying out of the grounds has been perfected. The trees and shrubs that clothe the hillside down to the road and to the brink of the river are valued by competent authorities at a great price. The shrubs are beautiful beyond description. There are shaded paths well nigh innumerable, with garden seats and quiet retreats where men may walk and talk and read in perfect peace. It is said that Dr Grattan Guinness spent £15,000 on the buildings and grounds. The outlook from the windows, no matter which way you turn, is one of the fairest in England. From one point in the gardens you can see, down the valley of the Derwent, the white walls and gleaming windows of Chatsworth.'[8]

'On the right, and below the hillside, is a park, with copses and a line of great beech trees shading the Drive up to the College ... the park slopes up to the white observatory, which crowns the shrubbery. The little Chapel has its own garden paradise. Below it, on a gently sloping hillside, is a great kitchen garden with fruit trees, beds of wintergreens, rows of green peas and everything necessary for the supply of the long dining tables. Beyond is a small farm with pigsties, from which a half a dozen creatures, fattened upon the spoils of the establishment, have just gone to be turned into money for the training of evangelists. There is a house for the three cows grazing in the meadow, and a stable for the horses. There is also a poultry farm.'[9]

The College had accommodation for sixty students in dormitories. The men looked after the premises, scrubbing the floors, cleaning the windows, making their beds and keeping the whole place in the most perfect order. The descriptions of the College at this time, give considerable signification to the fact that the student quarters were 'amply supplied with the very best lavatory and sanitary arrangements'.[10]

The present Common Room was a lecture hall, furnished with desks and chairs, a separate desk for each student. There was also, in the main building, a reading-room and a dining-room, 'beautifully furnished, and supplied with all the most modern appliances.' Cook was against mere luxury but he believed in fresh air, manual exercise and beautiful surroundings.

At the Committee of Management on 4 October 1905, Cook was able to report that the whole of the money needed for the purchase and renovation of the College had been raised. The total cost of the College amounted to £12,843 8s 6½d. 'Great satisfaction and thankfulness were expressed when the report was presented'.[11] That same meeting noted that, whilst fifty men had been accepted for training in the autumn, 'more than a hundred were waiting to come to the College for training'.[12] He had come to the conclusion that it was necessary to double the size of the College. At that point, mainly Local Preachers were admitted but it was obvious to Cook that it would become necessary to extend the training to other workers in the Church.

It is in this discussion we begin to see Cook's persuasive powers with the Committee. 'The fact that so many have had to be refused led to a serious conversation on how to provide additional accommodation. Several suggestions were made but nothing was definitely decided. The need of doing something was fully realised but it was considered advisable to defer the matter to be dealt with at a future meeting.'[13] The Committee also decided to meet twice a year, in April and October, instead of the four times a year established in 1903.[14] They were not to take account, however, of the industry and creative thinking of Thomas Cook. Between October and the next meeting of the Committee, Cook was not idle. The outcome remains a remarkable story with a mixture of faith and evangelical enterprise.

Cook had the idea of building a new wing in memory of Thomas Champness, who had died in 1905. The Committee was reluctant because raising almost £13,000 for the purchase and renovation of the property was a great achievement and might not be repeated. 'They deemed it unwise to launch an extension scheme so soon.'[15] Cook, as we have seen in chapter eight, raised donations to a level where the Committee was persuaded to undertake the work.[16] In the face of this, the Committee could not withstand his enterprise and, 'After considerable discussion the Committee unanimously recommended that the College should be enlarged by the addition of a New Wing, to be called the "Thomas Champness Memorial Wing" at a cost of £6000.'[17] Cook was so confident of the agreement of the Committee that he had already engaged Messrs Hemsall and Chapman of Sheffield to draw up plans, which were submitted to the Committee. 'These were carefully considered and with a few minor alterations were approved'.[18] The decision was so profound that a further Committee was called a few days later to confirm the decision.[19]

Tenders from ten building firms for the College extension were submitted at a meeting called for the 11 May but the lowest, from H. Boot and Son of Sheffield, was for £8,000. The architect was instructed to 'alter his plans that the amount might be reduced by £2,000'.[20] The Committee adjourned for a week and met with the architect, Mr F. Chapman, who had consulted with Messrs H. Boot and Son, revised the bill of quantities and, in consequence, reduced the overall cost neatly to £5,930.[21] 'The reductions were made by omitting the sick-room, the carpenter's shop and bicycle house, two bay windows and expensive masonry in the lower storey, also sundry leaded lights and panelling in the Lecture Hall and Class-rooms, by inserting iron baths instead of porcelain, lead hot water pipes instead of copper and substituting ordinary sash windows instead of Mason's Patent and sundry other items connected therewith.'[22]

The Committee accepted the quotation, set up a sub-committee to 'watch the building operations' and agreed unanimously that 'the work should be proceeded with without delay.'[23] There is a brief report about the progress of the work at the next meeting on 6 November 1906, but Cook's development thinking was moving apace and included the new wing, an extended dining-room and chapel, and a new Tutor's House. In the end the cost of the Champness Memorial Wing and Chapel Renovation was £10,408 5s 5d, of which over £8,000 had been raised but leaving 'a deficiency of £2,319 17s 10d.'[24] Cook clearly felt responsible for this debt and 'undertook to raise another £1,000 but the Committee agreed that they could not take any further action until the Home Mission Committee had considered the matter.'[25]

The stone laying for the extension took place on 21 June 1906. Already £5,000 had been collected of the projected £7,000 costs. Since the College could not be in session because of the building

Stone laying for the extension 21 June 1906

works, the costs of running the College (estimated at £350) were charged to the Building Fund. The Thomas Champness Memorial Wing was opened on Easter Monday, 1 April 1907, 'a bright and beautiful day'. They were £1,500 away from its cost of £7,500 at the beginning of the day. The new dining hall was used for the luncheon and the wing opened with ten listed preachers along with some as 'supporting preachers'. Dr H.J. Pope, General Secretary of the Home Mission Department, and therefore Chair of the College Committee, looking at what was really a quite large building dwarfing the existing Cliff House commented, 'The thing that impresses most deeply is the largeness of Mr Cook's faith'.[26]

The completed 'extension'.

Chadwick preached at the end; 'He had come to see his mausoleum. He had been told so often that he would be buried at Cliff, that he thought he had better come and see his grave. He looked rather lively for a corpse...' It should be understood that Chadwick was still at the Leeds Mission and, though he taught at Cliff part-time from its opening, he was not on the full-time staff until September 1907. His statement is curious, and presumptuous to say the least. However Cook in typically gracious style, 'when Mr Chadwick sat down ... called for the Doxology; the whole £7500 had been raised - Hallelujah!' Announcing the result of the offering after the final speaker, in typical Central Hall style, still continues today in some places.

At the same Committee, Cook 'reported that two ladies had offered donations of £250 each with a view to defray the cost of enlarging the Chapel on the estate.' Plans had been prepared in advance for a new wing, porch and vestry which were approved at that meeting.[27] On 23 May 1907, Whit Monday, the refurbished College chapel was reopened with Dr Bowman Stephenson preaching at the opening of the chapel.

Cook presented plans for a new Tutor's House prepared this time by Messrs Smith and Ensor, architects in Sheffield.[28] The new house, to become known as Cliff Park, was for the Chadwicks who had been designated for appointment to Cliff from 1907. The total outlay for the house was fixed at £1,200 and a loan was secured from the Home Mission Department at 3% interest.

Cook's Chapel

At that time Cook had three major building developments all taking place at the same time. Two were as large as any taking place in the Connexion, the 'Champness Wing' of the College and the extensive new house to be called Cliff Park. Cook's faith, endurance and sheer workload was considerable. That faith was rewarded as by 30 May 1907 he had 'received upwards of £8,000 towards the cost of the Champness Memorial Wing and the renovation of the Chapel. In addition to this, he had received £3,500 for the upkeep of the College and for the maintenance of the Evangelistic work in the rural circuits of Methodism.'

The cost of the work in building Cliff Park was in excess of the maximum set by the Committee of £1,200 but Henry Boot and Son agreed to undertake the work for £1,400. This did not include landscaping, pathways or, crucially, 'heating apparatus'.[29] In the end the cost was £1,600 and, though well built, there was a dispute

Cliff Park

between the architect and the contractor about the size of the building. This dispute lasted until June 1910 and was eventually resolved by asking another architect to 'complete the accounts' including settling the matter of the actual built size.'[30] A further surveyor was employed to confirm the second architect's and the contractor's figures.[31] There had been 'lengthened correspondence between himself and the Architect' and the bill for the second architect and the surveyor was deducted from the architect's bill.[32] Recent experience of building schemes suggests such correspondence can take considerable time and energy.

Undaunted by the scale of the building works, Cook placed before the Committee the issue of the water supply which in 'Droughty weather' was insufficient.[33] Negotiations with the Duke of Rutland's agent led to 'an additional water supply of 5,000 gallons daily' which would supply from the Baslow Waterworks all the College needs, including the busy laundry off Cliff Lane.

One part of his vision which Cook did not see built, was a proposed auditorium. Whilst the need for an auditorium was realised, especially with the numbers attending the Summer School, the Committee 'decided nothing could be done until the Tutor's House had been paid for'.[34] Into the College's possession has also come an architect's plan for ten 'Secular Tutor's Houses' which were to be built in a crescent at the top of the Cliff Park field prior to the observatory becoming a dwelling and the Cliff Cottages being built. The architects for this project were Smith and Ensor, who seemed so sorely to let Cook down over the technical aspects of Cliff Park. It should be said that Cliff Park is a superb dwelling, solidly built and a substantial manse. Notably Chadwick returned to Chapman and Co to design and supervise the building of the Thomas Cook Memorial wing.

Immediately after Cook died, the Committee met and Chadwick suggested a Memorial scheme that 'would go along the line of Mr Cook's own ideas and wishes. He produced plans ... providing in

The Cook Memorial Wing

the basement, Dairy, Larder and Laundry; on the first floor Office and Linen room, and on the second floor a Sick Room with accommodation for four patients; a Memorial Tablet to be inserted in a prominent place on the South front.'[35] In fact the Committee considered a further third floor, though that was never built.[36] The new wing and the memorial stone in All Saints churchyard, Curbar, cost £1,243.

There was little renewal of the property in the War years, though the minutes in 1915 refer to the 'special expenditure necessary on farm buildings and repairs and renewals within the College.'[37] These farm buildings were the series of buildings running along the orchard and now homes for staff known as 'Beulah', 'Maranatha' and 'Emmaus'.

At the reopening of the College, following World War I, Chadwick related that he purchased, with a generous donation from Mr Joseph Rank, some 'lands adjacent to our property which would be of very great value to the College.'[38]

Following the purchase of the lands by Chadwick prior to 1920, the Committee invited Sir Robert Kay to present a scheme for the settlement of all land and properties included within the Cliff College Estate. The Cliff College Committee became the tenant of the Home Mission Committee.[39] At the next meeting in June 1921, Sir Robert Kay gave a full statement concerning a proposal for the whole estate, the original Cliff estate and the additional lands purchased by Chadwick, to be given over to the Home Mission Board.[40] In fact the Committee had to return to this item in 1929 to cover the land and funds accumulated by Chadwick.

Chadwick proposed that certain renovations should be carried out in the College, 'concerning the installation of Electric Light and Laundry Plant, and also necessary repairs, painting and renewals' which, though not identified, were quite substantial with an estimated cost of £3,500.[41] The work was undertaken and the electric light was in operation from January 1921.[42]

Even at this point there was a discussion about an extension of the College, 'It was further arranged that the Principal and officials of the College Committee should go into the question of the other reconstructions which were needed, and carry them through if it should be found financially possible to do so.'[43]

In the summer of 1923, Chadwick indicated his plans to improve and extend the College. 'The accommodation of the College has never been adequate. More than half the students share a bedroom with others. They have no study, and every man ought to have a room where he can be alone for study and prayer. So I am resolved that each man shall have a separate bedroom … We also need a Library. At present the Common Room has to serve for a Library … The lavatory accommodation is neither adequate nor convenient and must be improved, for it is by these things an institution may be judged. The work will take a year and will be costly. We want the best. I hate poor workmanship, and will only do what can be done well. A Friend has promised five thousand pounds. It may cost seven … it has to be opened free of debt on Whit-Monday 1924.'[44]

The work was begun in the summer and a formal stone laying ceremony took place on 27 September 1923. Chadwick invited *Joyful News* readers to attend and help raise '£1,000 on that day.'[45] In fact, the work was delayed in the bad weather of that winter. The builders, being urged to meet their schedule, worked in conditions of frost and the end wall bows outwards slightly as a result. The next time you come to Cliff, stand in the rose garden underneath the wall, at the top of the steps and look upwards, and you will see the effect. Don't worry. It is very safe!

The College Committee did not meet between May 1923 and June 1926 during which time the Library wing was built. The extension was opened on the Friday of the Anniversary Weekend in early June 1924 by Dame Margaret Lloyd George, and The Rt. Hon. David Lloyd George addressed a public meeting in the evening. Lloyd George, who knew how to win his audience, spoke about the work of Wesley, Champness, Hugh Price Hughes and Chadwick. He finished his comments, 'The one thing that England needs now is not the material things which we politicians strive for, and which, in their own way, alleviate, assuage, soften, and perhaps improve the road. The thing that is needed in England is a 'spiritual awakening'. It is needed now more than ever. I believe there are signs that it is coming, and when it does, these young men will be taking the lead in it. (loud applause)'[46] It was a remarkable thing that a serving Prime Minister should be present at the opening of the College and it says a great deal for the place of Methodism and the non-conformist

churches in society and also for the impact Chadwick had among parliamentarians. On completion, the cost was £12,532 9s 0d and Chadwick had ensured that the whole amount was raised. The extension provided a new library, twenty-seven bedrooms and a 'sanitary annexe'.[47]

The Library

When the vision for the Treks came into being, and with it the need for storing bulky Trek carts, there came also the necessity for a building to house the carts and the bicycles and so the 'Trek Shed' was established.[48] This remains today, at the Calver end of the College Drive, though now it houses hundreds of benches and chairs used for the main public events of the College.

The opening of the Library with its oak shelving had highlighted the need to renovate the Common Room. 'That side of the old building has always been infested with rats. We filled up the vaults, concreted the floor and paved it with wooden blocks. Then I visualised a Dream of years, and it grew into a beautiful panelled room known as the Common Room. One thing suggested another and the Dining Hall cried aloud to be made to match its neighbour'.[49]

It was a Mr Soper of Barnsley who gave a 'handsome gift of oak for the panelling of the Common Room'[50] and in 1927 he again made a donation of oak panelling for the Dining Room.

In the editor's letter of the *Joyful News* Chadwick tells how he had always had a longing for a Leonardo da Vinci's 'Last Supper' and that he had seen a carving but it was too expensive. At the Southport Convention, he let it be known it was his jubilee as a preacher and he was given £50. With that he purchased the carving from a firm of sculptors and woodcarvers (Messrs Tory and Sons). He had it installed in the dining room and invited Councillor and Mrs Soper of Barnsley to the simple ceremony of unveiling. Councillor Soper had 'given all the oak for the panelling of the rooms and it was fitting that the carved panel should be unveiled by Mrs Soper.'[51]

The marble bust of Chadwick, in the 'Chadwick entrance' at the time of writing, was given to him to honour the fifteen years of being the Chair of the District in Sheffield. It was handed over at the Spring Synod 16 May 1928. It is a white marble bust set on a plinth of the very rare black marble found locally at Ashford-in-the-Water.

Prior to the annual meeting of the College Committee in 1928, Chadwick had acquired further agricultural land for the College, and 'Through the generosity of an anonymous friend … been able to purchase for the College the adjoining Grislow Field Farm of 76 acres.'[52] That same Committee noted that very few of the original Trustees of the College property were now living and Chadwick indicated that the investments representing the Reserve Fund for the College (which at that time were £2,500 on deposit at the bank and £13,921 in investments) were all in his name. He suggested that 'the property and Investments might be transferred to the Trustees for the Wesleyan Methodist Connexional Funds (Registered).'[53] The detail of the proposed Deed was brought to a Meeting of the Committee in June 1930 and Sir Robert Kay read the provisions which 'were fully discussed and suggestions made as to the safe-guards'.[54] In preparation for this, a number of tithes on the estate had been redeemed.[55] Later that year, the matter was in hand and investments were transferred in November 1930.

Stanton Ford

The house at Stanton Ford, known, until it was recently painted, as the 'White House', had been acquired prior to the Committee in September 1929, 'on a lease of 89 years, and had been put into habitable condition for a Tutor's residence'.[56] It is difficult to identify which, if any, Tutor resided there but after the death of Samuel, Mrs Chadwick lived in the house from 1932 until her death in August 1956.[57]

A request for an extension of the Curbar Churchyard had been received prior to the meeting of the Committee in November 1930. Some members of the Committee were entirely opposed to 'any gift of Cliff College land being made'.[58] However, Chadwick was finally given a free hand and it would appear that land was eventually made available to the Curbar Churchyard Committee. It seems that the request referred to land purchased by Chadwick from a Miss Kitchin which had caused a 'dispute with the Church Authorities' and Chadwick resolved the matter by selling the land back to her.

The Library and Chadwick Memorial Chapel

The conservatory, which is shown in so many pictures of the College in the early years, was in danger of collapse and beyond repair.[59] Chadwick had engaged an architect, Mr G.R. Bower, 'to prepare plans for a new entrance Hall and a new storeroom to stand on the site of the Conservatory'.[60] The entrance remains and the storeroom became toilets, when women were accepted as students in 1965.

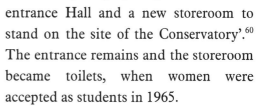

The Lamberts outside 'Ataraxia'.

Following his death, the question arose about a fitting tribute for Chadwick. Broadbelt proposed two possibilities, either a 'small chapel for the use of students' or a fund for the development of the 'Evangelistic Work of the College.'[61] The Committee chose the former, though Broadbelt managed to include both and Lambert, Dunning and Brice ensured the third, a granite cross on which is inscribed the College motto. By the meeting of the College Committee in March 1933, the plans for the Chapel were drawn up in draft and then confirmed.[62] No expense was spared in providing furniture for the chapel, including overhauling the organ, and providing a new oak carved case.[63] The architects were Potts and Hennings and the work which cost £5,427 3s 4d was met in the first year.

The ability of Broadbelt to fund building extensions had been noted around the Connexion. We see it being effectively used here. He not only built and raised the money for the Chapel and established the Chadwick Evangelistic Fund but also 'built three cottages on the College estate for Mr Roberts and two of the gardeners'.[64] These are now known as 'Laneside', 'Belmont' and 'Cartref'. In addition to this, 'The Principal also mentioned that some friends of his had given him some money to build a bungalow next to the cottages as a holiday home for old Cliff men and returned missionaries.'[65] Mr Wiseman called it a 'beautiful idea'. On completion the Bungalow was extensively used, though later, 'under changed circum-stances', extended to become the house now known as 'Lindum'. This was occupied by the Rev Joe Brice and, after his departure, Eric Haslock.[66] In that same year he adapted the observatory in Cliff Lane

Cliff Cottages and 'Lindum'.

to be a home for David Lambert who married Dorothy Wainwright in December 1933. Lambert called the house 'Ataraxia', the Greek word, meaning 'untroubled' or 'a place apart', which Chadwick had embossed in wood in his study.[67]

'Lindum' was described as 'a small bungalow near the Cliff Cottages'.[68] 'The holiday home is for any Cliff men either in the Ministry or in the ranks of the lay preachers, and for any missionary on furlough either of our society or of the Faith Missions such as the China Inland Mission or for any old local preachers who are helped by the Fund so splendidly organised by my friend and colleague "Metholay" at Christmas-time or for any minister of the Sheffield District'.[69] The holiday home was furnished by friends and paid for by additional donations. Applications for the use of the holiday home were to be made to Mrs Broadbelt.

1934 was a busy year for building, opening the Memorial Chapel on the 4 January, building the cottages and bungalow and supporting a mission hall in Sheffield. Broadbelt reopened 'Cliff Hall', in the Brightside area in East Sheffield. 'We have taken over an old and derelict Chapel ... (it) will provide us with a glorious opportunity for Aggressive Evangelism, we can put our theories to the test.'[70] Broadbelt had set aside two evangelists, Bros. Smith and Costain, 'who will give themselves to sacrificial service for the conversion of the people.' The Hall was re-opened and dedicated on 29 December 1934. I recall attending this Mission Hall in November 1967 at Fell Street, Brightside in Sheffield, with Howard Belben, just prior to the Hall being demolished.

There is correspondence between Broadbelt and Rank about the purchase of the Bridge Inn, Curbar. 'The Principal also reported on the possibility and advisability of buying Bridge Inn, if it should come into the market. The Committee approved and authorised the Principal to go forward.'[71] Broadbelt wanted to change its use to a bed and breakfast guest house and tea room but he did not get his way with this project.[72]

Cliff Hall

The largest project which Broadbelt undertook while he was Principal was the building of Cliff Hall. The Hall remains the largest single hall in the Peak District, apart from the Buxton Opera House. It is remarkable that such a vision was conceived when it was originally intended to be used on relatively few occasions. 'We propose to build a Cliff Tea Hall which will cost some £5,000 and which will house all our lunch and tea arrangements for the Anniversary and for the Derwent Convention.'[73] It was not until the early 1950s, when an organisation offering holidays for needy children in the Midlands, Midland Camping Venture, asked to use the Hall and Youth Camp that the Hall really began to fulfil its potential.

In addition to a proposed Assembly Hall, the new scheme included a warden's house, storerooms, a common room for Derwent Campers, sanitary accommodation and several garages. There was a tremendous transformation of the old farm site. 'The Anniversary crowds will occupy them only one day a year; and we expect developments of our spiritual work that will bring them into use regularly.'

In October 1938, Broadbelt laid out the plans for the Cliff Tea Hall, which were approved.[74] The building work cost £11,753 0s 7d to build the Tea Hall, improve the Stanton Ford Farm and make

necessary repairs to the College. All these funds had been raised by private donations without recourse to the College funds, such was Broadbelt's ability to raise funds among wealthy friends. [75] The hall was opened on the Saturday 27 May 1939,[76] at the Anniversary. Besides the Tea Hall, a home was made from existing farm buildings, 'a caretaker's cottage', garages and a

Cliff Hall was later used for student recreation

storehouse.[77] The immediate vision for the developing use of Cliff Hall was undermined by the declaration of War on Sunday 3 September 1939, at 11.00 by the Prime Minister, Neville Chamberlain.

During these seven years, Broadbelt had achieved a considerable amount of building and the minutes during the war pay tribute to this expansion. The minutes record that, 'The Principal reported that, during the last eleven years additions and alterations had been carried through, with the sanction of the Committee, to a total value of £19,000 – £10,000 for the erection of Cliff Hall, £5,500 for the Chadwick Memorial Chapel, £1,500 for the three Cottages, £1,000 for the Bungalow and £1,000 for the Tutor's house at Ataraxia.'[78]

Sometime prior to the outbreak of war, Broadbelt had made plans for the use of the College by a school, fearing that the military may require its use, as they had requested during World War I. 'The College is now occupied by the Sheffield Girls High School, and some two hundred lively and carefree girls of all ages from 6 – 19 years are enjoying our beautiful grounds. Some months ago, through the good offices of Mr S. Osborn J.P., a friend of the School and the College, we entered into negotiations with the Principal of the school that in the event of war the school should come out to Cliff. On the day before the declaration of war, the school authorities decided it was wise to evacuate the girls and they came in a fleet of cars on that very wet Saturday afternoon. It is a great privilege to us to provide a home for so many Sheffield girls and we shall do all in our power to make their stay, which I hope will be short, as happy as possible.'[79] The Head Teacher was Miss Macaulay with a staff of thirty teachers.[80]

Broadbelt had secured very satisfactory terms for the lease of the College to the Sheffield High School for Girls. The Committee were very content at the outcome and perhaps particularly so, recalling the possibilities during the First World War.[81] Cliff Hall was used for the Home Guard to meet and parade and, after the bombing of Sheffield, was used for housing blankets and stores in case of a further devastating raid. I believe that in the early 1980s I ate some of the bully beef left behind from the rations stored at the College!

Berith

J. Baines Atkinson, who had been a minister in the North Derbyshire Circuit and a visiting and valued Tutor to the College, retired in 1943 and asked the College Committee for permission to build a new home in the College grounds. Chadwick relayed this request indicating that permission had already been granted, 'the house to become the property of the College at their death. The Committee heartily concurred, expressing gratitude to Mr and Mrs Atkinson and the hope that they may live long in the enjoyment of their home.'[82] In the summer 'their new home is not yet ready' and so they took up temporary residence in the College. The house, when built, towards the top of Cliff Lane, was called 'Berith' and the Atkinsons enjoyed continuing contact with the College. When they passed away, the house came into the ownership of the College. Unwisely, the house was sold in 1973 and today is known as 'Fir Tree Lodge'.

At that same Committee Broadbelt 'expressed the hope that if at some future time it should seem desirable that his family should temporarily occupy the bungalow, the Committee and Trustees would be willing'.[83] The Committee agreed 'readily and heartily' but there were problems ahead about that.[84]

The School indicated in the autumn that they would terminate the tenancy on 30 December 1944, 'and would do inside repairs according to the terms of their tenancy'.[85] Sadly, there followed a long running dispute between the School and the College. The minutes bear witness to some bad feeling between the two. The minutes suggest that they had left the College in a poor condition. 'Six months' difficult labour had accomplished the task of reconditioning the College. The total cost had been £1,700 and this, according to the terms of the tenancy, should be borne by the School.'[86] It would seem that the School contested the scale of the re-decoration following their departure and initially paid only £650,[87] with the final payment two years later.[88]

Broadbelt and the Committee were clearly relieved the school had returned to Sheffield and were eager to prepare for the reopening of the College. They wanted to commence from the Easter of 1945, with twenty or thirty men 'a few of whom would be old students, to help in continuing the traditions of the College.'[89] In fact the College re-opened on 28 September, with thirty students. In the summer, Broadbelt had agreed the College may be used for a week's conference of the Moral Leadership Campaign for young men and women of the Forces.[90]

The name of Norman Dunning appears in the minutes again, this time making suggestions for his old College. One scheme related to the immediate post-war issue of the needs of ex-service men and Dunning's suggestion that the College be used 'for a period of one or two years for Service men was not approved.'[91] At the following Committee, a year later, he made an appeal to the Committee, 'to furnish a room in a projected training home near Hull' but the request was refused. He had been appointed to the Hull Circuit and, after one year refused to live in the manse preferring to live in Beverley Hall, a brick built substantial mansion on the edge of Hull

Cliff Hall (left) and the Youth Camp to its right

and, as its name suggests, on the way to Beverley. He had hoped to establish a College, and it would seem he wished to develop a 'Cliff' style of training with links to the Colleges in Hull.[92]

The Young People's Camp had been very successful in the immediate post war period and would not be able to expand if the College relied on marquees. Therefore, in the spring of 1947, seven Army huts were purchased, 'which were being erected by the labour of Evangelists and Students under the leadership of Mr T. Butler … within a month'.[93] The experiment was a great success and they had been used, with the marquees, by 500 young people at the Anniversary and 300 at the Derwent Convention of that year.[94] The following year Broadbelt announced 'We have been compelled to buy five more Army huts and are moving them from a park near Derby, and shall have them rebuilt on a site at Cliff. These huts are very costly, but very necessary for our work,' followed, of course, with a request for money.[95] The increase in numbers at the major events placed very considerable pressure on the water supply and toilet facilities, and caused a headache to the Committee.[96] The camp had been developed without attendant reference to the water supply, which at these major events was insufficient to service the toilets during these busy times. This created problems which were never completely solved until the building of the new conference centres, Broadbelt and Eagles, in 1988. These nissan huts, twelve of them altogether, were all given names: Faith, Hope, Charity, Humility, Kindness, Truth, Patience, Honour, Grace, Peace, Joy and Glory. When originally erected, these huts were used by women.

Large marquees were erected in Cliff Hall field to cater for the men who came to the major public events and they were given the names 'Bethel', 'Ebenezer', 'Peniel' and 'Zion'. Rows of iron bedsteads were placed in these marquees, in a field just vacated by cows, so the men had to be careful which side they got out of bed! There was also the smaller 'Fellowship Hut' from which Tom Butler ran the Cliff Fellowship, when it was established.

Broadbelt was granted permission in May 1947 'for the erection of two cottages, one for a gardener, and the other for Mr and Mrs Sainsbury.'[97] Sainsbury was a Lay Pastor with the Home Mission Committee and he was allowed to return to the College and work with Tom Butler in the development of the Youth Camp and take charge of arranging the Evangelists' Missions and organising the Book Department.[98] The two cottages were, in fact, formed from the old chapel and for many years have been known as 'Bethany' and 'Hillview'. Living accommodation for Ernest Steele as a married Evangelist was made above the Tea Hall premises.

When Broadbelt retired early, he remained at Cliff Park for a year and then was granted permission to enlarge 'The Bungalow' to its present proportions.[99] He was allowed to do so because the funds of the College were so buoyant. It should be remembered that it was Broadbelt who had looked after his staff by introducing pensions and offering accommodation free for the retirement of those who had given long service to the College. In fact Broadbelt never moved into the extended 'Bungalow' but retired to Wetherby. At the same time as the changes were being made to 'The Bungalow', Mr Haslock who lived there was to move to 'one of the two houses that are being constructed from the Old College Chapel.'[100]

Eric Haslock

The Farms at Grislow Fields and Stanton Ford had been purchased along with various other lands by Samuel Chadwick. Both Chadwick and Broadbelt had presided over the estate and, from the evidence of the Committee minutes had managed the estate efficiently and at a profit. In the years of Eagle's principalship the farms at Grislow Fields and Stanton Ford are dealt with as 'problems'. Gone is the entrepreneurial spirit of Chadwick and Broadbelt who saw these properties and lands making a profit for the College. The minutes of the Executive Committee are taken up with the 'problems' of ensuring they are kept in a state of good repair. The finances of the projects were not handled well in this period. The investment by the College for repairs and improvements to the Grislow Fields Farm during the period 1949 to 1951 was £4,000.[101]

At the same time, the rental, which had been £90 per annum, was proposed to be raised to £130 per annum. Even with government grants, this was a very poor return and indicative of the way the estate was handled at this time. In December 1954, the College funded joinery repairs costing £150,[102] but there is nothing in the minutes to recognise that the College was in fact subsidising the farms at Grislow Fields and Stanton Ford.

Indeed, when in 1953 Mr Horace Dalton acquired the tenancy, the finances were always going to work against the interests of the College, and so, for years the College invested money in the farms in excess of the annual rental received. The difference in business acumen of this period with either Chadwick or Broadbelt is considerable. Broadbelt, with the help of Sir Richard Kay, had ensured that the Sheffield High School agreement was on a self-repairing lease.[103]

The College Jubilee Fund was formed with the express aim to reconstruct the Lecture Rooms of the College and make them worthy of the rest of the buildings. 'We hope to provide two excellent rooms divided by a partition. The one to be normally used will be much lighter than the present one.'[104] The rough estimate presented to the Committee was for an expenditure of £2,000 but, at the meeting in February 1954, only £179 18s 9d had been received. This changed dramatically as a result of the successful Anniversary and the alterations were put in hand.

The Book Steward, Ted Budgell, was showing himself useful in redecorating parts of the College, Cliff Park and the Bungalow in advance of Dr Farndale coming to live there in the summer of 1953.[105]

Questions about whether the youth camp should be replaced were raised in June 1955.[106] The National Parks Committee had expressed the view that they wanted some more permanent structures than the nissan huts purchased from the Army. When the planners did not press the matter, the Committee prevaricated and finally the twelve huts were replaced by eight new structures in 1970.

When Tom Meadley was appointed Principal, he insisted that certain changes be made to the accommodation for the Principal and a door was placed at the College end of the corridor through the Principal's House to give him privacy. Not before time, a private kitchen was also installed in the Principal's flat. Prior to that, the Principal's family only had a small scullery on what used to be called the 'Bookshop Corridor', first door on the left.

It is not surprising that following the net outflow of funds on Grislow Fields the Executive Committee recommended that the Farm be sold with fifty acres of land. The property and some land

Ridgeway

was sold to Professor Eric Wilkes in January 1960 for £1,850. What is not clear, as good strategy, is the sale of Stanton Ford House. The Committee instructed the Treasurers to purchase the freehold and were willing to spend £800, prior to its final sale. The sale by public auction was for both the House and the fishing rights purchased by Chadwick in 1920 from the Duke of Rutland. The proceeds of the sale were £2,560. Both these sales had to gain permission from the College and the Home Mission Department but it revealed in both cases poor strategy. The Committee kept investments and sold the properties. The value of these farms and

Preparing for the concrete huts (above)
The 'new' Youth Camp (below)

Stanton Centre

houses has risen astronomically and both Stanton Ford House and Grislow Fields have changed hands a number of times. During 2003 Grislow Fields was offered for sale at around £750,000. This same mistake was made later when the Committee sold 'Berith'.

Berith was sold in 1960 and within three years the Committee realised there was a need for an additional house. Proceeds from the sale of Grislow Fields and Stanton Ford House enabled the building of Ridgeway on Cliff Lane. Howard and Jeanne Belben were the first occupants with their young family.

The next major building scheme for the College, after the considerable work completed by Broadbelt, came at the inspiration of Howard Belben. The main College building was in need of some repair and improvement. 'The scheme, which includes electrical rewiring of the College, refurbishing the study-bedrooms, installation of modern catering equipment, hostel accommodation for women students and new accommodation for staff'[107] was made possible in large part by a grant from the Joseph Rank Benevolent Trust. What the College Committee could not agree about, related to the need to replace the ageing Youth Camp nissan

Hut interior

huts which, twenty years after their 'temporary' relocation were leaking and rusting. The Committee membership was very large, with about fifty eligible to attend and its sheer size inhibited decisions. It was almost impossible to make final decisions, especially at a time of keeping the College financially secure. After many possible schemes had been debated, decided and then rescinded, a scheme was eventually agreed in the spring of 1968. The proposal was passed to build a Conference Centre, now called the 'Stanton Centre', which was opened on Wesley Day 24 May 1969. It was this development which began a new public ministry for the College, as indicated in chapter thirteen. The twelve nissan huts were demolished and replaced by eight similar structures made from pre-cast concrete. They were used for twenty years and were considerably warmer and cleaner but they did house thirty-two people in bunk beds. Those who slept in them faced a dilemma: the fan kept them awake at night, but without it the 'fug' the following morning was considerable.

There was some curious thinking in the Committee in relation to housing. Howard Belben gained planning approval for a new tutor's house in 1967. He wrote an explanatory note, 'It would then have cost about £9,000. The plans were abandoned when the amount of money coming in for the Extension Appeal was insufficient for this to be built as well as the Conference Centre. The house was planned to fit the contours of the land. It would have been situated between 'Ridgeway' and the car park.'[108] The Committee then sold 'Berith' in 1973 and within nine years was again seeking to build a four bedroom house for a new tutor, the Director of Evangelism, to be appointed from 1983. Hindsight of course is a wonderful thing but the sale of property was shortsighted and at this time the College could do with all the properties for staff or when vacant for rental.

The celebration of the *Joyful News* Centenary in 1983 prompted an appeal for £100,000 to build a house for the new post of Director of Evangelism, a post with Connexional responsibility besides being a tutor at Cliff. Only £71,000 was raised but the house Cartref was extended and modernised to make an additional tutor's house. Accommodation was made for the Evangelistic staff by adapting the Principal's House to make a two bedroom flat on the second floor, remodelling the Cliff Hall flat and investing £10,000 in a fund for training evangelists.[109]

During the time Dr William Davies was Principal, the Committee was agonising about the need to renovate the youth camp yet again. Coming back from London on the train, Bill Davies, Maurice Houghton, Brian Hoare and myself had an inspirational conversation with ideas coming thick and fast. It was a *kairos* moment! So that nothing was lost I wrote down the ideas on a serviette and then wrote them up as 'The Serviette Vision'. The only item not yet achieved is the swimming pool. The outcome was the building of Eagles and Broadbelt, the decision to make the 'Chadwick's Lounge' and install a heating system into Cliff Hall to make it usable in the winter. These developments were very significant for the public events the College could offer and they allowed new Conferences to take place. Changes to the entrance of the College were made and so the administrative office became much more accessible, a lay-by was built on Cliff Lane and new pathways laid through the orchard. In addition the house 'Emmaus' was formed from the 'Camp Common Room' to give accommodation for staff. These were big steps forward and Bill Davies, with Maurice Houghton as Administrative Officer, saw them through. In the College, the maintenance department

"Digging out" – space being created under Cliff Hall

moved to the Cliff Lane building, which was originally the laundry and for years had been used on Whit-Monday only as the Ladies toilet. The A.V.A. department transferred to a room where the maintenance department had been, and that then released a room for computers.

Since 1994 I had been indicating to the Committee and the Connexion that a further significant development needed to take place. A Development Group was established by the Committee, architects appointed, a viable scheme agreed, planning permission sought and a Connexional appeal launched. What we now call the 'grand scheme' would have cost £6.5million at 2001 prices. I was launched to speak at a series of meetings throughout the Connexion and to Trusts at home and abroad. Whilst we received many small contributions from individuals, churches and circuits, it became clear in the summer of 2002 that the grand scheme was not achievable. The arrival at the College of a new Bursar, John Steer, and the appointment of a new Estates Officer, Andy Barnett, brought new thinking and, within six months, a revised scheme had been devised and presented to the Committee, which delivered many of the requirements we originally desired, and crucially, could be achieved within a much smaller budget. The work began in earnest during November 2003 and the

Chadwick's Refectory on Centenary Day

Centenary Day, 3 March 2004, saw the re-opening of a renovated Cliff Hall by Mrs Jeanne Belben, wife of the late Howard Belben, a former Principal of the College. The newly refurbished hall includes the 'Chadwick's Refectory', the Chatsworth Suite, and the Haddon and Derwent Conference Rooms. In the summer of 2004, the old College Dining Room became the Howard Belben Library, disabled access was improved, the former library became a teaching space making available two seminar and two lecture rooms constantly through the year. The old library is the Thomas Meadley Lecture Room and the archive and research documents are placed in the Arthur Skevington Wood Research Library. These changes have enhanced the teaching and learning resources needed for the number of students involved in the present number of courses.

The removal of the Principal's living space from the main College building has meant that a new tutorial and administrative hub has been devised, and changes to the main entrance to the College could be reconsidered. At the time this book goes to press, over £900,000

Andy Barnett

has been raised towards the overall target of £1.5million. In this book I wish to pay tribute to the Estates' Officer, Andy Barnett and the Designer Peter Arnold for their committed approach to this project which has delivered a marvellous resource for the College. What the future holds, only time will tell, but I am sure that God has not yet finished with the development of the work and the College.

Chadwick's Refectory nearing completion

The Howard Belben Library

1   Joe Brice, 'The Romance of a House' in *The Cliff Witness*, Vol. 3, No 2, 1939, p.29.
2   Joe Brice, 'The Romance of a House' in *The Cliff Witness*, Vol. 3, No 2, 1939, p.30.
3   *Minutes of the Home Mission Committee*, 6-7 July 1903.
4   *Minutes of the Home Mission Committee*, 23 July 1903.
5   *Minutes of the Home Mission Committee*, 23 July 1903.
6   Joe Brice, 'The Romance of a House' in *The Cliff Witness*, Vol. 3, No 2, 1939, p.30.
7   *Joyful News*, 10 March 1904.
8   H.K., 'Cliff College,' *Leeds Mission News*, No 9, September 1904.
9   H.K., p.2.
10 Ibid.
11 Committee of Management *Minutes*, 4 October 1905. The minute indicates that the funds were raised in the following manner: 'Towards this amount the Home Mission Committee has contributed £5,759 18s 2d; made up from £3,302 15s 1d from the Twentieth Century Fund, and £2,457 3s 1d as special grants. The balance of £7,083 10s 4½d has been raised chiefly by donations and subscriptions'.
12 Ibid.
13 Ibid.
14 Ibid.
15 Joe Brice, 'The Romance of a House' in *The Cliff Witness*, Vol. 3, No 2, 1939, p.30.
16 *Minutes* of the Committee of Management, 1 Feb 1906.
17 Ibid.
18 *Minutes* of the Committee of Management, 1 February 1906.
19 A note to the Minutes of the *Minutes* of the 7 February 1906.
20 *Minutes* of the Committee of Management, 11 May 1906.
21 *Minutes* of the Committee of Management, 11 May 1906.
22 Ibid.
23 Ibid.
24 *Minutes* of the Committee of Management, 18 Nov 1907.
25 Ibid. The underlining is in the Committee Minutes.
26 *Joyful News*, 4 April 1907.
27 *Minutes* of the Committee of Management, 6 November 1906.
28 *Minutes* of the Committee of Management, 6 Nov 1906. The Ensor mentioned was in fact a great uncle of Mr David Ensor, Vice-President of the Methodist Conference 1981.
29 Ibid.
30 Minutes of the Committee of Management, 29 April 1909.
31 Minutes of the Committee of Management, 2 June 1910.
32 Ibid.
33 *Minutes* of the Committee of Management, 30 May 1907. My experience of this part of Derbyshire is that such extremes of weather are rare!
34 *Minutes* of the Committee of Management, 29 April 1909.

cont.

35   *Minutes* of the Committee of Management, 15 November 1912.

36   The builder appointed was Mr David Sheldon, at a cost of £866, *Minutes* of the Committee of Management, 28 January 1913.

37   *Minutes* of the Committee of Management, 22 November 1915.

38   *Minutes* of the Cliff College Committee, 7 May 1920.

39   *Minutes* of the Cliff College Committee, 7 May 1920.

40   *Minutes* of the Cliff College Committee, June 1921. No day is indicated and a new secretary is writing the minutes with abbreviated language.

41   *Minutes* of the Cliff College Committee, 7 May 1920.

42   *Minutes* of the Cliff College Committee, June 1921.

43   Ibid.

44   *Joyful News*, 31 May 1923 and Minutes of the Cliff College Committee, 4 May 1923.

45   *Joyful News,* 20 September 1923.

46   *Joyful News,* 12 June 1923.

47   *Joyful News,* 5 June 1924.

48   Joe Brice, 'The Romance of a House' in *The Cliff Witness,* Vol. 3, No 2, 1939, p.30.

49   Ibid.

50   *Minutes* of the Cliff College Committee, 21 June 1926.

51   *Joyful News*, 24 November 1927. The Sopers were a mining family and he became Mayor of Barnsley (*Joyful News,* 20 November 1938). See also the *Minutes of the Cliff College Committee*, 27 March 1928.

52   *Minutes* of the Cliff College Committee, 27 March 1928.

53   *Minutes* of the Cliff College Committee, 27 March 1928.

54   *Minutes* of the Cliff College Committee, 16 June 1930.

55   *Minutes* of the Cliff College Committee, 30 September 1929.

56   *Minutes* of the Cliff College Committee, 30 September 1929.

57   *Minutes* of the Cliff College Committee, 20 October confirmed this, offering Stanton Ford for 'as long as she required'.

58   *Minutes* of the Cliff College Committee, 4 November 1930.

59   *Minutes* of the Cliff College Committee, 21 July 1931.

60   *Minutes* of the Cliff College Committee, 21 July 1931.

61   *Minutes* of the Cliff College Committee, 14 December 1932.

62   *Minutes* of the Cliff College Committee, 7 March 1933.

63   Chadwick Memorial Chapel, file in the safe in the Principal's Study.

64   *Minutes* of the Cliff College Committee, 8 October 1934. The cost was £1500, *Minutes*, 26 Oct 1943.

65   Ibid. The 'man' is in the singular, presumably in error. The cost was £1000, *Minutes* 26 Oct 1943.

66   *Minutes* of the Cliff College Committee, 13 April 1943.

67   Mary Lambert, *D.W. Lambert: Singleminded* (private publication). She spoke at the 1932 Summer School as a returned missionary, at the suggestion of Lambert, who knew Dorothy in their teenage years. 'Thereafter "Peter and Wendy", as they called each other, used to meet regularly in the Peak District.' p.4. They married on 21 December 1933.

cont.

68 *Joyful News,* 15 November 1934.
69 Ibid.
70 *Joyful News,* 27 December 1934.
71 *Minutes* of the Cliff College Committee, 1 October 1937. In fact the Bridge Inn was sold from the Duke of Rutland's estate in 1920 and sold on again in 1950.
72 *Letter* to Joseph Rank, 20 May 1937.
73 *Joyful News,* 23 June 1938.
74 *Minutes* of the Cliff College Committee, 30 September 1938.
75 *Minutes* of the Cliff College Committee, 12 July 1940. Of the full cost of £11,753 0s 7d, £10,528 9s 9d on the Tea Hall, £909 15s 0d to improve the Stanton Ford Farm and £313 15s 10d on repairs to the College.
76 *Joyful News,* 1 June 1939.
77 Joe Brice, 'The Romance of a House' in *The Cliff Witness,* Vol. 3, No 2, 1939, p.30. The Caretaker's Cottage will be 'Maranatha', made from the farm buildings and the garages built at that same time. The storerooms became the camp toilets and the 'Camp Common Room' which is now a house, 'Emmaus'.
78 *Minutes* of the Cliff College Committee, 26 October 1943.
79 *Joyful News,* 14 September 1939.
80 *Joyful News,* 5 October 1939.
81 *Minutes* of the Cliff College Committee, 12 July 1940.
82 *Minutes* of the Cliff College Committee, 13 April 1943.
83 *Minutes* of the Cliff College Committee, 13 April 1943.
84 Ibid.
85 *Minutes* of the Cliff College Committee, 15 November 1944.
86 *Minutes* of the Cliff College Committee, 16 November 1945.
87 *Minutes* of the Cliff College Committee, 15 November 1946.
88 *Minutes* of the Cliff College Committee, 21 November 1947.
89 *Minutes* of the Cliff College Committee, 15 November 1944.
90 Ibid.
91 Ibid.
92 I visited Beverley Hall at the invitation of Mrs Fay Dunning, and learned of his plans, which never materialised. He clearly had hoped to follow Chadwick at Cliff and, after these hopes were dashed, he determined to start his own college on Cliff lines. In the end his dreams were unfulfilled and he resigned from the ministry.
93 *Minutes* of the Cliff College Committee, 12 May 1947.
94 *Minutes* of the Cliff College Committee, 21 November 1947.
95 *Joyful News,* 11 March 1948.
96 *Minutes* of the Cliff College Committee, 22 September 1948.
97 *Minutes* of the Cliff College Committee, 12 May 1947.
98 *Minutes* of the Cliff College Committee, 21 November 1947.
99 *Minutes* of the Cliff College Committee, 18 May 1949.
100 *Minutes* of the Cliff College Committee, 18 May 1948.
101 *Minutes* of the Cliff College Committee, 13 June 1951.
102 *Minutes* of the Cliff College Committee, 14 December 1954.
103 See the section on the Second World War.

cont.

104 *Joyful News,* 28 January 1954.
105 *Minutes* of the Cliff College Committee, 2 October 1953.
106 *Minutes* of the Cliff College Committee, 24 June 1955.
107 *Cliff Witness*, March 1968.
108 'New Tutor's House, Proposal 1967', file in Principal's safe.
109 *Cliff Witness,* Autumn 1984.

CHAPTER 10

The Beauty of Holiness

It is indisputably the case that holiness has been one of the key charisms of Cliff College. The considerable number of books written by Principals and other members of staff are testimony to that. The College evangelists considered holiness and evangelism connected because those who were interested in holiness would be the first to want to share the good news with others. The teaching of the doctrine has not always, curiously, been harmonious within the College, but at its best has offered a clear rendition of the Wesleyan hope for sanctification. The College's motto, a confident declaration of the wholeness of redemption of God in Christ, is 'Christ for All – All for Christ'. It is a combination of Arminian lavish grace, Christ died for All, and also an enthusiastic Wesleyan call that Christians should give their All for Christ. There is not room in this chapter to explore the doctrine fully, and it deserves further research, if we are to discover a relevant restatement of the doctrine in the twenty-first century.[1]

One of the issues in dealing generally with the literature on holiness is that of terminology. 'Perfection', 'Christian Perfection', 'Second Blessing', are all terms which have been used. Wesley, in formulating the doctrine for the people called Methodist wrestled with the terms but 'Christian perfection' was not one of his choices. 'I have no particular fondness for the term,' he explained to Dr Dodd, 'it is my opponents who thrust it upon me continually, and ask me what I mean by it.'[2] He used and defended the term 'perfection' because it was a biblical word and concept.[3]

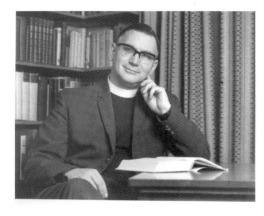

*Dr Arthur
Skevington Wood*

The theology of holiness owes so much to Wesley, therefore it is vital we consider his teaching. Dr Arthur Skevington Wood's legacy was that he helped people to gain a clear understanding of Wesley's teaching on holiness. He wrote a classic book about John Wesley, *The Burning Heart*[4], and gave an inaugural lecture to the Wesley Fellowship in 1985 entitled 'Love Excluding Sin'. Dr Wood had retired as Principal of Cliff College in 1983, and the lecture is the considered reflection on Wesleyan holiness teaching by a life-long Wesley scholar. Arthur Wood identified Wesley's sermon on the 'The Scripture Way of Salvation' (1765) as a key text in the exposition of Wesley's doctrine: 'He spoke of entire sanctification, of expressions like "full salvation" and "perfection" as used in the letter to the Hebrews. "But what is perfection? The word has various senses: here it means perfect love. It is love excluding sin; love filling the heart, taking up the whole capacity of the same."'[5] Wood makes the point that the same emphasis is given in a letter to Walter Churchey in 1771: 'Entire sanctification, or Christian perfection, is neither more nor less than pure love – love expelling sin and governing both the heart and life of a child of God. The Refiner's fire purges out all that is contrary to love, and that many times by a pleasing smart. Leave all this to Him that does all things well and that loves you better than you do yourself.'[6]

The doctrine was discussed at the first Methodist Conference in 1744 where the question was raised, 'What is implied in being a perfect Christian?'[7] The answer given was, 'The loving the Lord our God with all our heart, and with all our mind, and soul, and strength (Deut, 6:5; 30:6; Ezek 36: 25-9)'.[8] In a letter to Hannah Ball, the pioneer of Methodist Sunday Schools, Wesley wrote, 'All that is necessarily implied therein (i.e. in Christian Perfection), is humble, gentle, patient love, love regulating all the tempers and governing all the words and actions.'[9]

The Jackson Portrait of John Wesley watches over the Principal's study

Dr Wood's conclusion was that the terms to be employed in relation to Christian Perfection or Holiness, if we are to follow Wesley are '"Love" – "pure love" – "love expelling sin" – "perfect love": these were the descriptions which Wesley employed to express the heart of what he meant.'[10]

Arthur Wood gave interesting advice to those arguing about the eradication of sin. 'Whether sin is suspended or extinguished Wesley refused to dispute. He told Joseph Benson that he used the word "destroyed" because Paul does: "suspended" he could not find in his Bible. He preferred to regard sin as excluded or expelled by love. It was a matter of displacement. Love and sin cannot live together. There is no room for both.'[11] It is clear that Wesley's doctrine expressed the optimism of grace, teaching deliverance from inward as well as outward sin: 'It undoubtedly implies salvation from all sin, inward and outward, into all holiness.'[12] Arthur Wood concludes that 'Wesley's outlook was existential. His was the theology of the present moment. In this moment the believer may be free from sin. That does not guarantee even the next moment. But at least this moment may be sinless; and from the angle of God's enabling grace, if this moment, why not the next and indeed every moment?' The dilemma of being on the one hand delivered from sin, and on the other with sin ever present, is expressed by Wesley using metaphors from Paul: 'a man may have the Spirit of God dwelling in him, and may "walk after the Spirit", though he still feels "the flesh lusting against the Spirit."'[13]

Wesley considered the question of whether sanctification or holiness occurs suddenly in a crisis experience or as a maturing process. In a letter to his brother Charles he wrote, 'Go on, in your way, what God has peculiarly called you to ... Press the *instantaneous* blessing: then I shall have more time for my peculiar calling, enforcing the *gradual* work.'[14] Wesley recognised that the issue created tensions between his preachers and wrote quite candidly to them, 'The point is not determined, at least not in express terms, in any part of the oracles of God. Every man therefore may abound in his own sense, provided he will allow the same liberty to his neighbour; provided he will not be angry at those who differ from his opinion, nor entertain hard thoughts concerning them...Be the change instantaneous or gradual, see that you never rest till it is wrought in your own soul, if you desire to dwell with God in glory.'[15] In the process of sanctification Wesley referred to the crisis in a number of ways: a 'second change', 'farther change', 'blessed change', 'the instantaneous blessing', 'the second awakening', 'second work of grace', 'second blessing', and 'the second blessing'.[16] This use of language regarding holiness would become controversial in Methodism and at Cliff.

Dr Wood had come to the conclusion that holiness was primarily a process. He explained his reasoning with clear awareness of Wesley's teaching: 'The verbs in his description of the Christian's life are all in the present continuous tense. "God is continually breathing, as it were, upon the soul, and his soul is breathing into God. Grace is descending into his heart; and prayer and praise ascending to heaven; and by this intercourse between God and man, this fellowship with the Father and the Son, as by a kind of spiritual respiration, the life of God in the soul is sustained; and the child of God grows up, till he comes to the "full measure of the stature of Christ". Elsewhere Wesley speaks about the continual inspiration of the Spirit filling the heart with love like a well of water springing up into everlasting life.'[17]

There is no doubt that Wesley taught that 'perfection was the natural consequence of the total process of salvation, and he saw it as God's special gift to the Methodist people.'[18] This view has been taken up as one of the charisms of Cliff College. It relates to the conversion of a person as well as their continuing discipleship. In a nutshell, conversion may be considered as the moment when the love of God entered a person; sanctification as the process in which the love of God filled that person; holiness as the continuing experience of being filled by God's love "to the exclusion of Sin". Holiness in this understanding is not earned, but is the gift of God imparted to the Christian and gives rise to a lifestyle of total devotion and commitment to the Lord Jesus Christ. The words of Paul as translated by J.B. Phillips catch the implications of this holiness theology, 'Don't let the world around you squeeze you into its own mould, but let God re-mould your minds from within, so that you may prove in practice that the plan of God for you is good, meets all His demands and moves towards the goal of true maturity' (Romans 12:2-3).

The Cliff tradition of holiness teaching begins with Thomas Champness. During the twenty years he published the *Joyful News* and proclaimed his views on holiness, both Cook and Chadwick were preaching, teaching and writing on the subject. A summary of their teaching will give an assessment of their beliefs. Champness was a down-to-earth preacher and teacher, and in *Plain Talks on Christian Perfection*[19] he set out his views in which perfection is described as growth in sanctification. He cautioned against impatience: 'perfection is not a question of a moment. It is growth, not a leap'.[20] He illustrated his approach by reference to a photograph and its likeness to the real person; as the Christian grows in sanctification so they become more like the real thing, Christ. The call to perfection, he wrote, is to be like Christ: 'What is needed, is a Christianity that is Christlike ...(that) is Christian Perfection.'[21] The pattern he recommended in moving towards perfection is one of commitment, dedicated service, a consecrated life. 'If we follow the pattern the Lord Jesus left us we shall find that Perfection will become an accomplished fact.'[22] Champness believed that after conversion the Christian disciple should, though not all did, seek a deepening sanctification. His teaching in this respect was not dissimilar from the 'Keswick' teaching which was emerging at this time. Champness did not agree with Cook about regarding the eradication of sin which he thought owed more to the hymns of Charles Wesley than the Bible.[23] Champness maintained that such expressions as the eradication of 'the root of sin' do not occur in the scriptures and he thought they led to misconception.[24]

Thomas Cook, on the other hand, was much more deliberately Wesleyan, but he had a romantic view of biblical exposition. Vallance Cook, his brother, indicates that Thomas yearned for holiness from the beginning of his Christian experience. 'He determined, cost what it might, he would not only be saved, but he would be saved to the uttermost'.[25] Cook focussed his search on biblical texts which in turn determined his theology of holiness: "I will sprinkle clean water upon you, and ye shall be clean: from all your filthiness, and from all your idols, will I cleanse you. A new heart also will I give you, and a new spirit will I put within you: and I will take away the stony heart out of your flesh, and I will give you a heart of flesh." (Ezekiel 36:25-26); "Wherefore also He is able to save to the uttermost them that draw near to God through Him, seeing He ever liveth to make intercession for them." (Hebrews 7:25); "If we walk in the light, as He is in the light, we have fellowship one with another, and the blood of Jesus His Son cleanseth us from all sin" (1 John 1:7).

Cook came to the view that God's offer of salvation involved both forgiveness leading to conversion, and cleansing which imparted holiness. This was not a shadowy ideal but could be a living experience, and Joshua Dawson encouraged him. And so it was that three years after his conversion, after struggling and striving, that he accepted 'by simple faith' that God wished him to be holy: 'at last, by a simple effort of faith, deliverance came, the last enemy was cast out, sin's stain was cleansed away, and great peace filled his soul.'[26] What he had experienced, he preached.

An example is his exposition of 1 John 1:7, 'The Blood of Jesus His Son cleanses us from all sin'. Cook gave an analysis of what he called the 'twofold character' of sin in a sermon published under the title *Entire Cleansing*;[27] Smart included it in his book about Cook's early ministry. The distinction Cook pressed is that 'we must discriminate between guilt and depravity...sin committed is the transgression of the law, but depravity is in-bred, inherited.' In a somewhat romantic illustration he explained his point; 'A mother puts upon her child a clean pinafore, and says; "now this is not to be soiled". But the child disobeys. She may forgive the child for her disobedience, but she cannot forgive the pinafore clean; she must wash it. So God may forgive the wrong that we do, but He cannot

Thomas Cook pictured in 1904

forgive a depraved heart. Heart-sin must be cleansed away, and it is to this cleansing the text refers – "The blood of Jesus Christ, His Son cleanseth us from all sin"'.[28] He built an argument in the sermon that not only can God cleanse from all unrighteousness, but also impart entire cleansing: 'the heart is cleansed by the Holy Spirit taking full possession, and it is only kept clean by His remaining... We preach, therefore, a moment by moment salvation, maintained by a perpetual faith in the cleansing blood.'[29] This is the eradication theory in which not only is the Christian strengthened to resist sin, but the root of sin is taken out. It is true that Cook considered that temptation remained possible and will come, but his concept of entire cleansing is predicated on the belief that such temptation will be resisted because the experience of 'blessed assurance' is lived in a continuing way.

Since Cook focussed on 1 John 1:9, we should consider the meaning of the text. The letter of John does appear to argue that the Christian does not and cannot sin. However there are two kinds of 'perfectionism'; one John condemned as heretical, as in 1:8, 'If we say we have no sin we deceive ourselves and the truth is not in us', and 1:10, 'If we say we have not sinned, we make him a liar and his word is not in us.' The other kind of perfectionism he viewed as orthodox as in 3:6, 'No-one who abides in him sins.' It may be that the apparent paradox is understood by the more practical approach of 2:1, 'I am writing these things to you so that you may not sin. But if anyone does sin we have an advocate with the Father, Jesus Christ the righteous.' That is, John makes a call for righteous living, but acknowledges that Christians may not always live such a righteous life.

The precise text Cook used is 1:9, 'If we confess our sins, he who is faithful and just will forgive our sins and cleanse us from all unrighteousness.' It is perfectly true that John moves the argument along in the sentence. When we acknowledge our sin, God will forgive and καθαρίση ἡμας πω πασης αδικίας, 'purify us from all unrighteousness'. It is the death of Jesus (1:7) which makes the cleansing, or purification possible, but it relies upon the acknowledgement of sin which inevitably results in God's forgiving and purifying response. What is cleansed is αδικία meaning 'unrighteousness', the opposite of the nature of a holy God who is both righteous (δικίαος) and faithful (1:9, though often translated in English as 'faithful and just'). The Greek αδικίας will not bear the translation 'depravity'.[30] There is a Greek word which carries that meaning, ασωτία, which means an 'abandoned dissolute life' and which might be translated 'depravity', as in Ephesians 5:18, 'Do not get drunk with wine, for that is (ασωτία) debauchery; but be filled with the Spirit.' The Greek καθαρίζω, normally translated 'purify', may mean 'the removal of sinful desire in general as well as the guilt attaching to actual sins'.[31] Consequently it would appear that the verse does speak of a twofold process, but it is a cleansing from the effects of sin rather than eradication of sin. However in questioning Cook's exposition I do not wish to diminish the influence of his writing and preaching on the development of holiness teaching in the late nineteenth century.

Cook recognised that the work of God did not make people 'faultless', but the crucial thing was our intention: 'Perfect love is not always a successful achievement; it is a childlike purpose, *a sincere aim in all we do to please God.*'[32] Whilst for Cook, holiness did not mean the absence of temptation,[33] he did challenge the view that sin was inevitable for the Christian.[34] However Cook maintained there was a second definite experience that should be sought and claimed, and which imparted entire sanctification.[35] He then maintained that purity, when achieved, was not the goal of Christian devotion but the beginning of a new maturing process, 'a new starting point on a higher plane.'[36] In that sense he agreed with others that 'Holiness is both a *crisis* and a *process*'.[37] He interpreted cleansing as a continuing process, 'We teach, therefore, not a *state of purity*, but a *maintained condition of purity*, a moment-by-moment salvation consequent upon a moment-by-moment obedience and trust.'[38] It is in this understanding that Cook is revealed as having a conditional theory of the eradication of sin, that is, it is dependent on the faith of the disciple. Therefore the Christian should be a 'God-possessed Soul',[39] seeking the love and grace of God which is '*bestowed*, imparted, given to us as a gift'.[40] This experience would bring the Christian to evangelical perfection, by which he meant those who are 'fully fitted and equipped for the service of God.'[41] This experience would then be in the fullness of the Spirit, a conscious walking with God, an experience of intense spirituality (which he sometimes called Beulah land[42]), a serenity and peace in the midst of life which he referred to as 'soul rest'.[43] Cook maintained throughout that this is a blessing that all Christians may and should enjoy, and which would give power for service. The theme of consecration is present but what makes his view of holiness distinctively Wesleyan is the insistence that perfection is attainable and sin may be eradicated. His book concludes with advice to enable those who know the experience of perfect love to maintain that state; which is characterised by a desire for greater illumination, a life of simple trust, times of prayer and Bible meditation, active Christian work, and always a desire for more.[44]

Henry T. Smart acknowledges that between his two friends there were differences; Champness taught that perfection was a matter of spiritual growth, rather than the eradication theory. 'Mr Cook's view was that sin is a sort of microbe, and that it is to be destroyed by the indwelling of the Spirit of God. Mr Champness could not accept this 'microbe theory'.[45] When confronted by the Wesleyan holiness hymns which speak about the 'root of sin' Champness simply indicated they were not biblical and 'after all the Methodist Hymn Book is not of equal authority with the Word of God.'[46]

At the same time as Champness, Cook and other Wesleyans were teaching and preaching holiness to such considerable effect in Britain, there were other strands of holiness teaching developing. The American glass manufacturer Robert Pearsall Smith gave the holiness movement a new impetus in the United States.[47] Pearsall Smith came to Europe to recuperate from a serious illness. He conducted holiness conferences in London during the Moody campaigns of 1874–75. Between 29 August and 7 September 1874 he joined about 1,000 men and women of the Evangelical Alliance for the 'Oxford Days of Blessing' where he and his wife, Hannah Whitall Smith were invited to speak. Their emphasis was that in the life of faith Christians were challenged to 'maintain close fellowship with God and to gain victory over all known sin.'[48] The Smiths had been influenced by Phoebe Palmer who with her sister held 'Tuesday Meetings for the Promotion of Holiness' in their home in New York. They edited *A Guide to Holiness* and their teaching shaped holiness thinking in America and Britain. Palmer popularised what she called 'altar theology' which emphasised human consecration. She urged people who wanted to be sanctified to lay their desire for holiness on the 'altar' and trust God to deliver entire sanctification. The hymn 'When we walk with the Lord' comes from this period. The American preachers, of whom Hannah Whitall Smith was reckoned the best, met with a ready audience. For years previously William Pennefather,[49] who wrote the hymn 'Jesus stand among us', held the Mildmay Conference with the express purpose of spreading the holiness movement. Grattan Guinness was also a speaker at these conferences and it seems possible that Ann Elizabeth Hulme attended. The longing for holiness and exploration of its teaching led in 1875 to the Brighton Conference 29 May - 7 June.[50] Out of these meetings came the Keswick Convention under the direction of Harford-Battersby, Evan Hopkins and later, F.B. Meyer. They stressed 'holiness through faith' and the offering of life in dedicated service.[51]

The Keswick Convention set a different course from the Wesleyan theology of Champness and Cook. 'Keswick denied traditional Wesleyan convictions that Christians could experience entire sanctification, teaching instead that through the entry into 'the rest of faith' sin was not eradicated but "perpetually counteracted"'.[52] Keswick denied the idea that holiness was attainable through the efforts of Christian service. 'Evangelical conceptions of holy living achieved through sustained struggle were replaced, in the spirituality purveyed at Keswick, by the idea that sanctification, like justification, was attained through faith, not works.'[53]

The call to holiness at Keswick had in the 1870's been described as the 'higher Christian Life' but in the early twentieth century the heart of the message was described as the 'normal Christian Life'.[54] This Bebbington describes as the democratisation of holiness teaching.[55] The Convention still maintained the theme of holiness by faith and laid a stress on the believer's consecration to Christ.

Chadwick took the view that the 'second blessing' should be preached, and saw that as the most important element of the training at Cliff. 'Learning is not the chief thing ... scarcely a man comes that does not get his Pentecost'.[56] Part of the hagiography surrounding Chadwick relates to an event in October 1920, which occurred after Chadwick had preached about holiness at a Class Meeting. The *Joyful News* records: 'There should have been an algebra class after supper, but the men asked for a prayer meeting instead. What a meeting it was! It lasted until long after the ordinary bedtime. We studied the Bible passages relating to the gift of the Holy Spirit; we sang, then we prayed. All over the room men were pleading that they might have the assurance of full salvation ... Suddenly one of the brethren jumped up to shout Hallelujah! Glory had come into his own soul. At the top of our voices we sang, "'Tis done the great transaction's done"... soon, in every part of the room, men were praising God that they had entered into the blessed experience. We were all aflame.'[57]

Samuel Chadwick whilst Minister in Leeds

Chadwick set out his views on holiness in the *Joyful News* and shortly after his death a selection of these, edited by Joe Brice, was produced: *The Call to Christian Perfection*.[58] This collection of articles is like the man: clear scholarship, straightforward and blunt. He admitted that 'It is easier to prove the doctrine of a Second Blessing from John Wesley, than from the Bible.'[59] Like Cook he made a call for Christians to follow the scriptural pattern and to seek perfection, holiness and sanctification. He also agreed with him that Christ came to save from sin, and that 'Christ redeems, that He may cleanse and restore.'[60]

His view relating to the theory of eradication changed. On the one hand Chadwick criticised the holiness teaching of Count

Zinzendorf, who began the Moravian movement and was influential on Wesley's thinking. He maintained Zinzendorf was 'utterly without warrant'[61] when he had taught that 'all true believers are not only saved from the *dominion* of sin, but from the being of inward as well as outward sin, so that it no longer remained in them'.[62] On the other, in a thinly disguised attack on the Keswick movement he criticised the teaching of 'Christian Perfection as "metaphysically attainable"', and yet which denied 'the fact of actual attainment … but regards it as an imputed perfection and not an actual possession. In this teaching inbred sin is not eradicated but repressed, and holiness is not imparted but imputed.'[63] Dunning reports that Chadwick contrasted Keswick with the Southport Convention, which stood 'for the doctrine of eradication of inbred sin and imparted holiness, as against the Keswick teaching of repression of sin and imputed holiness.'[64] In a passage which was highly critical of Keswick Chadwick accused Keswick speakers of proclaiming a theological fiction, 'a process of sheer make believe, by which God shuts his eyes to our real state and agrees to accept a fiction for a fact.'[65] Some years later he was more accommodating and described the differences between Keswick and Southport as being, 'different interpretations of the same experience'.[66] However he contrasted the Methodist interpretation of eradication with the Calvinist under-standing of counteraction (which is how he saw Keswick), but concludes: 'There is a very real difference, but there is no essential antag-onism'.[67] All of these criticisms appear in published articles but his preaching highlighted the positive. The Chadwick sermon collection in the College archives has three series of sermons preached on holiness. In these there is neither criticism of Keswick theology nor a detailed exposition of the eradication of sin. Throughout, however, there is a powerful call for inward cleansing and holy living.[68]

Perfection, according to Chadwick, should be sought as a definite experience, a second blessing, and maintained by prayer and devotion. However, he did not commend people to testify to the experience,[69] even though 'It has been the chief glory of Methodism to proclaim this experience as the duty and privilege of all.'[70]

One additional emphasis which he brought to holiness teaching related to καθαρίζω as translated 'fitness' or readiness for service.[71] He explored the uses of καθαρίζω in the New Testament: the mending of nets to make fit for use (Matthew 4:21), the praise which is set in order so that the discordant notes are eliminated in the harmony (Matthew 21:16), the restored company of believers who are of the same mind and judgement (1 Corinthians 1:10), to supply or complete what is lacking (1 Thessalonians 3:10) and the bringing into being of the physical world, which was pronounced 'good' (Hebrews 11:3).

There are some aspects of Chadwick's life which are curious, such as his writing about 'sleepy hollow'. Another relates to his thinking about holiness. On the door of the study and written on the front page of his diary each year was the word *Ataraxia*. He explained this in some detail in an article now only found in his papers. *Ataraxia* is the state of '"undisturbedness", i.e. serenity or restfulness of spirit'.[72] The basis of this peace is a confidence in God. He described the experience in a way which echoes the Keswick teaching about 'resting in God', as 'the untroubled heart of John 14, the perfect peace of Isaiah 26:3, and the unafraidness of Psalm 112:7, and the care-free peace and joy of Philippians 4:6 and 7.'[73]

Chadwick, for all his call for holiness, was aware of the limitations; there is no romanticised theology here. He made clear that perfection 'does not lift a man above the possibility of temptation … neither can it bring immunity from frailty, limitation, and ignorance, for humanity is sanctified without being absorbed. It cannot be final for it is still probationary … It is a restoration of relationship, a renewal of nature, a sufficiency of grace that makes it possible to live in all things according to the will of God.'[74]

Cliff College and the *Joyful News* shared the promotion of holiness teaching in Methodism along with the Southport Convention. Champness and Cook were speakers at the first Convention in 1885 and Cook, Chadwick, Broadbelt and Baines Atkinson were all Presidents of the Convention. Southport had a significant impact on Wesleyan teaching in Methodism and beyond. By 1893 the Southport Convention has achieved 'a Connexional importance … from the fact that a large number of people, Methodist and others, have been able to date from the meetings of this Convention clearer views of holiness and a new inspiration for the attainment of the blessing.'[75]

J. Baines Atkinson

The Convention was supported locally by the Rev W.H. Tindall, Superintendent of the Southport Circuit, who had written the article 'Try Women' for the *Joyful News* and was the first Convention President. The speakers were many of the famous preachers of the day, Dr T. Bowman Stephenson, Dr W. Fiddian Moulton, and John Hornabrook who for years was the Secretary of Conference for the Wesleyans. Along with these also came some of the finest Central Hall preachers including Scott Lidgett and Luke Wiseman.

The Convention was not universally welcomed. The *Methodist Times* indicated that many ministers were very concerned when one of their members had received 'the blessing' at the Convention, and asked why of all the people in Methodism these seemed the 'most difficult, awkward, cantankerous, obscurantist and touchy people.'[76] Nevertheless, the Convention had a close relationship with Cliff, and for many years the Cliff Trekkers visited Southport to preach in the open air and help at the Convention, a practice begun with students from the *Joyful News* Home. The holiness meetings attracted many hundreds each year to its Convention site in Mornington Road, Southport, where more recently the title has changed to 'Summer Fire' and continues the Wesleyan influence. Holiness teaching has not been prominent in Methodism for decades, and in this regard both Southport and the Cliff holiness tradition, 'conveyed a picture of a lonely school of prophets at odds with Methodist progress-iveness.'[77]

J. Baines Atkinson was closely associated with the Southport Holiness Convention, being its President for 14 years. His considered reflections on holiness were published in the book *The Beauty of Holiness* in which Atkinson brought together the best from his predecessors, without their romanticism or confusion.[78] His is the finest of the extended works from Cliff writers and the book deserves to be widely available today. His work was the forerunner of Arthur Wood's shorter and influential article, 'Love Excluding Sin'. Atkinson began consideration of holiness with an exploration of the holiness of God,[79] then of biblical terms which suggest that holiness is a condition which

The 'Joyful News' Prayer Meeting c. 1965

Christians may enjoy. He has many allusions to Wesley and is deeply Wesleyan especially in his insistence that holiness is a gift of God and is attainable now.[80] He puts forward a different element from either Cook or Chadwick, in his insistence that holiness has a 'social, ethical and practical ideal'.[81] Atkinson does not go so far as to suggest that holiness impinges on the social or political theory, and like Wesley and Chadwick he sees the beneficial effects to society emerging from the changed lives of individuals. 'The environment or atmosphere of holiness in Scripture is always communal. It deals with the individual, but it is related to society'.[82] The penultimate chapter of the book is concerned with character, or 'fruits of Perfect Love or Entire Sanctification.'[83]

College
Chapel

Tom Meadley towards the end of his time as Principal reflected on the major issues confronting the future of the College. He set out in a paper the challenges to Cliff as being, primarily, that it should 'demonstrate that it can adapt itself to change of unprecedented speed and size without losing continuity with its organic origin.'[84] Meadley had found at the College a definition and style of holiness preaching with which he was clearly uncomfortable, and dealing with that he considered 'the profoundest challenge'. He set out the issue as he saw it: 'The Wesley doctrine of Entire Sanctification, which has largely disappeared from Methodism, has been preserved at Cliff, expressed in terms of Second Blessing, a casual phrase of Wesley's which has become a technical term. The idea is that the root of sin can be removed completely in a moment of time, and this experience can be known and testified to as a continuous blessing of perfect fellowship with God and prefect love towards our fellowmen.'[85] He was conscious in his paper that to question this interpretation of the doctrine was an emotive issue at the time, and he referred to the 'violence with which any suspected deviation is regarded…(by the) … charmed circle.'[86]

Meadley called for a more open discussion; 'The truth of this matter needs much more sober and searching investigation, and a willingness to tolerate varieties of interpretation. The whole separatist supposition that it is possible to cut oneself off from the actual world of events and responsibilities, is alien to the Gospel and fatal in its spiritual consequences, but so also is the almost complete absorption in the spirit of the

The Rev Tom Meadley

world of the average church life. The challenge to full commitment, and a total work of grace in the soul is one of the requirements of effective mission, but how to state this truth and exhibit it in relevant terms is one of the supreme challenges to Cliff.'[87] My view is that this remains one of the greatest challenges for the contemporary Church but it is no longer a divisive issue in the College.

In 1969 Tom Meadley published his own thinking about holiness in *Top Level Talks: The Christian Summit Meeting*, in which with characteristic style he gave the doctrine a restatement.[88] Meadley had the knack of splicing together Wesleyan doctrine, contemporary biblical exposition, and at the same time helping the reader to consider ideas in a new and creative way. The title of the book came from a statement by Winston Churchill calling the leaders of the world's most powerful nations to have an unfettered and wide ranging 'conference on the highest level'.[89] In the book he deplored the tensions of his day. 'A whole set of associations has gathered round the subject and rendered it for many either taboo or touchy.'[90] Second blessing theology and preaching had clearly divided people in the College. When Cliff preachers latched onto the language of second blessing as a necessary second experience prior to Christian maturity, and quoted Wesley, they did not, according to Meadley, take hold of the breadth of Wesleyan theology at this point. Meadley referred critically to the way Cliff College evangelists expressed Wesley's doctrine 'in terms of the Second Blessing',[91] and it would appear that Meadley had been wounded by criticism. 'Once the challenge is raised, anyone's spiritual integrity and foundation is involved one way or another, for or against, so that calm investigation and impartial discussion are hard to achieve.'[92] What is achieved in the book is a refreshing explanation of a practical holiness. Meadley wants a holiness which is 'not righteous overmuch',[93] he cautions against 'finicky censoriousness',[94] 'doctrinal fastidiousness',[95] 'morbid introspection' and using the doctrine as a 'tranquillizer', a kind of comforting providential coma, to avoid the hard realities of Christian discipleship in the modern world.[96]

Meadley contends for a holiness which affects every part of life and the church liturgy. He calls for an outworking which can be visible in the Christian's life, which he refers to as the 'Holiness highway code',[97] and for a quality of love which is mature and enduring in the midst of difficulty, a 'weather proof love'.[98] The doctrine is firmly placed as the key element of the evangelical revival which led to 'most of the great humanitarian reform movements of the nineteenth century in Great Britain.'[99] He quotes Wesley with evident agreement, 'the Bible knows no holiness but social holiness'.[100] Moreover, he pleads that within the Church holiness doctrine should not be individualised, 'true sanctification is corporate', it is for the benefit of the whole community of God's people.[101]

The dispute about the nature of a second definite experience remained unresolved and was at times an unhelpful distinction among some students and staff. However, resolution came when the Charismatic Movement began to have an effect on the whole British Church in the late 1960's and influenced Cliff College. The language of 'second blessing' was overtaken by a phraseology of 'Baptism in the Spirit'. The charismatic theologian Thomas Smail, and Bill Davies as Principal, both prompted the view that baptism could mean either 'initiation' or 'a flooding'. Thus, in the sense of 'initiation', people are baptised in the Holy Spirit at conversion (new birth) but in the sense of 'being flooded by' believers are baptised in the Holy Spirit when they are filled with the Spirit. This view sees the phrase 'baptism in the Holy Spirit' referring to 'both conversion and fullness, which are theologically <u>one</u> but in <u>experience</u> may be separate.'[102] The phrase 'second blessing' disappeared entirely and instead students and staff sought and preached the experience of 'being filled with the Spirit', being 'open' to the Spirit.

One of the unique expressions of Cliff College holiness teaching is

A College Class Meeting

the insistence that holiness and evangelism are related. Joe Brice captured the assumptions of the Chadwick era in an article entitled 'Evangelism and Holiness', where he stressed that evangelists are 'created in holiness, sustained by holiness and live to spread holiness'.[103] The main assumption is that, 'every holiness preacher in earnest is an evangelist, and every evangelist in earnest is a preacher of holiness'. At conversion and entire sanctification the preacher and believer are open to the grace of God and the desire to be committed to him. Brice, who was no mean scholar, prized the experience of holiness for the evangelist above all other things. The evangelist 'needn't be academic – but he *must be saintly*.'[104] Brice understood the experience of holiness to be one which propels people to share their faith, and he calls upon the Methodist church to renew its interest in Wesleyan holiness teaching as well as evangelism.

It is this same call which I have heard in the preaching of Donald English, Arthur Wood, Bill Davies, and D. Paul C. Smith. Holiness is an experience of a God who is holy, it is illuminating and life transforming, but it is not to be kept a secret. It is this kind of winsome Christian experience which has always been present in the Cliff ethos.

1   The Rev C. Paul D. Smith has begun this process in a lecture given as one of the Cliff College Centenary lectures.
2   John Telford (ed.), *The Letters of the Rev John Wesley, Standard Edition* (London, Epworth Press, 8 Vols. 1931) (*Letters*), 3.167.
3   *Letters,* 4.212.
4   Arthur Skevington Wood, *The Burning Heart* (Calver: Cliff College Publishing, 1999).
5   Arthur Skevington Wood, 'Love Excluding Sin' in Mellor and Taylor, *Travelling Man* (Calver: Cliff College Publishing, 1994), p.66, quoting, *Sermons*, 2.448.
6   *Letters,* 5.223.
7   Thomas Jackson (ed.), *The Works of John Wesley,* third Edition (London: John Mason, 14 Vols. 1829-31, (Works), 8.65.
8   *Works*, 8.65.
9   *Letters*, 6.266.
10 Wood, 'Love Excluding Sin', p.67.
11 Wood, 'Love Excluding Sin', p.75.
12 *Letters,* 2.213.

cont.

13   Edward H. Sugden (ed.), *The Standard Sermons of John Wesley* (London: Epworth Press, 1921, (Sermons), 2.373-374.

14   *Letters,* 5.16.

15   *Works,* 6.490.

16   *Letters*, 5.215; *Sermons*, 2.391; *Sermons* 2.395; *Works*, 8.329; *Letters*, 5.16; *Letters*, 6.144-5; *Letters*, 4.133; *Letters*, 3.212, 5.315; *Letters*, 6.116.

17   Wood, 'Love Excluding Sin', p.76 quoting *Sermons*, 2.234.

18   Gerald R. Cragg, *Reason and Authority in the Eighteenth Century* (Cambridge: Cambridge University Press, 1964), pp.168-9.

19   Thomas Champness, *Plain Talks on Christian Perfection* (Rochdale: Joyful News Book Depot, 1897)

20   Champness, *Perfection*. The pages of this short book are not numbered. The sentences appear in a section entitled 'Perfection a matter of Growth'.

21   Champness, *Perfection,* in the section, 'What is meant by Perfection'.

22   Champness, *Perfection*, in the section, 'A lofty Ideal'.

23   Henry Smart, *The Life Of Thomas Cook* (London: Charles H. Kelly, 1913), p.281.

24   Smart, *The Life of Thomas Cook,* p.281.

25   Vallance Cook, p.45.

26   Vallance Cook, p.46.

27   Henry T. Smart, *Thomas Cook's Early Ministry* (London: Charles Kelly, 1892) where the sermon is reproduced in full, pp.134-151. *Entire Cleansing* was more recently republished, undated, by the Revival Movement, N. Ireland.

28   Smart, *Thomas Cook's Early Ministry,* p.135.

29   Smart, *Thomas Cook's Early Ministry,* p.144-145.

30   Thayer, *Greek-English Lexicon of the New Testament* (Edinburgh: T&T Clark, 1961edition), p.12 and see p.138.

31   Stephen Smalley, *1,2,3 John – Word Biblical Commentary* (Dallas: Word, 1984) p.32.

32   Thomas Cook, *New Testament Holiness*, p.10. The italics are his.

33   Cook, *Holiness*, pp.12-15.

34   Cook, *Holiness*, p.16.

35   Cook, *Holiness*, pp.22-32.

36   Cook, *Holiness*, p.37.

37   Cook, *Holiness*, p.43. The italics are his.

38   Cook, *Holiness*, p.43. Again the italics are his.

39   Cook, *Holiness*, p.46.

40   Cook, *Holiness*, p.52.

41   Cook, *Holiness*, p.60.

42   Cook, *Holiness*, pp.82-87.

43   Cook, *Holiness*, pp.88-95.

44   Cook, *Holiness*, pp.139-146.

45   H.T. Smart, *The Life,* p.281.

46   Ibid.

47   Paulus Scharpff, *History of Evangelism* (Grand Rapids: Eerdmans, 1966) p.215.

48   Scharpff, p.215.

cont.

49 R. Braithwaite, *The Life and Letters of Rev William Pennefather* (London: 1878).

50 Orr, *Britain,* pp.218f.

51 Paulus Scharpff, p.197.

52 Ian Randall, *Evangelical Experiences* (Carlisle: Paternoster Press, 1999), p.14.

53 Ian Randall, *Evangelical Experiences*, p.14.

54 Ian Randall, *Evangelical Experiences*, p.27.

55 David Bebbington, *Evangelicalism,* p.173.

56 *Joyful News,* 3 June 1920.

57 *Joyful News,* 4 November 1920.

58 Samuel Chadwick, *The Call to Christian Perfection* (London: Epworth Press, 1936). Joe Brice had begun to edit the material prior to Chadwick's death. They were based on articles first published in the *Joyful News* 1912.

59 Chadwick, *Christian Perfection*, p.68.

60 Chadwick, *Christian Perfection*, p.71.

61 Chadwick, *Christian Perfection*, p.71.

62 Ibid.

63 Chadwick, *Christian Perfection*, p.75.

64 Dunning, *Samuel Chadwick,* p.148.

65 Chadwick, *Christian Perfection*, p.76.

66 *Joyful News,* 16 June 1932. Ian Randall suggests this softening of Chadwick's criticism came through contact with the Keswick movement, *Evangelical Experiences,* p.100.

67 *Joyful News,* 16 June 1932. He cannot resist the temptation however, to contrast the views of the two conventions and describe Keswick theology as absurd: 'the definitely and immediately attainable and the eternal approximation to the unrealisable'.

68 Cliff College Archives, E22. Handwritten notes from which he preached. 'Holiness Series I', given at the Southport Holiness Convention, June 1910. 'Holiness Series II', given at the Southport Holiness Convention 1911, 1913 and 1923, though the final sermon on the 'Whole Armour of God' was preached 29 times in that period and all noted on the flyleaf. 'Holiness Series III', given at the Southport Convention in 1914.

69 Chadwick, *Christian Perfection*, p.93.

70 Chadwick, *Christian Perfection*, p.77.

71 Chadwick, *Christian Perfection*, p.31.

72 Cliff College Archive, E21. Seven unnumbered volumes containing typed articles, lectures and sermons by Chadwick. This one entitled, '*Ataraxia*', p.2.

73 Ibid.

74 Chadwick, *Christian Perfection*, p.35.

75 A. Skevington Wood, *Let us Go On* (Ilkeston: Moorleys Print and Publishing, 1985), pp.15-16.

76 *Methodist Times,* 24 June 1926, p.10.

77 Ian Randall, *Evangelical Experiences,* p.81.

78 J. Baines Atkinson, *The Beauty of Holiness* (London: Epworth Press, 1953).

79 Atkinson, *Beauty of Holiness,* pp.1-32.

cont.

80   Atkinson, *Beauty of Holiness*, pp.77-93.
81   Atkinson, *Beauty of Holiness*, p.94.
82   Atkinson, *Beauty of Holiness*, p.103.
83   Atkinson, *Beauty of Holiness*, p.123.
84   Tom Meadley, 'The Challenge to Cliff College Today'. Archive document, which appears not to have been published. This paper, dated July 1964, came at the end of his time as Principal, and since it criticised the 'charmed circle' within the College may have been written for the Committee.
85   Tom Meadley, 'The Challenge to Cliff College Today', p.2.
86   Meadley, Ibid.
87   Meadley, Ibid.
88   T.D. Meadley, *Top Level Talks: The Christian Summit Meeting* (London: Epworth Press, 1969).
89   Meadley, *Top Level Talks*, p.x. Winston Churchill, House of Commons, 11 May 1953.
90   Meadley, *Top Level Talks*, p.2.
91   Meadley, 'The Challenge of Cliff College today', p.2.
92   Meadley, *Top Level Talks*, ibid.
93   Meadley, *Top Level Talks*, p.109.
94   Meadley, *Top Level Talks*, p.96.
95   Meadley, *Top Level Talks*, p.100.
96   Meadley, *Top Level Talks*, pp.98-99.
97   Meadley, *Top Level Talks*, p.184.
98   Meadley, *Top Level Talks*, p.187.
99   Meadley, *Top Level Talks*, p.106.
100 Meadley, *Top Level Talks*, p.107.
101 Meadley, *Top Level Talks*, pp.107-8.
102 Thomas Smail, *Reflected Glory* (London: Hodder and Stoughton, 1976), see chapter 6 'Birth and Baptism in the Spirit'. William R Davies, *Spirit without Measure* (London: Darton, Longman and Todd, 1996), pp.22-41, and his Christian Doctrine student handout, CD 13 'Sanctification and Power' 1983-1994.
103 *Joyful News,* 30 June 1932.
104 Ibid. Joe Brice undertook his ministerial training at Richmond College and gained a PhD at London University through a research dissertation, 'The Influence of Hume in British Theology' (undated). A copy is in the Cliff College archive library.

CHAPTER 11

Samuel Chadwick

Samuel Chadwick was born on 16 September 1860 at 8 Baldwin Street, Burnley, to a devout and humble couple. Within months, they had moved to 6 Back Hammerton Street, 'It would be difficult to imagine…anything more drab, prosaic, and uninteresting than our street. Its name was its only distinction, for it was named after the only distinguished man of letters Burnley has produced. There was not a blade of grass, a tree or a flower in our area. It hummed with the noise of factories from the morning until night. The only playground was the kerbstone.'[1]

Samuel Chadwick in 1909

Samuel's father worked in the mill at Burnley and was never in a position to earn more than two pounds a week.[2] Dunning's biography has many stories of Chadwick's childhood and upbringing because he clearly loved to portray himself as the man who had emerged from the terraced houses and back streets of Burnley.[3] Dunning reports intriguingly that 'His father was sincerely pious, though not aggressively religious. His mother was deeply religious, though not particularly pious.'[4] It is clear that the Christian faith was a significant part of his childhood and family life. His grandfather had been converted by one of Mr Wesley's preachers and devoutly led the Sunday early morning prayer meeting in Burnley.[5] In his childhood, the Christian faith was central, with the symbols of faith and desire for respectability. 'We had a mahogany chest in our Cottage home ... that was the sign of our respectability and proof of our piety. On the top stood a family Bible and a ponderous Life of Christ.'[6]

After the death of his father in 1909 he wrote, 'He was the kindest and most lovable man I have ever known but his eye was keen and his judgement just, though his heart was tender and his spirit kind. In him and Mother was a rare combination of gaiety and grace.'[7] He held his mother in high esteem and he wrote of her in a way which mirrored the manner in which he preached, 'She was intellectual without learning, regal without vanity, saintly without ritual, capable without fussiness, witty without venom, humorous without malice and merry without being frivolous ... She never kissed her children once they were weaned but no-one doubted her love. The discipline was stern but no-one knew it, for the home abounded in laughter and goodwill.'[8]

From the age of eight, Samuel went with his father to assist him in his work at the nearby Oak Mount cotton mill. He went 'as a half-timer to the mill when he was eight and at eleven finished his education (!) receiving no more teaching until, twelve years later, he went to Didsbury College as an accepted candidate for the ministry.'[9] The work in the mill was demanding and involved long hours, working from six in the morning until six at night, 'but by seven o'clock he was at his books, and for five hours struggled over grammar and arithmetic, geography, and history, theology and the Bible.'[10] There was at an early stage a conscious call to the ministry. His spiritual journey clearly began in the ethos of the home but it was at a Sunday School Anniversary in 1870, when he was aged ten, that Samuel determined he would serve Christ in the best way he could. At the age of fifteen he felt the call to ministry but it was when Josiah

Mee came to the Burnley Circuit that Chadwick was really encouraged to preach and to study. Josiah Mee was already a significant influence in the life of Champness and now in Chadwick he identified a young man with potential.[11] Wesleyan Methodist ministers moved every two or three years and Mee was succeeded by Dr Waddy Moss who was a 'giant in intellect, a prodigy in learning, and a master in exposition'.[12] Even allowing for Dunning's capacity for fulsome praise, clearly Waddy Moss was a significant help to the young preacher. The training was rigorous and at his oral examination at the Local Preachers' Meeting Chadwick was closely questioned for an hour and twenty minutes before being given, 'a hearty and unanimous vote'.[13] Dunning goes on to record that the next minister was not so well disposed to Chadwick and 'told the young preacher with brutal frankness that, years before, he had made up his mind that he would never open the door to the ministry to an uneducated man'.[14] However Josiah Mee, now Superintendent of the nearby Bacup Circuit, was instrumental in Chadwick becoming the lay Evangelist at Stacksteads, and so it was in 1881 that, at the age of twenty-one, the significant ministry of the young Samuel Chadwick began in this mill village at the edge of Bacup.

What actually happened at Stacksteads has become overlaid with hindsight and so Dunning speaks of it as a time of revival. What is interesting is that the young Samuel kept a *Journal* from the time he began his work at Stacksteads on 23 July 1881 until 28 April 1883.[15] The Journal, the only one he wrote, was clearly a way of recording his work and to be shown to the superintendent minister to confirm how he had spent his time. 'It does not go beyond the day when it ceased to be necessary'.[16] The first entry, in a copper-plate writing is:

Saturday, July 23rd

Arrived here to enter upon my new work at 12:5 a.m. Spent the aft.
with Mr Disley; & in the evening he kindly introduced me to about ½
doz. families connected with the place. At 7 we attended the Band-
meeting 12 present - good meeting.

After being at Stacksteads for two months he reflects on Saturday
the 17th September, in the following way:

During the past fortnight, I have been much encouraged with the
apparent success of the open air and cottage meetings. Many people
have come out from their houses and listened attentively to "words
whereby they may be saved" - The cottage (services) have been well
attended by those who do not generally attend such services – we
always get our places well-filled, and although we do not see
immediate results I am persuaded some good is being done by these
services. When I have visited amongst the neglecters of public
worship – I have – as a rule – been well and kindly received – several
have promised to come to chapel. Some I have seen there, others have
not yet redeemed their promise.

I am sorry to find a looseness among some of our tract distributors
about going regularly with their tracts, several have expressed their
sorrow that they don't come every week, for they always read them.
On the whole I think God's work is progressing at Stacksteads –
slowly but surely, God's Kingdom is extending in our midst. Let us
pray for a grand "reaping time" and according to our faith, it shall be
done onto us.[17]

As he spoke of this time some sixteen years later, Chadwick
recalled the time at Stacksteads:

It was a large chapel, comparatively new, in the midst of a crowded
population of quarrymen and factory workers. There I was a stranger,
without experience, faced with the problem how to get those godless
people inside the house of prayer. I was innocent enough to believe

that my sermons would do it. But, alas! I soon came to the end of my little stock and nothing happened. Eloquence and logic, however profound, make but little impression on pillars and pews. I became anxious and in my anxiety betook myself to prayer. Soon thirty or forty people signed a covenant to pray daily for a revival of God's work.[18]

Chadwick felt called to preach and 'prided himself on his sermons'[19] and spent many hours in their construction and in the search for illustrations. He had arrived in Stacksteads with fifteen sermons 'of which he was very proud, and he believed would bring a revival of religion'.[20] Fifteen years later he recalled how one Sunday evening the Rev J.D. Brash preached and gave a testimony that awakened his interest in the doctrine of Scriptural Holiness. 'But instead of seeking the blessing, I set myself to study the subject. Much reading, however, only led to confusion; and at last I turned away from all the other books on the subject to the Bible. For weeks I read nothing else.'[21] He had a deep spiritual struggle and a testing of motives, 'Some things that were precious to me had to be given up. Then finally the battle raged over my preaching. About three o'clock one Sunday morning my little pile of sermons was burnt, and I started afresh.'[22] With the sermons went his pride; if revival were to come to Stacksteads then it would be because of the work of God not his proficiency in preaching. 'That day seven people were converted: one for each of my barren preaching years.'[23]

It is impossible to identify this experience in the *Journal* though we do have the reflections noted above. Within a few days of arriving at Stacksteads, on Wednesday 27 July 1881, he records, 'Divine Service in the evening, Mr Brash preached a grand sermon. Text Rom 5:3-5. Had some conversation with F. Sutcliffe about preaching.'[24]   On Monday 15 August he reports, 'I have felt greater freedom and blessedness in my work today than usual.'[25]

Early on he discovered something which stayed with him throughout his ministry. He had no theory or policy for social or community betterment but he became convinced, through the experience at Stacksteads, that social ills and community needs would be met as people became converted. This was also why he was so involved in the Temperance movement. His reflections after nine months working at Stacksteads were written in his *Journal*, 'I was frequently told today that brawls and quarrels were everyday occurrences before we began to work or visit amongst them but now they never hear such a thing. Many who never entered a place of prayer have gone to their own Church and 2 or 3 have come to our own Chapel. Had a long and serious conversation with Mrs Sharpe about her soul. She was deeply impressed about 12 months ago with a message from her dying mother and the impression has never left her. She says her husband is not like the same man since we began to have our meetings at their house.'[26]

From time to time we catch real glimpses of northern life from his Journal, as on Saturday 10 March 1883, 'Funeral – Tea-party and Entertainment.' Often people in Lancashire referred to funeral arrangements and a meal afterwards, as a person being 'buried with a ham tea' sometimes foreshortened to being 'buried with ham'. In the humdrum life of the mill workers, no opportunity for entertainment or enjoyment was overlooked and if someone had lived a long life then, whilst the funeral service was solemn, afterwards there was an energetic wake. Some of the housing would be very inadequate. 'Was in a place today I've never seen before, There are a lot of cellars, down some steps above the chapel. Wretched places.'[27]   Indeed though he was a great believer in the power of prayer there were some situations where he felt the effects of prayer were limited. 'I don't always offer prayer in their houses – sometimes I don't think it would do any good – on Friday I prayed in almost every house, on Thursday only in a few.'[28]

Temperance teapot

The link with the Temperance Campaign would seem to be at the heart of Chadwick's concern. Dunning, with a typical sweeping statement, describes this time as one in which 'The Blue Ribbon Movement was sweeping through Lancashire like a prairie fire.' People who signed the pledge and became members wore the blue ribbon badge with pride. Chadwick entered this campaign with evangelistic zeal and was soon made President of the movement in the district.[29] The evangelical gospel and the call for abstinence from alcohol were seen at this time as inseparable. Clearly this had an impact on the local people; 'Great meetings were held everywhere, in public halls, churches and schools and in the open air. In six months more than three thousand people signed the pledge … Chadwick used to say that he pinned the blue ribbon on the coats of the local Member of Parliament, Councillors, Magistrates, Clergy, Doctors and Employers of Labour.'[30] So successful was Chadwick in persuading leaders of the community to join that the local brewers and publicans called him the "Methody Devil".[31]

His Journal carries accounts of the conquests, some of which relate to individuals and the difference made in their lives. 'Visited about 6 families in the evening. Robt Whitehead is coming to Chapel tomorrow night. Total abstinence has made a great difference in that man's home but if he only gets the love of Christ shed abroad in his heart, it will be better still.'[32] Though he was very keen about Temperance he did place the issue in a wider context of the need for salvation. One reflective entry in his *Journal* makes this clear, 'During the past months eight persons (adults) have signed the pledge. It is not my intention to substitute temperance for religion but as a stepping stone to religion, for I find it impossible to do anything with people who are slaves to the demon drink, until they are willing to give it up.'[33]

Other entries show the considerable effect of the Temperance Movement and enthusiasm with which it was greeted. 'Visited about 6 families in the main road. And then answered an invitation to Knot Hill House full of curiosity as he had promised to tell me something "that would serve my purposes". I was greatly delighted when both he and his wife expressed their willingness to become members of the Blue Ribbon Association. There are few things for which I have longed for more earnestly and so with unspeakable pleasure I handed over the Card and ribbon. Which were duly signed and donned. Bless the Lord. The meeting in the hall that night was indescribable. Amid the wild enthusiasm and thunders of applause Mr W. Mitchell took the ribbon. Over 50 new pledges taken in that service.'[34]

Chadwick was in the same Wesleyan Methodist District as Champness and the latter was a real encouragement to him. They were both concerned about drink and enthusiastically supported the Temperance movement. The number of occasions in which their meetings are recorded in Chadwick's Journal are not numerous. However, significantly, the two are together the week the first edition of the *Joyful News* was published. On Monday 19 February, Chadwick wrote: 'Spent with Mr Champness at Facit. Visited from house to house in the afternoon and rendered what assistance I could at the services.' Again on Wednesday 21 February, he records: 'spent the whole day with Mr Champness at Facit, same as Monday.' There is no mention about the *Joyful News* which was launched on the 22 February, but they are together conducting a mission in the Bolton area. Like Champness he was interested in other fine preachers, 'Went to Manchester to hear Messrs Moody and Sankey',[35] but there is no further comment.

Like many things about Chadwick, there were events which grew in stature and importance with the telling. One event relates to the conversion of a well known scoundrel in the community. It was surely such a transformation of character that it was like a resurrection, not dissimilar to Lazarus being raised. And Chadwick related the story in the *Joyful News*:

> One night there came to a meeting the most notorious drunkard in the town. His name was Robert Hamer, but everyone knew him as "Bury Bob" and he himself had forgotten his proper name. He had been guilty of every brutal crime in the calendar except murder and the exception was of grace. He had fought a fierce bull-dog with his hands tied behind his back, worried rats with his teeth, eaten glass, swallowed knives, smashed furniture, wrecked public-house bars, mauled policemen, and fought all comers. He was a terror. His presence in a religious meeting was a sensation. When he walked to the table and asked for a pledge card the excitement was overwhelming. There was a stillness like the silence in heaven as he took the pen and made a cross opposite his name. The following Sunday he was gloriously saved... The next Sunday morning the town turned out to see Bob go to chapel. One would have thought the Mayor and Corporation were going. On the steps Mr Chadwick announced that in the Evening Service Bob would testify to the grace that had saved him. The common people, the disreputable people, the scoffing people, the praying people, all sorts of people came that they might see Lazarus whom Jesus had raised from the dead. The

revival went on for months, and hundreds of the very worst people were gloriously saved.[36]

The *Journal* does not refer to the intention of 'finding a Lazarus' though there is [37]reference to 'James Hamer, an inveterate drinker, signed the pledge.' The *Journal* further notes that he cared for Mary Hamer who was seriously ill and 'died happy in the Saviour's love'.[38] The entry for the 4 January, besides noting her death, indicates, 'Eliza Hamer has promised to come back to school and Chapel.'[39] If James Hamer was related to the notorious 'Bury Bob' it may be that Chadwick's ministry to the family had real effect on Robert who was soundly converted. The absence of information may be because the *Journal* does not cover the whole of his time in Stacksteads for two reasons. It is clear that he had another Journal or Diary, 'The Report of work done from March 19th to April 1st was entered in my other Book'[40] and the period 29 April to 19 December 1882 is lost. We are therefore dependent on Chadwick's detailed reflections of 1921 in the *Joyful News* and the earlier article, 1897 in the *Methodist Recorder*. The secondary sources follow the *Joyful News*.[41]

The most dramatic entry in his journal so far as converts are concerned is found on Sunday 14 December 1882, but there is no mention of Hamer. After the evening service he noted, 'In the prayer meeting six persons were at the communion rail seeking for mercy. Several of them found peace. The most notorious amongst them were Harry Pegg, E. Hayhurst, and Jas Dearden (Jimmy Sheddy). May God hold them up'.[42]

Chadwick candidated for the ordained ministry during the winter of 1882. The Superintendent minister of the Bacup Circuit, the Rev John Hay, supported Chadwick's candidature for the Wesleyan Methodist Ministry as 'a young man of good understanding, sound judgement and mature piety.'[43] There are not many indications in his *Journal* about this process, though on Tuesday 21 February 1882 he noted that he was 'Having to preach a trial sermon today at the Mount. A great part of the time was devoted to study'. Again the following week there was another trial sermon, on Monday 27 February, 'Preached another trial sermon at Shawforth. There was a good congregation. Mrs Walker being amongst the number as critic'. Chadwick was unanimously recommended by his District but rejected by the Special Examination Committee, known as the 'July Committee' because of the month in which it met.[44] This Connexional committee recommended acceptance or rejection of candidates to the Methodist Conference of that year. Chadwick was turned down. The *Journal* is silent about these incidents due to the missing pages. Whether his thoughts were entered into the 'other book' referred to earlier, we do not know. It may be that in this absent book, Chadwick wrote his more personal thoughts and reflections.

Whilst at Stacksteads, Chadwick had Greek tuition from a Church of England clergyman[45] and he recalled later in life that he was given the opportunity of entering the Anglican Ministry when he was first declined as a candidate. In his Presidential address at the Wesleyan Methodist Conference at Manchester in July 1918 he remarked, 'You handled me rather roughly at the beginning and would have made a free gift of me to the Egyptians quite cheerfully, if I had been willing to go.'[46] However he persisted at Stacksteads for another year and was then accepted as a candidate for the ministry. He still had to undertake examinations, 'I have to devote almost the whole of my time during the day to studies in preparation for my exams. which are now close at hand.'[47] The following week he had his District trial sermon. 'During this week I have been busy preparing my trial

Sermon which has to be preached at Bury on Monday next'.[48] The Superintendent minister, the Rev George Scott, mindful of the criteria considered important in the church at that time, commended Chadwick in the following way: 'Mr Chadwick's moral and religious character is irreproachable and he is faithfully attached to the doctrines and discipline of Methodism. He has read the *Large Minutes*, the *Standard Sermons of Mr Wesley*, also Mr Wesley's *Notes on the New Testament*. He has no matrimonial engagement, takes neither snuff, drams nor tobacco and is free from debt. His offer is without any restriction and his health is good.'[49] This is the penultimate entry in his Journal, and he emerges as an accepted candidate and was admitted to Didsbury College in Manchester.

Chadwick had a good time at Didsbury College, though 'There were times when he was uncomfortable in his new surroundings. He was of a retiring disposition, and found the way of approach to other students not of his immediate circle extremely difficult. He took no part in the sports life of the College and everything in his nature revolted against the "ragging" to which some of the students were subjected'.[50] Chadwick enjoyed and benefited from the wise tuition and mentoring of Luke Wiseman as Assistant Tutor, Dr Pope and A.J. French who taught him the use of English. It is clear that at Didsbury the education he had missed in his early life was supplied. Like many students he would eventually meet at Cliff College, it was often the people who had missed out earlier who made the greatest strides forward. Luke Wiseman became a lifelong friend and preached at his funeral.

Chadwick is portrayed by Dunning as a very intense, quiet person, focussed on the need for study and avoiding sports and other pastimes.[51] He was probably very aware of his own lack of learning and that at the young age of twenty-three he had not been in education for ten years, probably also of his humble background. His father had to subsidise his training from his meagre wages. Chadwick insisted that his father had a holiday during one of his vacations and covered for him in the mill.[52] Chadwick repaid his father in full while he was a Probationary Minister.[53] One of his fellow students was Edward Davidson who had also been a lay worker and evangelist and a friend of Thomas Cook. Chadwick went to hear Thomas Cook preach at the evangelistic meetings he was conducting in Manchester. 'The sermon puzzled me. My critical faculty was at a loss to account for its power, but when the appeal was made, hundreds went into the enquiry room. The preacher looked a mere boy and the sermon was certainly not mature, but in the after-meeting the ruddy-faced youth was a great Master of Assemblies.'[54]

Chadwick's first appointment in 1886 was a year in the Edinburgh, Nicholson Square Circuit, where, at the same time, preachers such as Henry Drummond were at the height of their powers. 'It was during this period of his probation that he first held Passion Week Services, and the experiment was repeated year by year in subsequent spheres of labour. Samuel Chadwick was a pioneer in this direction as far as the Methodist Church was concerned. Some people thought he was dangerous. They feared Popery and Anglicanism but he was sure of his leading and others were quick to follow.'[55] This delight of celebrating the Christian festivals remained through his ministry. When on his delayed passage to South Africa in the spring of 1916 to preach to the Conference he wrote, 'I am praying God will open my way to preach in Passion Week. I began Holy Week Services at Clydebank in 1887 and it will be a pity to miss this year.'[56]

Chadwick had been approached by the newly opened Birmingham Mission[57] but the Chairman of Scotland persuaded him to remain north of the border so, in 1887, he became the first minister of the newly opened Church at Clydebank, Glasgow, where, initially, only a few people worshipped and Chadwick had to gather the congregation.

> The first people saw of him was at a street corner on a Saturday night preaching the Gospel. Nobody knew him and he found a place which he thought was ideal for an open-air meeting. There was a row of houses opposite so he went to the end cottage, and knocked at the front door. It was opened by a big, bulky, strong-looking woman with her sleeves rolled up above her elbows. Mr Chadwick asked her if she would let him have a chair for an hour. "No!" she said, banging the door in his face. The young man was not dismayed. His first impulse was to ask at the cottage next door but, thinking that he might get the same reply, he ventured to knock at the same door again. The same woman answered. The second time he asked for the chair. "I told you once," she said, "you won't get it," and again the door was closed. He knocked a third time. The woman opened the door in a rage. "I want to give you a shilling for the loan of your chair," said Mr Chadwick. The woman was hesitant for a minute, then she replied, "Why didn't you tell me that at first?" She brought the chair and he put his hand in his pocket and gave her a shilling, saying, "I'll give you another, if you will come and hold it for me while I stand on it." The big woman walked across the square with the frail looking minister. He put the chair where he wanted it, stood on it, and told her to put her hand on the back of it. Then he turned round and gazed at her. What a scene for the middle of a Scottish town on a Saturday night! A young man standing on a chair, gazing down at a big, masculine-looking woman![58]

Chadwick had a very creative ministry at Clydebank, partly because he was in effect planting a church and as a result the organisation of the church was invented as they went along.

Chadwick was ordained at the 1890 Wesleyan Conference and at the third reading of the Stations,[59] Thomas Champness intervened by proposing that Chadwick should be sent as the Superintendent of the Leeds Mission. This was a prestigious appointment and a newly ordained minister was not what the Circuit Stewards had expected. 'I arrived at Leeds, a bachelor, carrying a canary that someone from Clydebank had given to me.[60] The stewards who came to the station to meet me, did not know me. They passed me on the platform and I arrived without them at the Superintendent's house with my sister, who was to be my housekeeper, and a maid she had brought with her.'[61]

Sarah Chadwick née Crowther

He was not welcome as the Superintendent, because the stewards had wanted a much more experienced minister and threatened to reduce his stipend. However, with typical forcefulness, he assured the stewards he had not asked to come to Leeds, he had never received a reduction, would not start now he was Superintendent and if he did well he expected a rise![62] The community around the Wesley Methodist Church was a needy one with drink and gambling posing significant problems. In the end he had a very fruitful ministry. During this time his sister met and married the Rev W.W. Hollings, and he met Sarah Crowther.

The Cliff College Archives contain the diary of Sarah Chadwick, hand written in pencil in an exercise book. It covers the period of her life from 1886 until 1895.[63] Sarah was born in Leeds on 2 February 1868 at Wellfield House, Churwell. Her father died when she was only eight and the family moved to Boston Spa. She was educated privately and in her teens became a member of the Methodist Church and the Band of Hope.[64] In 1885 they returned to Chapel Allerton, Leeds, where the family fortunes must have improved for they moved to Wetherby in July 1887.[65] She had a considerable interest in the arts and in Leeds, Manchester and London attended galleries, music recitals, and oratorios. Her visits to the capital reveal an interest in architecture and, though the Crystal Palace 'did not come up to my expectations'[66], she clearly appreciated the charm of Kew Gardens where she spent 'a long and delightful time'[67] and the Regent's Park Zoological Gardens where on her first visit she lists all the thirty different types of animals seen.[68]

She and her mother and sometimes friends, travelled to London and to Kent, Wales and Scotland, besides the trip to Norway which was to affect her life significantly. They usually stayed in hotels in some luxury, and in Wales there was always the 'carriage awaiting' to return them from a walk in the hills to the hotel. This is the life of an upper middle class young woman who, in the late nineteenth century, had both time and resources to see the world and rejoice in its beauty and form. She was a committed member of the churches where they lived and always had a Sunday School or Bible class with the names of those attending listed in her diary. She attended demanding lectures such as one on 'Unwritten Languages' by a Dr Hellier in Oct 1887[69], and the following year heard the Rev W.L. Watkinson lecture on 'A few encouraging signs of the present Day'.[70] She studiously read the scriptures, deciding on 1 January 1889 to read the Bible through and finishing on 2 April 1892.[71]

Sarah and probably her family returned to Boston Spa in 1889 where her mother had an entrepreneurial spirit, because in March 1892 she opened a Convalescent Home and kept it until August 1893. Sarah lists the names of all the one hundred and nine women under the heading 'The Inmates'.[72]

Her first mention of the Rev S. Chadwick simply names him, with no comment, as being a preacher at the Tadcaster Convention in

1890.[73] However, with her mother, she embarked on the S.S. Albano from Harwich on 11 June 1892 for a two-week trip to Norway. The trip was to be a turning point in her life, for it was there on board that she met Samuel Chadwick. The sea was rough with a heavy squall getting up so that the crew were affected as well as the passengers. 'Terrible squall all night – had to hold on with one finger by the ring of the Prt hole, bitterly cold. Not known so rough for 30 years at that time of the year … First Mate not very well. Both stewardesses very bad – laid full length on our cabin floor'.[74] Eventually the weather calmed and they reached Norway. On Tuesday the 14 June she records, 'Then sang hymns till bedtime at 10:30p.m. But were disturbed about 12 p.m. by what sounded like a jumping match on deck above our heads, and on inquiry found it was "only the gentlemen trying to keep themselves warm, by racing round, headed by the Revd S. Chadwick.' [75]

After this frightful journey, they visited beautiful scenery in the Hardanger Fiord, and 'had a delightful drive back again, enlivened by songs from the Revd S. Chadwick and Mr Rogers.' Chadwick is referred to occasionally as one who conducts Prayers and Hymns and on one occasion conducts a service 'by request'. I wonder if it was from Sarah.

The trip to Norway concluded on 24 June and a further touring holiday was taken by Sarah with her mother and her brother Fred in Scotland, during 13 August to 26 August 1892, 'My First Holiday to Scotland'. They arrived in Edinburgh and, significantly, they were called on in the evening by Mr Chadwick among others. The following day they heard Chadwick preach in the morning at the Albert Hall. Her entry introduces him proudly as 'the Revd S. Chadwick of the Leeds Central Mission'. Later that day she and her party, which included Miss Chadwick, attended an evening service at the Synod Hall 'conducted by Mr Chadwick and we all sat on the platform'.   Neither Chadwick nor his sister appear to have accompanied them from Edinburgh on the tour of Scotland.

The next time Chadwick is mentioned is March 1893 where Sarah records, 'Went with Mother to the Central Mission Chapel Anniversary, Leeds'. The next entry is a few days later, 'March 21st Tuesday – The Lord has answered my long, long prayer and so kindly, how I thank him words cannot express. I must try and show Him by my action I now know what two kinds of happiness are.'

In early April, Sarah was in Ambleside and on the 5 April recorded, 'Day of Days – Wordsworth Stine – Red Hill "After Supper"'.[76] Is this when Chadwick proposed to her? The diary does not divulge that, but after two days which simply record their journeys, she writes on the 8 April, 'Home again – to St Ives - the 1st parting'. The next entries are at the beginning of May when she clearly attended Leeds. 'My first Sunday at Wesley'. The description of the ministry on the second Sunday is very full, concluding with the comment, 'A most Sacred Day - May the Spirit of God never leave us – Sat up till 12:30pm in close fellowship.' The following entry is Thursday 18 May, '"Dearest" off to America – a long separation.'

Then there is a new page and an underlined heading, 'A New Epoch' followed by the entry, 'Wednesday August 23rd 1893, 12 a.m. (Presumably she meant 12 noon.) The Day. Dr Moulton – Guests without end. 1p.m. In a cab – alone with Dearest off to York. Thence by train to Dunbar. Arrive 8 p.m. supper at the Royal Hotel, and to Bed at 9:30. !!!!!!!.....'[77]

After their honeymoon, they were appointed to the Shoreditch Mission in Hackney Road, returning a year later to Oxford Place

Chapel, Leeds. Sarah then virtually disappears in the published literature. Dunning hardly mentions her, with only the slightest mention of Chadwick's marriage.[78] Fiddian Moulton, Lambert and Cresswell hardly mention Sarah in their histories of the College.

Sarah Chadwick

How would this cultured and able woman deal with marriage to a young and already famous preacher in Wesleyan Methodism? There are a few clues to her ability. At Oxford Place each week they distributed a leaflet which on the front cover advertised the services of the following Sunday and on the inside and back pages was a devotional article under the overall title of 'Home Service Series', each with a number. Typically they had a theme, two or three verses of a suitable hymn, a scripture passage, a prayer and the text of the article. Most of the articles in the archives are written by Samuel Chadwick but some are written by 'Mrs S. Chadwick'. The leaflet advertising Sunday 16 December 1900 is headed inside 'Home Service Series, No 39', with the subtitle 'The Church in Thy House'. The message has the theme 'Killed or Sold' and is a call for temperance and concludes, 'Stop drinking yourself. Refuse to have it in your house. Forbid your children to fetch it. Sign the pledge, and encourage others to do the same.'[79] Another has the theme 'The Shepherd King', and drawing on Isaiah 40:10-11 and Rev 7:17, uses the prophecy and apocalypse to show Jesus the Shepherd King who Knows, Provides, is our Protector and Companion.[80] The 'Home Service Series No 122' is written by Sarah and titled, 'Hanging the Wrong Man' based on Mark 15:15 where Barabbas is released and Jesus delivered to be crucified. She concludes with the urgent call of a preaching woman 'Oh sinner, you are crucifying your Lord afresh. You are endorsing the act of Pilate and condemning the wrong man. It is you who ought to be punished. It is you who ought to die. But He has died in your place. He has overcome the devil and conquered death for you. His death is your life. Will you not give yourself to Him who gave Himself for you? He is your Saviour. Come to Him today.' [81]

She was also a contributor to the *Leeds Mission News* and in May 1904 wrote an article 'Mary Jones and her Bible' with not only the story of the little girl but also a summary of the work of the British and Foreign Bible Society.

An Open Letter from Mrs. Chadwick

TO

The Women in the neighbourhood of Cliff College.

There is an interesting article from the *Methodist Recorder* 13 October 1932, which concerns the re-opening of the Ventnor Street Mission, Leeds (closed for three years), a new venture as a result of the Methodist Union of that year. 'To Mrs Chadwick, wife of the much esteemed and loved Principal of Cliff College, was entrusted the duty of unlocking the door and leading the people into the re-conditioned sanctuary. She said that many people were saying that Union would mean the closing of a large number of Churches and she was glad that that day they had an illustration of Methodist Union re-opening one. She passed on a gracious message from her husband who wished "God's richest blessing upon this venture of faith." ... Mr W. Challoner, who has had much to do with the opening of the Church, Mrs Chadwick, the Rev A. Lowe and the Rev Norman Dunning gave stirring addresses.'[82]

When the Chadwicks came to Cliff in September 1907, Mrs Chadwick began a Bible Class and to advertise it initially she wrote a leaflet entitled, *An Open Letter from Mrs Chadwick to the Women in the neighbourhood of Cliff College*, which is undated but refers to their arrival 'last September to live in the new Tutor's house at Cliff Park'. She explains that she had been used to 'hundreds of women to whom I had been a helper and friend'. She writes about the difference in moving from the vigorous life at Oxford Place, 'I cannot tell you how desolate it felt.' The services are to be on Sundays between 3 - 4 and held at the College Chapel. They are for 'Young women, Wives, and Mothers. Any woman over sixteen years will be welcome.' The services are to be 'bright, hearty and homely' and the first address to be given by Sarah was to be 'Can a Woman satisfy Jesus Christ?'[83] There are over a hundred different leaflets in the College archive which advertise the Bible Class, each with a subject and an address given by Mrs Chadwick.[84] The leaflets run from 8 March 1908, the first meeting, to 31 March 1912, presumably when it ended, prior to the Chadwicks' departure to the South Yorkshire Coalfields. Mrs Chadwick is the advertised preacher on each occasion with the exception of 3 March 1912 when the Mr C.E. Oxenborough Rush was to give the address.[85] Clearly she was a welcome speaker but there is no suggestion that after her husband became the Principal she continued the Bible class, nor that she ever invited Mrs Cook or Mrs Moulton to take part. Very strange!

Chadwick's sojourn in London Shoreditch Mission was a brief year, 1893-4, though he rescued the church from debt. He was then recalled to Leeds to serve the central and prestigious Oxford Place

Methodist Church. His welcome to Leeds was not warm on either occasion, and in this case the Quarterly Meeting voted against his appointment. However, it is the Conference which decides and to Oxford Place Chadwick was sent.

Dunning, in his usual optimistic presentation of Chadwick's ministry, indicates that the church was full from the first morning service. In his foreword to a Centenary booklet about the Leeds City Mission, the Rev Luke Wiseman refers to Chadwick's ministry at Wesley Chapel as giving a 'headstrong young minister named Chadwick the opportunity he craved.'[86] Wiseman indicates that when the Meth-odist churches of central Leeds were realigned (closing St Peter's and retaining Wesley and Oxford Place), 'Samuel Chadwick, whom God had so mightily used at Wesley, was brought from London to take charge. As was foreseen, this did not suit everyone but Mr John Raynar, whom one might describe as not merely a pillar, but one who, like the psalmist, bore up pillars, gave the young missioner his wholehearted support. That settled matters. If conservative, sagacious, refined, devout John Raynar was convinced and satisfied, who need hesitate? Let the preacher have his way! And soon all Leeds knew that another Samuel was established in its midst as a prophet of the Lord.'[87]

At the first Quarterly Meeting after Chadwick's arrival, he reported the membership as being 294, with 12 on trial. At the next meeting a decrease of 31 was reported, but with 47 on trial. After that there were regular increases until, in the Quarter before his transfer to Cliff, the membership was 957 members, 108 on trial and 145 'junior members'.[88]

Congregations grew considerably in this period, moving from an average of 400 to large congregations filling the chapel. When, in

January 1907[89], Oxford Place was being cleaned and restored, the worshippers removed to the Coliseum which seated 4,000 and it 'was crowded before the time for the service.'[90] Chadwick's preaching is often referred to as 'unique'. He demanded a great deal from his congregations: 'To go through Dr. Pope's compendium of theology is hardly to be expected of a man who hopes to hold a congregation of 4,000 in a great public hall, but such was the case with Mr Chadwick during the second occupation of the Coliseum. He loved preaching, and was a master of the expository method. His sermons were the outcome of a long and intensive study and evidenced a profound knowledge of the Bible and of human nature. They were always used, as a means to an end – that of bringing men to God, and there was an urgency – a directness – a power in them which held men and women in close attention for an hour at a time; but of course, it was not only a sermon – it was the man himself that held your interest. Slight of stature, with a striking head, an aggressive nose, eyes that seemed to be looking both inwardly at some vision, and out through to the heart and mind of the object in front; with hands that could be very expressive and very tender; a voice that carried well though not loud except in moments of tense emotion; a manner somewhat assertive and pugnacious – without any trace of indecision or fear, consequently dominating most men and circumstances; yet, withal as gentle as a child, as humble as the poorest, as self-forgetful as a saint. Indeed, as you sat in the service of a Sunday evening – the place full to the doors – and watched him come up the stairs on to the rostrum – an insignificant slip of a man except for the head – you instinctively felt that he was coming directly from the presence of the Most High with a message to a waiting people. He spoke as an ambassador – without apology, indecision, or self-consciousness – but with something of the rugged authority of a prophet'.[91]

In addition to a considerable increase in the membership and congregations, the mission was involved in social action and caring ministries. The *Leeds Mission News* for December 1904 speaks of the importance of finding homes and work for poor people. 'Is it any use attempting to save these people without social appliances for their rescue? They are homeless, penniless, workless, and worthless ... It is useless to give them money ... Is there anyone who will help us to start social work on a definite and organised scale? We want to provide temporary work and a temporary home for these hopeless, helpless creatures for whom Christ died. Indiscriminate charity is worse than useless. Who will help us to tackle this problem in a Christian and sensible way? Mr Myers and his helpers are prepared to undertake the work if friends will find the means.'[92]

It has to be understood that Chadwick was a master of raising funds, but this issue of *Leeds Mission News* shows his awareness of the social and economic issues facing the City of Leeds, even though there is the hint of urging people to give generously. 'Trade is worse in Leeds than it has been for many years. There are thousands out of work who never demonstrate. Little children are starving. Schoolmasters tell us of the children who do not go home at dinner-time because there is no dinner, and their little school fellows share with them their scanty crust.' He acknowledges that the City Council are putting a considerable fund of £10,000 'to provide work for the unemployed'[93] and which at today's values would be at least £500,000. He is keen, as a good fundraiser, to place the Mission's work at the forefront of this social enterprise, 'The strain on the resources of the Mission is very great. We visit the sick and starving empty-handed. Our resources are exhausted and we shall be glad if those who can will help, especially in our work among the sick. Our appliances for nursing need replenishing and we need funds to provide nourishment for the suffering. As Christmas approaches let everyone try to brighten and gladden somebody's home. That is the correct way to secure a happy Christmas for our own.'[94]

During this period he held what today would be described as an evening Bible School. In the winter of 1896-7 he held 'Studies in Christian Doctrine' on a Wednesday at 8:00pm, with the following robust topics for people to study:

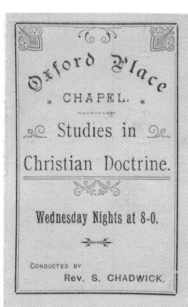

Oct 28	The Make-up of the Bible
Nov 4	The New Testament and its Writers
Nov 11	The Inspiration of the Bible
Nov 18	The Christian Doctrine of God
Nov 25	The Person of Christ
Dec 2	The Atonement: What it reveals of God and what it does for the Human Race
Dec 9	The Conditions of Salvation
Dec 16	The Holy Spirit
Dec 23	The Scriptural Doctrine of Holiness
Jan 6	The Church
Jan 13	The Sacraments
Jan 20	Christian Ethics [95]

The life of the Church is summarised in the centenary booklet in the following way: 'The various activities such as Bible Classes, Guilds, Women's Meetings, Cottage Services, Open Air meetings, Sunday Schools and Social Relief Work. A weekly tract – written by Mr Chadwick – was distributed to 2,500 houses by voluntary workers; visitation of the sick in the infirmary and of prisoners in the cells, was a regular weekly ministry. The place became a hive of activity and the meetings instant with life and power.' [96]

The *Leeds Mission News* also records that 'A great experiment' had been undertaken by taking the Coliseum on Sunday evenings. 'The Oxford Place people have stood loyally by the Chapel, and at the Coliseum there have been from twelve hundred to fourteen hundred, mostly men, and of the class we want. Mr Dinsdale preaches at Oxford Place, and Mr Chadwick is preaching at the Coliseum a series of sermons on "God's Appeal to Men of Reason". We believe religion to be the sanest and most reasonable thing in the world. At either place all are welcomed on the broad basis of humanity and brotherhood.'[97]

During this period of his ministry Chadwick undertook, with the Trustees of the Oxford Place Chapel, a significant building scheme which began in 1896 and was concluded in 1902, with the whole of the expenditure of £30,429 (at today's values over one and half

million pounds), being raised by the end of 1906. Such a building scheme was a quite remarkable feat in the midst of this vigorous ministry. 'So ended a tremendous undertaking – the whole carried out in faith and by prayer and brought to a successful conclusion without any other means than by plain statement and appeal to the goodwill and generosity of the members and friends of the Mission.'[98]

Chadwick had a remarkable ministry there for thirteen years during which he became a leading preacher amongst the Wesleyan Methodists. In 1902 he was elected a member of the Legal Hundred, the group of one hundred ordained Wesleyan Ministers who held power within the

Revs Thomas Cook and Samuel Chadwick (1906)

Church.[99] His ability as a writer as well as a preacher and teacher was recognised by the astute Champness, who invited him to be the

Editor of the *Joyful News* in 1905, a task he undertook with the help of Annie Douglas, until his death in 1932. From the opening of Cliff

College in 1904 he was a part-time tutor coming each Monday evening to lecture and stay over until Tuesday for further lectures. At his last Oxford Place Mission Anniversary in 1907 before leaving to take up the full-time appointment at Cliff College, the Lord Mayor of Leeds, Mr Joseph Hepworth, chairing one of the meetings, turned to Chadwick and said,

Cliff Park

'You have done well, sir! What you have done here and in this city will live for generations, and I thank God that you ever came. You will take away with you the blessings of tens of thousands of people, who will watch your work and rejoice in everything that you do'.[100]

He preached at the Great Missionary Thanksgiving Meeting in the Royal Albert Hall, 29 April 1907, with the King and Queen present. Chadwick was still only forty-seven, but already recognised as a great preacher, though many years from being the President of the Conference. Nevertheless it was Chadwick who was invited to preach, and a special illuminated leather-bound booklet was produced for the occasion.[101] On the inside cover, in Sarah Chadwick's handwriting it says: 'The King and Queen, Edward VII and Mary were at their first Methodist Service. Queen Mary wished to speak to "S.C.", after the service, and said, "Your address greatly moved me". Tears were in her eyes, and overflowed as she said, "Thank you".'[102]

Miss Annie Douglas

In 1907 he was appointed by the Conference to join Thomas Cook at Cliff College to be the tutor in Biblical Studies and Theology. It was here that he began the work for which he is most remembered. Cook had built Cliff Park for the new Tutor and Samuel and Sarah lived there along with Miss Annie Douglas and a maid. Chadwick had always felt a close affinity with the College and had nurtured the notion of teaching in a College for over ten years, 'There are not many occasions on which I have had premonitions, but my visit to the Bible Institute at Chicago in 1893 made an impression on me which was increased with every visit.'[103] It was for this reason, encouraged by both Champness and Cook, he had agreed to take on the task of teaching at Cliff, even though he had an extremely busy ministry in Leeds. 'Mr Champness was the first person to tell me that my greatest gift was not preaching but teaching' and then 'When Cliff opened I agreed to lecture twice a week to the men on the Bible.'[104] His appointment at Cliff as Tutor was the beginning of an era in which he built on the work and vision of Thomas Cook.

Samuel and Sarah Chadwick

Chadwick was recognised as a leader within the Church and was appointed the Chairman of the Sheffield District in 1911 whilst still a tutor at the College, and remained Chairman until 1926. He left Cliff in the summer of 1912 to become the Superintendent of the newly formed South Yorkshire Coalfields Mission and lead evangelistic work there. The untimely death of Cook meant that he not only remained in that work but also was from late September the Acting Principal. Chadwick took up the task of Principal in the year 1913 with ideas for the development of the public ministry of the College, but these were dashed by the outbreak of War in the summer of 1914. The College persevered through the year, though with a smaller number of students, 'the numbers for the three terms being 72, 49, and 41.'[105] In November 1915 the number of students had reduced to 20, 'some are medically unfit for military service but others will in all probability be required to meet the national needs.'[106]

Chadwick had received an indication that the 'Military Authorities' may require the new Champness Wing for troops. During the meeting of the Committee a demand was received by telegram to billet 160 troops in the College, 'requesting that the building be placed at their disposal with the least possible delay.'[107] The response of the Committee was laudable and they unanimously adopted the following resolution:

> While loyally bowing to military necessity the Committee would greatly prefer that the new wing of Cliff College should be used as a convalescent hospital rather than for the billeting of troops and approves the suggestion that Mr Chadwick should make every endeavour to secure that arrangement.[108]

The military did not come, there were no students from December 1915 to the reopening in 1919, and no meeting recorded of the College Committee between November 1915 and May 1920. Chadwick was not idle during this period, visiting South Africa on behalf of the British Conference in spring of 1916. He kept a diary which was typed and bound in an illuminated copy and placed in the archives. As he approached South Africa, he was aware of the great evangelistic ministry Cook had there some years before. 'I begin to be appalled at what lies ahead, and I want to fit myself in every possible way for the task ... Mr Cook was here in 1892 and had some wonderful Missions

Norman Dunning

... He was at the zenith of his powers and his Missions were mighty. I expect I shall find many of his converts even after twenty-five years ... He was away from April to December and saw over 6,000 conversions.'[109] There is just that hint of rivalry under the surface. Chadwick visited, preached or lectured in Cape Town, Port Elizabeth, Grahamstown, East London, Kimberley, Bloemfontein,

Johannesburg and Durban. In each place he also preached in a number of surrounding townships. Whilst there, he saw firsthand the plight of the black Africans and wrote a personal log of the injustice he had seen, while at the same time commenting on the gracious welcome afforded by both the white and black community.

Rev J.I. Brice

In the Connexional Year 1918-19 Chadwick was President of the Methodist Conference. His presidential address; 'The World Crisis and the Age' was masterly, calling for integrity in politics as Europe moved towards peace, a world-wide move towards justice and peace, an overturning of the drink trade, and a revival of Methodism.

As a result of the South African experience, he was determined to put a more missionary element into the course. 'I have resolved to put a Missionary course into the Curriculum at Cliff. It makes me mad to think of all that was happening when I was in College and to remember that I knew nothing about them. There ought to be a course on the history and the happenings of the Field - anyway we will have a try at it.'[110] He was deeply impressed by an Anglo-Catholic Priest, Father Norton,[111] who was a missionary, and a Mr Clarke who was a life-long missionary and member of the Plymouth Brethren, with stories which delighted Chadwick.[112] Clarke was on the same boat returning with his second wife for mission work in Southern Africa. Many of the students graduating from the College went overseas to Canada, Australia, Southern Africa. Dunning reported that of the 42 ministers in Western Australia 21 were Cliff men. [113]

After the war Chadwick reopened the College and immediately began to build a new team of Tutors. Norman Dunning arrived in the first year. Chadwick was not well, even in the early years of the

Mr D.W. Lambert

1920s. 'Grave apprehension was expressed concerning the Principal's health and he was earnestly exhorted in the general interest to spare himself as far as was possible.'[114] Again there was concern for his health in that the Committee approved a plan for a Garden Party at Cliff during the Sheffield Conference of 1922, along with a Summer School and Conferences, but they also 'expressed the opinion that The Principal should be relieved as far as possible from the extra burden involved.'[115]

Chadwick in later years with Dunning, Lambert and Brice on whom he relied.

Nevertheless, despite his illness, in 1922 he became the President of the National Council of the Evangelical Free Churches, preaching widely around the country. W.H. Heap recalled that ill health dogged him all his days and at one point his complaint was diagnosed as 'consumption of the bowels'.[116] Chadwick was severely ill in the early part of 1932.[117] Dunning clarifies for us the extent of Chadwick's illness but nowhere do we read what kind of surgery he had. 'During the last ten years of his life he scarcely knew what it was to be free from pain. An operation in 1927 was followed by a more serious one two years later.'[118]

Arthur Myers, a minister who knew Chadwick well and wrote the Diamond Jubilee tribute about the *Joyful News* and its Editors, wrote about Chadwick, 'His versatility was amazing. A strong Protestant and yet a high Churchman, though not a sacredotalist.'[119] J.I. Brice, who worked with him so closely at the end of his life, recalled that, 'there was often a suggestion of Catholic mysticism in his adoration of Jesus'.[120] Reflecting on his life Strawson described him as a 'high church Methodist'.[121]

Samuel Chadwick and David Lloyd George

There is a very interesting insight into the world of Cliff College through a presentation, which Sarah Chadwick evidently used to describe the College. It is entitled *Cliff – Past and Present, The story of how two great ventures became one.*

The traditions of the old Cliff remain with the modern Cliff. Community singing has echoed through the house and grounds from the beginning. "The voice of prayer is never silent". And the Holy Spirit of God is the Spirit of a Divine Love which shows itself in the brotherhood of men who dwell together for a season under one roof and then go out to seek and to save the lost, both in their country, and in lands beyond the sea.

A little ought to be said about the college programme of work. In the lecture hall the study of the Bible still has first place. Secular studies such as grammar, history, literature are necessary as many men have had very small educational opportunities. But how to study the Bible, the books of the Bible, their relation to each other, and the Bible in relation to preaching, which is seen in the Clinic, are all of great value.

For over twenty years the Principal's lecture has begun with a prayer offered by the students in song, 'Break thou the bread of life'.

Manual labour has come down from the beginning. Adam earned bread by the sweat of his brow and Cliff men are not spared. As in the days of Dr Grattan Guinness, Thomas Champness and Thomas Cook, so now in these later days the students take their share of labour for the upkeep of the College. Men with trades can keep their hand in, and their muscles firm. Miners still can heave coal, stone masons can build walls, foresters cut down trees and joiners, painters, electricians, stenographers, hairdressers, postmen, chapel-keepers, cobblers, waiters and farm labourers all find a duty to fulfil. The men who have come off an office stool and have no hard places on their hands are not left out. They have a chance to develop some muscle, for there are potatoes to plant and harvest, digging, hoeing, weeding, grass cutting, and the sweeping up of leaves in Autumn. There are also [poultry to feed, pigs to wash,] (these words are crossed out in the original text by a later hand) windows to clean, and knives and brasses to polish. There is work for all, and all accomplish their work in the Cliff Spirit.[122]

There is a final word about finance in the text of Sarah Chadwick. It is interesting that at the close of the presentation of the work of the College, Sarah Chadwick has written before the announcement of the final hymn, 'collection'. Few things change. The text about the finances of the College reads:

> From the first God has honoured the faith and work of an Evangelist, and has seen that he lacked no good thing. How the money came, and how the money still comes is one of His Miracles of Grace. God takes into partnership the man of faith.
>
> How the College was bought and equipped, a Champness Memorial Wing built, also a chapel and organ at a sum total of £25,000, was a story Mr Cook was never tired of telling, and his friends were never weary of hearing. Towards this amount, £155 was received in pennies from poor folk, readers of the *Joyful News* who wished to add their mite to the Memorial of their friend.
>
> After Mr Cook's death the 'Cook' Memorial Wing, taking the form of a Sanatorium, Office, and Laundry sorting room was built at a cost of £1,100 and the total amount was quickly provided from the spontaneous gifts of many friends who wished in this way to pay their tribute to his memory. The expenses of the present age are greater even than in the past. The 'New Wing' built for the sake of efficiency was opened at our 'Coming of Age' Anniversary in 1925, free of debt. 1,930 subscriptions were sent, in response to our appeal, varying in amount from sixpence to one hundred pounds. The annual cost of the institution is great, and in addition to the weekly contributions of the students, the gifts of the poor as seen week by week in *Joyful News*, and other sources of income which come to us in answer to prayer, we have a great Anniversary at Whitsuntide, at which we make up the Balance, an average of £2,000 a year, and if God sends us more than we ask for, we know that it is for us to use in improving the place and developing the work for His honour and glory.[123]

Dunning, who through the 1920s, except when on his overseas preaching tour, had been acting as a Tutor at the discretion of the Home Mission Committee, was from 1930 designated as a 'Tutor at Cliff College'.

The College Committee endorsed Chadwick in January 1932 as the continuing Principal but did discuss his successor. In the June of that same year Chadwick discussed the matter of succession with Dunning. The only indication we have comes from a short article in the *Joyful News* in the week after Chadwick's death entitled, 'My beloved Principal has gone'. In it Dunning recalled, 'the emotion of a June night four months ago. He had made a very important decision in which he felt I did not acquiesce. He was sure he was right, but he grieved for me. Hour after hour he talked; he poured out his soul. We knelt to pray.'[124] In fact at the May meeting of the College Committee, at which Dunning was not present, the question of succession was considered. 'It was now a question of a colleague who would take responsibility with a view to succession. It would be disastrous to make Cliff a College pure and simple. The man appointed must be in full sympathy with the work, share the same type of religious experience. His own choice would be the Rev J.A. Broadbelt.'[125] Clearly Dunning and Brice had been devoted to him, Lambert admired him immensely but none of them was to be the Principal. Brice was appointed by the Conference in 1932 to the Derby Mission. Broadbelt came that summer to live at Cliff Park as the Principal-in-Waiting.

Chadwick died on the 16 October 1932 at Cliff, and his funeral was held on the College terrace. Students formed relays to carry the coffin down the drive to the graveyard at All Saints, Curbar, close to Cook's memorial. On the day of his funeral the Committee met afterwards, gave tribute to Chadwick, made arrangements for Mrs Chadwick's housing at Stanton Ford and confirmed Broadbelt's appointment. Luke Wiseman 'reminded the committee that at the last Conference, the Rev J.A. Broadbelt had been appointed as Mr Chadwick's colleague. The Home Mission Committee and the Conference understood that when Mr Chadwick retired Mr Broadbelt should be appointed in his place as Principal.'[126]

Chadwick's funeral service on the Terrace

Chadwick's grave in Curbar Churchyard

Broadbelt was, as ever, prepared for this moment 'saying that Mr Chadwick could have no successor. He was unique but it was a source of strength to know that this was Mr Chadwick's own wish and there would be no change of policy in the work of the College but we should carry on as he desired us to do.' [127]

Chadwick was a great statesman of the Church, remarkably well read in theology and philosophy and abreast of world events as his preaching and writing reveal. He was devout and disciplined, 'Ataraxia was not merely a word on a card hung on his study wall and written each year on the front page of his diary, it was the very atmosphere in which he lived.'[128] He arose early each day at six, 'having a cold bath summer and winter' and often working until midnight.[129] He was a great editor and contributed also to *Out and Out* and *Experience*. W.H. Heap, who wrote the lengthy obituary for Chadwick, entitled 'The Warrior Saint', summed up his eulogy: 'Whether as preacher, evangelist, social reformer, or Editor, he must be ranked as in the first class.'[130] At his funeral his friend Luke Wiseman preached on the text, 'Samuel was established to be a prophet of the Lord'. Indeed he was.

1   Norman Dunning, *Samuel Chadwick,* (London: Hodder and Stoughton, 1933), p.27.
2   Dunning, *Chadwick*, p.26.
3   Dunning *Chadwick,* pp.23 – 39 See also T.A. Seed *The Rev'd Samuel Chadwick* ca 1908 E43 and W. Fiddian Moulton, *The President of Conference* E43 1918.
4   Dunning, *Chadwick,* p.23.
5   Dunning, *Chadwick,* p.24.
6   Dunning, *Chadwick,* p.28.
7   Dunning, *Chadwick*, p.24.
8   Dunning, *Chadwick*, p.25.
9   W. Fiddian Moulton, *The President of the Conference;The Rev Samuel Chadwick* (E43: undated but published during his presidential year, 1918-19).
10 Dunning, *Chadwick,* p.37.
11 Dunning, *Chadwick,* p.37.
12 Dunning, *Chadwick*, p.37.
13 Dunning, *Chadwick*, p.38.
14 Dunning, *Chadwick*, p.38.
15 Samuel Chadwick, a black note book which is simply called *Journal,* Cliff College Archive, E44.
16 *Joyful News,* 18 August 1921.
17 Archive E 44, *Journal,* entry for 17 September 1881. The underlining and double underlining is his.
18 Samuel Chadwick, 'How I became a Missioner', in *The Methodist Recorder Winter Number* Vol. XXXVIII, No. 2092, Christmas 1897, pp.43-47, p.44.
19 Dunning, *Chadwick*, p.43.
20 Dunning, *Chadwick*, p.43.
21 Chadwick, *Methodist Recorder* 1897, p.44.
22 Ibid.
23 Ibid, and see also Dunning, *Chadwick*, p.43.
24 *Journal,* 27 July 1881.
25 *Journal*, 15 August 1881.
26 *Journal*, 2 March 1882.
27 *Journal*, 28 November 1882.
28 *Journal*, 14 October 1881.
29 Dunning, *Chadwick*, p.41.
30 Dunning, *Chadwick*, p.42.
31 Dunning, *Chadwick*, p.42.
32 *Journal*, 25 February 1882.
33 *Journal*, 7 January 1882.
34 *Journal*, 9 March 1883.
35 *Journal*, 8 March 1883.
36 *Joyful News,* 25 August 1921 and related also by Dunning in *Chadwick*, pp.44-45.
37 *Journal,* 8 December 1881.

cont.

38 *Journal,* Chadwick visited her on the 30 December and she died on the 4 January.
39 *Journal,* 4 January 1882.
40 *Journal,* The entry prior to Sunday 16 April 1882.
41 There are some details in Chadwick's own account in the *Methodist Recorder Winter,* 1897; Dunning's account pp.40-47; David Howarth, *Samuel Chadwick and some aspects of Wesleyan Methodist Evangelism 1860-1932* (M. Litt. thesis University of Lancaster 1977). See also Ken F. Bowden in his *Samuel Chadwick and Stacksteads* (Stacksteads Methodist Church: Bacup, 1982).
42 *Journal,* 14 December 1882.
43 'Minutes of the Bolton District Meeting, May 1882' in *District Minutes* 1881-1882, Vol.2, in the Methodist Archives collection at the John Rylands Library.
44 Dunning, *Chadwick,* p.47.
45 Dunning, *Chadwick,* p.47.
46 Bowdon, *Stacksteads,* reports, 'It is probable that his friendship with the Vicar of Waterfoot was a factor in this. The Rev Alexander James Harrison had been a minister of the Methodist New Connexion until 1871, serving in eight circuits in ten years. In 1871 he resigned and became curate of Shuttleworth, and after ordination as priest moved some five miles up the road to Waterfoot in 1873. He had given the young lay missioner his first lessons in English subjects, as well as Greek, Latin, Euclid, and Samuel Chadwick, reviewing Harrison's autobiography twenty years later remarked: 'He was the first to give me real help in the difficult task of self-education, and I have treasured the memory of his kindness with reverent gratitude.' p.17-18.
47 Chadwick, *Journal,* 17 April 1883.
48 Chadwick, *Journal,* 25 April 1883.
49 *District Minutes,* and reported by Bowden, *Stacksteads,* p.20.
50 Dunning, *Chadwick,* p.59.
51 Dunning, *Chadwick,* pp.59-60.
52 Dunning, *Chadwick,* p.63.
53 Dunning, *Chadwick,* p.67.
54 Dunning, *Chadwick,* p.62.
55 Dunning, *Chadwick,* p.64.
56 Chadwick, *An Evangelistic Tour in South Africa* (A Bound Diary 1916, in the Archives of Cliff College, E52). In the Diary he refers to Clydebank in 1887 but he was in Edinburgh in that year and the first Holy Week in Clydebank was 1888. So this is possibly a slight mistake of year or place. I suspect the year, since he would 'see' in his mind's eye the place in which these took place. The Archives also contain a series of sermons used in Holy Week over the years.
57 His friend the Rev Luke Wiseman was in fact appointed to the Birmingham Mission. The fortunes of these two men were to rise in parallel ways over the years.
58 Dunning, *Chadwick,* pp.65-66.
59 Methodist ministers are appointed, or stationed, to particular circuits. The 'reading of the stations' happens three of four times in the Conference after which

cont.

all the ministers are appointed for the following Connexional year. The practice still continues.

60 In those days Methodist ministers might move annually and all furniture and furnishings were provided by the Circuit, including crockery and cutlery. A minister and his family could move by carrying their possessions on the train, sending their books ahead. Dr Marcus Ward explained the predicament to me in 1969, with reference to his own experience as a 'child of the manse' and one whose grandfather had been a Wesleyan Methodist Minister. It was only in 1971 that finally Methodist Ministers and their families owned the furniture in the manse they occupied at the time.

61 Dunning, *Chadwick*, p.69. Heap recalls that Chadwick's sister 'kept house for him', *Joyful News,* 20 October 1932.

62 Dunning, *Chadwick*, p.69, where Dunning clearly supports Chadwick's request for a rise. Dunning himself was a flamboyant man and minister. Here and at Clydebank Dunning reports with uncritical support that Chadwick's remuneration package was above that normally afforded a minister.

63 Archive E1 *Diary* of Sarah Elizabeth Crowther 1886 – 1895. The diary is handwritten in pencil in an exercise book. The pages are not numbered but I have indicated the page numbers for reference.

64 Sarah, p.1, 'Became a member of the "Wesleyan Methodist Society" on 8 March 1882 under the Rev J.H. Horrell. Became a member of the "Band of Hope" in April 1883.

65 Sarah, *Diary,* p.18.

66 Sarah, *Diary,* p.8.

67 Sarah, *Diary,* p.22.

68 Sarah, *Diary,* p.13. 'Lions fed, Tigers, Leopards, Yaks, Elephants, Camels, Zebras, Kangaroos, Wild Ass, Hippopotamus fed, White Brown and Grizzly Bears, Hyena, Antelopes and Deer, Tortoise, Wolfe, Crocodile, Buffalo, Wild Hog, Dog Fox and Goats, Beaver, Puma, Moose, Monkeys, Hawks, Peacocks, Cockatoos, Eagles, Kites and Bats, Kingfisher, Rattlesnakes.'

69 Sarah, *Diary,* p.20.

70 Sarah, *Diary,* p.25.

71 Sarah, *Diary,* p.27.

72 Sarah, *Diary,* p.77.

73 Sarah, *Diary,* p.31.

74 Sarah, *Diary,* p.37.

75 Sarah, *Diary,* p.39.

76 Sarah, *Diary*, p.79.

77 Sarah, *Diary,* p.83 and all the exclamation marks are hers.

78 Dunning, *Chadwick*, pp. 75, 76, 144. At no point is the date or place of the wedding indicated nor any attempt made to relate Sarah's ministry.

79 Sarah Chadwick, Home Service Series, No 39, dated 16 December 1900.

80 Sarah Chadwick, Home Service Series, No 66, dated 8 September 1901.

81 Sarah Chadwick, Home Service Series No 122, dated 5 July but with no year indicated.

cont.

82   W. D. Lister, 'Beginning a New Chapter at Leeds' in *Methodist Recorder,* 13 October 1932.

83   Sarah Chadwick, *An Open Letter from Mrs. Chadwick to The Women in the Neighbourhood of Cliff College*, undated, but published in the spring of 1908, Cliff College Archives E4.

84   Section E4.

85   Cliff College Archives, E5.

86   B.L. Austick and H B Jobbings, *A Century – Not Out!, The Story of 100 years of Worship, Work and Witness at Oxford Place Chapel, Leeds,* (Leeds Methodist Mission, 1935) p.3.

87   *A Century – Not Out!,* p.3. Indeed curiously the Quarterly Meeting had preferred to appoint the Rev F. Luke Wiseman who became great friends with Chadwick, see p.23.

88   *A Century – Not Out!,* p.23.

89   *8 Days Mission,* a leaflet describing the mission conducted by Josiah Nix and Chadwick 20 - 27 January 1907.

90   *A Century – Not Out!,* p.23.

91   *A Century – Not Out!,* p.24.

92   *Leeds Mission News,* December 1904, p.9.

93   *Leeds Mission News,* p.9.

94   *Leeds Mission News,* p.9.

95   *Studies in Christian Doctrine*, Cliff College Archives E14, Material concerning Leeds City Mission.

96   *A Century – Not Out!,* p.23.

97   *Leeds Mission News,* p.9.

98   *A Century – Not out!,* p.25.

99   The Legal Hundred consisted entirely of ordained ministers who were in fact the Connexional Trustees and the real power within the Church. Cook and Chadwick were members of the Legal Hundred.

100   *A Century – Not Out!,* p.26.

101   Published by Novello, with all hymns and anthems included.

102   Archive C24, *Hymns and Anthems* (Novello: London, 1907). All the Methodist 'greats' were there and signed the booklet; Henry H. Fowler, Albert Clayton, Henry Haigh, R.W. Perks, Marshall Hartley, Charles H. Kelly, W. Lamplough, C.J. Dale.

103   *Joyful News*, 16 August 1906. The article is entitled 'Why I Accepted the Invitation to Cliff College' and in it Chadwick confides in the readers, as Champness had done about his thoughts, why in this case he had decided to move to Cliff.

104   Ibid.

105   *Minutes* of the Committee of Management, 31 May 1915.

106   *Minutes* of the Committee of Management, 22 November 1915.

107   *Minutes* of the Committee of Management, 22 November 1915.

108   *Minutes* of the Committee of Management, 22 November 1915.

109   Chadwick, *An Evangelistic Tour In South Africa*, Unpublished, 1916, p.10.

cont.

110 Chadwick, *South Africa,* p.11. He has come to this opinion after considerable conversation with a Roman Catholic priest, Father Norton.

111 Father Norton, a member of the Society of the Sacred Mission, urged Chadwick to visit the College at Kelham (near Newark). Chadwick was impressed by his spirituality as well as his learning: 'Father Norton preached…The talk was poor enough, but the shining of his eyes was arresting, and what he said was strangely impressive.' p.3. 'He seems to have written on most things, and gave me an account of the Early Saints and Martyrs of Africa.' *South Africa,* p.6.

112 On board were a Mr Hoste, who is 'doctrinaire' and Mr and Mrs Clarke with whom Chadwick struck up a warm relationship. 'He has had a life full of adventure with Lions, Alligators, and the like. The Colonists think he is much too good a man to be giving his life to the natives.' *South Africa,* p.13.

113 *Minutes* of the Cliff College Committee, 30 Sept 1929.

114 *Minutes* of the Committee of Management, June 1921.

115 *Minutes* of the Cliff College Committee, 15 December 1921.

116 *Joyful News,* 20 October 1932.

117 *Minutes* of the Cliff College Committee, 9 May 1932.

118 *Joyful News,* 27 October 1932.

119 *Joyful News,* 25 February 1943.

120 *Joyful News,* 27 October 1932.

121 James Strawson, 'Methodist Theology 1850-1950', in A. Raymond George, *A History of the Methodist Church in Great Britain,* Vol. 3, p.221.

122 Sarah Chadwick, *Cliff – Past and Present, The story of how two great ventures became one,* pp.20-21.

123 Sarah Chadwick, *Cliff Past and Present,* p.22-23. This final section is entitled, 'The Final Word must be about Finance'.

124 *Joyful News,* 20 October 1932.

125 *Minutes* of the Cliff College Committee, 9 May 1932. An invitation was sent from the meeting. A very different process from the one we presently suffer.

126 *Minutes* of the Cliff College Committee, 20 October 1932. In fact the typed words, 'when Mr Chadwick passed away' have 'passed away' almost entirely rubbed out and 'retired' inserted.

127 *Minutes* of the Cliff College Committee, 20 October 1932.

128 D.W. Lambert writing in the *Joyful News,* 20 October 1932.

129 Ibid.

130 *Joyful News,* 20 October 1932.

CHAPTER 12

Here come the Trekkers

I t became the received wisdom in the College that the advent of the 'Trekkers' came from Chadwick himself. In the 1948 booklet published to advertise the work of the summer missions, there is 'A Short History of the Cliff College Trekkers', in which we read the following: 'In one of his periods of illness, Samuel Chadwick, then Principal of Cliff College, saw a vision of bands of young men going forth from the College to tramp the roads of England, Wales and Scotland, preaching and singing the Gospel of Jesus Christ as they went. That vision resulted, in 1925, in

The first Trek to leave Cliff College 1925. D.W. Lambert on the right

335

Mr Cook's Gospel cars described as the "Flying Column of Methodism" were the forerunner of Trekking.

the sending out from Cliff of the first band of Trekkers. Each year since, groups of men, in teams of eight or nine each, and in an ever-growing number of teams, have set forth from the College to tramp and, in later years, to cycle the roads of the country. The only gap in the programme was that caused by the war years.'[1] Students in the 1920s supported this notion: 'We can say it was Mr Chadwick's idea. It was one idea but I don't think that is the right word. It would seem to me we could safely say it was "Vision"... Sometimes we would hear the Principal talk of Sleepy Hollow where the thing began to germinate and eventually grow. Just what or where Sleepy Hollow was I don't know but something came new out of it and, by the end of the last term, the vision had formed into reality. Plans had been made, and the trek carts were ready and volunteers for the trek were ready for the road. The whole exercise was an act of faith. Plans were made for each cart to visit certain places; it was all walking; the places and distances would have to be planned so the trekkers would get there in a day'.[2] There was some confusion over the dating of the Treks' beginnings. Dunning in his obituary of Chadwick suggests it was after the illness in 1927 that Chadwick 'established the Order of Methodist Friars'.[3]

However, the Trekkers or Methodist Friars were in fact the logical outcome and built upon previous work of the College in the days of Champness and Cook. The Joyful News Mission had always employed people on mission as lay workers who, depending upon their ministry, were known as Joyful News Evangelists, Joyful News Female Evangelists and indeed the Joyful News Missionaries. On the whole they worked alone but it was not uncommon for them to work in small teams. Similarly the work of the Gospel Cars normally involved two people with a horse and substantial caravan. George Boak, a student at Cliff 1924-5, recalls his first meeting with the ministry of Cliff in the form of one of these Gospel Cars. 'I can just remember one of Thomas Champness's vans put down on the village green. It was drawn by a horse, and was the living quarters of a student at Cliff College training for the work. He had Christian literature to sell; and held meetings in the chapels, mainly for the evening services in each. During the day the people were visited and no doubt invited to the meetings he was conducting and to stimulate spiritual growth amongst the people of the village.'[4] George was born in 1898 and if the student did come from Cliff, which is likely, then of course it would have been one of the Gospel Cars which were at that time under the auspices of Thomas Cook rather than Champness.

When the work moved from Rochdale to Cliff College the ministry of the Gospel Cars continued and Cliff students were sent to join them on preaching days and weekends. It is clear from the reports that this was seen as an important element in the College's life.

During the First World War, the older evangelists were able to tour the villages. H.H. and Mrs Roberts 'toured for fifteen weeks through the summer of 1915 in the "Joshua Dawson Memorial Car" through the rural districts, singing and preaching the Gospel'.[5] So the concept of evangelists moving around the country preaching wherever they could was part of the ministry of the College from the beginning.

A particular event in the College's life during the autumn of 1920 was the spark of enthusiasm which gave students and staff the compulsion to look outwards. 'There has been a wonderful spirit of evangelism in the College. Early in the October term there came a mighty baptism of the Spirit. For weeks we were in a state of glorious revival. Out of that experience there came a passion to get

Seaside Mission: Tom Butler and Colleagues.

people saved. Groups of men have conducted open air services in the market place in various towns, and seen over a hundred grown-up people kneeling in a ring seeking salvation. There have been many striking and dramatic cases of conversion.'[6]

The effect of that was to place within the College a desire for evangelistic enterprise and, from the reports, it is clear that Dunning was the instigator, along with other staff. 'During the Christmas and Easter vacations, evangelistic campaigns were organised. A more extensive programme has been arranged for the summer. Pilgrim preachers will go in companies of two or three through the villages. They will trust to God for the supply of their needs. They will preach and pray but they will not beg. They will go as they are led, and stay in each place until either something happens or they are distinctly led to move on. Another set of men will conduct open air missions at seaside resorts, beginning at Skegness, and finishing at Southport.'[7] This 1921 *Report* set out the main elements of what became known as the Trekkers, a small group of students, preaching in chapels and the open air as they travelled, staying where they could and gladly receiving what was given, not asking for money nor pleading poverty.

That same year Norman Dunning led seaside missions during the summer vacation: 'during the holiday months the "Pilgrim Missioners" going on foot from village to village and "taking nothing in their purse" continue their fruitful witness.'[8] The Home Mission Report to the Conference of 1922 contained a full report by Norman Dunning about seaside evangelism:

> During the summer of 1921, we organised a series of open air meetings among the holidaymakers at half a dozen of our English seaside resorts and the general results were of so encouraging a nature, that this year we felt led of God to organise a Campaign of Seaside Evangelism on a much larger scale. From the beginning of July until the end of September, about forty of our young preachers were engaged in the exacting but blessed labour of seeking to influence for righteousness, thousands of people who were spending day after day holiday-making, without much thought to eternal things. The preachers included several well known ministers, and a large number of Students from Cliff College, in addition to one or two Evangelists, Undergraduates from the Universities, and Students from the Theological Institutions.[9]

The following year was the year which sealed the idea of students and evangelists having times of concentrated evangelistic mission as an integral part of the College course. For the report of the Twenty-fifth Anniversary of the College Chadwick recalled, 'In the year 1922 we began the Team method. It came unsought. The Free Churches of Chesterfield invited the Staff and Students to take possession of the Churches for ten days, and being persuaded that it was of the Lord, the invitation was accepted.'[10]

This invitation from the Chesterfield local churches and clergy for a mission over Easter 1922, was the impetus for what would become a significant development in the evangelism strategy of the College. The mission was apparently very successful. Chadwick took the wise decision to appoint Norman Dunning as leader, 'with absolute control over all the Evangelists'.[11] 'The men were entertained by friends in the locality and gave their whole time and strength to the work. They held services many times a day in the Churches and in the open air. Every house in the town was visited three times. The whole town was stirred. Memorable scenes occurred in the Market Place, scores of men and women openly professing themselves seekers for Christ. On the Saturday night a 'Procession of Witness' many hundreds of yards long walked through the streets singing and inviting people to a late service. The crowd filled four large chapels to overflowing. The special theatre services were thronged. In all upwards of 2,500 persons gave in their names as converts. The work is still progressing.'[12]

It was this experience which confirmed both the work in teams and the purpose of evangelistic endeavour. 'We shall organise Team Missions again but they will be for purely Evangelistic ends'.[13] In fact, Norman Dunning clearly considered that the development of Team Missions had a very positive effect on Methodism. 'During the last decade, the Team Mission did much to restore to Methodism her spiritual vitality. All over the world, ministers and lay preachers organised themselves into groups, and laid siege to town after town. Here was a method of doing evangelistic work which was acceptable to the Church and effective in the world. The first Team Mission was organised from Cliff, and conducted by Cliff men.'[14]

In 1923 the evangelism which is described by Norman Dunning looks very much like the later Trekkers but still without the carts. There is no indication of how they travelled around the country. 'From the middle of July until the end of September there were forty students engaged in the work of preaching the Gospel in unusual places. Groups of half-a-dozen men preached three times a day for a fortnight at Llandudno, Eastbourne, Margate, Yarmouth, Skegness, Redcar, Saltburn, Whitby, Scarboro', Filey, and Bridlington. In addition, a party of eight missioners conducted meetings on the various racecourses where race meetings were held between July and September. They visited Nottingham, Redcar, Stockton, York, Derby, Manchester and Doncaster and, in the midst of difficult circumstances, witness was born of Christ's Power to Save.'[15]

It was during 1925 that the title, so fondly used by Chadwick about these student missions, 'Trekkers' first appeared. Previously they were referred to as 'pilgrim missioners'. Samuel Chadwick had been ill and near to death, during which time he had a vision of the developing ministry of the College, which is related for us in a number of places. As we have seen, he curiously referred to an experience of 'Sleepy

Methodist Friars

Hollow' in which presumably he was recovering from illness and able to reflect on the College and its ministry. It is likely that the GP would offer him laudanum for his condition, which could explain the enhanced sensation of a visual experience:

> Sleepy Hollow has often been to me a place of vision, voices and vocation. It was in sickness that there came the call of God to the work of ministry while I was yet a lad in obscure poverty ... On another occasion, an Angel of the Lord found me baffled, beaten and bruised, after my first encounter with the kingdoms of darkness; and it was he who instructed me in the way of the Lord and showed me my way about in the Scriptures ... Three years ago I lay deep in the valley of shadows. The gates of death were not far away ... Suddenly the finger of God touched me ... vividly there came to me a vision of the world as my Lord had seen it.[16]

The comments from Chadwick all came four or five years after the reported events and contained the main characteristics of the trekkers: 'The men were to go in groups and I was to read to them the tenth chapter of Matthew ... they were to go as Witnesses, proclaiming everywhere the Gospel of God in Jesus Christ His Son. All other subjects were to be left to others; our business was to save souls. The Evangelists were to avoid vain and unprofitable controversy, though ready always to give a reason for their faith and hope.'[17]

The title Trekkers and possibly the advent of the Trek carts did begin in 1925 but the idea had developed over five years under the leadership of Dunning. The appointment of David W. Lambert in September 1924 brought a significant impetus to the development of the trekking missions. Lambert took charge of the missions work and deliberately built on this tradition. He wrote of the summer of 1925, 'The special feature of the year has been the trek of "Methodist Friars". The team missions began at Cliff and now the "Trekkers" lead a campaign of evangelism to those outside the Churches. They have a trekking outfit, and go without money and no set programme. They evangelise as they go. They make no collections, ask for no accommodation, seek no patronage. They sleep under canvas, prepare their own food, give their own testimony. They were on trek six weeks, covered 400 miles, and held services as often as three or four times a day. They never lacked a meal, never had a day's sickness and all their needs were wonderfully supplied. As shoes and stockings wore out, supplies were always at hand. At the end of the Campaign the trek account balanced to a penny.'[18]

When Chadwick, Dunning and particularly Lambert reflected on these treks, they saw themselves as the successors of disciples who had left everything and gone out in small groups to proclaim the gospel. Certainly in the Jubilee issue of the *Joyful News*, Lambert traces the trekkers back to the Matthean commission. 'In fulfilling the "Go" of Christ's evangelistic commission, they prove the "Lo" of His abiding presence'.[19] The Cliff Trekkers are called Methodist Friars because 'they seek to combine the joyous adventure and passionate devotion of St. Francis with the assured experience and world embracing Gospel of John Wesley.'[20]

T. Fred Wilson, who also became an Assistant Tutor at Cliff before the war, recalled that the first time he met a Cliff Trek he was converted under their ministry.[21] 'Attracted by their unconventionality, I went to hear the Cliff men at one of the Village chapels. When they came into the pulpit I was rather amused. It was the first time I had seen preachers dressed in shorts and khaki shirts. They looked like scouts. Soon amusement had given place to conviction and, before the service ended, I had surrendered to Christ.'[22] Wilson met a number of trekkers and had an idealised view of their life whilst on the road. However, he later became a student and discovered the reality of the situation. 'Soon I found that the adventure was not just what I had thought it was. Tramping in heavy shoes results in blisters; and when blisters are rubbed off and the raw flesh is chaffing, they can be really painful. Shall I never forget the day when I tramped with feet like that, the sun beating down upon us, the road sticky beneath us, and having a feeling of intense nausea caused by something in our diet? How I longed for the end of that journey. How I wondered if ever I would get there.'[23] He discovered, as many Cliff students have on mission, that the camaraderie of the team which can be so fulfilling can also be very demanding: 'After a few days there came the shock of finding that the whole team was as human as I was. It had always seemed to me that Trekkers were different from myself and that the frailties of human nature would not count in such fellowship. Not so ... I found that in living in such close proximity to one's fellows, as one must whilst on Trek, all the little points of temperament and personality are magnified and often become irritating. The first impulse is always to tell the other man what you think about him. The Christian way is to ask God if there is something in you which is affecting the other man in the same way'.[24]

Ready to leave Cliff - first stop Buxton

By 1927 the trekking method of these 'Methodist Friars' had become a firm tradition: 'We pioneer in evangelism. These missions are developing. Last summer we had three bands of Evangelistic Friars. This year we have seven. The work is a venture of faith. Each group carries its own outfit for sleeping and cooking. They take no collections, ask no favours, beg neither food nor money. They beg nothing neither do they refuse anything. Their needs are met, and to a penny all expenses are provided. As they go they preach, crowds are gathered, souls are saved. These Cliff College Friars have had campaigns at Blackpool, Southport, Leeds, Bristol, and Warrington with glorious results. These treks are experimental and preparatory. God has sent

344

us £500 towards the organisation of an order of evangelists who will be Knights of the Cross, seeking to win for Christ the multitudes outside the Churches.'[25]

Lambert cherished the hope that this trekking method would have wider implications in the British Church and saw the Cliff Trekking method as a work in progress. In the 1927 *Report* he wrote, 'The vision has not yet taken actual and abiding form but it is on the way. Meanwhile, during our summer vacations, we have sought to do for a few weeks, and in a small way, what we hope the Methodist friars of the future will do on a big scale and for many months together.'[26] By 1930 the idea had spread and Lambert was able to report, 'The evangelisation of the land by means of Trekking preachers holds the imagination of Methodism today. Each summer the roads are full of Trekkers. There are Missionary Trekkers, Theological Institution Trekkers, and University Trekkers. The Trek movement, as it exists today, was born at Cliff. We pioneer in evangelism and are delighted when others follow the track we have blazed.'[27]

In 1929 the large team mission was brought into question, though for the next seventy years the large team was to have a significant impact on a town or region. 'The trekking Friars is our latest adventure. For a few years we organised Team Missions but accommodation and comprehension dissipated their power, and the Churches were not ready for large accessions of converts. The Friars are detached from Church organisation. Their appeal is to those outside the Churches.'[28] The strategy of the Treks had now matured and was set out for the wider Church:

Some Facts about the Friars

1. The Methodist Friars are Cliff College men who give up their vacation to Campaign Evangelism.

2. They go on trek, carrying their outfit on a hand-pulled cart. They march from place to place, camp in the open or on schoolroom floors, and preach, sing and testify at every opportunity.

3. They take no collections, solicit no subscriptions, ask for no hospitality – they go forth in faith, and all their needs of every kind are met.

4. The first band of Methodist Friars set out in August, 1924. In six weeks they tramped four hundred miles and saw scores of men and women openly confess Jesus Christ as their Saviour and Lord.

5. During the summer of 1928 there were twelve Trek Parties out on campaign. In twelve weeks they tramped over three thousand miles, preached to thousands of people, and saw hundreds of conversions. They preached and testified in over two hundred towns and villages, conducted services on the sea-shore, on village greens, in market places, city squares, racecourses and at pleasure feasts and fairs.[29]

Lambert with the Irish Trek

The Anniversary Report for 1929 records: 'New features were added in 1928. In that year the first Irish Trek was undertaken from Belfast to Londonderry and back. At a week's campaign in the Leeds City Square there was a crowd every night of more than five hundred people, almost entirely men. In this year the Methodist Friars made their first appearance in Hyde Park and gave their joyous testimony in a Mission in Hyde Park, London, where the sure and joyous testimony of youth silenced the jeers and arguments of materialist and atheist alike.'[30]

Musical Trekkers

The gospel message which was preached had a Wesleyan optimism of grace and the reports of the work from the Trekkers reflected this: 'Hundreds have knelt on the coats of the Friars or on copies of *Joyful News* in the Market Place, Public Square, or open thoroughfare.'[31]

There was a song written for the Methodist Friars, which first appeared in the fourth edition of *Cliff College Choruses* in 1946, though it was probably formed in those days when the talk of the Methodist Friars was at its height.[32] Lambert maintained that music was always a part of the trekking experience, 'a choir of men who wanted to carry their message round the country'.[33]

> For we are the Friars, the Methodist friars;
> We'll go forth with Fire and Blood,
> And we'll bring them back to God
> With salvation to ev'ry nation,
> We will conquer with the Fire and the Blood.

In the 1929 *Cliff College Report*, the report of the treks is entitled, 'The Order of Methodist Friars' but the title did not survive Chadwick, except in the reports from Lambert who kept the idea of the Friars alive. Regularly in his accounts of the Treks in *Joyful News* he refers to himself as the 'Methodist Friar' or entitles his article as 'Friars' Corner'.[34] In a duplicated page given to students going on Trek in 1936, there is attached a 'Manifesto of the Methodist Friars', with, at the top, a Note Bene: 'This statement has been loyally accepted by each new generation of Friars. Please keep up the tradition. D.W.L.'[35] The Manifesto is then set out:

1. We travel by way of faith. (This means an attitude of constant prayer).

2. Our ONE and ONLY aim is to bring men and women to Jesus Christ and to extend His Kingdom.

3. We gladly give our TIME and STRENGTH, and ALL we have and are for this end.

4. Having done our part faithfully, we are prepared to leave the rest with God.

5. We realise that what we ARE is more important than what we <u>say</u> or <u>do</u>. Therefore we would ever be in an attitude of constant and utter dependence upon God.

6. While on Active Service we are prepared to follow with absolute loyalty the Appointed leaders.

7. We pledge ourselves, while on duty, not to spend money on ourselves, nor time on anything but work. (We need all our spare time for rest and devotion).[36]

Stanley B. Smith (Cliff 1929-30) indicates that he went on trek at Easter: 'At Easter 1930, many of us went trekking over the Pennines to Barnsley, where we conducted services in many Methodist churches there. We pulled a small wagon with our belongings on it. We were equipped at the College with stout boots and some sort of uniform. The first day's march was to Sheffield. My boots felt alright to begin with, but when my feet began to swell they became very painful. One of our students, from Cornwall, happened to have a motor-cycle, so I had to share it with him for the rest of the journey to Barnsley. After the services there, we went home for the Easter holidays.'[37]

Time for a "cuppa"

Eating was important for men travelling up to 20 miles a day pulling a cart. 'The midday meal was eaten en route. We pulled up. One would go off to get boiling water, free of course, for tea. For over eleven weeks, every midday meal included pineapple cubes, bought at Woolworth's 6d. (2½ p) per can. For long afterwards, I could not face pineapple.'[38] There were occasions where money was given and a feast was prepared. Ben Mackay recalls: 'I looked at the coins, they were two half-crowns (25p). When we arrived at the church we found the kitchen open for us. I spotted a frying-pan, and went to one of the others. "Here go to the butcher's down the street and get sausages and eggs with this," passing him the half-crowns. He was soon back, the butcher having given him a good supply for the money ... the sausages were soon in the pan, while hungry men smelling the cooking waited for the feast.'[39] The Trekkers were given food by people along the way: 'By this time we had accumulated a good amount of stale cake which showed that we got more than hot water when we visited a house to get some. The Methodist minister's daughter collected it from us and made a delicious pudding.'[40]

In 1930, and in a way which suggests a summary of the work of the College, there is a further reflection about the trekking. 'In 1925 the first Cliff Trek set out. Some ten men tramped over four hundred miles, sleeping on schoolroom floors or in a tent, living under camp conditions. All the way they preached and testified, and everywhere they saw men and women converted. They became known as the Methodist Friars; they combined the universal Gospel and assured testimony of the early Methodists with the joyous sacrifice and the simple life of the first Franciscans. Each year in increasing numbers but in the same simple way, the Cliff Friars have taken to the road. In parties of eight to ten, they have trekked a distance totalling over five thousand miles. They have borne witness on village greens and market squares, on crowded pleasure beaches and racecourses, to crowds of every size and kind. Everywhere they found a ready

Cycle Trek

response to their appeal. Men and women, living apart from God and His Church and with 'no use for religion' were arrested by their message and savingly converted. On the other hand, young people brought up in Christian homes and nurtured in religion felt the pull of their real and joyous message and were led to confess Christ, and so to find a personal experience of Him.'[41] Other ministers were supportive and J.A. Broadbelt spoke very warmly of the work of the Cliff Trekkers: 'God bless the Trekkers, and if you meet them be kind to them and help them.'[42]

The long summer vacation was given up to trekking and most of the students participated. In 1931 sixty students were on trek for more than ten weeks. Four parties moved around England, massing for great weekend campaigns at strategic centres like Manchester, Bristol and London. One trek crossed to Ireland and another pioneered its way into Scotland. The seaside campaigns at Blackpool and Bridlington have become features in the summer programmes of those popular resorts.'[43]

Colporteur carts had been known for much of the nineteenth century, both in this country and overseas. However a team of six, eight or even ten young men pulling a large cart was unusual. Pulling the trek carts was not the easiest of tasks, and the students trained by pulling them up and down the steep lane to Curbar Gap. 'The worst position on the cart was holding

1955 Trek

the shaft. Both hands had to be used to prevent the cart tipping backwards. Walking the fairly long daily distances, holding the shaft was much more tiring than pulling the ropes where arms were free.'[44] Ben Mackay who was a Scottish sailor and probably a strong man recalled, 'I did a lot of walking by the shaft.'[45] The design of the carts meant that they could carry all their goods, with tents, blankets and primus stove, plus literature. Shorts, shirts and shoes were supplied by the College. 'At the rear of the cart and at the bottom was a cupboard for foodstuffs, and utensils. When the cart was tilted back, it rested on this attachment.'[46] The carts weighed half a ton when loaded, and were painted black with a text on one side and the College name and badge on the other, in gold lettering.[47] They went long distances; Ben Mackay recalls in 1935 doing 610 miles between 24 June and 2 September and in 1936, 575 miles from 23 June to 7 September.[48]

There are memories of these Treks and Missions which are full of embellished comment. The leaders are built up: 'that splendid host of evangelists so magnificently captained by brothers Dunning, Brice and Roberts, whose song and speech in the streets and sanctuaries wrought exploits which oft have reminded me of Wesley.'[49] It is possible that the impact and the outcomes of the missions were exaggerated. 'Men and women by thousands found themselves in the glory-zone; ice-bound souls were strangely warmed; an infectious enthusiasm compelled hitherto undreamt of ministries; the challenge of splendid happenings silenced the gibes and obviated cynicism. Churches which had ceased to function save in feeblest form, proved themselves accoutred with the whole armour of God, and counted as Heaven's instruments'.[50]

Joseph Pearce speaks of the evangelists as 'God-intoxicated men, every chink, cranny and corner of their being under the dominance of the Divine … This was one of their outstanding assets, that they were purveyors of a pleasing gaiety, disbursers of the largesse of celestial vision, channels through which flowed the ever gladdening river of grace.'[51]

After World War II, the treks continued in the summer though most of the teams returned for or during the Derwent Convention. Traffic on the roads had increased in volume. Even on rural roads speed became dangerous and an accident befell one of the Treks.[52] The last treks, in the sense of teams of students pulling carts, were in 1959 when five of the seven trek teams were walking.[53]

Carts long left behind, but khaki shorts and shirts were not replaced until the 1966 Bridlington Trek

One further Trek took place in 1983 as part of the Centenary celebrations of the *Joyful News*. The idea came from a former student and evangelist, Steven Wild, who was at that time training for the Ministry and in his final year at Wesley College, Bristol. The vision, as optimistic as the reports earlier in the century, was to reach at least one hundred converts in that centenary year, by trekking, as had the students in the 30s, wearing the khaki uniform, shorts, and shirt. A replica Trek cart was constructed and a team of twelve former students walked with the Trek cart from Cliff to Blackpool and returning to Cliff between 8 July – 29 July. The team lived by faith during the Trek. Each day the group walked about fifteen miles and in the evening held a rally in a local church. The route and rallies were all arranged well in advance with a prayer card inviting people to pray and support the Centenary Trek. The Centenary Trek was

Centenary Trek

greeted as a great success, with many converts, and the team returned with optimistic stories to great acclaim on the Friday of the Derwent Week.

The last word on Trekking is left with D.W. Lambert, who was above all, the man who carried the vision through fifteen years:

> Behind the Treks there is something more than a mere attempt to fill up the summer vacation with evangelistic activities. The Cliff Treks came out of a vision, born of a burning passion to save the

masses of men and women outside the Church...Trekking is not a picnic, it is warfare, and at times the conflict is fierce...Cliff Trekkers learn to endure hardness as good soldiers of Christ Jesus...Trekking is not compulsory...the Cliff Boys carry the joy of their Lord in their faces because it is their hearts. They are bearers of *good* news, of *glad* tidings.'[54]

Trek "Send-off" 1947

355

A word of encouragement from Principal Tom Meadley for

one of the last teams to pull a cart 1958

1   *The Cliff College Trekkers. A Photographic Record.* (Calver: Cliff College, 1948).
2   George H. Boak, *Reminiscences and Reflections* (Scarborough: Pindar Print, 1980) p.2
3   *Joyful News*, 27 October 1932.
4   George Boak, *Reminiscences and Reflections*, p.2.
5   *Report of the Wesleyan Home Mission Fund* 1921, p.64.
6   *Report of the Wesleyan Home Mission Fund* 1921, p.60.
7   *Report of the Wesleyan Home Mission Fund* 1921, p.61.
8   *Report of the Wesleyan Home Mission Fund* 1922, p.73.
9   *Report of the Wesleyan Home Mission Fund* 1922, pp.68-72.
10 *Cliff College Report* 1929, p.17.
11 *Cliff College Report* 1929, p.17.
12 *Report of the Wesleyan Home Mission Fund* 1922, p.73.
13 *Cliff College Report* 1929, p.17.
14 *Cliff College Report* 1930, p.29.
15 *Cliff College Report* 1924, pp.35-6.
16 *Cliff College Report* 1928, pp.3-4.
17 *Cliff College Report* 1929, p.18.
18 *Report of the Wesleyan Home Mission Fund 1926,* p.85.
19 *Joyful News*, 1 June 1933.
20 *Joyful News*, 1 June 1933.
21 T.F. Wilson, 'Trekking' in *The Cliff Witness,* Vol.3, No.4, p.49. The Minutes of the College Committee record that a young man should be appointed in January 1939.
22 T.F. Wilson, 'Trekking', p.49.
23 T.F. Wilson, 'Trekking', p.50.
24 T.F. Wilson, 'Trekking', p.50.
25 *Report of the Wesleyan Home Mission Fund* 1927, p.111.
26 *Cliff College Report* 1927, p.35. There were three trek teams in the summer of 1926.
27 *Cliff College Report* 1930, p.29.
28 Report of the Home Mission Fund, 1929, p.76.
29 Report of the Home Mission Fund, 1929, pp.76-77.
30 *Cliff College 25th Anniversary Report* 1929, pp.34-36.
31 *Cliff College 25th Anniversary Report* 1929, pp.34-36.
32 J.H. Stringer (ed.), *Cliff College Choruses* (Calver: Cliff College Bookroom, 1946), No. 84.
33 *Joyful News,* 17 May 1934.
34 *Joyful News,* 4 September 1930.
35 Item L4 in the College Archives.
36 Item L4 in the College Archives.
37 Stanley B. Smith, *Far to Go* (Leicester: The Encore Press) p.32.
38 Ben Mackay, *A Tale that is told,* (Unpublished) p.295. He was a student in 1934 and the following year was on the evangelistic staff.
39 Ben Mackay, *A Tale that is told,* p.295.
40 Ben Mackay, *A Tale that is told,* p.296.
41 *Home Mission Fund Report* 1930, p.88.
42 *Joyful News,* 9 July 1931.

cont.

43 *Home Mission Fund Report,* 1931 p.88.
44 Ben Mackay, *A Tale that is told,* p.291.
45 Ben Mackay, *A Tale that is told,* p.291.
46 Ben Mackay, *A Tale that is told,* p.291.
47 Ben Mackay, *A Tale that is told,* p.291.
48 Ben Mackay, *A Tale that is told,* pp.292 and 319.
49 Joseph Pearce, 'Memories of the Cliff Crusaders' in *The Cliff Witness* Vol.2, No.3, 1938, p.46.
50 Joseph Pearce, 'Memories of the Cliff Crusaders' in *The Cliff Witness* Vol.2, No.3, 1938, p.46.
51 Ibid.
52 *Minutes* of the Cliff College General Committee, 9 October 1959. Five were walking, one cycle and one Van trek. The following year only one trek was walking and that was for part of the way to Morecambe, *Minutes,* 6 October 1960.
53 Letter, from Dr Wood to Steve Wild, 8 October 1982, when he was planning the centenary trek, expressing some caution from the College Committee, 'Mr Frank Blackwell remembers an accident that befell one of the last treks.'
54 *Joyful News,* 21 September 1933.

CHAPTER 13

Choose Life

Thomas Cook proposed to the College Committee that a 'Summer School should be held for 10 days in 1908 for the benefit of those who cannot come to the College for a lengthened period of training. The proposal is to have special lectures, morning and evening, on Bible Study, Christian Evidences, Sermon Construction, Elocution and kindred subjects, and to set the afternoons apart for recreation.'[1] Before approaching the Committee Cook had floated the idea with others and was sure of the 'success of the undertaking'.[2] With this proposal Thomas Cook and his wife, Jessie, followed the practice of the Guinness family in inviting people to join them for the summer period or holidays at other times.

Mrs Cook undertook this responsibility and even after her husband's death she hosted the visitors during the summer of 1913. However this practice ceased immediately Chadwick was appointed, for he 'did not see his way to make arrangements for summer visitors to the College on similar lines to those adopted by Mr and Mrs Cook, but hoped to submit proposals at a later meeting of the Committee for a Bible Conference in August.'[3]

The first Summer School of 1914 was brought forward to the first week in July, and Chadwick planned for a 'Bible Conference during the first three weeks of August',[4] though the plans did not materialise, 'A number of unforeseen circumstances arose that made it necessary to abandon them for this year'.[5] This clearly was the outbreak of War and the Committee hoped it would be possible to continue, 'in the confident expectation that the Providence that had so mercifully and wonderfully watched over the Institution from its commencement would not fail us in the time of National Crisis.'[6]

After the War the summer schools continued and in the summer of 1926 they were held in the first and last weeks of August when these days of inspiration and teaching were mainly attended by local preachers.

From 1905 an anniversary had been held, at first in March at Carver Street Chapel, Sheffield.[7] In 1907 the celebration of the anniversary was combined with the opening of the Champness Wing on Easter Monday at the College.[8] This pattern was followed until the first Anniversary Whitsuntide Meetings at Cliff in 1911.[9] It was in the period after the war that the Anniversary weekend at Whitsuntide really took hold of the imagination of the Methodist people. They came in buses from all parts of Britain for the day, and many people stayed locally for bed and breakfast in people's homes. Special trains were put on and from 1929 the 'Hallelujah Express' ran from London to Grindleford, stopping at many places on the way as advertised in the *Joyful News*. By the early thirties the whole event was a work of considerable precision, overseen by the notable Sheffield business-man and Cliff evangelist, H.H. Roberts. He arranged the serving of tea to the crowds who came; 'the organisation of the tea is a work of art. Twenty minutes are allowed for eating, and within ten minutes the tables are cleared and filled again ... It is half past five and the last sitting-down has just finished. The students are clearing the tables off the lawn. Within twenty minutes or so the tables will be gone and the lawn laid with seats for the evening meeting.'[10] It was the success of these events and the delight in singing new songs that prompted the publication of the first volume of *Cliff College Choruses*, at the Anniversary in 1934.[11] Immediately they sold well.

A profound impression of the scale of numbers of people attending the Anniversary Monday was gained for the public when Broadbelt, still at the height of his powers as an entrepreneur, had a photograph taken of the crowds filling the Terrace in 1935; this he then used at every opportunity. The impression was given of thousands of people attending this remarkable event. The weather was always a problem for them as this comment in 1936 reveals. 'I never saw the tables so wet at 2 o'clock in the afternoon and then "something happened" and we had not another drop of rain until well on into the evening.'[12] The story of the rain holding off from the Terrace through the prayers of H.H. Roberts became one of the faith stories of the event. 'It never rained on

Tea on the Terrace

H.H.R.'s tablecloths' was the tale – an accusation often relayed to staff on more recent Bank Holiday Mondays when rain poured down and swept the crowds into the marquees and Cliff Hall. It was told as though somehow those who now led the work at Cliff were to blame. Ernest Steele, a Cliff Evangelist, used to say; 'It didn't rain on his table cloths because he never put them out if it was raining!'

The Summer Schools continued into Broadbelt's time and in 1938 became known as the Derwent Convention with a week of Bible teaching and seminars for deepening the spiritual life and witness of those who attended. It was at a Committee in October 1937 that the plans were laid for the Whitsuntide Camp, 'for a long weekend in the field at the back of the College. Also the enlargement of the Summer School by the formation of a camp for men, the women to be accommodated in the College, and the Summer School meetings to be held in a tent. It was hoped thus to accommodate five hundred students at the Summer School, and to give it a new name, 'The Derwent Convention'. The programme was to be threefold:- Bible Study, Scriptural Holiness and Evangelism at Home and Abroad,'[13] and the evening worship, 'in a Tent in the Park'.[14]

All of this occurred in the beautiful Derbyshire Dales and with trips out from the College to experience the countryside. Broadbelt captured for the late thirties the possibility of coach trips, and the genius of the holidays which Guinness and Cook had offered in those years earlier. To facilitate these events he took one of his boldest decisions, to build the substantial Cliff Hall. 'We propose to build a Cliff Tea Hall which will cost some £5,000 and which will house all our Lunch and Tea arrangements for the Anniversary and for the Derwent Convention.'[15] Though affected by World War II the Derwent Week emerged as a very successful recipe for combining a family holiday, Bible study and training for Christian leadership.

During war years the Anniversary soldiered on. In 1940 there were three days of meetings though the crowds were smaller, and the day finished early before the blackout. H.H. Roberts reckoned that almost 2,000 people had taken tea. In 1941 some people stayed in the village, though over the weekend only 150 people were present and some three to five hundred on the Monday.[16] The Youth camp was retained as part of the Anniversary weekend. In 1943, one hundred and thirty young men and women had attended, 'who taxed all possible accommodation to the utmost.'[17] The number of young people was a new feature and 'they made the weekend ... the camp has been an unqualified success. We shall do it again.'[18] The 1944 Anniversary was very small because of the difficulty of travel in May 1944. The war preparations for the D-Day landings meant that fuel was rationed and travel passes were not readily available. The advertisements in the *Joyful News* that year for the Anniversary had been very confident: 'forty years on' celebrating the work and ministry. However those who attended came mostly from the local area and travelled mainly by cycle or foot. The *Joyful News* in late May announced that the main public meetings and the camp were cancelled.[19] The post-war Anniversary in 1945 was the 'Sixth War-Time Anniversary and Victory Gatherings'.[20] Broadbelt announced through the *Joyful News* that the College would be opened in September to receive students but that the Derwent Convention was postponed from August 1945 to 1946,[21] indicating there was simply too much work needing to be done to prepare the College for the autumn term.

In 1942, due to the war, the Derwent Convention was moved to Green Street Methodist Church, Morecambe and held during Holy Week, concluding on Easter Monday. The report is written in glorious tones by Joe Blinco.[22] In 1944 the theme, preparing people

Derwent 1948

for the post war needs of the country and Christian mission, was 'Scriptural Holiness expressing itself in Social righteousness and Aggressive Evangelism.' The first Derwent Convention after the War in 1946 set the pattern for the future and was the dream Broadbelt had in the late 1930s. Following the war he hoped to increase the Young People's Camp from 250 to 600 at the Derwent.[23] The main events were in full swing in 1946 with 500 applications for the 350 available places in the Young People's Camp at the Anniversary. Though there had been torrential rain the 'Meetings had been crowned with blessing'.[24]

These two main public ministries continued and were built upon after the war. It was at the 1953 Anniversary that an Upper Tent for the Whit-Monday was in place for the first time. Before this an overflow meeting had been held on the Principal's lawn with the speaker standing in the porch. The slope of the land in the Upper Tent caused the seating, mainly forms, to fall over and Tom Butler made an appeal for £2,000 to have the plot for the marquee levelled. This work was carried out before the following year and the 'top tent' evening meetings became the platform for Tom Butler and Herbert Silverwood whose humour and skill in leading a meeting became legendary.

The Jubilee day of the opening of the College was celebrated on 3 March 1954, Ash Wednesday, and those present walked in the snow to All Saints Parish Church, Curbar, and had a luncheon at the College after which the President of Conference, Dr Donald Soper, brought a message.[25]   He called for people 'with emotion for the truth, a heart that was on fire, with a fire that was directed and disciplined by faith and knowledge above all things.'[26] He expressed admiration for the work and ministry of Cliff, 'outside the porch before people could be brought into the pew', even though he could not subscribe to 'some of the bylaws'[27], by which he presumably meant the strict college rules for the student body. The Jubilee was also the occasion for an appeal for £2,000 to improve the lecture facilities, but as indicated in chapter eight, this did not reach its target.

Joe Blinco and Billy Graham emerge from the Cloisters

The greatest Anniversary meeting was undoubtedly that of 1954, the Jubilee of the College and the year Billy Graham came to preach. Eagles had the wisdom to identify Billy Graham as one of the great preachers, and from the outset the *Joyful News* supported Dr Graham in the face of criticism from many church leaders. Cliff evangelists and students went to Haringey to support the mission there. The *Joyful News* of 11 March carried commendations of the ministry of Billy Graham from Christian leaders in this country and America.[28] Apart from Sangster the attempt was unconvincing since it really needed support from a senior Bishop, but the criticisms of Billy Graham were fierce.[29] 'Most Britons were antagonistic when he came over. They deplored the linking of American ballyhoo with religion. Only a Suffragan Bishop and a Conservative M.P. were eager to attach their names to his Greater London Crusade.'[30] Graham agreed to come to the Cliff Anniversary on the Monday. This was a stroke of genius on the part of Eagles and gained the College an immense amount of good publicity. There were articles in the major Christian and local press.[31]

(Above) H.H. & Mrs Roberts with their team preparing teas in the new Cliff Hall, 1939. (Below) 'Volunteers' washing up.

The *Joyful News* carried a map with the parking arrangements for coaches and cars, and eating arrangements for the day. The event was planned with military precision and the advance publicity in the *News Chronicle* spoke of 50,000 expected.[32] In the event 60,000 people attended and no one who was there will forget that rainy day.[33] The *Sheffield Telegraph* inflated the numbers to 70,000 and the *Daily Express* claimed 40,000 but the other papers carried the police estimates.[34] Tom Butler was in charge of feeding and coping with this crowd with 370 volunteers. The *Derbyshire Times* ran away with enthusiasm for numbers, 'Over seven tons of food were used to feed the people in relays, of 1,000 in Cliff Hall. As they waited to be served

the visiting crowds sang hymns (and were entertained by Herbert Silverwood). Over 5,000 packed lunches were served, and 10,000 snacks provided in four buffets situated at various points in the grounds ... they had used 4,500 cakes, 130 gallons of milk, 336 pounds of tea, 1,500 loaves, 150 boxes of biscuits, and 350 dozen bottles of mineral waters.'[35]

Wilson Grady from the Graham team, with Canon Bryan Green, had been the main speakers for the weekend. The huge crowds attending on the Monday, travelling in vehicles on the then narrow roads into the heart of the Peak, caused Billy Graham to be delayed and he arrived late. People came in a thousand coaches, hundreds of cars, and buses which ran a shuttle service from Sheffield and

Chesterfield, or used the shuttle bus from Grindleford station to Calver Sough. Many people walked the two miles in the rain from the bus terminus at the neighbouring village of Baslow. 'The roads through the village were a sea of people with coaches and cars edging slowly through, nose to tail. Mr Graham himself, travelling from Manchester, was delayed for 80 minutes by the throng. Sun bronzed and smiling, he mounted a simple wooden platform and began with a joke about the weather. Within two minutes the rain had stopped and while he was preaching the sun broke through for the first time.'[36] The meeting was in Cliff Park field with a temporary platform made of new wood, erected towards the bottom of the field. With the ground being saturated the huge crowd of people stood anywhere they could up the hillside. Billy began the address by saying, 'This is a wonderful English Day. It's wonderful to be here'.

After the morning meeting, the crowd mostly remained where they were in the rain on the Cliff Park field. 'A huge cloud seemed to pour its whole contents upon the patient multitude who were waiting for Dr Graham's second and last appearance in the evening. Evangelist Herbert Silverwood seeing the plight of the crowd rushed to the empty platform with some colleagues helping, and began by saying amid tumultuous laughter that he was by no means a dry preacher. Many other witticisms followed, interspersed with rousing choruses for half an hour or more, during which the crowd still more increased in size until the park (i.e. Cliff Park field) was almost full to capacity. Then as previously, at the time appointed for the evening meeting, the rain stopped as suddenly it had begun. Exit a dripping Silverwood, and the platform party arrived.'[37]

Billy Graham showed, while at Cliff, the deft touches which have made him such a world-renowned preacher and leader. He showed the personal touch too, by visiting Evangeline Haslock, wife of the Secretary Eric Haslock, who for four and half years had been bed-ridden with kidney trouble.[38] Ever gracious, he showed an awareness of the place of Cliff in Methodism and commended his hosts and his audience. 'I have never seen Dr Graham so amazed with his audience, "Nothing can quite be compared with this – not in the whole of my ministry. In the U.S.A., after a few drops of rain the crowd would melt away. You have got something here we have not got in America."'[39] His preaching began with reference to contemporary issues, in this case the atomic bomb, and stories of people he had met, and then moved to the spiritual issue he wanted

CROWD A RAIN-SOAKED HILL TO HEAR BILLY GRAHAM

60,000, crowd a rain soaked hill to hear Billy Graham

to bring home to his hearers and the address concluded with a clear invitation to respond. No one does this better than Billy Graham.

In the afternoon he preached from John 16:8-11 about the Holy Spirit coming to convict of sin and righteousness and judgement. 'This world is in a very serious condition. Unless, somehow we can solve our problems quickly we are heading towards a third world war of H-bombs that can wipe out great areas of civilisation ... God says every soul is going to face a judgement of God. That will be 10,000 times worse than the H-bomb if you are outside Christ[40] ... some of you came out of curiosity or because somebody brought you in a coach ... but if you refuse Christ when you have this opportunity to-day you will stand before the judgement of God.'[41] Despite the weather, 'A great hush fell on the crowd as with ease and simplicity he expounded the words from John.'[42] In the evening from Deuteronomy 30:19, 'I have set before you life and death. Therefore choose life.' The plans for counselling enquirers on the Tennis Court, half way up the hill, were put aside with such large crowds and the problem of moving on a muddy field. People were invited to hold up a hat, handkerchief, or the hymn sheet produced for the occasion, as a sign that, 'I'm going to receive Christ, obey Christ, live for Christ' and they prayed a prayer of response after Dr Graham.[43] Thousands did this, particularly at the evening meeting, when there was a sea of white handkies and hymn sheets. After the prayer Billy Graham invited people to write to the Principal and he would respond with literature for them. Remarkably, by the end of June four hundred had done so.[44]

Another view of the human story from this event came from the *News Chronicle*, which reported, 'Ordeal of the 60,000; rain, mud and chaos at Billy Graham's last rally'.[45] It focussed on the 'many' who fainted, had cuts and bruises, or were lost in the crowd. The article paints the impression of a bronzed American evangelist who kept people spell-bound by his preaching and then abandoned the scene with the people 'left in a sea of mud.'[46] Apparently twenty people were left stranded, unable to find their coach which after waiting had returned home. Those who remained camped down in the college and five took a taxi home.[47] Other papers had the story that heroically the local farmers had pulled out the cars and coaches, which were axle deep in the mud from the fields. Local memory has it they were paid 2s 6d by each grateful car and coach driver. Horace Dalton, at the time the College's tenant farmer of Stanton Ford Farm, received special mention for his efforts, though in typical style he was concerned about the land, 'we shall have to write this pasture land off for weeks'.[48]

This event, one day in 1954, lives on in the memory not only of those who attended but, for some considerable time, of all who then lived in the Hope Valley, the day that Cliff College brought the valley to a stand-still. All those who are supporters of Cliff recall it as the 'great feast' when so many attended and so many responded, leading many to conclude that in all its history Cliff has not had an Anniversary like it before or since. Cyril Powell who was at that time one of the Cliff Tutors summed up the experience as follows: 'No one present will ever forget it. It would have been so easy at many stages on the Sunday and on the Monday to have lost heart: the weather seemed to be so adverse. But that never happened. Everybody was marvellously sustained, and the story is one of victory. As so often

happens, God turned the very adverse conditions to His advantage, and if some of our prayers weren't answered quite in the form that we asked them, they were answered in a way that exceeded our greatest expectations ... this day at Cliff will be for thousands present a never-to-be-forgotten day. For thousands faced the choice and responded.'[49]

371

Billy Graham indicated that he might return to Cliff the following year; 'he hoped to visit Cliff next year during his campaign to the North'.[50] That did not occur. The Anniversary of the following year, 1955, set the scene for the meetings[51] right through to 1984 and the

Sunshine Corner
Whit Monday 1952

event began to have the ethos of a celebration of a bygone era. Nevertheless there were some glorious and memorable events over the years. The numbers attending the bank holiday Monday meetings were considerable for many years, with 16,000 reported in 1955,[52] and 15,000 in 1958.[53]

Tom Meadley was keen to ensure that the centenary of Chadwick's birth was celebrated and on Saturday 17 September 1960, a day after his birth date, Norman Dunning and Joe Brice spoke at a 'two hour convention'.[54] The third member of that trio who worked with Chadwick through the 1930's was D.W. Lambert, by this time Principal of the Lebanon Bible College, and he spoke at the Derwent Convention evening meetings for that year. On the whole this was a low key celebration, but the book edited by Lambert for the centenary of Chadwick's birth sold very well, *Through the year with Samuel Chadwick*, a series of devotional readings for every Sunday of the year.[55] Meadley, who was very keen to increase the College library provision, requested donations for a Chadwick Library fund. The money was invested and is still contributing to the Library expenses of today.

Centenaries began to come thick and fast, with the outstanding one being the Centenary of the *Joyful News*. Dr Skevington Wood, as a renowned historian and writer, ensured that booklets were written about the three pioneers of Cliff: Champness, Cook and Chadwick;

John Moorley, on behalf of the Cliff College Fellowship, compiled *Cliff in Pictures* and the College republished Amos Cresswell's booklet, *The Story of Cliff*. The Centenary Day was 22 February 1983 and in a cold Cliff Hall an Anniversary Meeting was held, though Donald English as the main speaker warmed those who attended the rally. The Centenary Fund was launched seeking £100,000 which provided funding for further staff accommodation. That summer, as we have recounted, a former student, the Rev Steven Wild, led a Centenary Trek, setting out on 8 July and returning three weeks later during the Derwent Convention. Arthur Wood wrote, 'Replicas of the old-style carts are being specially constructed and the team of past students who are undertaking the journey to Blackpool and back have already gone into training. Their prayer is that the Lord will give them a hundred souls en route to mark the Centenary.'[56] In fact only one Trek cart was made by Steve Wild's father, and is still used by the College today.

The Anniversary changed its name in 1984 to become the 'Celebration Weekend', continuing the great traditions but the numbers attending gradually reduced. Through the eighties it was estimated that 6-8,000 people came depending upon the weather. There were marvellous moments. Who could forget being seated on the Terrace on a warm Monday evening with Donald English preaching on 'Living a Holy life' with the scent of wild garlic in the air, caused by people walking on the prayer paths, or recall great moments when 'sons of Cliff' came as President of the Methodist Conference to preach at the morning meeting on the Terrace, first the College Principal Bill Davies and then the Rev Brian Hoare. Over the years it was evident that the crowds were slowly diminishing and in an attempt to stem the tide, new ventures were tried in music with 'City of Gold' and on the Monday evening a greatly appreciated service for Healing and Wholeness.

It became clear, however, that a totally new venture was needed. Gone were the days when the Cliff Anniversary was the only event of its kind. Now there were Spring Harvest, Easter People, Greenbelt, Soul Survivor, and many others. Both for Derwent Week and the Celebration Weekend it was time for a thorough overhaul, new thought and reconsideration. The College had changed too; no longer were there only two courses with most students staying only one year, which could be a long one. Now the

College dealt with over two hundred students and offered fourteen courses. The effect of this increased workload across the year on both teaching and support staff, with these two major events at the end of the year, was telling. The creative work which gave rise to major changes was undertaken in the winter of 2001, and 'The Festival' was launched for 2003. It attempted to take the best of both events and mould them into a new event running from Saturday of the Spring Bank Holiday weekend to the Friday breakfast. The first in 2003 was a great success especially for those who experienced 'Festival' for the whole week. Numbers were nowhere near those of previous years,

 but it was believed then and believed now, that a new type of event has been born onto which it will be possible to build for future years. What then of the future? The Staff hope and pray that the 'Festival' will go from strength to strength, and there are in addition many other events at the College which now have a greater strategic influence on the church in this country.

Building the Conference (now Stanton) Centre in 1968 meant that the College could host a series of weekend conferences and receive church and other groups who hired the premises. Initially Mary Lambert had the promotion and organisation of the Conferences as her remit and a plan quickly developed. In the first year of operation the College had an ambitious programme of six 'weekend courses' between October 1969 and the following May covering the topics: Leading the Church, Understanding the Faith, New Ways of Evangelism, Vocation, House Groups, The Holy Spirit.[57] The next programme appeared for the year 1971-72 with three conferences. These became the pattern for future years. In that year the topics for the new 'Cliff Conferences' were: 'A Faith for Today' with Dr Stephen Travis, 'Counselling' with Dr Frank Lake, and 'Vocation' led by the Cliff Tutors.[58] The pattern of various conferences continued through the next two decades with the best attended ones being on 'Healing and Wholeness', 'Prayer' and 'Counselling'. Some were ground-breaking, such as the invitation to the gracious Roman Catholic Father Ian Petit; or the dramatic weekend in November 1987 entitled 'Prophecy Today' with Dr Clifford Hill who caused quite a stir. Mostly the weekends were reflective and people found nourishing teaching, good fellowship and, under Bill Davies's leadership, inspiring worship. All these contributed to thirty years of regular conferences. In the late eighties the College held a series of four-day conferences on 'Approaches to Evangelism' and 'Working in Church and Community'. These proved small but valued consultations, and in the early nineties, the College embarked on short 'exposition' consultations at the suggestion of Donald English who was concerned to develop the next generation of expository preachers. People came by invitation and met with scholars such as Professors Jimmy Dunn, Frances Young, John Rogerson, and of course Donald English and Bill Davies.

The renovation of Cliff Hall in 1988 and crucially the installation of heating throughout the hall enabled the College to offer larger conferences and a new constituency. The first of these major conferences was a regional consultation in May 1988 of the World Methodist Evangelism Institute. 'Regional' in this context meant Europe, including for the first time Eastern European countries where travel was available in a new way. The driving force behind the W.M.E.I. were Dr George Morris and Dr Eddie Fox who had raised support from the United States for the travel and accommodation costs of delegates from the developing world. The conference was a great success and it was that experience which led to the College hosting the World Methodist Evangelism Institute, Fifth International Seminar in January 1993. One hundred and thirty-seven people representing forty-two countries attended a seminar which 'proved to be of deep fellowship, providing a new framework

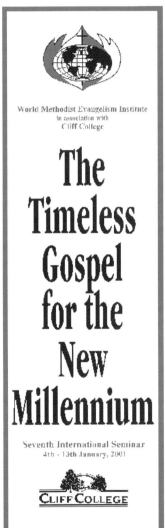

World Methodist Evangelism Institute
in association with
Cliff College

The Timeless Gospel for the New Millennium

Seventh International Seminar
4th - 13th January, 2001

CLIFF COLLEGE

for inspiration, teaching, sharing and challenge.'[59] The experience of hosting this conference convinced the College staff that they now had the facilities and the know-how to run complex, high profile conferences. The second International Seminar was held in January 2001 with the theme, 'The Timeless Gospel for the New Millennium'. There were over two hundred delegates from forty-three countries and every continent.

A number of other conferences were planned by the College in the nineties, and in January 1994 the first of a series of six preaching conferences took place having the title 'Preaching – A Lost Art?' with Fred Craddock, Donald English and Colin Morris. Over two hundred people attended from Britain and Ireland and the feedback was excellent: 'The conference was a milestone, a watershed in my life ... I have never before had access to such high quality teaching or an opportunity to explore such issues. I have felt affirmed in my call, been encouraged, challenged, horizons expanded and my desire to learn more and preach 'better' increased.'[60] It became clear that the College had learned a way of delivering conferences on subjects which ministers, local preachers and lay workers considered vital. The four annual conferences which followed built on this success, promoted as 'The Art of Preaching', but were widely known in Methodism simply as 'The Preaching Conference'.[61]

The most recent of the these major conferences called 'Shapes of Future Church' was held in January 2004 led by Dr Martyn Atkins with speakers who are at the leading edge of thinking about the issues facing the church. The chief aim of the conference was to explore and reflect upon some of the patterns of church beginning to emerge in Britain in the early 21st century in the hope of discerning more clearly where God is leading, but also 'giving permission' to faithful Christian people, many of them Methodist, to think new thoughts about church and its place in God's missionary and redemptive purposes today.

Most people associated with or observing the ministry of Cliff would see its public face as being primarily the 'Anniversary' or 'Celebration Weekend', but in the past twenty years that focus has moved. The public ministry is now and will be in the future a multi-faceted approach. The College already has plans to promote a series of short courses, linked to a reformulated Open Learning Centre, under the banner of 'Horizons – Learning for Christian Living'.

---

1 Minutes of the Committee of Management, 18 November 1907.
2 Ibid.
3 Minutes of the Committee of Management, 24 October 1913.
4 Minutes of the Committee of Management, 18 May 1914.
5 Minutes of the Committee of Management, 31 August 1914.
6 Minutes of the Committee of Management, 31 August 1914.
7 *Joyful News,* 15 March 1906.

cont.

8 *Joyful News,* 28 March 1907.

9 *Joyful News,* 8 June 1911. Two of the three previous Easter Mondays had suffered from bad weather, and in 1908 sudden squalls of snow fell. Therefore they moved to the later and warmer Whit weekend.

10 *Joyful News,* 8 June 1933.

11 Tom Jones (ed), *Cliff College Choruses Vol. 1* (Calver: Cliff College, 1934).

12 *Joyful News,* 8 June 1936.

13 Minutes of the Cliff College Committee, 1 October 1937.

14 *Joyful News,* 23 June 1938.

15 *Joyful News,* 23 June 1938.

16 *Joyful News,* 5 June 1941.

17 Minutes of the Cliff College Committee, 26 October 1943.

18 Joe Blinco writing in the *Joyful News,* 24 June 1943.

19 *Joyful News,* 25 May 1944.

20 *Joyful News,* 10 May 1945.

21 *Joyful News,* 21 June 1945.

22 *Joyful News,* 23 April 1942.

23 Ibid.

24 Minutes of the Cliff College Committee, 15 November 1946.

25 A handwritten note from Eagles, on the back of the invitation, indicates, 'The weather at the Jubilee was very wintry with much snow. This prevented many people coming on the day. The House party numbered 80. The College chapel was absolutely full on the Tuesday evening, with extra seats in the aisle and vestibule. There were 150-160 for lunch. Attendances at the services at the Parish Church were approximately, Morning 300, Afternoon 350, Evening 320.

26 *The Derbyshire Times,* Friday 5 March 1954, p.10.

27 *The Methodist Recorder,* 11 March 1954. The *Joyful News* did not report that point!

28 *Joyful News,* 11 March 1954. The Church leaders were the Rt Rev H.R. Gough, Bishop of Barking, the Rev Dr W.E. Sangster, the Rev Dr F. Townley Lord, the Rev Preb. Colin C. Ferr, the Rev Dr D.G. Barnhouse, First Presbyterian Church, Philadelphia, and the Rev Dr John Weaver, Dean of Detroit Cathedral. Alf Lawson wrote on the ministry of Billy Graham 25 March 1954, and Joe Blinco had an article almost every week about Billy Graham and the London Crusade.

29 It was widely rumoured that the Archbishop had asked him not to come to London and the Christian and daily press had been critical of this young brash American preacher.

30 *Sheffield Telegraph,* 7 June 1954. The article does go on to reveal that The Prime Minster, Winston Churchill, Dr Fisher, the Archbishop, the Lord Mayor of London and the Dean of Westminster changed their minds. Fisher wrote, 'Though it started with much publicity, it was not publicity that collected those great audiences and held them with increasing effect over three months.'

31 Of course the *Joyful News* each week but also the *Methodist Recorder, Christian Herald, The Christian, The Sunday Companion, Derbyshire Times,* and *Sheffield Star.*

cont.

32 7 June 1954, an article written the previous day.

33 The following papers covered the event next day, 8 June, most with a reporter present: *The Daily Express, The Daily Mail, News Chronicle, Daily Despatch, Daily Herald, The Sheffield Telegraph, the Star,* and on the 10 June, the *Joyful News* and *Methodist Recorder,* 11 June *The Derbyshire Times. The Manchester Guardian,* on 8 June carried a brief piece.

34 *Sheffield Telegraph*, and *Daily Express,* 8 June 1954.

35 *The Derbyshire Times*, 11 June 1954.

36 *Daily Mail,* 8 June 1954.

37 *Methodist Recorder*, 10 June 1954.

38 *Derbyshire Times,* 11 June 1954.

39 Eric Tattersall, in the *Methodist Recorder*, 10 June 1954.

40 *Daily Despatch,* 8 June 1954.

41 *Derbyshire Times,* 11 June 1954.

42 *Derbyshire Times,* 11 June 1954.

43 *Joyful News,* 10 June 1954.

44 *Joyful News,* 1 July 1954.

45 *News Chronicle,* 8 June 1954.

46 Ibid.

47 Ibid.

48 *Sheffield Telegraph,* 8 June 1954.

49 *Joyful News,* 10 June 1954.

50 *Methodist Recorder*, 10 June 1954.

51 *Joyful News,* 19 May 1955.

52 *Sheffield Telegraph,* (precise date lost) June 1955.

53 *Sheffield Telegraph,* 26 May 1958.

54 *Joyful News,* 18 August 1960.

55 D.W. Lambert, *Through the Year with Samuel Chadwick* (London: Epworth Press, 1960).

56 *Cliff Witness,* Summer 1983, Vol 20, No 2.

57 *Cliff Witness,* December 1968.

58 *Cliff Witness,* November 1971.

59 Taken from the opening paragraph of a twenty-one page report summarizing the outcomes of the conference for the delegates.

60 Comments taken from the assessment forms completed at the end of the conference.

61 In January 1995 the main speakers were the Rev Brian Beck, Dr William Davies, Professors Ella Pearson and Henry Mitchell. In January 1996, Drs Donald English and Debra Washington, and Professor William Abraham. In April 1997, Professor Fred Craddock, and Drs Colin Morris and Judith Rossall. In Jan 1998 Drs Donald English, Ben Witherington III and the Rev Jim Graham. In January 2002 with J. Geoffrey Stephenson, Dr David Wilkinson and the Rev Graham Horsley.

CHAPTER 14

Evangelise or Perish

The desire to engage in evangelism was the driving force for the development of the *Joyful News* Training Home and Mission. What today we would call a 'seminar', Champness called the 'Grindstone' in which he offered training on the practical aspects of mission and ministry. He focussed on the methods of winning people for Christ and enabling their nurture. His book, *Soul Saving Preaching*, was an urgent call for preachers to see evangelism and the saving of souls as their main aim.

He published a remarkable book about street preaching in 1901 by a Mr W. Foster, who was known widely as 'Praying Billy', the title of the book. The *Joyful News* regularly made a call in its pages for its readers to engage in winning people for Christ.

One of the purposes of the *Joyful News* was to publish reports of revivals, and from its first issue the work of Thomas Cook, the Connexional Evangelist, is noted, inviting people to support his meetings. Details of the ministry of D.L. Moody and his meetings in Britain appear in most issues from the second edition, with the

---

THURSDAY, FEBRUARY 22, 1883.

BIRMINGHAM.

The Rev. T. COOK

Begins a MISSION in

ISLINGTON CHAPEL,

ON SUNDAY, MARCH 4th.

METHODISTS OF BIRMINGHAM
Rally round him, and expect that hundreds will be converted the first week.

---

commendation, 'Here Mr Moody is at his best directing penitents to the Saviour'.[1] The Champnesses had met Moody years earlier: 'It was about the year 1871 or 1872 that we met for the first time. He called upon us when he came over prospecting. We were then in Leeds.'[2] A weekly list of 'Evangelistic Engagements' first appears in the *Joyful News* from 11 September 1884 and shows the names of the Revs Cook, Champness, Stuart and Waugh with a Mr Sampson and Cawood, and the town in which they were preaching.

During April 1885 the lead article in the *Joyful News* dealt with the training of lay evangelists. The burden of the article was that 'something should be done to begin a scheme for the training of evangelists to work in the villages of this country.'[3] Champness was keen to promote evangelism by all means and, in April 1885, published a plan for the 'Revival of the Work of God' suggested by the Rev John McKenny, a Wesleyan Minister.[4] He was keen about the scheme which, if adopted by all Methodists would, he judged, have the twin benefit of filling all Methodist chapels, and 'in time empty the public houses, which means seeing the prisons and workhouses without tenants also.'[5] It is clear that he linked evangelism and social reform based on the conversion of individuals, as did Chadwick, and essential to that was a move towards temperance. The proposed plan for revival was simple: 'Let each member of the Church strive for the conversion of one soul during the year, and feel the responsibility of the task he undertakes ... if prayer, faith and effort be combined, our Churches MAY be more than doubled. There will be great improvement in piety, and increase of Members.'[6] Those who were office-holders were invited to seek to bring more than one person for conversion; Class leaders were asked to recommend this to their Classes, and set aside time at noon each day, to pray for this work.

It must be remembered that one of the driving motivations for Champness was to call the Church to evangelism. In May 1885, a further article appeared about the training of lay evangelists. Their earlier article had an impact, and caused discussion in the Theological Institution Committee, 'that while the committee deeply sympathises with the necessity of making Lay Agency as efficient as possible, it be represented to Mr Champness that the question properly belongs to the Home Missionary Committee.'[7] Champness refused to think of this as a way to shelve the matter, one which he considered was so important; 'we wish the Home Mission Secretaries would take the matter up and give us a plan.'[8] The impression Champness gave was of a church dragging its feet on mission and evangelism while he was pioneering new initiatives. Notice that within the initial aims of the *Joyful News* he wanted no church politics, but he was prepared to engage in discussions of strategy, if it touched on evangelism.

In May 1885 it became clear that the issue of training lay evangelists would come before the Conference. Champness commented in the *Joyful News*, 'In the meantime, the Editor of this paper means to do something himself. During the past year, he has had some young men living with him and working under his eye and the success he has met with has encouraged him to go on in the same direction until the Connexion takes the matter up.'[9]

By September, Champness had his first trainees, Reed and Seager, for Village Evangelism,[10] and during October he referred to his manse as a 'Home for Village Evangelists'.[11] From the beginning he had more invitations than he could manage; 'Let us say once and for all that we do not have a large stock of ready-made preachers on hand, wholesale, retail and for exportation. We have chosen a few young men and two or three of them are going out at once; but the others need teaching and training, so we must ask for your patience and prayer to the Lord of the Harvest.'[12] The title 'Joyful News Evangelist', with the names of Reed and Seager, appears in the list of evangelists for the first time on the 22 October 1885, one year and seven months after the launch of the paper. 'The friends, who are interested in Rural Methodism, will see we are moving on in the direction of Village Evangelism. Four of the men are at work in various circuits ... Five other young men are preparing for that same blessed employment'.[13] Champness was assisted in their training by colleagues in the Bolton Circuit.[14] He wanted practitioners to train his students.

In January 1886 the *Joyful News* Evangelists are listed separately; Brittain, Doran, Reed, Seager, Simpson and Wardle. Miss Tindall, daughter of Rev W.H. Tindall who was involved in the Southport Convention was named in the ordinary list.[15] Champness's vision grew substantially from these humble beginnings and after five years of publishing the *Joyful News*, he listed fifty-five evangelists including Sister Fervent, the 'Bible woman' in Spain. Many missionary organisations employed colporteurs, men and women who distributed scriptures. Sister Fervent was supported by Champness to distribute the scriptures in the Barcelona region.

Over five years they had trained and employed sixty-eight *Joyful News* Evangelists. He referred to the '"Joyful News" Movement as giving real impetus to the work of evangelism at that time ... just in the nick of time, when agricultural depression points to the necessity for doing something to relieve circuits in the rural parts of England from some of the financial strain which has been very severe and cannot be endured much longer.'[16]

Champness referred to similar movements which were developing in other denominations at the time. He could never shake off an antipathy towards the Church of England, something which would land him in prison later. His feelings were reflected in his otherwise positive comment that the developing Church Army in the 'Church of England, so called, will send forth hundreds of Lay Agents.'[17] However, he was warmer in his comments about another branch of Methodism: 'In Birmingham also our friends of the Primitive Methodist Church have started a similar movement.'[18]

He was always restless about the state of the Church and the urgent need for evangelism. 'There ought to be at least a Thousand Young Men at work among the cottages and farmhouses of the land; and we appeal to Ministers to look out for these men and let us train and employ them. The Rev. Samuel Atkinson, of Tredegar, is doing something like what we are doing; but we feel there ought to be at least fifty Homes where, in large or small numbers, these men should be fitted for the task of saving the villages.'[19]

The work had grown and the Home Mission Committee recommended that he devote his whole time to the *Joyful News* Mission. Champness had earlier been offered the possibility of release from the work of circuit responsibilities but at that time he had been reluctant. However on this occasion he gladly concurred with their decision. 'The Committee determined to recommend to the Conference that we should be released from Circuit life at the next Conference and thus have time to develop the "Joyful News" Mission ... We have come to the conclusion to take a larger house, and to lay ourselves out for doing a greater work than ever for village Methodism.'[20]

The key development in the work during 1888 and 1889 was the decision to train and appoint female evangelists. The work had grown considerably and increased from fifty-five to eighty people the list of *Joyful News* Evangelists, of whom thirteen were overseas, and eleven were *Joyful News* Female Evangelists.[21]

The next development came with the horse-drawn caravans, which he referred to as 'Gospel Cars' and were used to mission in rural areas. As we have seen, Champness became enthusiastic about Gospel Vaans when he attended a dedication of one at York with

Josiah Mee. It was intended that an evangelist would live in it 'gipsy fashion', and combine preaching, door-to-door visiting and selling books.[22] Champness was impressed with the idea and so it was that David Pilgrim was given the task of taking a horse from Cheshire to hitch to a van in Kent and return to Rochdale and begin the work.

The first horsedrawn Gospel Car

There was the "Joyful News" Caravan No 1 & 2 under the *Joyful News* Evangelists, called the Village Mission Cars – 'Faith' and 'Hope'. The work of the Gospel Cars developed slowly and, five years later, there were three *Joyful News* Caravans, the third being the 'small van', sometimes referred to as the 'little Ark' in reports.[23] In addition he was also training men for the *Joyful News* Circuit No.1 where three of the evangelists were serving. This was based around the work at Rydall Grove near Pershore. At first it was called the 'Joyful News Worcestershire Mission' and met in a converted wheelwright's shop.

These various developments were not always smooth or welcomed, for in March 1889 Champness was having to defend himself against the charge that the *Joyful News* Evangelists would undermine the ministry of the Local Preachers. The Rev James Ernest Clapham was most anxious that 'no work done by the "Joyful News" Agents should take the place of voluntary labour.' Champness did not consider his evangelists were undertaking the same ministry; he therefore readily agreed.[24]

Thomas Cook was involved with one strand of mission which Champness supported in his newspaper, 'Out and Out'. Champness was developing so many ideas associated with the *Joyful News* movement and in January 1888 he made a substantial link with 'Out and Out' and with his friend Thomas Cook's ministry. An extended article appeared in the form of a letter from Cook and Gregory Mantle which set out both the need and the optimism of that era:

> Perhaps never in the history of our Church had we more Evangelistic power amongst us than we have today; but if we cannot keep in the love of Christ those we win for Him, as it has been clearly demonstrated we have not been doing the last few years, of what avail is all our effort? Could anything be more paralysing to Christian faith and activity than to know that we are losing our members as fast as we can gain them? It is surely time the facts of our leakage were faced and the question carefully and patiently considered, whether something more cannot be done to keep those we gather and to establish them in the faith. This is unquestionably the problem of the hour.
>
> Profoundly moved by the conviction that some remedy should be attempted, we have given ourselves to prayer that we might be led to adopt some course that would contribute at least towards the better conservation of the fruit of our Evangelistic labours. The formation of the "OUT AND OUT BAND" is the outcome of our deliberations.[25]

The main purpose of 'Out and Out' was to nurture new Christians, organise meetings, promote Bible reading, prayer, evangelism and the search for holiness. The organisation was supported by a monthly magazine published by the Marshall Brothers, London, a well known non-denominational evangelical publisher. The only recorded work between the *Joyful News* and 'Out and Out' came in the missions associated with the five 'Out and Out Band Gospel Mission Cars', Faith, Hope, Charity, Victory and Peace with their headquarters at 76 Micklegate, York. The *Joyful News* carried information about the missions.[26] A further link with the College came because one of the co-founders, the Rev Gregory Mantle, was the first Superintendent of the huge Deptford Mission which seated 2,500 and had two full services each Sunday evening with a different silver band for each service. John Broadbelt served with Mantle as a young minister and undoubtedly learned a great deal from him.

The ability of Champness to run the *Joyful News* Home, the newspaper and many other publications, and to administer evangelists and missionaries, shows a man of considerable stamina as well as vision; but the mid 1890s was a difficult period for him. The Missionary Controversy in May 1890 had been a real blow to Champness's hopes for the missionary work and one he felt deeply. In 1894 he had more evangelists than at any previous time, 115 in all. It was then that his funding income reduced 'accompanied by a decline on our Book business'.[27] The announcement in July 1895 of the dismissal of sixty evangelists must have been a real blow to Thomas and Eliza though they retained thirty-two *Joyful News* Evangelists.[28] It is curiously comforting to know that even Thomas and Eliza Champness experienced problems of cash flow. However, then, as at other times, supporters of the newspaper and the mission gave generously and the accounts to 31 August 1896 showed a healthy

Thomas Cook with Gospel Car No 21

balance of over £943 in an outlay of £5009 6s 5½d. The *Joyful News* in which Thomas and Eliza relayed this information took the form of a joint article which had a confident tone, missing for the previous two years.[29]

When in March 1904 the work transferred to Cliff College there were altogether thirty Gospel Cars with thirty-five 'men'.   During the winter, they were employed in the rural districts and in the summer at the holiday resorts.[30] It would seem that women were never used in the Gospel Cars and did not feature at Cliff for another sixty-two years. The work of Cliff College, from the beginning, was linked with evangelism and 'for a comparatively small outlay we have fifty evangelists and local preachers in continual training. More than sixty evangelists are at work in the rural and most needy circuits of the Connexion, and thirty Cars, in charge of competent Agents, scattering good literature and conducting Open-air services. Surely nothing could be more in harmony with the best types of Methodism, old or new, or anything more practical and economical than the work we are doing.'[31]

Gospel car with many texts

By 1909 Thomas Cook, who had also been enthusiastic about the Gospel Cars, discovered their limitations. 'Though the Gospel Cars were not in as much demand as formerly, there was an increasing demand for the services of Cliff College Evangelists. The explanation was that they could be supplied at a much cheaper rate than a Gospel Car.'[32] The cost of the caravans, needing horses to be hired to pull them from place to place, became prohibitive and the number of Gospel Cars reduced though the number of evangelists increased. In 1909 there were only four Gospel Cars though a healthy number of evangelists, forty-one.[33] Two years later there were two Gospel Cars and forty-five evangelists.[34] The impending World War reduced the evangelists to twenty and saw the end of the caravan Gospel Cars.[35]

When the College became established at Cliff, Cook devoted his creative energy during the first two years to raising the funding for the Champness wing and persuading the Methodist Church to support the College with another full-time Tutor. However in the summer of 1907 the work of the evangelists moved from the villages to new areas of mission: 'We are now busy making ready for our summer campaign at the seaside. By this means, we hope to reach the masses who are not ordinarily reached by our Church agencies.' He sent out the Gospel cars and added, 'Our students will go to these places at the end of the term, to assist the brethren in charge of the Cars and to gain evangelistic experience.'[36]

Evangelists Bennett and Slack with their motorised Gospel Van in 1923

By the early 1920s their view of the Gospel Cars was different. The Committee, presumably at Chadwick's recommendation, 'resolved to respectfully call the attention of the Home Mission Committee to the urgent need for the Revival of the Gospel Car as an agency of aggressive Evangelism.'[37] Curiously in the *Joyful News* of November 1921 Chadwick reproduced a picture of a car, pulling a kind of caravan, being a motorised replacement for the Gospel Cars. He made an appeal for some at a cost of £280 each.[38] The following autumn there is a photograph of a new Motor Gospel Car, property of the Wesleyan

Methodist Home Mission Committee; with it were evangelists, Bennett and Slack who were past students of the College. The Car was dedicated by Luke Wiseman at the College. Chadwick writes, 'If Methodism will provide the cars, we will find the missioners'.[39]

Evangelism was always viewed as one part of the whole of the Church's mission and the holistic nature of Chadwick's view of this appears in a series of articles in the summer of 1907 as he prepared to come to Cliff as a tutor. He considered the importance of evangelism in the life of the Church's work and referred to the nature of the open

Bicycles purchased in November 1905 to be used by students preaching in the Peak District

air evangelism,[40] promotion of holiness,[41] class meetings,[42] Church membership,[43] the nature of ministry,[44] and evangelistic preaching.[45]

Evangelistic preaching was also expected from the students in their Sunday appointments around the Peak District and, for this purpose, in November 1905 they received twenty new 'state of the art' bicycles each with its own carbide lamp. In those days, bicycles were much to be preferred to walking. Students also reached out to the workers during the digging of the Derwent Waterway, which took water from the recently built Derwent and Howden Dams south to the Nottingham and Derby area. Some labourers were housed at Stoney Middleton and two attended the Wesleyan Reform Church. Students visited the inns in the village during the evening to talk with the men and they invited them to come to the chapel. One did come and was converted in the prayer-meeting. They gained permission to preach in the lodging houses, 'We could hardly see across the room for the tobacco smoke.' During the winter of 1906/7 they took simple services and were well received by the men.[46]

'It was reported that Mr H.H. Roberts, one of the Cliff College Evangelists, was in the habit of taking his daughter, Cissie, with him,

and allowing her to give addresses in his meetings, and that she had been designated with her father as a "Cliff College Evangelist". This was considered to be misleading, in view of her tender age and inexperience, so the committee decided that it could not sanction the continuance of this arrangement. It was resolved that Mr Roberts should cease to be recognised as a Cliff College Evangelist unless he was willing to meet the wishes of the Committee in this matter.'[47] One student, John Newbould, recalling his student year wrote of 'H.H.R.'; 'Harry Roberts was one of the most original evangelists I have ever known ... It was interesting to see him when he wanted to get a crowd for an open air meeting. He had

Harold H. Roberts

an old banjo. He couldn't play it. He hadn't a note of music in him, but he could twang it. He would take his old banjo and take his stand in the street. He would twang it for a while until the kiddies began to gather round. Then he would strike up and sing … over and over again until people began to gather round. I guess that sometimes they thought at first he was a cheapjack selling something for nothing but they some found out that Harry was offering something to them that money could never buy.'[48]

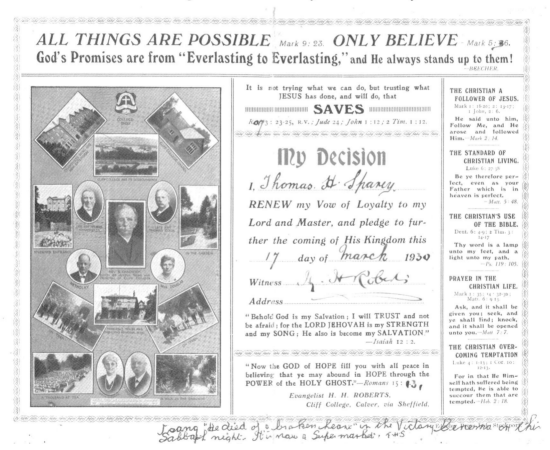

The Decision Card of Thomas Sparey who became a student , witnessed by H.H. Roberts

Bridlington 1923 – H.H. Roberts is 3rd from right

The work of the evangelists gained a good reputation and they were invited by circuits, 'where for financial reasons additional ministers cannot be maintained'.[49] This is not what Cook had in mind for his evangelists but it showed the acceptance by the Connexion for the work being done at Cliff as early as 1909.

The face of evangelism was changed at the College by two experiences. The first was the mission in Chesterfield at Easter 1922, which years later Chadwick would refer to as a 'daring experiment' and following which Cliff promoted the importance of town-wide missions with large teams.[50] The following year they also appointed teams for mission working with the churches of Rotherham and much later the Sunderland mission was greatly influential.[51] The College was self-consciously a training ground for evangelists in this period, with Dunning and Lambert, two of the leading thinkers about practical mission. 'We train Evangelists, that was the whole aim at the beginning and is our aim still ... and all our work is subject to the demands of Evangelism'.[52] In a paragraph reproduced in the Home Mission Fund Report, Lambert recalls that 'Cliff exists to train evangelists. For this purpose it was founded, and to this end it continues. Its unique mission is to inspire the evangelistic passion of the New Testament, that is the Pentecostal order, and to instruct and equip for evangelistic service that shall be effective in this day and generation.'[53] The point is emphasised in the Home Mission Fund Report to the Conference: 'We train Evangelists. We send forth Evangelists. We pioneer Evangelism'.[54]

The Wesleyan Methodist Conferences leading up to the Union in 1932 were times when the various departments placed their own issues as key for the coming new Methodist Church. In 1929 both the Primitive Methodists at Tunstall and the Wesleyan Methodists in Plymouth presented significant reports and proposals about evangelism.[55] Chadwick wrote a lead article in advance of the report being discussed and the following week printed the report in full.[56] He was clearly attempting to influence the debate and placed evangelism as the first priority of the emerging united church. He challenged Methodism regarding apathy about evangelism; called for a return to the original purposes of Methodism, of which evangelism was one, and commended the Primitive Methodists for putting 'evangelism at the forefront'. He stressed the Report's call for Methodism to be a missionary church both at home and abroad and commented that the best way to ensure this is to preach Christian Perfection, because of which experience, Christians are constrained to share the good news. The real Union of the churches would come in a shared 'passion of an evangel' and the lack of young people in the church would be resolved if the church engaged in evangelism. Evangelism would deal with the issues before the Conference in other reports, related to social reform, public morals and international relations. Indeed, evangelism, indicated Chadwick, with some powerful evidence, was the key to finance. He concluded the article by placing evangelism as the key to all the elements before the Conference: 'The agenda demonstrates on every page the need for a Revival of Religion, and calls the Church to seek the gift of Pentecost that we may be strong in the Lord to do exploits in His name.'[57]

Chadwick was not only making a point about evangelism but, as a senior elder in the ministry, was calling for the coming United Church to make evangelism the key element for future strategy and the need to take the ministry of Cliff College seriously. It was the view of Chadwick's supporters that under his leadership, 'Cliff was the greatest force for evangelism in modern Methodism.'[58]

The phrase 'Evangelise or Perish' first occurs at the turn of the 1930s. It was first used publicly as the title of a booklet by the leading Methodist Dr J.E. Rattenbury, commenting about the uniting of the three Methodist Churches. 'Whatever Evangelism is for other churches,' this pamphlet declares, 'it is essential and vital for Methodism. A Methodism which does not evangelise may have names and numbers, but it lacks meaning'.[59] Apparently a mission across London was planned to take place at the same time as the Uniting Conference, with the Revs Ensor Walters and Rattenbury in charge of it. The phrase was taken up in the *Joyful News* above the list of evangelists' engagements from September 1934 until the war years, to emphasise the importance of the evangelists' ministry.[60] It

was to become a real watchword for Broadbelt and appeared on the 1946 edition of the *Cliff College Choruses*.

In October 1932 the Cliff Committee, following Chadwick's death, set up in thanksgiving to God for his life and ministry the 'Chadwick Evangelistic Fund', and Joseph Rank, who was Circuit Steward

Cliff Evangelists with cap and CE badge

when Broadbelt was at the Tooting Mission, gave £20,000.[61] In his Cliff Letter in the early spring of 1933 Broadbelt was placing his imprimatur on the mission of the College. He linked his ministry with the legacy of Chadwick, as all the tutors believed they had to at that time, and then indicated that because of the recently formed 'Chadwick Memorial Fund for Evangelism', he has been able to 'pull to earth the castle the late Principal built in the air'.[62]

At this time, Broadbelt supplied the evangelists with their grey double-breasted suits and the overcoats, peaked caps all with the CE, (Cliff Evangelist), badge sewn on them. Ben Mackay recalls: 'As evangelists, we were supplied with grey double breasted suits with an embroidered badge, one on each lapel in light grey, with CE in the centre. The idea was taken, I think, from the Church Army uniform. There were also peak caps with the same design on the front. I never wore mine, like many others on the staff.'[63] 'We were given £1 a week, paid monthly, so, being given hospitality and expenses, like fares paid, we were solvent. Most places gave us a gift of money which went towards paying for our fares home.'[64]

A new strategy for evangelism was unfolded in which twenty evangelists were available for invitation by circuits to conduct

"Men in suits"

evangelistic missions over two weeks, including three Sundays.[65] The first week was to prepare the Church, and then 'the mission proper' to begin on the second Sunday and run across the third weekend, 'finishing with a great rally on the Monday with a visit of some member of the Cliff staff.'[66] They did not have long between missions,

'As was customary, we rested for four days at Cliff before the next mission.'[67] This was the strategy for the winter months and then in the summer the evangelists became part of and led the Trek teams. The College decided to engage in some longer stays for trek itinerary.

Early in 1935 they publicised an offer to circuits of three, four or five days of 'intensive work at various chapels'.[68] This practice was found to be of benefit to the work and staying longer in certain places became more regular.[69]

They were not always welcomed partly because Methodism was not committed to evangelism but also because some evangelistic practice was not good.

Dedication of Mr Broadbelt's first Gospel Car

Such people were easily caricatured, and Leslie Weatherhead, a Cliff student in 1912-13, represented the view of many about their ministry as follows: 'An evangelist is a man with two suitcases and twenty sermons drooping with age and dripping with emotion, leaving poor ministers to clear up the mess'.[70]

Broadbelt had spent much of his ministry in the city centres and it is not surprising that he felt a commitment to work in the East End of Sheffield. 'We have taken over an old and derelict Chapel ... (it) will provide us with a glorious opportunity for Aggressive Evangelism, we can put our theories to the test.' He set aside two evangelists 'Bros Smith and Costain, who will give themselves to sacrificial service for the conversion of the people.'[71] The Hall was re-opened and dedicated on 29 December 1934.

Herbert Silverwood with the Cinema Van

They also advertised the open-air cinema, which was a removal van with a back projector and used at the seaside.[72] Herbert Silverwood was a past student and an evangelist who worked with them from time to time and often used the Cinema Van.

In 1936, in an attempt to provide pensions for long-serving staff including evangelists, housing was provided in retirement. H.H. Roberts was the first and became an honorary evangelist who would 'help the younger evangelists by his prayers'.[73] Broadbelt also tried to increase salaries and established the policy that all staff would be in the Home Mission Pension scheme. Matt Brown and Bros Butler, Blinco, Barrett and Binnington were paid £200 per annum and the others £100.[74]

In October 1936 there was a call for *Joyful News* readers to pray for the evangelists at 12 noon each day and encourage links between the supporters and the College evangelists. The work had grown under Broadbelt, mainly because of the funding from the 'Chadwick Memorial Evangelism Fund', and at that time he listed in the *Joyful News* forty-two evangelists.[75] They normally worked in pairs with the

exception of Matthew Brown, W. Barrett, Tom Butler, P. Binnington and J.D. Blinco.[76] The evangelists were mainly engaged on missions around the country but, if they returned to the College when it was full of students they used the old Chapel across Cliff Lane as a dormitory. This rudimentary accommodation was necessary through the 1930s when the College was carrying this large number of evangelists.

Herbert Silverwood preaching, George Chapman 2nd from left

A young Tom Butler

The outbreak of war on 3 September 1939 brought an abrupt end to the treks and the missioners returned to the College immediately. 'Many of our Evangelists who have done such fine service for some years in the Churches, are now free for Pastoral Work in the Circuits.'[77] There was nevertheless a residual group of evangelists on the staff; Butler, Booth, Blinco and Sainsbury were taking some missions.[78] Inevitably, the creative work of the evangelists came to an end and the energies of the remaining Cliff staff went to support churches and those who had been connected with the College. Broadbelt wrote his letters to students, the correspondence courses were developed and the staff held 'Cliff Weekends' to promote the cause of evangelism, discipleship and holiness.

Even during World War II the College had 'four evangelists fully employed … and four had been partially employed.'[79] The mission work, which the College had developed at holiday resorts, was severely curtailed, and missions at Bridlington, Skegness, Lowestoft and Yarmouth were all cancelled.[80] However, a team led by Herbert Silverwood was still missioning at Blackpool and Morecambe. By the spring of 1943, only Butler and Wilson remained on the staff, because all the others had been transferred to the Home Mission Staff as Lay Pastors,[81] and in the later part of the War only Tom Butler remained on the staff at Cliff.[82] However he continued with the Cliff Weekends, as did Broadbelt and other tutors, and the Morecambe Seaside mission. After the war Broadbelt quickly rebuilt his team of evangelists and by the summer of 1946 there were eleven evangelists on the staff, who organised seaside missions not only at Morecambe but also Bridlington, and under the leadership of Herbert Silverwood, at Lowestoft and Yarmouth. Vivian Evans, a 'very valuable evangelist', was to receive a wage of £4 a week and board for

L -R Ernest Steele, Jim Beasley and Tom Butler

himself and his wife at the College. It is unclear where he actually lived. Mrs Evans became an Assistant Secretary.

At this point tribute should be paid to three evangelists who between them influenced the College's strategy on evangelism for fifty years, Tom Butler, Herbert Silverwood and Ernest Steele. Herbert Silverwood was a student from January - December 1926 at the same time as a friend from Barnsley, John Whitehouse. They were both sponsored by a Mr J. Barlow and, after training, these 'Cliff boys' conducted missions across the country. Known as the 'Yorkshire Firebrand', the handbills for his missions announced the preacher had come 'from coal-pit to pul-pit'. Herbert became a Connexional Evangelist and in the summer months at least worked with the trekkers at the seaside, most notably at Morecambe,

Herbert Silverwood in later life

Lowestoft and Bridlington. He had a great wit and infectious humour born of a keen observation and love of people. In 1936 he pioneered the use of film in the open air, 'The technique here was that of keeping the audience together and interested after the film ended, when Herbert appeared "to say a few words" ... Herbert's story telling and Walt Disney cartoons made a very effective partnership in evangelism.'[83] He was at his best in the open air, responding to the jibes of the crowd or keeping the people queuing for tea happy at the Anniversary. An incident from the Commando Campaign in London is typical. A team of Anglican and Congregational clergy spoke nervously in the open-air:

Each gave a brief word, but only a handful of people stopped to listen and then walked on. However when it came to Silverwood's turn he asked all the ministers to stand in a circle. He then saw a fellow who was walking past wearing a bowler hat. He went to him and asked him if he could borrow his hat for just a moment. The fellow reluctantly handed it over, then Herbert borrowed a white handkerchief, from another reluctant donor. All this time the clerical brethren were getting more and more embarrassed, but not Herbert. He placed the white handkerchief on the ground and black bowler hat on the handkerchief. By this time a few more people had stopped, wondering what these parsons were doing and what was under the hat. In less than five minutes a crowd of fifty had gathered and it grew and grew – folk thought there must have been an accident. Then Herbert spoke. He explained who we were, why we were there and gave them a really helpful message. Then he returned the hat and the handkerchief.[84]

It was in the 'Top Tent' that he continued his ministry at the Anniversary Monday, where he 'told stories, led choruses (to piano accordion accompaniment) and gave off the cuff sermonettes.'[85] He had a quick wit and in 1968 at the afternoon meeting Herbert, seeing the three speakers approaching the Tent, remarked 'Here they come, Freeman, Hardy and Willis!', causing uproar in the crowd and bemusing the preachers. Yorkshire Television invited him to be the preacher, representing the best of 'old fashioned preaching', in a 1975 documentary about Grisedale, 'The Dale That Died'.

Tom Butler was a student in the autumn of 1932, as Chadwick died. He with Blinco and Barrett was a powerful influence in the College and the following year he joined the evangelistic staff. The evangelists undertook missions and always they returned to the College with stories of 'great blessing'. The Rev Amos Edwards wrote concerning a mission at Holmes near Southport, 'The services on Sunday were full of power! For many, it was a day of much heart searching. At the end of the day the rail was filled with those who desired to make a fresh committal of themselves to Christ and to claim the gift of the Holy Spirit. Only eternity will record the full story of the last ten days at Holmes.'[86] Tom worked very well with Broadbelt, built up the Youth Fellowship, organised the camp, and undertook many missions across Ireland as well as in all other parts of Britain over a period of twenty-three years. His imprimatur remained on the Anniversary for many years afterwards.[87]

"Bacon for how many?" Malcolm Pears and Ernest Steele with two of their volunteer team before the College opened its doors to female students.

Ernest Steele had been a cook in the Navy before coming to the College as a student in 1946 and seemed an ideal choice as evangelist and supervising the cooking in the fast growing needs of the Youth Camp. Ernest remained at the College succeeding Tom as Senior evangelist in 1956. He became a senior candidate for the ministry and, in the summer of 1963, took an appointment at the Prudhoe Street Mission, Newcastle. He left after seventeen years at the College but like Silverwood and Butler often returned. For many years he supervised the catering for the Anniversary and Derwent with a dedicated team, Malcolm Pears, Clive Taylor, Len Ball and Russ Houghton. Students on this team worked very hard and for long hours, but found the whole experience a pleasure, for they created an atmosphere of joy and spiritual care. Even when he had retired he and his wife Olive came to support the students and staff in these busy times.

After the War a number of changes were made. The Committee considered the 'best modes of trekking'[88] and the Summer Treks of 1949 had not begun from the College but from an industrial centre. 'The carts had been overhauled at a cost of £610 and new boots, clothes and accordions purchased at a cost £303'. Discussion also took place in the College about Tent Missions, which were proving very popular where missions were held in rural areas after World War II. The Committee approved the purchase of a tent for £250, which would hold 250 people seated, and could be used by senior Evangelists around the country. The first call would be 'new areas, and places where we contemplate opening new causes.'[89] The committee was nervous about expenditure, Eagles as Principal was not able to raise the money and the project was abandoned.[90]

The next clear initiative came, not from Cliff itself, but from the Home Mission Department. The Rev Colin Roberts, himself an ex-student of Cliff, had launched the idea of 'Christian Commando Campaigns' which today seems a rather dramatic title for an evangelistic mission.[91] The young Maurice Barnett grasped the vision and wrote with enthusiasm in the *Joyful News*.[92] Maldwyn Edwards was similarly engaged and the inference in the *Joyful News* write-up was that this form of evangelism had great sympathy with the work of the trekkers.[93] The Commando Campaigns were supervised from the Home Mission Committee,[94] and they were a feature of Methodism for some years.[95] Some students were involved

Shooting Brake equipped with loudspeakers for open-air work

in the Greater London Christian Commando Campaign, in a team of two thousand, 'drawn from all participating denominations, from Anglo-Catholic to Quaker.'[96] The members worked in twos or small groups, depending on the task. The purpose was to reach to where people worked or spent their leisure, taking the gospel message out to where people were. They targeted the workplace speaking to a gathered meeting or holding 'an open-air talking point outside the factory gate, often with the use of a loudspeaker car.'[97] David Lawrence, a student in 1946/7 recalls that 'theatres gave us the stage for five minutes during the interval. Rank's Saturday morning Children's Clubs were just beginning and included a commercial for local Sunday Schools. Some offices allowed us in for brief prayers to start the day. Hospitals, clubs, universities, schools and prisons, all were approached and many doors were opened to us.'[98]

In these post-war years the initiative for evangelism in Methodism moved from Cliff to the Home Mission Department. It was not

Blackburn 1958

surprising, therefore, that Tom Butler, who had been at the College for 23 years, resigned from the staff in February 1956 and transferred to the Home Mission Evangelistic Staff in the summer. There he had the renowned Rev Dr W.E. Sangster as his boss and Butler became a 'Lay Connexional Missioner'.[99] Nevertheless many missions were very significant. Jim Beasley, a 'handsome dark haired evangelist', had a remarkable ministry but died tragically in 1957 aged only thirty-two.[100] At Crosland Hill Methodist Church in Huddersfield in 1948, Jim Beasley with Ernest Steele, Bill Parkinson

Eric Birkinsaw, Andy McCabe and John Neilson led a mission which became the talking point in the community. So many people responded at the meetings that enquirers could not all come down the aisle. The mission had a long-term impact for mission overseas, ordained ministry, and committed lay ministry, the consequences of which are seen fifty-five years later.[101]

The appointment of Tom Meadley as Principal was controversial in some quarters because he had not previously been associated with the College. In September 1957 he was introduced as offering contemporary thinking to the ministry of evangelism, 'One of Mr Meadley's special gifts is to put evangelical teaching into modern pattern'.[102]

Recognition of the ministry of Evangelists has always been a problem both for the College and within the Church. On a number of occasions an 'Order of Evangelists' has been proposed. Twice the Committee Minutes record that such an Order was considered and, in December 1950, a paper was presented (though we do not have a copy) but 'further consideration was postponed.'[103] The matter resurfaced again in June 1951 but the proposal was 'further postponed, until the time appeared more opportune.'[104] There is no suggestion in the *Minutes* why the matter was at that time inopportune but there were criticisms voiced at the same meeting about the Cliff College Youth Fellowship and, after a 'full and frank discussion', there was a typically Methodist response of establishing a sub-committee. The Fellowship was run in effect by the evangelists, and if they were seen as lacking competence, then a Connexional

Sunshine Corner, Ogmore Vale Mission 1965

Order, with them at the centre, would be risky. More recently the recognition of the role and ministry of the Evangelist has taken greater priority in the Church of England for nationally recognised ministries. In 2000 Brian Hoare, then a Secretary at the Home Mission Division, presented a report to Conference entitled 'The Role and Recognition of Evangelists in the Methodist Church'. The Conference responded warmly to Brian, accepted the report and thus endorsed the ministry of evangelists in a new way. The Rev Graham Horsley, Secretary for Evangelism and Church Planting at the Methodist Conference in 2003, successfully gained their agreement for an Order of Service for such recognition. This is intended to further promote the recognition of evangelists, and deepen the ministry of evangelism in British Methodism.

Occasionally a matter arose when students and even staff had to be disciplined, otherwise the name of Cliff could have

Cliff College – moving with the times!

been brought into disrepute, as for instance in June 1955, when two ex-students were engaging in evangelism 'which had somewhat unworthy features'.[105] Every Principal I have known has unfortunately had to expel students.

The costs of the missions under Cook and Chadwick had always been met by generous donations. Broadbelt established the 'Chadwick Evangelism Fund', but the issue of financing the evangelists was a significant one. In the mid-1950s the committee had to reflect on the costs to the College of the missions and decided to make a charge of £15 per ten-day mission.[106]

The missions conducted by the evangelists adopted a particular pattern. The 'Sunshine Corner' children's work,[107] the evening rallies, the 'Cliff Night' with slides, along with visiting homes and taking Sunday services in churches, became the feature of Cliff missions across the land from the war years through to the early 70s.

'Refreshment'

Then guitars appeared instead of the ubiquitous accordion, and Cliff quickly followed in the footsteps of the 'Glorylanders', Malcolm and Alwyn, Ishmael and Andy, with its own group 'Refreshment' which produced an album in 1978. Gill Hargreaves, Colin Stephenson, Desmond Curran and David Savage formed 'Refreshment' and cut the record but it was dated from the beginning being launched around the same time 'Spring Harvest' came on the scene with a whole new wave of Christian music.

It was groundbreaking for Cliff in those days, but already the Christian music scene had moved on from the quiet guitar-strumming group more reminiscent of the sixties to the higher tech and certainly louder rock music. 'Out of Darkness' were the first group to deafen Christian ears around 1970, followed by many others. Ishmael and Andy reworked their style and music to become 'After the Fire', 'Trinity Folk' became 'Parchment' with their best known song, 'Colours of Day' and at the same time came the brilliant 'Re-generation' whose manager was later to be a Principal of Cliff! It has to be said that Martyn Atkins also played in a Christian band but, as yet such experience has not become a requirement for the post of Principal.

The Evangelistic Team 1991/2: The Rev Howard Mellor, Mr Alf Waite, Mr Greg Alexander, Mr William Porter, Mrs Shirley Alexander and Miss Carole Thomas

The College realised that the 'hit and run' missions of a week or ten days had a limited impact in the more complex society of the late seventies and a link was made with the 'One Step Forward' Campaign pioneered originally by Bryan Gilbert.[108] This was training material designed to help churches move towards being a missioning community and therefore ready to receive a Cliff team. The 'One Step Forward' Campaign had three main stages: 1. Operation Agape (Loving), focussing on the church and seeking to renew and deepen spiritual devotion. 2. Belonging, considering the worship and caring

410

ministry of the church, and, 3. Sharing, which was designed to help the congregation share their life and faith with the community.[109]

The College developed during this time a pattern of mission where the whole College, tutors, evangelists and students, would go on mission. There was a weekend in the Autumn, ten days at the end of the Spring term leading up to Palm Sunday, and three weeks in the Summer. The Summer missions were often student led though the evangelists were involved in the larger teams and more complex missions. The whole process was to encourage students to discover their gifts and to take responsibility for mission events. In this way they learned new skills, became more confident in leading and developed in their christian discipleship.

In 1981 a decision was made to appoint a Director of Evangelism, a Methodist minister known in the Connexion who could lead the evangelism team, teach evangelism and counselling in the College and promote the cause of evangelism across the Church. The post was the clear next step for me, and, with some trepidation, I applied and was appointed.[110] Therefore with great joy in 1983 Rosie and I moved to Cliff and initially, and for what was to be a sabbatical year, we lived in the Cliff Hall flat. Brian Hoare carried the responsibility at that time for the evangelists and the year gave me the opportunity to listen to the tutors, evangelists and students and then to make proposals both for the team and new courses. From the end of the first quarter I took responsibility from Brian for all the forward planning of the missions to ease his workload. That summer with the backing of Bill Davies and the Committee the new way forward was considered. The evangelists should become full members of staff. Their names had previously appeared not on a staff list but at the top of the 'Student List'. The team was to work under the Director and new strategies were envisaged. In addition a new Diploma year would begin from September 1984. I recall those years as halcyon days, touring the country, promoting the College, meeting as many people as possible, running the Diploma course and building on the excellent teaching which Arthur Wood, Robert Mason and (standing in for a year) Brian Hoare had undertaken.

Evangelists team: Gini Carlin, Mark Chambers, Andy Smith, the Rev Phil Clarke, Mike Robinson and Susanna George

The work developed quickly and we wrote material under the title *Growing Together in Christ* to prepare churches. Initial contact with churches led to the booklet *Thinking About Mission* and WHAM days, 'We're Having A Mission'. The need for good and reasonably priced literature led to the founding of Cliff College Publishing with evangelistic tracts and a number of booklets designed to prepare churches for mission. When he was appointed the Director of Evangelism, the Rev Philip Clarke wrote books with intriguing titles; *The Hedgehog Scenario*, *Over-flow* and *Jesus at Tesco*. Now Cliff publishes tracts, booklets, books and a well received Academic Series.

The work developed in the 80s and 90s under the leadership of myself and Philip Clarke, with the College being recognised and respected as one dedicated to the teaching and practice of evangelism. The problem was always that the Connexional 50% of the Director of Evangelism became too thinly spread across the Connexion and other denominations. It was therefore a great blessing when the Forum for Evangelism began. Though with few at first, Districts began to appoint more Evangelism Enablers and Circuits followed suit. More ministers saw their work as intentionally about evangelism and so the numbers of people attending the Forum, meeting normally at Cliff, grew to fifty-five people employed by local churches, Circuits or Districts as evangelists.

The decision by the Methodist Conference to recognise the Ministry of Evangelist and to prepare an Order of Service for that purpose, was itself a tremendous step. The challenge always was to help the church, national, regional and local to see the vital importance of the task.

The Evangelists 2003, Rev Paul Dunstan, Sue Peat, Helen Edwards, Brian Rice and Eva Walkers, the European Evangelism Enabler, who comes originally from Albania, and began work at Cliff in 2002 after completing a BA degree at Cliff.

In the summer of 2004 the Rev Steve Wild became the fourth Director of Evangelism. He brought the gifts of a holiday camp showman, the experience of Circuit, District and Connexional work, as well as working with many organisations not least in television and at major events such as Easter People and Spring Harvest. He had been a student and evangelist at Cliff and more recently gained an MA in Evangelism Studies. Steve is a man of prayer with an overwhelming desire to share the Good News of Jesus with others. To him falls the privilege and responsibility of taking the evangelistic team and strategy for the College into the new millennium. All who know him and know of his work have welcomed his appointment at the College. We look forward to the ministry which will now unfold.

The Rev Steven Wild,
Director of Evangelism

1   *Joyful News,* 1 March 1883.
2   *Joyful News,* 10 August 1899.
3   *Joyful News,* 9 April 1885.
4   *Joyful News,* 23 April 1885.
5   *Joyful News,* 23 April 1885.
6   *Joyful News,* 23 April 1885.
7   *Joyful News,* 7 May 1885.
8   Ibid
9   *Joyful News,* 28 May 1885.
10 *Joyful News,* 10 September 1885.
11 *Joyful News,* 8 October 1885.
12 *Joyful News,* 27 May 1886.
13 *Joyful News,* 22 October 1885.
14 Ibid.
15 *Joyful News,* 21 January 1886.
16 *Joyful News,* 24 May 1888.
17 *Joyful News,* 11 October 1888.
18 Ibid.
19 *Joyful News,* 1 November 1888.
20 *Joyful News,* 13 December 1888.
21 *Joyful News,* 7 February 1889.
22 Joe Brice, *The Crowd for Christ,* (London: Hodder and Stoughton, 1934), p. 39, see also pp.71-72.
23 *Joyful News,* 13 September 1894.
24 *Joyful News,* 28 March 1889.
25 *Joyful News,* 5 January 1888.
26 *Joyful News,* 28 July 1904.
27 *Joyful News,* 11 July 1895.
28 *Joyful News,* 11 July 1895.
29 *Joyful News,* 22 April 1897.
30 Report of the Home Mission Fund, 1905, p.126.
31 Ibid.
32 Minutes of the Committee of Management, 1 December 1909.
33 *Joyful News,* 16 September 1909.
34 *Joyful News,* 14 September 1911.
35 *Joyful News,* 11 September 1913.
36 *Joyful News,* 6 June 1907.
37 Minutes of the Committee of Management, 15 December 1921.
38 *Joyful News,* 3 November 1921.
39 *Joyful News,* 26 October 1922.
40 *Joyful News,* 13 June 1907.
41 *Joyful News,* 20 June 1907.
42 *Joyful News,* 1 August 1907.
43 *Joyful News,* 9 May 1907.

cont.

44 *Joyful News,* 25 July 1907.
45 *Joyful News,* 8 August 1907.
46 This outreach lasted through the winter of 1906–7 when the Champness wing was under construction, and fewer students admitted. It is possible that the students had more free time and made contact with the working people through the builders at Cliff some of whom lived locally.
47 *Minutes* of the Committee of Management, 31 March 1908.
48 John Newbould, *The Roots and Early Growth of Cliff College* (Unpublished typescript in the archives. He wrote it after 45 years of ministry, c. 1950), pp.72-73.
49 *Minutes* of the Committee of Management, 1 December 1909.
50 *Joyful News,* 27 April 1922.
51 *Joyful News,* 7 April 1932.
52 Dunning in *Joyful News*, 28 April 1928.
53 *Joyful News,* 28 April 1932.
54 Report of the Home Mission Fund, 1929, p.75.
55 *Joyful News,* 18 July 1929.
56 *Joyful News,* 18 and 25 July 1929.
57 *Joyful News,* 18 July 1929.
58 *Joyful News,* 17 May 1934. Dunning wrote the phrase as he left Cliff. Maybe it was veiled criticism of Chadwick's successor or more likely, sadness that he himself had not been made Principal.
59 *Joyful News,* 29 January 1931. In fact the Rev Ensor Walters first coined the term.
60 *Joyful News*, 27 September 1934.
61 *Joyful News,* 26 July 1956.
62 *Joyful News,* 16 February 1932.
63 Ben Mackay, *A Tale that is told,* p.302.
64 Ben Mackay, *A Tale that is told,* p.302.
65 Ben Mackay, *A Tale that is told*, p.300.
66 *Joyful News,* 16 February 1932.
67 Ben Mackay, *A Tale that is told,* p.337.
68 *Joyful News,* 24 January 1935.
69 *Joyful News,* 12 March 1936.
70 Ben Mackay, *A Tale that is told,* p.313 and taken from the *Evening Standard,* 1936.
71 *Joyful News,* 27 December 1934.
72 Ibid. The van and its equipment were donated by Lord Rank.
73 *Joyful News,* 17 September 1936. Thirty years later, this method of providing accommodation would lead to insufficient housing being available on the estate.
74 *Joyful News,* 1 October 1936.
75 *Joyful News,* 15 October 1936.
76 *Joyful News,* 17 September and 1 October.
77 *Joyful News,* 14 September 1939.
78 *Joyful News,* 23 November 1939 and 4 January 1940.
79 *Minutes* of the Cliff College Committee, 25 April 1941.
80 Broadbelt, *Letter,* 19 July 1940.

cont.

81 *Minutes* of the Cliff College Committee, 13 April 1943.

82 *Minutes* of the Cliff College Committee, 15 November 1945.

83 David Lazell, *Firebrand* (Bromley: Foundation Publications, 1971), p.70.

84 Eric Challoner, *It so Happened* (Alsager: Fairway Folio, 1998), p.93.

85 David Lazell, *A Happy Man from Yorkshire* (Loughborough: David Lazell, 2003), p.125.

86 Marie Butler, *They called him "Brother Tom"* (Ilkeston: Moorleys Print and Publishing, 1985).

87 Tom went to work with Dr Sangster at the Home Mission Department between 1956 and 1964, and for the Movement for World Evangelization between 1966 and 1972.

88 *Minutes* of the Cliff College Committee, 14 October 1949.

89 *Minutes* of the Cliff College Committee, 14 October 1949.

90 *Minutes* of the Cliff College Committee, 30 May 1950.

91 Colin Roberts, *These Christian Commando Campaigns,* (London: Epworth Press, 1945).

92 *Joyful News*, 11 November 1943.

93 *Joyful News*, 13 April 1944.

94 *Minutes of the Home Mission Committee,* 6 July 1944.

95 *Joyful News*, 13 July 1944, 27 March 1947.

96 David Lawrence, *Memoirs and Extracts from the Diaries of David Lawrence* (Norwich: personal publication, 1995), p.33.

97 David Lawrence, p.34.

98 David Lawrence, p.34.

99 *Joyful News*, 30 August 1956.

100 John Wood, *A Year to Remember* (private publication, c. 2003), recalls mission at Loftus. Jim Beasley preached in the cinema and 64 responded to the gospel.

101 Not only did people enter the caring professions engaging christianly within the community; they began 'Huddersfield for Christ', became missionaries and preachers, and the next generation are serving God. Bill Parkinson, *Memories* (a typescript copy was presented for the archive, 2004) indicates that 'The parents of the Rev H. Mellor, the author of this book, were blessed and helped by the mission at Crosland Hill', p.30. Subsequently published by Scotforth Books, Lancaster, 2004.

102 *Joyful News,* 12 September 1957.

103 *Minutes* of the Cliff College Committee, 13 December 1950.

104 *Minutes* of the Cliff College Committee, 13 June 1951.

105 *Minutes* of the Cliff College Committee, June 1955.

106 *Minutes* of the Cliff College Committee, June 1955.

107 Clive Pugh, *Aims and Methods of Sunshine Corners* (Calver: Joyful News Bookroom, undated). Cliff College Archive Library.

108 In fact David Greenaway came and worked with Robert Mason, Tutor in charge of the Evangelists, on the materials.

cont.

109 All the materials were written by Bryan Gilbert or developed by David Greenaway. A full set of the final shape of the material is contained in the Cliff College Archive Library.
110 Actually I could not believe I had been appointed, and phoned Stuart Rhodes the Chair of the Interview Panel the following morning, just to check I had heard him correctly.

CHAPTER 15

Cliff College Fellowship

rom the beginning, students who studied at the *Joyful News* Training Home wished to keep in touch and they did this at first in correspondence with Thomas and Eliza Champness and through the issues of the *Joyful News*. Champness wrote to each Joyful News Evangelist and missionary each week. Normally they were typed letters of two or three pages though when he was touring the country and preaching he wrote postcards.[1] It would appear that when the work came to Cliff College, and the numbers of students increased, then Cook and Chadwick relied on the *Joyful News*. In hand-written ledgers a detailed summary was kept of each student who had attended the College from March 1904. The summary gave opportunity for ongoing comment and up-to-date information of their ministry was added over the years.[2] These continued for many years as the main forms of record-keeping and contact. From 1937, there were a few years when the *Cliff Witness* was published, and its main purpose was keeping a 'special link with all old Cliff men, and there are thousands now all over the world.'[3] The beginning of the Second World War brought about the end of the *Cliff Witness* but the need for an effective alumni organisation had been identified. Throughout the War, Broadbelt returned to the practice of Champness and sent an occasional duplicated foolscap letter to immediate past students and evangelists. Dunning and Lambert personally kept in touch with students and

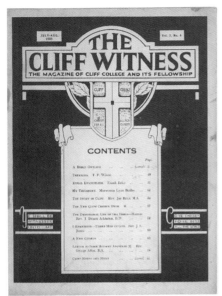

Dunning said that he travelled the world visiting past students. Lambert too seemed to have a significant letter-bag, sending postcards to past students, rather in the fashion of Thomas Champness.

The first appearance of an alumni group of any kind, in the *Minutes of the College Committee*, is June 1949. The 'Cliff Men's Fellowship' came into being during that year and published its first handbook in 1950. It was often referred to both in speech and in the College Committee Minutes as the 'Old Cliff Men's Fellowship' and sometimes more kindly as the 'Cliff Student's Fellowship'. The membership in 1950 was 461 and the Fellowship held a two-day conference that year at the College, which was very well received.

However it is clear from editions of *The Cliff Witness* published in the 1930s that 'The Cliff Fellowship' was the link between all old Cliff students. In 1937 the membership fee was 1s per annum and the Secretary was the Rev John Roberts of Kirton, Boston, Lincs.[4]

Regretably the early minute books of the Cliff College Fellowship appear to have been lost in a fire at the then Secretary's house and so a detailed record of the history of the Fellowship pre-1977 was lost. Also the reports to the College Committee of the Cliff Men's Fellowship tended to be extremely brief. However, in 1957 greater analysis is given. There were 614 members of the Fellowship, 169 in the Methodist ministry and 65 ordained overseas, 27 lay pastors and 265 local preachers. There were 1 Presbyterian, 20 Baptist, 12 Congregational, 3 Anglican, 5 Salvation Army and 47 lay pastors or preachers in other denominations. Altogether the members were

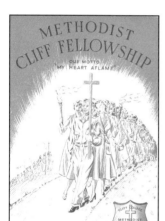

86% Methodist and other churches 14%.[5] This shows a considerable predominance of Methodists, which would not be reflected today, especially in the postgraduate work.

After the War, there also emerged a 'Cliff College Youth Fellowship', Tom Butler's brain child, begun in response to the numbers of young people attending the Young People's Camp. It was 'designed to band together in closer unity young people reached by the Camp and by the Evangelists' Missions.'[6] The work grew and, within the year, Butler reported 1,700 young people in the Cliff College Youth Fellowship with meetings happening regularly and locally all over the country.[7] By September 1948, it had grown to be 2,800 and, 'apart from very rare exceptions, it was proving itself soundly Methodist and sensibly enthusiastic.'[8] There was a magazine published with its badge, and motto, 'My Heart Aflame'. The magazine became titled *The Crusader*, with Bible studies, information about missions, a message from the Principal and invitations to the Anniversary and Derwent Convention.[9]

The Committee was concerned about 'dangers incidental to the great success and popularity of the camp, these were frankly discussed and are being guarded against very carefully.'[10] With 500 young people all enthusiastically brought together it would be amazing if there were not issues to deal with.

At the first meeting of the Executive Committee, the first item referred for their consideration was the Fellowship, presumably because of possible reported problems. 'The Principal reported that he had made wide and careful enquiries, and that the vast majority of branches were working in absolute loyalty to Methodism. There had been three difficult cases but these either had now been solved or were in course of solution'.[11] The detail of the cases is not revealed by the archives.

By October 1949, the numbers had increased to 3,320 (93% were Methodist) with 93 groups meeting, though there were a number of complaints being received and these were investigated by the College. The size of this group must have mirrored the growth of the MAYC (Methodist Association of Youth Clubs) which was just in its infancy at that time. The Cliff College Youth Fellowship was a real force and an organisational structure was developed with a 'Manifesto of the Cliff College Youth Fellowship'.[12]

The earlier difficulties of the Youth Fellowship meant that the College needed to set out a constitution which should be presented to and agreed by the College Committee. This was first discussed in May 1950 but took two year's consultation in the College before the constitution was formally presented. The agreement of the Home Mission Board and the Conference was required. The proposed Constitution has fourteen detailed clauses and a 'preamble'. This highlighted what were presumably the besetting problems faced by local churches with lively groups of keen young Christians. The preamble for the *Proposed Constitution of Cliff College (Youth) Fellowship* was as follows:

> The Fellowship came into being largely as a result of Missions conducted by the College Evangelists, and its purpose was to give definite training in Bible study, prayer and active evangelism.
>
> The members naturally have a close relationship with Cliff College and contact has been maintained with them by a bi-monthly bulletin and by Youth Camps held at Whitsuntide and at the Derwent Convention, and by periodical visits of the College Staff to Cliff Fellowship Rallies.

The basis of the Fellowship is essentially Methodist, and its chief intention is
to help the Methodist Society in which it is found. Where possible its
greatest activity is on Saturday nights, which are given over to Bible study,
prayer and evangelism, as in earlier Methodist days.

It is strongly desired that this close relationship between the Fellowships and
the College should be maintained – always subject to the kindly
understanding of the Minister and Officials of the local Methodist Society. [13]

Eventually the Constitution was ratified at the Conference in July
1953.[14] This was a cumbersome procedure taking a very long time for
the agreement of a relatively minor document. Whilst it can be assumed that this constitution was designed to deal with the besetting sins of an enthusiastic youth movement which in some places did not relate well to the local church or minister, it reads like a draconian document, designed by ecclesiastical bureaucrats rather than a youth organisation designed for growth and renewal. The

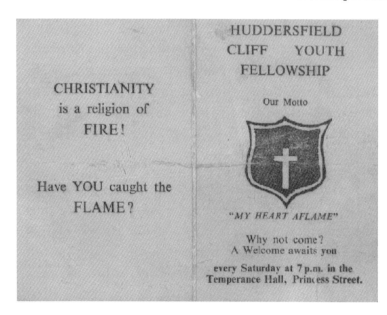

inclusion of 'Methodist' took away the distinctive edge of the name
but wisely the College kept the badge simply as the 'Cliff College
Youth Fellowship'. Intriguingly the *Crusader* did not carry the
manifesto, which suggests that the leaders at the time, including Tom
Butler, thought the publication of the constitution would not help
the life of the Fellowship. The following June 1954 the membership

was 4,600 with 90 groups meeting, and the Fellowship donated £445 to the College in subscriptions and gifts.

When Tom Butler left, it would seem the administration of the Youth Fellowship was not dealt with in the same detailed way and the reports were very generalised in terms of members and costs. The College Executive Committee meeting on 15 April 1958 had been asked to look at the matter. They found that the Fellowship had been in action for 12 years, 'it had received in that time 7,389 members of whom in 1958 there were 2,200 subscribers. The number of groups ... were 32 though in 1951 there were 134.'[15] Despite this apparently detailed information, the same meeting brought particular attention to the fact that: 'At this point there was no record of the names of leaders and secretaries of the Fellowship, nor is there any record of where these groups meet. This information is now being tabulated for future reference.'[16]

In 1959 'after a great deal of time pruning and looking into the membership of the Fellowship, we feel it safe to report that there are 1,500 fully paid up members ... We believe that, with more time given to the Fellowship, a new vision will come to the work, causing many new members to be enrolled ... and thus the Fellowship will play the part it was always intended to play, that of setting the hearts of men aflame with the love of God and a passion for souls.'[17] The key to its renewal was to place the responsibility once again into the hands of the senior evangelist, at that time Ernest Steele.

The renewed Youth Fellowship had an influence in bringing young people to the Anniversary and the Derwent Convention. In 1962 Ernest Steele noted that, 'one of the outstanding influences has been amongst those of the Fellowship who are students in Universities and Colleges; these have brought new friends along to

the Camps.'[18] The Fellowship always had to guard against the criticism that members did not take an active part in the life of the local church or that the Groups were in competition with the Christian Endeavour or the Wesley Guild. Ernest Steele noted that many of the Youth Fellowship were active as Local Preachers and as Mission Band leaders or members.[19] He was also convinced that one of the benefits of the Youth Fellowship was the link that its members had with the College.

When Ernest Steele left the evangelistic staff of the College in the summer of 1963, it was decided to bring the Youth Fellowship administration into the main administration of the College. 'The Cliff Fellowship is increasingly becoming a personal link with the College, rather than group meetings and this is what we wish to encourage. It is hoped to bring all members into a "Friends of Cliff" relationship and slowly incorporate the membership of the fellowship into the existing College records.'[20]

The 'Friends of Cliff' came into existence as the *Joyful News*, renamed *Advance* for two years, finished publication. Of the approximate 9,000 subscribers, though numbers had been falling, 1,000 people returned a pre-paid card indicating they would wish to continue contact with the College. The first issue of the *Cliff Witness* in January 1964 gave recognition to the strands of people who would now be receiving this publication, the past members of the Youth Fellowship, the readers of *Advance*, Cliff supporters and past students.[21] The 'Friends of Cliff' had a badge and any person could join by making a donation to the College. They were then eligible to receive the *Cliff Witness* and purchase from the College the 'Friends of Cliff' badge. Supporters of the College and past students now receive *Cliff Today* as a way of keeping in touch with the College and, since 1964, there has also been a monthly column in the *Methodist Recorder* about life in the College.

The ending of the Youth Fellowship in 1963 and the admittance of women students in 1966 made it inevitable that the 'Old Cliff Men's Fellowship' would need to make a change of name. What has since that time been known as the 'Cliff College Fellowship' (CCF) has kept the College in touch with past students and produces an annual list of all the members. The question of membership and

subscriptions was always a tricky one. In 1979 the membership was recorded as 1,379 but only £467 had been received in subscriptions at £1 per head. CCF had a deficit of £60 that year and the Committee resolved that a "strong letter be sent out".[22] On several occasions during the 80s appeals were made, and those who had not responded had their names "removed". John Moorley was co-opted on to the Fellowship committee in 1976 to introduce computer technology to records and from that time he gave the Fellowship positive administrative direction.

In 1983 the centenary of *Joyful News* was marked by CCF with the publication of the excellent *Cliff in Pictures*, a facsimile of the first edition of *Joyful News*, and the sale of 1,500 commemorative mugs.

In 1988 when the Secretary/Treasurer Howard Spratt stood down, a thorough review of the CCF was undertaken, and the CCF Committee used the situation to reconsider the Fellowship's position on finance and membership matters.[23] It was decided that a new office of Membership Secretary would be more appropriate to the future shape of CCF and John Moorley was elected to this position at the 1988 Annual General Meeting. A new structure was implemented by changes to the constitution – CCF ceased to collect subscriptions and everyone completing a residential course at the College would be automatically included in CCF and would remain a member:

> Membership shall continue as long as a former student supports the College: in that (a) they are committed to pray regularly and (b) they support the work of the College through CCF, as the Lord enables (All cheques payable to Cliff College who administer the finances of the Fellowship).[24]

All donations, which increased as a result of the changes, were sent directly to the College for immediate use, whereas previously funds were only transferred annually.

A further significant change was approved at the AGM in 1992. It had been recognised that tutorial staff became Vice-presidents and so maintained their links with their former students but there was no similar opportunity for non-tutorial staff. Therefore Associate Membership was made available for those who were not already included by virtue of being a former student.

We rejoice in the present numbers of students who are registered on courses, full-time and part-time, initial and ongoing training. The College has been grateful to the Cliff College Fellowship Committee and particularly its current Membership Secretary, John Moorley, who has spent endless hours ensuring that we can properly keep in touch with people. It is a labour of love which he personally gives, but one of diligent work and attention to detail which enables the College to be in touch with all its past students and present supporters. (The number of past and present students on the database is currently 2,146).

The Cliff College Fellowship supports the College in a number of ways. Past students often return to help with the running of major events or to give a week working in the grounds. The Fellowship also supports the College through gifts, mainly to the General Funds, but sometimes to the Student Welfare Fund and at the centenary by supporting the renewal of the Prayer Paths into 'Pilgrim Paths' which individuals or groups can use for prayer and meditation.

The major strength of the CCF has been that it has maintained tangible links between its membership, which result in mutual prayer support, a means of continuing contact amongst peer groups and an accessible base of support for the ongoing work of the College.

CHRIST FOR ALL

cliff

COLLEGE FELLOWSHIP

ALL FOR CHRIST

Handbook 2004/5

News, Reports etc and a Devotional item p2-7
Current students and Directory of Members
Help save the lost (Inside back cover)
Minutes of the AGM p77-78
Response slip p77

Please check your entry and return response slip even if there are no changes - we need to know you are still there!

As this book goes to press the Cliff College Fellowship Committee has set up a working party to review and as necessary to redefine the structure of the Fellowship to meet the needs of the College community as it develops. Today there are more students than at any point in the College's history. However, a higher proportion of these are only in College for short periods compared with those who are resident full-time. There is a groundswell of feeling that all staff should be actively included in the Fellowship rather than only becoming Associate Members on leaving Cliff.

If CCF is to be effective in the future it must continue to be sensitive to the changing needs of recent generations but also supportive of former students who trained at Cliff in a very different world.

1   The archives contain the letters to Ernest Cooper in China, normally from Thomas but sometimes written by Eliza. He wrote postcards to evangelists with news of a new appointment.

2   The information is kept in three ledgers and includes all students from 1904 – 2000. With the permission of present students a summary is held on computer and the College complies with the Data Protection Act.

3   *Cliff Witness*, Vol.1, No.1, p.1.

4   *Cliff Witness*, Vol.1, No.5, p.82.

5   *Minutes* of the Cliff College Committee, 19 September 1957.

6   *Minutes* of the Cliff College Committee, 15 November 1946.

7   *Minutes* of the Cliff College Committee, 21 November 1947.

8   *Minutes* of the Cliff College Committee, 22 September 1948.

9   We have a number of copies in our archive, with the first dated 1949, and the final copy October 1958.

10 *Minutes* of the Cliff College Committee, 22 September 1948.

11 *Minutes* of the Cliff College Executive Committee, 14 December 1948.

12 *Minutes* of the Cliff College Committee, 30 May 1950.

13 The Constitution was presented to the College Committee in June 1952, approved by the Home Mission Board in time for the Conference of 1953.

14 *Minutes* of the Cliff College Committee, 2 October 1953.

15 'Cliff Youth Fellowship Report', *Minutes* of the Cliff College Executive Committee, 15 April 1958.

16 Ibid.

17 'Cliff Youth Fellowship Report', *Minutes* of the Cliff College Committee, 9 October 1959.

18 'Cliff Youth Fellowship Report', *Minutes* of the Cliff College Committee, 26 October 1961.

19 'Cliff Youth Fellowship Report', *Minutes* of the Cliff College Committee, 11 October 1962.

20 'Cliff Youth Fellowship Report', *Minutes* of the Cliff College Committee, 3 October 1963.

21 *Cliff Witness*, January 1964, Vol.1, No.1.

22 *Minutes* of the Cliff College Fellowship Committee, 27 May 1979, 'After lengthy discussion it was proposed by the Rev D. Coombs and seconded by Mr H. Silverwood as follows: To ensure that the present membership of The Cliff College Fellowship should reflect active members only, we resolve that (1) a strong appeal should be sent out to all non-active members (with the next mailing) and (2) and that after a period of 4 years, non-active members will be notified that they will (a) deleted from the Cliff Handbook and (b) cease to receive the Handbook. This was unanimously agreed.'

23 Due to a fire at the then secretary's home all *Minutes* and archive prior to 1977 were lost.

24 *Constitution of the Cliff College Fellowship*, Section C (ii).

CHAPTER 16

A Learning Community

Under Champness, the 'Grindstone', the name given to his
morning Bible studies, typified
the heart of the teaching for the *Joyful News* evangelists. These
seminars were homely wisdom, insight from ministry and, whilst
undoubtedly informed by the scriptures, they treated a series of
issues which fall under the heading of 'practice theory'. Their
purpose was to enable the evangelist to be a good practitioner, to
speak in public, to deal with hecklers in the open air and to nurture
people in the faith. Champness had been an ordained minister for
some twenty-seven years before he began to train people. He lacked
the initial theological training from which Chadwick later benefited
but he had a keen sense of the issues relating to ministry.

He did, however, have the great sense to bring in others to help.
The training initially was given largely by Champness but he was no
theologian. He enlisted help from the Rev J. Finnemore, 'He is one
of our greatest helpers, for he has from the beginning of our work in
training Evangelists, taken great pains in teaching them by
correspondence.'[1] Champness, like Cook after him, called on good
teachers to train the *Joyful News* evangelists but the primary training
was an apprenticeship with experienced practitioners. Champness
later invited the Rev Joseph Todhunter to teach theology and, from

431

1889, when the Home moved to Castleton Hall, Chadwick came from the Leeds Mission to teach biblical exposition and preaching.

Cliff College Time Table.

23

MONDAY	9¼–10. Orthography.	10–10¾. English History.	11–11¾. Catechism.	11¾–12½. Mathematics.	2–3½. Manual Labour.	3¼–4¼. Candidates' Class.	6–7½. Bible Study, Preparation.		7½–8½. Biblical Lec. Rev. S. Chadwick.
TUESDAY	8¾–9¾. Biblical Lec. Rev. S. Chadwick. 9¼–10.	Arithmetic.	English Literature	Geography. Preparation.	Manual Labour.	Candidates' Class.	6–6¾. Geography.		Class Meeting. Rev. T. Cook.
WEDNES.	English Gram.	Reading.	Algebra.	Science.	Manual Labour.	Candidates' Class.	English History.	6¾–7½. Biblical Analysis.	7½–8½. English and Arithmetic, Preparation.
THURS. ...	English Gram.	Arithmetic.	Writing.	11¾–12¾. Theological Lecture. Rev. J. C. Greaves.	Manual Labour.	3¼–4. Geometry.			Preaching Service. A Student.
FRIDAY ...	Catechism.	Arithmetic.	Composition.	11¾–12½. Algebra.	Manual Labour.	3¼–4¼. Candidates' Class.	Geometry.	Greek.	Geography and Bible Preparation.
SAT'DAY	Geography.	10–11½. Pastoral Lecture. Rev. Thomas Cook.		Biblical Analysis.					

The emphasis on the practice of evangelistic ministry continued into the work of Cliff College. As a Connexional Evangelist Cook had been concerned to ensure that new converts were given good guidance. Not surprisingly, when he took over as Principal of Cliff, his primary aim was not only to give students an education but to put them on the right lines of self-improvement.[2] Cook had high hopes for the future of the College, and great expectation of the training offered by the College. His vision was not just confined to the Methodist Church nor the British Isles. His was a far greater missionary vision, 'The promise we see of future usefulness and ability fills us with large hopes and expectations. We are growing seed-corn for the conversion of the world.'[3] He therefore gathered

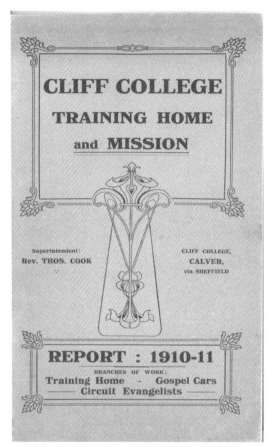

CLIFF COLLEGE
TRAINING HOME
and MISSION

Superintendent:
Rev. THOS. COOK

CLIFF COLLEGE,
CALVER,
via SHEFFIELD

REPORT : 1910-11
BRANCHES OF WORK:
Training Home - Gospel Cars
Circuit Evangelists

around him a group of able men and women as the team of tutors: the Revs Samuel Chadwick, J. Clapham Greeves, A. Bingham, to teach theology and biblical studies. Mr C.E. Oxenborough Rush BA, was appointed senior Lay Tutor and, in effect, the Director of Studies, a role he was to have for twenty years; and Miss Lilian Hovey came over from Sheffield to teach English and elocution. Each year he also had two young tutors who were either competent students or graduates looking for experience, and in 1904 they were T.W. Thompson BA, and J.J. Studley. With typical grace, Cook thanked this team 'for the earnest, patient, and skilful work they have done during the year. We speak of them with affection and esteem because they have toiled hard for the benefit of the men.'[4]

The effectiveness of the training was measured in ways distinctive to Methodism; firstly the relationship with local preaching and secondly the acceptability of ex-students as candidates for ordained ministry. Champness was concerned that people should know that the studies at Castleton Hall had been successful in training local preachers. 'The experiment we have made in training Local Preachers has been so far successful that we feel we cannot serve Methodism better than by extending this part of our work.'[5]

The move from the 'Home' in Rochdale to the 'College' in Derbyshire demanded that student attainment was robust academically and in terms which would be understood by

Methodists. Thomas Cook in his first report as Principal of Cliff College wished it to be known that not only were there good numbers of students wanting to attend the College in its new venue but also that the outcomes of their training were more than satisfactory. There was considerable emphasis on the acceptability of students as Local Preachers or as Ministerial candidates. 'More than a hundred men have been in training, of whom twenty-five have been qualified for evangelistic work. Twenty-seven have been recommended by the District Synods as suitable candidates for the ministry and the remaining fifty have returned to their homes and secular vocations, greatly helped in their work as Local Preachers by what we have been able to do for them.'[6]

Again in 1908 he measured the achievements of the College by the same criteria, 'Our estimate is that 40 men who have been trained at Cliff College are accepted annually for the Ministry at home or abroad.'[7] This recurred in 1911 with the following summary of the efficacy of the work of the college: 'During the last seven years 725 students have passed through the College; 119 of these have been accepted for the Home Ministry; 79 are in Canada, 62 in the United States, 42 in Australia, 10 in South Africa and other parts of the world; 61 are Lay Agents and Evangelists in this country, while 352 have gone back to their circuits as Local Preachers.'[8] It is interesting that the same yardstick was used many decades later to measure the academic merit of the courses. In a series of articles about Cliff students in theological training in the *Joyful News* during the autumn of 1957, the implication was given that the Cliff training fitted a person well for theological training, as though that gave Cliff some credence.[9]

CLIFF COLLEGE.

Wesleyan Lay Workers' Training Home,

CALVER, via SHEFFIELD.

TABLE OF HOURS.

MORNING:

A.M.	6-30.	Rise. Household Work and Private Devotion.
"	7-30.	Roll Call.
"	8-0.	Breakfast.
"	8-30.	Morning Worship.
"	9-15 to 12-45.	Classes.

AFTERNOON:

P.M.	1-0.	Dinner.
"	2-0 to 4-0.	Manual Labour.
"	4-0 to 5-0.	Free Hour.
"	5-0.	Tea.

EVENING:

P.M.	6-0 to 9-0.	Classes and Preparation.
"	9-0.	Supper.
"	10-0.	Each Student to retire to his own room.
"	10-30.	Gas out.

In 1907 when Samuel Chadwick was at the height of his powers as Superintendent of a large city church, his appointment as Tutor was crucial to the development of the College. Cook had recognised the importance of a second tutor with complementary skills to his own. He wrote, 'The appointment of the Rev Samuel Chadwick, who will act as my colleague with special reference to the Biblical and Theological training of the men, will add greatly to the efficiency of our staff, and will be of incalculable benefit to the men.'[10]

Cook and Chadwick established at the College a theological stance which was from the beginning both evangelical and evangelistic. Bebbington's now famous typology of nineteenth century evangelicalism with the Bible, the Cross, Conversion and Activism as key elements fit almost exactly the major themes of Champness, Cook and Chadwick.[11] There are however other emphases which emerged as the College developed as a learning community, not least that of holiness teaching.

Cook, as we have seen, established the College firmly as a place where evangelical theology was taught and upheld: 'At Cliff College, definite doctrines are held and taught. We hold by the doctrines of grace and teach ruin, redemption and regeneration in the old-fashioned way.'[12] Similarly Chadwick, preaching at the Anniversary of 1909, at the Easter Monday rally in Sheffield, declared that Cliff

435

'stood for the teaching of positive truth, definite experience, and passionate salvation.'[13]

Chadwick was proactive in his defence of evangelical doctrine and challenged theologians who sought to undermine it. Early in 1907, before his appointment to Cliff as a tutor, he remarked in a *Joyful News* article that the 'Rev R.J. Campbell of the City Temple, has stepped into the open and proclaimed himself the apostle of a New Theology.'[14] Campbell had written in the *Daily Mail*, and Chadwick refers to his 'theological oscillations. For some time he has walked in a mist, and his friends have striven in vain to discover his attitude to the fundamental doctrines of the evangelical faith ... In the enthusiasm for his own propaganda he fails to do justice to the orthodoxy he repudiates, as when he speaks of those who believe the Bible was "let down from heaven on a string".'[15] With this editorial, Chadwick shows his understanding of philosophy and theology and his ability to mount a theological defence which would be understandable to his readers.[16] He defended biblical theology, without falling into Campbell's caricature, and then challenged the proponents of the new theology to 'put it to the test in the slums of East London. Of what avail is it to tell drunkards and harlots, swearers and thieves, of their duty to the universe, and that through endless stages of perfecting they will attain to the Absolute?'[17]

He returned to the task of defeating this 'New Theology' the following week, a task he clearly enjoyed. He saw this as a 'protest against the tyranny of evangelical faith ... they complain of its narrowness and want of elasticity.' He placed the debate firmly in the context of evangelism and concluded: 'There is no place for uncertainty in the presence of peril. Literalism may be provoking, but emasculation is fatal. Better be narrow and mighty than broad and powerless.'[18]

Chadwick's summary of the 1911 Fernley Hartley lecture, *Christ and The Gospels* by Professor Holdsworth, shows a real engagement with the lecture and understanding of the contemporary writers. It is proof of his commitment to scholarship on the one hand, and the Bible as devotional text: 'A spiritual faith cannot live on abstractions, and many will be reassured that by the assurance of so competent a judge that the historical basis of the living Christ stands firm, whether or not the theory of "Q" be true or not.'[19]

For all his emphasis upon an evangelical understanding of theology, Chadwick was not a narrow biblicist as David Howarth has firmly concluded in his unpublished thesis on Chadwick.[20] The Bible for Chadwick was 'inspired', but he would have nothing to do with narrowness or bigotry and wanted his own view, and therefore that of the College, to be understood as 'broad-based'. His final word was, 'Stand together for the Word of God, but not in any stupid sense'.[21] Earlier he had contended with the leaders of the Wesley Bible Union who complained that the *Joyful News* had 'so often expressed subversive principles'.[22] Chadwick regarded the Bible Union as contentious controversialists, having a 'nagging' manner.[23] He upheld the revelation of God through the scriptures but insisted that 'inspiration was not dictation'.[24]

He had to defend the College and his teaching from the ardent evangelicals on the one hand and the liberal scholars on the other, insisting to both: 'The work of the College is based upon the Word of God and the doctrines of grace. We have no quarrel with knowledge, new and old, scientific or historical, philosophical or psychological, but we believe in the Holy Ghost who spake by the prophets. We teach the Bible intelligently, systematically and reverently. Nothing we teach ever needs to be unlearned, and no Cliff College evangelist despairs of any sinner this side of the grave. The College stands

437

frankly for Full Salvation, as interpreted in Methodist doctrine. The efficiency of the evangelist is in the equipment of Pentecost. The Gospel saves, and Full Salvation works. Our faith is scriptural, supernatural and rational. The experience of grace is as psychologically sound as it is scripturally true. The work of the College is proved in the adventure of faith that goes unafraid to challenge the world.'[25]

Chadwick was aware of the learning in other disciplines and wanted to place the academic provision of Cliff in the context of developing thought in the early twentieth century but with a distinctive emphasis. 'The world we are sent to evangelise is a very different world from that which John Wesley claimed for his parish. The romance of science has brought a new world of consciousness, a new sense of democratic power, a new standard of values, and a new right of inheritance. The new democracy claims the world. There is a new social order, a new economic conscience, and a new conception of religion'.[26] As a result he was confident that the standard and quality of the teaching and learning at the College would provide a good foundation for those who undertook courses at Theological Colleges which were at that time alive with Liberal Protestant theology.

The Library Cliff College, Calver.

If the theological stance of the College was evangelical with a significant emphasis on biblical understanding and theology, the focus of the work was evangelism and the training of evangelists. Thomas Cook commented in his first report to the Conference: 'Our men are not only taught how to

C.E.O. Rush

preach but they are employed in preaching and taught how to become fishers of men. Our great aim is to help them to win multitudes of souls for Christ. It is remarkable how some have developed the soul-saving gift, and how skilful they have become in this work. We cannot bestow the soul-saving gift, but we can help to enrich it by suggesting ways and methods which we have learnt by observation and experience.'[27] Cook was also keen to ensure that the training in evangelism was very practical: 'It is not sufficient that men who do this work should be zealous; special training is necessary, or their hearers will be repelled by their incompetence and ignorance. Socialists are alive to the importance of instructing their propagandists in principles, facts, and arguments and we must lay ourselves out to help our men to secure the necessary equipment for work so momentous as the saving of souls. Neither piety nor learning can take the place of knowing how to pull in the net. Evangelists need training in this particular more than in any other, and we do our best to teach them what we have learned by observation and experience.'[28] The overriding purpose of the training was to equip men as evangelists and this was confirmed in an early report from Chadwick: 'Our work is to train men for effective Evangelism, and perhaps our greatest service is in those who return to their circuits better equipped for the work of the Church and fired with enthusiasm for all that is implied in aggressive Evangelism.'[29] Chadwick, reflecting on the work of the College in 1928, wanted to make quite clear that evangelism was a key charism of the academic and pioneering work of the College: 'we train evangelists for Twentieth Century Evangelism.'[30]

Chadwick's book review of *The Social Mission of the Gospel* reveals his opinion that social change would come about by personal conversion. It also betrayed his own considered view, 'The social can only be attained through the spiritual, and society can never be reconstructed from without. It is not a system but an organism; and social redemption can only come by individual redemption'.[31] So evangelism was doubly important for it would not only bring individual conversion but also social change.

In what was to prove his final report to the Conference Chadwick set out the primary purpose of training at Cliff as evangelism: 'Our specific purpose is to train evangelists, and the whole curriculum of the College is based on this. Our standard of work, both in its nature and its scope, is that which will worthily furnish and prepare an effective evangelist for service in these modern days. The Bible is central to all our work. We seek to turn out men who will reverently, intelligently and effectively handle the Scriptures in the spiritual warfare to which they are called. A knowledge of the Book as a whole, detailed exposition of chosen portions, and analysis of separate books, form the biblical substance of the timetable. Because the evangelist must have a clear grasp of the doctrines of grace, theology occupies an important place in our scheme of study, and to this the catechism is a useful auxiliary. Because the evangelist needs to express himself in language that is correct, clear and convincing, we include in our syllabus English Language and Literature, and kindred subjects of a general nature.'[32]

Similarly, then as now, there was an emphasis on praxis, the interrelation between serious study and practical application. This is neither practice alone, nor is it theory alone, but practice theory, or praxis. 'The College combines training with teaching. Every Sunday practically all the students are preaching in the villages. Open-air services and Visiting Bands are organised, and most weeks there is the joy of the harvest.'[33] As Cook had phrased it in the initial years:

'Repentance and faith and holiness are still our watchwords, and to these doctrines we are true, not only in our public ministry, but in the instruction of the classroom. The result is that our men are filled with an all consuming desire to save souls, and never a Sunday passes but we rejoice with the joy of the harvest.'[34]

The educational aims were set out in what today would appear to be quaint ways of speaking but they carry the same desire for students to broaden their horizons, deepen their understanding of the scriptures, the church, ministry and the world around them: 'There is an infection of intensity. The eyes are opened to vast reaches of far stretching lands. New enthusiasms are kindled and loins girded.'[35] It was expected, then as now, that students have an 'aptitude for study'. In 1920 this was reported in a rather intriguing way. 'There has been equal zest in study. The students are dogged in the secular studies that are difficult to adult minds but they are then as sleuth-hounds in the study of the Scripture, Theology and Homiletics. The progress some of them make is really amazing.'[36]

The desired outcomes were not confined to the academic learning nor the ability to move on to new areas of ministry, but focussed on the development of personal qualities for ministry. 'We ask also for the prayers of God's people that every man who comes to Cliff College may receive power he never had before to help God to make the world better.'[37]

In the early years and before the Treks began the Cliff course was short and intensive, with three ten-week terms. In those days, few of the students came for the whole year. Normally it was for a term or part of a term, in some cases for as long as their funds allowed. Some had seasonal work and needed to return, for instance, to the farm. In the first year, 'The period of training has averaged four and a half months, but several men have remained with us for the whole year.'[38] In these years the curriculum was adapted to the needs of the men who came, but always with a purpose of preparing for ministry.[39]

The intention of the College from the time of Champness was always to offer open access to people who otherwise may not have qualification or be able to attend a college. Cook set out his view that 'Our men are mostly sons of the poor, such as come from the factory and plough. The majority of them have no intention of seeking service for which there is monetary remuneration. They come seeking better equipment for the service of God and the church, and return afterwards to the circuits and secular employment.'[40] Years later, Chadwick commented that, 'It is no uncommon thing for a man to enter with hardly a notion of study, and to close his course in the front rank of capable students.'[41]

Some of the students attended Cliff College to 'test a call' and for help in candidating for the ministry. Cook commented, with his own experience in mind, that many of the Cliff students have had 'slender educational advantages, (and) have little chance of being accepted for the Ministry apart from such help as we can give. They come to us bent on making the most of their opportunity and it is remarkable how many have given proof of their call and fitness for the work.'[42]

The remarkable scholar W. Fiddian Moulton, from a dynasty of biblical and missionary scholars, when writing the *Report* about the College in 1914, rejoiced that the college was the 'College of the underprivileged.'[43] He used the phrase as his subtitle for the Silver Jubilee booklet in 1928.[44] Fiddian Moulton was a tutor from 1913 until his sudden death in 1929, and echoed the desire of Champness to reach the 'man in the smock frock', but Moulton extended the invitation to the underprivileged of the industrial towns.

Samuel Chadwick,
Fiddian Moulton,
Norman Dunning
Oxenborrow Rush

The main criteria of acceptance was the quality of character, Christian commitment and willingness to learn. 'We refuse no man who is earnest in spirit, keen in purpose and set upon getting people saved. The strain is considerable, for we believe in work and the time is short. There is fervour, enthusiasm and joyousness that has come to be known as 'the Cliff Spirit'. Some of the men are very poor; but the poorer they are the merrier they seem to be, for God is always doing surprising things for them in answer to their prayers.'[45]

The theme of Lay Training is very significant through the work of Champness, Cook and Chadwick. They wanted Cliff to be recognised along with the theological colleges but they did not imitate them. Cliff was for lay training. Chadwick wanted to emphasise the College as a lay training college with a distinct emphasis on evangelism, which he championed for the next twenty years.[46] There is a recurring theme within the literature which elevates lay training and distances the College from being a place of preparation for ministerial training. 'Let it be clearly understood, we are not primarily an institution for training men for the ministry. We are a Lay Preachers' College first and foremost; and although we are glad to render assistance to those who are wishful to enter our ministry; that is only an incident in our work, although we do try to give special help to candidates during the critical Summer Term. The majority of our men go back into the circuits, and to their old employments, strengthening – we are convinced – the preaching plan and the administrative organisation of those circuits.'[47] He was also concerned that people considered the College as a 'forcing-house for

D.W. Lambert

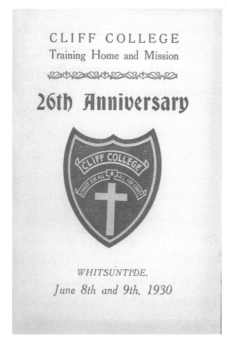

CLIFF COLLEGE
Training Home and Mission

26th Anniversary

WHITSUNTIDE,
June 8th and 9th, 1930

candidates for the Ministry.'[48]

Links with other Colleges seem to be limited. That might in part have been because Chadwick was critical of theological training: 'A ministry that is College-trained but not Spirit-filled works no miracles ... Some preachers have finished their ministerial training with the confession that they learned less about their Bibles than about any other subject; ... Enthusiasm does not often accompany scholarship.'[49] Despite the urgent need to show Methodism that the teaching and learning at Cliff was at least comparable with other theological colleges, both Cook and Chadwick distanced themselves from engagement with the Colleges even though the *Joyful News* carried news of the Methodist College open days. Curiously it was with a college in United States that there was most contact initially. Champness knew Dwight L. Moody, the American preacher and evangelist, who opened 'Northfield' near Chicago in 1889 as a Bible Training School, and Chadwick taught there on a number of occasions.[50] However there is no evidence of contact with other Bible Colleges until Lambert went to the Faith Mission and much later Stringer joined the staff of the newly formed London Bible College.

Through the articles of the *Joyful News*, the College was associated with the great missionary conferences. The Edinburgh Missionary Conference 14–23 June 1910, presided over by the Methodist layman John R. Mott, was covered in some detail with leading articles by Chadwick and on the 9 and

23 June, W.H. Heap dispatched to report on the Conference deliberations.[51] Chadwick gave an Address at the 76th Anniversary of the Evangelical Alliance, a prestigious event for all leaders of the denominations. That year Chadwick was the President of the National Council of the Evangelical Free Churches. The address was printed in full in the *Joyful News*, and he set out the Charisms of the College, Biblical, Evangelical and Witnessing as he saw they related to the Evangelical Alliance.[52]

Joe Brice and D.W. Lambert with students

Chadwick and the College benefited from the care and diligence of Oxenborrow Rush who had joined Cook in 1904. When he left for the mission field in the spring of 1924, Chadwick wisely chose David W. Lambert to take his place. A generation younger, well trained and with experience of teaching, Lambert proved very successful as a teacher and also in the application of leadership in the Trek missions which were developing. 'The new members of staff, Mr D.W. Lambert, B.A. (Cambridge) and Mr Young, have won the esteem and affection of their colleagues and of the students.'[53] One of Chadwick's great friends from the United States, the Rev Dr J.G. Bickerton of Philadelphia, visited the College each term and delivered a course of lectures on the Gospels and the Pauline Epistles.

At the end of the Chadwick era, there was the clearest indication of the College's policy of integrating academic learning with evangelistic ministry preparing students for Christian leadership, ordained and lay. In his booklet published to celebrate the Silver

The Rev Howard Belben's lecture to the first mixed year (1966)

Jubilee of the College, Fiddian Moulton, who had been involved with the College for almost twenty years and knew the College better than most, set out the principles, aims and methods of the College and for the teaching and learning process identified five key elements:

1. Biblical teaching which aims at covering all the books of the Old and New Testaments, with special attention to selected examples of different types. Each book is studied in outline. Criticism is not ignored, but content is our chief concern. Each term one or more books are studied exegetically, so that in addition to a general knowledge of the books of the Bible each student is taught methods of minute and exact study. Most men who come to us leave with a sense of having found the Bible, which is the inspired word of God that abideth for ever.

2. Special attention is given to the vocabulary of the New Testament. The great words of evangelical doctrine are studied and expounded.

3. Dogmatic theology is taught, and emphasis is placed on the central and saving truths of the Faith.

Mr Frank Blackwell, and the Revs Malcolm White, Howard Belben (Principal), and Amos Cresswell, 1966.

4. Homiletics, the art and calling of preaching, have a place all their own. We cannot make preachers, but the blame is not with the College if any

Late 70s: the Revs John Job, Dr Arthur Skevington Wood, Brian Hoare and Mr Robert Mason.

man leaves it without a practical knowledge of the art.

5. General education includes every-thing a man needs for efficiency and effectiveness in the work of evangelism.[54]

Broadbelt had many strengths, but academic development was not one of them. He followed the trajectory set out by Chadwick. However, after the Second World War the position of learning had been elevated by the 1944 Education Act and the post-war period made demands on colleges not present before. When Cliff College reopened in 1945, the Committee determined to grant to students 'who had fulfilled a course of study at the College, and had been in every respect satisfactory to the staff' a College Diploma.[55] This must have been the first time such recognition had been given even though the College was self-validated. The College had already agreed with the Local Preachers' Department that where Cliff Students passed the College exams 'on text books prescribed by Conference for Local Preachers, and were satisfactorily passed, this would be accepted as Equivalent to passing the Connexional Local Preachers Examination.'[56]

Howard Belben, when he became Principal, was particularly concerned to gather to the College a group of Tutors who were scholars in their own fields. He attracted the Rev Malcolm White to teach biblical doctrine, and in the spring of 1966 announced, 'subject to Conference' the appointment of the Rev Donald English to join the College staff in September.[57] Unfortunately the Conference chose

The Rev Royston Emms holding a Tutorial in the Library

to send Donald to Hartley Victoria College in Manchester but the young and able scholar the Rev Royston Emms came to the College. He was an exceptionally good teacher and eventually, like Malcolm White, took a career in secondary education. The Rev David Sharp, the Rev John Job, Dr Arthur Skevington Wood, Mr Robert Mason and the Rev Brian Hoare, by their appointments, continued the trend of fine scholars who had shown their ability as evangelists and pastors.

The College Certificate course had hardly changed between 1967 and 1983 with the exception that different subjects were offered for 'A Level' examination. There were still many students who had been sent by their ministers 'to test a call', and along the way to gain sufficient 'O Level' subjects, and for those who might be able to undertake a Degree course, two 'A Level' qualifications. Religious Education was offered with Sociology, and Malcolm White taught British Government at 'A Level' in the late 1960s. The Rev Dr Stephen Mosedale and the Rev Kathleen Bowe continued this same standard of teaching and training in the 1980's with a special emphasis on pastoral ministry. During this time Mr Ron Abbott was also a tutor at the college, making other alternatives available. When a student arrived and indicated a pressing need to study an obscure subject (Mathamatics, Geography and the like) Ron looked into the middle distance and commented sagely, 'Well I might be able to help, I used to teach that some years ago.'

The Tutors 1987 - the Revs Howard Mellor, Dr Bill Davis (Principal), Dr Stephen Mosedale, Kathleen Bowe and Mr Ron Abbott.

The first very considerable change to the curriculum came in 1990 under the leadership of Dr Bill Davies, when the College espoused the newly formed training package for Local Preachers, called *Faith and Worship*. The course had sixteen taught modules and, across the certificate year, it was decided to teach an adapted version of the course, using a module each week. This was the first of a series of dramatic changes which had the positive effect of unlocking a tired academic schedule but it too closely webbed the College in with the Methodist Local Preachers' course. For the first two years, the College pioneered the course and was ahead of the Connexion. From the autumn of 1993 a new version of the Certificate was devised by Stephen Mosedale and Richard Woolley, because it became clear that people who had completed the local preacher training, *Faith and Worship*, wanted to come to Cliff to 'test a call' or have further training for differing types of Christian ministry. It was realised this would cause difficulties in future years and the dilemma was in itself a spur to further academic developments.

The Cliff College Certificate was not recognised by the Methodist Church and the hard-won concessions which Howard Belben had achieved became increasingly irksome, as the teaching developed at Cliff under the leadership of Bill Davies. The Division of Ministries was approached to see whether they would allow students who had successfully completed the Cliff Certificate to use this to offset the academic hurdle of six 'O Level' qualifications, the exception being that all students would need English. The reply was that the Division would ask a 'Schools Inspector' to attend the College and assess whether the Cliff Certificate had the equivalent academic value of 'O Levels' and, if so, how many.

This letter was not well received at Cliff and it created a determination to approach the University of Sheffield. The Tutors were convinced that the Cliff Certificate course equated in large measure to the first year of a degree course, and some had first-hand knowledge from studying both the Cliff Certificate and then later the University of London, Diploma in Theology and the BD. The initial contacts with Professor John Rogerson in April 1991 were so very

Tutorial Team 1998

promising that the College was determined not to pursue the matter within Methodism but to press on to gain validation from Sheffield. The matter took much longer than anticipated because the University of Sheffield was at that time developing its structures to enable links with validated Colleges. The visitation to the College by a panel from the University took place in November 1993 to review the College's academic provision and two programme specifications, one for the Certificate in Biblical and Evangelistic Ministry and the other for the degree of Master of Arts in Evangelism Studies. In this process, we learned the importance of providing complete and detailed information and, because Sheffield is a deliberately secular University, the need to defend the academic study of evangelism and the training of reflective practitioners in the mission and ministry of the church.

The news that the Senate had accepted our application came in January 1994 and meant that the courses could commence in the September. I was to become Principal in the September, and would have to lead the MA in Evangelism Studies, so we delayed the start of that course until a 1995 intake. By that time Paul Ashby, Peter

Phillips and Phil Clarke had also proposed to Sheffield a Diploma in Biblical and Evangelistic Ministry and the following year a Level 3 course to take students to a BA (Hons) in Biblical and Evangelistic Ministry. At last we had courses which would gain proper recognition across the world and even in Methodism.

Lecture in progress

The Methodist Church introduced a process of vocational discernment called 'Foundation Training'. A number of students entered Foundation Training as they proceeded through the three-year course and some students came to Cliff to undertake foundation training. However this process has had a negative affect on student recruitment at Cliff since from the beginning of the College there had been a constant stream of students sent by Superintendent Ministers to 'test a call'. Now they were going to a number of other institutions.

The Revs Peter Philips, Dr Martyn Atkins, Mrs Suzanne Garnett, Principal Howard Mellor, and the Revs Phil Clarke and Paul Ashby

Developments seemed to happen at a rapid pace when these courses were created and validated. I went to meet the Rev John Finney, then the Bishop of Southwell's Advisor in Evangelism and later to become Bishop of Pontefract, with the intention of inviting him to lecture on the MA course. He accepted but in turn spoke about a programme in which he was involved, developed by David Watson and which since David's death John had taught at Fuller Theological Seminary. A British version of the programme was devised called 'The Changing Church Course' taught mainly by Anglicans for clergy who were experiencing renewal in their congregations and wanted to harness this outflow of spiritual energy rather than experience the church dividing or exploding. I looked at the course with one of the then staff members, Felicity Lawson, and translated the heart of it into what became the Diploma in Leadership, Renewal and Mission. Prior to his death David Watson had suggested to Bill Davies that Cliff would be the place for the course. Bill wisely felt at that time the College was not ready for it, but under changed circumstances the time was right.

This new course with its delivery team joined the College, and the first Postgraduate Diploma in Leadership, Renewal and Mission ran from the autumn of 1996. It began as the Rev Dr Martyn Atkins joined the staff as Postgraduate Tutor in Missiology, Evangelism and Apologetics. These courses became the bedrock of the postgraduate department and have now gained international recognition. Another course came about as a result of co-operation with Dr George Lovell. Across a period of over twenty years, I had admired the work of George Lovell and, as a result of his involvement with the MA in Evangelism Studies, he asked whether Cliff could join with Westminster College, Oxford and the Urban Theology Unit, Sheffield, to offer a course to train people in consultancy. This course commenced, using the resources and staff of the three institutions, but unfortunately it was complex to administer and insufficiently anchored in any one of the institutions. A change was precipitated when the Methodist Church unwisely gave Westminster College to Oxford Brookes University. At that time George Lovell had produced significant writing about consultancy and ministry, so the next natural step was to bring that course to Cliff. This was negotiated and the MA in Consultancy, Mission and Ministry was launched in autumn 2000. One course, at postgraduate level, which did not reach its potential was the MA in Training and Theology in Church and Community. Perhaps it was the length of the title which put people off, but only four people enlisted for the first cohort. The following year the numbers were even smaller and so the initial group of four were the only group which completed the course. It was a necessary but unwelcome step because as the external examiner commended the course as a 'unique opportunity for church workers to engage in study of this nature'.[58]

It became clear that we needed to respond to people who wanted to undertake research degrees leading to an MPhil or PhD. We were receiving regular enquiries and, therefore, in the autumn of 1994 I wrote to the University of Sheffield requesting a meeting to discuss the issues involved. The Academic Development Committee of the Senate, meeting in early 1995, recommended that Cliff College be granted Designated Status. The effect was that the Board of Collegiate Studies of the University conferred on the College an *Agreement of the Award for Higher Degrees by the University of Sheffield to the students of Cliff College*. The legal arrangement was signed on 4 October 1995 and this was probably unique in the modern history of Higher Education. In effect, it gave Cliff College the status of a University Department with our own Higher Degrees Committee to accept, supervise and recommend for acceptance, students for research degrees in the University. At the revalidation of the College in 1999 there were five people studying as part-time research students, and, so far, the Rev Barrie Cooke has gained an MPhil and Rev John Job a PhD with others close to submitting.

While these postgraduate courses were being developed and promoted, we were approached by people who wished to study a thorough course preparing people for Children's ministry. Ian White, who at that time, was the Evangelism Enabler for East Anglia, had contacts with Scripture Union. Alan Charter and Max Reynolds from Scripture Union committed time to help in the development of the course. This alliance between Scripture Union and the College gave birth to the Diploma in Children's Evangelism and Nurture. It became the most controversial of all the courses, and was challenged in the Senate of the University. We had carefully made sure the course proposal was absolutely sound on academic grounds, so that even those within the University who were philosophically opposed to such a course could not derail the application on academic grounds. The course, we knew, was the most thoroughly prepared application we had made to the University. It was accepted and agreed. A launch day was planned to advertise this unique course to small groups of invited journalists in a hotel reception room in London's Piccadilly. That same day the *Independent* newspaper ran a story with the heading, 'Christians are coming to get your Children'. The media picked up the story on Radio Five Live, and I was interviewed on the Radio 4 PM programme. It was the best publicity we have ever had!

The Children's Evangelism and Nurture course was a runaway success, under the leadership of Ian White along with Scripture Union staff and the best lecturers available. This made us consider the possibility of other undergraduate courses. We then developed the Diploma in Music, Spirituality and Worship with the help of the Rev Brian Hoare, Chris Bowater and others, then curiously, the course which never had an applicant, a Diploma in Holiness Studies. We were grateful to the Rev D. Paul C. Smith for his detailed work on the subject, along with Martyn Atkins and myself on what would have been a unique and intriguing course. Although available for a further two years, it never had any applicants. I have even marketed it in churches suggesting ministers should nominate people for whom such a course would be beneficial!!

A further development was the relocation of the Methodist Churches Open Learning Centre to Cliff College. The Open Learning Centre was in financial trouble and Cliff made a bid for the whole enterprise. Two of its programmes were linked to other Institutions but the rest came to Cliff and we have continued to trim, edit, and commission modules. All the Open Learning Centre courses are presently being remodelled and will be launched in this Centenary Year as 'Horizons – Learning for Christian Living'. The delivery of the modules will be even more linked to the 'Cliff experience', ensuring that students who enlist have the opportunity for short periods of study at the College.

The full inventory of the academic development over the last ten years would be incomplete without mention of the International Learning Centre. That came about because the Rev Richard Jackson,

who is Assistant Tutor in the Postgraduate Department, had served as a minister in Sierra Leone, and came with a vision for delivering a part-time course there, in the manner we had developed at Cliff. As Sierra Leone was emerging from twenty years of war and the church was growing rapidly, there was a great need for the training of leaders. Therefore, the International Diploma in Applied Ministry and Mission was established with the help of the World Church Office of the Methodist Church and with mission partners in Ireland and Europe. We have been grateful to *Feed the Minds* and the Methodist Church in Ireland for their help and donations of books and resources. One hundred students applied for the first course! Since the largest lecture room available to us only held fifty people, every lecture was delivered twice. Tutors from the UK and Europe were linked with a local tutor to deliver the subjects and the whole experience became a learning experience for everyone involved. It has been a remarkable vision and is likely to become a model for the delivery of courses in other parts of the World Church in the future. The summer of 2004 saw the first Graduation for the course and it was an enormous privilege to attend the ceremony in Freetown, Sierra Leone and preside at that event. It is our hope that with mission partners there, and with the continued support from the UK and Europe, the College will be able to run the course again for the region of West Africa and in so doing prepare people to take it on themselves for the future. Our great hope is to establish the course in different parts of the World Church in the future.

The next few years will be most interesting to watch. With the appointment of the Rev Dr Martyn Atkins we have one of the country's leading missiologists as College Principal. The academic staff has been strengthened by the appointment of Dr David Firth as Old Testament Tutor, and, in summer 2004, by the Rev Dr Philip Meadows taking Martyn's place as the Director of Postgraduate Studies. The appointment of the experienced Rev Steven Wild as Director of Evangelism confirms the commitment by the College to the training and practice of evangelism. This strong and innovative team has now forged links with the University of Manchester. The relationship with the University of Sheffield has been very important for the development of the College, allowing new courses at both undergraduate and postgraduate levels. However, it became clear in the Spring of 2003 that Sheffield could not accommodate all the developments which we believed were necessary to carry forward the next phase of Cliff's academic development. Therefore as this book

Dr David Firth

goes to press a new arrangement is being forged with the University of Manchester, and an enormous amount of detailed preparation is being undertaken by all the staff, but particularly by the Rev Dr Peter Phillips and Dr David Firth. One new course will be in Youth, Mission and Ministry and the detailed work for this programme proposal is presently being undertaken. Other new courses will emerge in the future, existing ones will be transformed, and I believe the international reputation of the college will continue to be enhanced.

Rev Dr Martyn Atkins

1   *Joyful News,* 18 November 1886, and the Rev H.S.B. Yates followed in this work.
2   H.K. *Leeds Mission News,* September 1904.
3   *Report of the Wesleyan Home Mission Fund,* 1905, p.125.
4   *Report of the Wesleyan Home Mission Fund,* 1905, p.126.
5   *Joyful News,* 5 September 1895.
6   *Report of the Home Mission Fund,* 1905.
7   *Report of the Home Mission Fund,* 1908.
8   *Report of the Home Mission Fund,* 1911.
9   *Joyful News,* articles through October and November 1957.
10 *Report of the Home Mission Fund,* 1907.
11 David Bebbington, *Evangelicalism in Modern Britain* (London: Unwin Hyman, 1989), pp.2-17, listed by him as Conversionism, Activism, Biblicism and Crucicentricism.
12 *Report of the Home Mission Fund,* 1907.
13 *Joyful News,* 11 March 1909.
14 *Joyful News,* 24 January 1907.
15 Ibid.
16 Ibid, He wrote: 'His theology is neither Biblical nor historical, but speculative. Spinoza westernised Pantheism and Campbell has modernised Spinoza. He does not deny the divinity of Jesus; on the contrary, he declares every man a Christ, and as really a manifestation of God as the Christ Himself. Religion is defined as man's responsibility - not to God but to the universe; the recognition of the essential oneness between the soul and the Over-soul called God. Since every man is a manifestation of God, no man can be lost; every soul must return to the Absolute from whence it came.'
17 *Joyful News,* 24 January 1907.
18 *Joyful News,* 31 January 1907.
19 *Joyful News,* 17 August 1911.
20 Howarth, *Samuel Chadwick,* Chapter 6, pp.179-208.
21 *Joyful News,* 20 October 1932.
22 *Journal of the Wesley Bible Union,* 1919, p.275. The Wesley Bible Union was formed in 1914 to uphold, 'The Absolute and Final Authority of Holy Scripture' (see *Journal,* 1924, p.123).
23 *Joyful News,* 15 January 1920.
24 *Joyful News,* 15 January 1920.
25 *Report of the Home Mission Fund,* 1928, p.110. Years earlier he had declared, 'We seek to make men skilled craftsmen who know how to handle the Holy Scriptures.' *Report of the Home Mission Fund,* 1913, p.99.
26 *Report of the Home Mission Fund,*1928, p.110.
27 *Report of the Wesleyan Home Mission Fund,* 1905, p.125.
28 *Report of the Home Mission Fund,* 1908, pp.104-105.
29 *Reports of the Wesleyan Home Mission Fund,* 1915, pp.98-99.
30 *Report of the Home Mission Fund,*1928, p.110.

cont.

31 *Joyful News*, 29 November 1906. The details of publication are not given.
32 *Report of the Home Mission Fund*, 1931, p.86.
33 *Report of the Home Mission Fund,*1913, p.99.
34 *Report of the Home Mission Fund*, 1907.
35 *Report of the Home Mission Fund*, 1913, pp.98-99.
36 *Report of the Home Mission Fund*, 1920.
37 *Report of the Home Mission Fund*, 1913, p.99.
38 *Report of the Home Mission Fund*, 1905, p.124.
39 *Report of the Home Mission Fund*, 1913, p.99.
40 *Report of the Home Mission Fund*, 1908, p.104.
41 *Report of the Home Mission Fund*, 1913, p.99.
42 *Report of the Home Mission Fund*, 1908, p.104.
43 *Report of the Home Mission Fund,*1914.
44 *Report of the Home Mission Fund*, 1914, p.119 and the Silver Jubilee booklet, *The Story of Cliff, the College of the Unprivileged*, 1928.
45 *Report of the Home Mission Fund*, 1924, p.80.
46 *Report of the Home Mission Fund*, 1913, pp.98-99.
47 *Report of the Home Mission Fund*, 1914, p.119.
48 *Report of the Home Mission Fund*, 1913, pp.98-99.
49 Chadwick, *The Way to Pentecost,* pp.15-17.
50 *Joyful News,* 28 June 1906. Champness had met Moody the evangelist, Chadwick had visited to lecture there.
51 *Joyful News,* 9 and 23 June 1910.
52 *Joyful News,*13 July 1922.
53 *Report of the Home Mission Fund,* 1925, p.73.
54 Moulton, *The Story of Cliff* (Epworth Press: London, 1928), pp.39-42. *Report of the Home Mission Fund*, 1828, pp.68-9.
55 Minutes of the Cliff College Committee, 12 May 1947.
56 Minutes of the Cliff College Committee, 15 November 1946.
57 *Cliff Witness,* January 1966.
58 Professor Ivan Reid, in his report as External Examiner, 30 October 2003.

CHAPTER 17

Proximity and Polarity

The *Joyful News* Training Home and Mission had been from the outset deliberately distanced by Champness from the Connexional structures. Thomas Champness made it quite clear that in taking on the proposed newspaper he wished to be the editor on his own terms which were without payment and therefore without supervision. After some initial reluctance the Wesleyan Methodists welcomed his proposal. Champness saw himself as standing for a kind of Wesleyanism which could affect the whole beneficially: 'We must keep the fires burning while the frost lasts', was a favourite phrase of his. This suggests that he saw the *Joyful News* Mission as both over against and yet crucially connected to the Wesleyan Church. There was a real and creative tension between them.[1]

From the beginning Champness's view of the *Joyful News* was that it should not engage in 'Connexional politics' – however, as we have seen, Champness was not afraid of using the *Joyful News* as a campaigning publication. His most critical article of the ministry came in 1888 in a leading article under his own name entitled, 'The Parasite Ecclesiastic'.[2] He was very critical of ordained colleagues, referring to them as 'Mistletoe Ministers' who do not work hard, and have a parasitic life in circuits, indicating that they move on when their batch of sermons are preached. This did not endear him to the

461

Conference in July 1888 where exception was taken to the article, which was read out from the platform to cries of 'Shame'. He was unrepentant, writing the following week in the *Joyful News*, 'None of those who cried 'Shame' when the article was read in the Conference denied the truth of it.'[3]

He also had to suffer considerable criticism in 1890 about the way he conducted the *Joyful News* missionaries, as chapter six makes clear. That criticism almost made him leave the Church, but he remained loyal though he felt the 'Controversy' had curtailed the vision he had for the missionary work. On the other hand he trusted the Church in 1903 when he handed over the Training Home; standing back, he allowed the Church to make its decisions. That took great courage and wisdom, and his faith was rewarded both in the appointment of Thomas Cook as Principal and in the initial purchase of Hulme Cliff College.

From the outset Cliff College was well connected to the Methodist Church. Key Methodist Leaders who supported his work such as the Revs H.J. Pope, Luke Wiseman, John Hornabrook, Samuel Collier, and other able and influential laymen including William Lamplough, T.H. Bainbridge, Joseph Rank, and Sir Robert Kay were members of the Cliff College Committee. As we have noted Champness, Cook and Chadwick were members of the 'Legal Hundred', the company of one hundred respected ministers who were the real Trustees of Wesleyan Methodism.

Cook had been very faithful to the Wesleyan Methodists who honoured his ministry, and had released him as a Connexional Evangelist for twenty years of ministry. His nine years as Principal were visionary years and in that time the relationship between the College and the Home Mission Department was very cordial. Cook found the lack of vision in the Cliff Committee and the Home Mission Department irksome but almost always found the initial funding which enabled him to proceed with his schemes and dreams.

Chadwick benefited from his considerable standing as the renowned preacher from the Oxford Place, Leeds. He had been the chosen preacher for the Centenary Celebrations of the Wesleyan Methodist Missionary Society in the Albert Hall with the King and Queen present. In common with Nonconformist leaders of his day he was known to politicians, and was a good friend of Lloyd George. In 1918 the Church honoured Chadwick by voting him President of the Conference. Chadwick ran the College as an independent entity, raised the funding, appointed a superb team around him, promoted the College and sought no recourse to Connexional funds, whilst at the same time adding to investments and purchasing land and property for the College. He was supportive of the Wesleyans, and was critical of the Wesley Bible Union which campaigned against a united Methodist Church. He supported the proposed Union and in an account of the discussion at the 1922 Methodist Conference at Carver Street, Sheffield, Chadwick concluded, 'Yours in the fellowship of our Lord's Prayer that His People may be one as He and the Father are One.'[4] Similarly ten years later at the point of Union he remained positive: 'We are all of one mind in our rejoicing over the United Methodist Church, and pray with one heart and one faith that the year may abound in grace, power and glory, to the salvation and sanctification of the Redeemed.'[5]

In 1922 while the Conference was in Sheffield, the College arranged a Garden Party at Cliff for the Conference delegates. This took place one afternoon during the Representative Session and according to W. Fiddian Moulton so many of the delegates were interested in the work of the College that between 1,000 and 1,600

463

attended.[6] Since the Conference numbers were about 600 there were either many friends attending, or an evangelist was counting! So many attended the garden party that according to W.H. Heap there was some question about whether a quorum remained in the Conference.[7]

Trek teams on mission

However at the Conference of 1930, Chadwick who had been ill for most of the previous two years had to defend Cliff and his position. He was clearly upset by the criticism, which focussed around the concern over his successor, the appointment of Dunning as Tutor, and therefore his second in command following Moulton's death. A different method of appointment for Cliff Tutors was used than existed for other theological colleges since Cliff was under the direction of Home Mission Committee, but the cutting criticism was that he, Chadwick, was an autocrat.[8] He wrote an editorial piece about the situation defending himself against the charge of being defensive, but he clearly was. Chadwick wrote to Crowlesmith, 'There is something sinister about the whole move – a group of men have set themselves out not to oppose Cliff but to capture it...They hate our theology and still more our aggressive soul-saving evangelism. I have a feeling they don't like us and the things for which we stand.'[9]

The tense feeling in the country in 1939 spurred the Methodist Church to new evangelistic efforts. According to one commentator, the Methodists not only urged their own church but also other free churches and the Anglicans to renewed efforts in evangelism. [10]

'The gospel was taken to thousands of unchurched in factories, clubs, business houses, schools, universities, hospitals, theatres, and prisons. Millions were confronted with making a decision for Christ, and great stress was placed on follow-up meetings and instruction classes. A new interest arose in the Christian message and in the church. The evangelistic zeal of ministers and of their lay workers was kindled afresh.' [11]

Towards the end of the War a 'Rural Commission' was established by the Conference of 1945; unfortunately the College which undertook so much work in rural England was not represented on that Commission. This was very different from the experience of Champness who had been invited by the Conference in 1896 to speak about the rural work of the *Joyful News* Mission. The Cliff Committee commented on its findings after they were published, and 'ventured to suggest that the Commission was imperfectly acquainted with the actual work the College is already doing in this direction, and would recommend to its notice a recently published leaflet on the history and present work of the College. Every possible aid to Village Methodism will still be loyally and enthusiastically rendered in the discharge of our specific responsibility for the training of Evangelists. The Principal outlined further possibilities in the direction of Village Missions by Cliff Evangelists.' [12]

From the beginning of the *Joyful News* movement until the end of World War II the purpose and policy direction of the College was set by the Principal and restated regularly in the Annual Reports to supporters, the Home Mission Report to the Methodist Conference and in the *Joyful News*. The first major discussion about the policy of the College with a suggestion of a change of direction, came in 1945 with the 'Report of the Sub-Committee appointed by the Home Mission Committee to consider the proposals made in the Rural

Methodism Commission Report concerning Cliff College, and certain criticisms of the teaching given at Cliff College by one or two members of the Home Mission Committee at its meeting on February 8th 1945'.[13] A letter from Broadbelt in February 1945 to Sir Robert Kay, who had been Chadwick's friend and solicitor to the College for many years, has a weary tone. 'You will remember that when I called to see you some time ago I said there was a section of Conference that seemed to think they could do better work with Cliff College than the training of evangelists. They are on the warpath again and a Committee is to meet in London on Thursday this week at which they propose to discuss the matter. I shall be going up to London ... Have you anything ... that you think will fortify me when I attend the Committee?'[14] The response is requested to be sent to the Waverley Hotel, off the Strand.

The Revs Baines Atkinson, Howard Belben, Principal Eagles and the Rev John Broadbelt

The sub-committee Broadbelt attended included key decision-makers of Methodism and was chaired by the Rev J. Oliver Hornabrook, Secretary of the Conference and Rev Colin A. Roberts, General Secretary of the Home Mission Department. At the next Home Mission Committee on 23 March, Hornabrook read the special report of the sub-committee and moved its adoption which was carried without discussion. W.H. Heap gave considerable space to the report in the *Joyful News*[15] emphasising that 'their findings are emphatic', and the article carried the headlines 'Cliff College - a complete answer to its critics'. The report was very supportive of the College, but the issues of the special nature of the College, its differences from other theological colleges and its place as a full part of Methodism were emphasised.

The place within Methodism was rehearsed by reference to the 'origin and the purpose of the foundation of Cliff College as set forth in the Deed[16] and as defined by the Conference of 1903 when it came under the direction of the General Home Mission Committee.' This set the issue of governance clearly for the Home Mission Department, though the decision-making process was always delegated to the College Committee which had the standing of a sub-committee of the Home Mission Department. The work of the three Principals is noted, though the fact that all three, and particularly Chadwick, had been critical of Methodism was not mentioned. Nevertheless the report stated, 'Cliff College is an integral part of Methodism and therefore is eager at all times and in all practical ways to work in close co-operation with all other departments of our Church work.'[17] The charge that Cliff was teaching things contrary to 'Our Doctrines' or too narrowly, was confronted. 'The theological teaching embodies the essential truths of Christianity. It is certainly not "obscurantist" or "fundamentalist", and the criticisms given by one or two members of the Home Mission Committee are quite unfounded.'[18] Moreover the Church had benefited from the training because 'scores of men have gone back to their Circuits as local preachers fired with a new and informed enthusiasm, and many have later received the call of God to the Ministry.' Indeed many students became Lay Pastors under the direction of the Home Mission Committee.

There was also the charge which was levelled at the College in further reports that the emphasis on scriptural holiness was more about the second blessing than the Wesleyan doctrine. Nevertheless the sub-committee affirmed the College to be within the Methodist teaching on the doctrine of holiness: 'The Committee is convinced that by its emphasis on evangelism, both in its teaching and in action, and on the mission of Methodism to spread Scriptural Holiness throughout the land, Cliff College is making a very valuable contribution to the life of Methodism.'[19]

Some suggestions involving Cliff being used primarily to train class leaders and the placing of students in circuits during term time for practical training were rejected as 'impractical'. The academic veracity of the College was underlined by reference to the exchange of tutors between Cliff and the theological colleges and the breadth of the curriculum, described as: 'Methodist Theology; Bible Study (with special reference to background as well as to content); Church History (including Methodist History); Homiletics; English Language and Literature; Evangelism and Social Righteousness at Home and Abroad.'[20]

The College and the *Joyful News* welcomed the report and 'as its conclusions will prove of special interest to our readers I give the report in full ... I venture to hope this report will show the critics of Cliff and its work, the value to Methodism the College really is. It should greatly encourage all the workers and friends of its special work.'[21] There is no doubt that the College needed to keep stating its purpose and importance to the Methodist Church, which in almost every decade has questioned its continuance.

In October 1953 the College itself decided to consider all the options and to set up a Committee of Exploration into the Future of the College. It was charged with considering 'all matters concerned with the present use, and future possibilities, of the College.'[22] Things were at a low ebb in terms of student numbers and vision for the

468

future. However by the following Committee in February 1954 the picture had changed considerably. There were increased numbers of students, and proposed 'Schools of Evangelism', and therefore the matter was allowed to 'lie on the table'. This suggests the Committee was mainly worried about the numbers of students, and they had been persuaded to revisit the purpose of the College. The anticipated visit of Billy Graham put new heart into the College, and new impetus to the work and funding.

The College Committee in October 1964 heard that the Home Mission Committee had appointed a Special Committee to 'consider the place of Cliff College in Methodism today and all things pertaining to its well-being.'[23] The Chairman of the Leeds District,

Tom Meadley encourages a student

the Rev E. J. Prentice, had been appointed the Convenor and the Special Committee had already met residentially on the 24 and 25 September. The issue seems to have been in connection with the theological emphasis of the College and therefore whether, in finding a successor to Tom Meadley, an examination of the candidate's theology should be sought. The minute which is headed 'Appointment of Principal 1965', reads like a summary of late night talks at ACAS: 'A full and frank discussion followed, though no resolution was passed.'[24] The main issue was the theological base of the College. 'It transpired that some of the members of the Committee understood that the College was traditionally committed to what is now known as the Conservative Evangelical position, and also to the Second Blessing interpretation of Scriptural Holiness.'[25] I take it that this was the view held by the protagonists in this discussion and one which pervaded the College as I came as a student in 1967. What happened in the discussion which followed was extremely important for the years ahead:

> The Principal (Tom Meadley) pointed out that the only documentary authority available as a basis of discussion was the Inter-Varsity Fellowship Manifesto, which was a human document without unequivocal divine authority, and subject to scrutiny in the light of Scripture and reason like any other Christian Confession. The policy of the College, while basically evangelical, was not aligned to any special party in the Church, but to enable those of differing points of view within the Christian Fellowship to learn from each other on a basis of open investigation of the Scriptures. The same principle applied to teaching on holiness.

> Rev Dr Colin Roberts spoke as the elder statesman with the longest and most intimate knowledge of the College as student, for many years the General Secretary of the Home Mission Department, and Chairman of the Cliff College Committee. He made it quite clear that the College had never been officially tied to a particular party in the Church. The gifts of the past were from men who loved the straightforward Methodist Gospel and longed to see effective evangelism, and were not contingent upon maintaining the Conservative Evangelical Creed only, even though the main emphasis was for the most part in accord with such teaching.

> It was clear that the point must be established one way or the other. There was no doubt about the basis on which the present Principal was appointed. Mr Douglas Brown, Vice-President of the Methodist Conference expressed the view that no doctrinal test should be expected other than that applied to all Methodist ministers that they adhere to the historic creeds, the principles of the Reformation, the Forty-four Sermons of John Wesley, embracing the doctrine of Universal Redemption, Assurance, and Scriptural Holiness. This view met with a strong murmur of approval.[26]

This discussion set the scene not only for the appointment of Tom Meadley's successor but also the tone which remains today. Chadwick would never have submitted to a doctrinal test, even though he agreed with Cook that at Cliff College definite doctrines are held and taught. Chadwick declared that he 'stood for the teaching of positive truth, definite experience, and passionate salvation.'[27] Neither of them, however, referred to the doctrinal basis of the Evangelical Alliance in the way that Mrs Hulme had insisted in drawing up her Deed in 1872. Chadwick knew of the Alliance and preached at its Jubilee celebrations. Similarly Chadwick would not align himself with the Wesley Bible Union, which professed to be the true Wesleyans and was scandalised by talks of Methodist Union.[28] It was critical of Chadwick because he would not join the Union, or give it outright support through the *Joyful News*, and 'thus few of us have

The Rev Howard Belben

any hope from it at the present time'.[29] Chadwick maintained that he was a man of the Bible but not in any obscurantist manner. His final message began, 'Stand together on the Word of God, but not in any stupid sense...'[30] His spirituality was also broader than that usually found in evangelical preachers of his day, with his interest in the Christian Festivals.

The appointment of the Rev Howard Belben, was a stroke of genius by the appointing committee: He upheld the traditions of devoted loyalty to the Scriptures, had an admiration and understanding of scholarship, a warm spirituality and an enthusiasm for mission, and understood Cliff and its supporters. He was welcomed on all sides of the debate; to the 'Old Cliff Men' he was the respected person to uphold the traditions of the College, and to the Connexion the person to bring in change.

The 'Special Committee' recommended changes to the internal structure of the Cliff Committee.[31] It also cleared the air regarding the decision-making process. The Conference and the Home Mission Committee were the ruling body, although powers had been delegated to the Cliff College Committee, but it was clearly a sub-committee of the Home Mission Committee. The paper laid to rest the issue of the appointment of staff with which all this issue had begun: 'The Cliff Committee has never appointed the Principal of the Staff, nor has it any authority to do so. The nominations are made by the Home Mission Committee, but always after consulting the Cliff Committee. Appointment is made by the Conference.'[32] The situation today is similar, and the College is protected in this by Standing Order 341, which states that the appointment of the Principal and Tutors, ordained or lay, shall be Conference appointments.[33] In fact the contemporary practice is also to forward the reasoned statement regarding the appointment of the Bursar to the Methodist Council as it is a senior appointment.

In July 1969 the College General Committee appointed an 'Ad Hoc Committee' to look at its life and finances. The committee found that expenditure was agreed by seven people in the organisation without reference to each other. They recommended that from 1970 the appointment of an 'Administrative Officer' be made, 'who shall act under the Principal of the College and the local Treasurers.'[34] The Administrative Officer would be responsible for:

1. maintaining the organised life of the College with responsibilities similar to those of a school Bursar,

2. administering the Conference Centre,

3. all the day to day management.[35]

The same Committee indicated that the Conference of 1969 would be asked to agree to a restructuring of the Connexional Departments into 'Divisions'. The proposal at that time was for the College to move from Home Mission to the 'Division of Ministries'. The sub-committee expressed its dismay at this recommendation, and questioned that possibility, 'without the Charity Commissioners agreeing to alterations to the Deed under which the property at Cliff is held. But apart from this the Committee sees Cliff as a weapon of lay evangelism. They are convinced that the policy of Cliff must primarily be with mission.'[36] The Committee in October 1969 argued that the College should remain with the Home Mission Division because of its commitment to evangelism. The distinctiveness of Cliff would be compromised if moved to the Division of Ministries, along with general lay training, and the 1903 and the 1930 Deeds linked Cliff to the Home Mission Department and its successors.[37] The submissions made to the working party for Department Structure and Function were acted upon, the College remained with Home Mission and the matter faded from the minutes.

What is not made clear in this exchange is that Cliff staff and supporters were concerned that the College would be swallowed up by the Division of Ministries, with its emphasis on a more liberal theology, certainly in the appointments made in the colleges. At a time when the Methodist Church was closing Didsbury College Manchester, Headingley College Leeds, and eventually Richmond College Surrey, the gaining of Cliff as a centre or an asset was also considered to be part of the underlying and real purpose of the proposal. Cliff had felt 'at home' in the Home Mission Department, though the Department had not always taken proper responsibility for investing in its wholly owned asset. The College minutes always speak of 'gratitude' for the Home Mission grant but in reality from

1904 – 1948 the Principals had found willing people to give financial support to the College. Meadley refers to them indicating that 'the day of the merchant-princes who make large scale benefactions has long past'.[38] It was a great shame that towards the end of Bill Davies's time the Home Mission Fund did not write-off the debt owed on the Eagles and Broadbelt Buildings and that funds raised by Cliff for Home Mission were not passed back when funds were 'stream-lined' after restructuring in 1996.

Mr Jack Henderson

One benefit to the College from the intervention of the Home Mission Division was the appointment of an Administrative Officer. This was key as 'the ultimate responsibility for finance will be his no matter who happens to be doing the actual work.'[39] The benefits were that there would be proper control and management of the College's finances, which would benefit the College enormously. The danger in such an appointment was that finance, not visionary leadership would by default set the priorities for the college. Mr Jack Henderson was appointed in 1970 as the first person to hold this post, a businessman from Halifax who was told by the Rev George Sails, then General Secretary of the Home Mission Division, to 'keep the purse strings tightly closed'. Given the financial difficulties being experienced at that time it was not bad policy. Jack was followed in this role by Maurice Houghton in 1982, and Maurice gave detailed attention to the work for twenty years before

Mr Maurice Houghton

stepping down in 2002. It was during Maurice's time that many changes took place in the College including the major development of the Eagles and Broadbelt buildings.

A Home Mission Commission considered the place of Cliff College within Methodism and reported to the College committee in March 1973. It did not make substantial suggestions, except that all student applicants should be interviewed as part of the process (previously most of the interview process was by letter and written references), though it did set a criterion that non-Methodists should be restricted to 25% of student places.[40] That is the kind of recommendation administrators love, but is impossible to apply.

The matter of the doctrinal position of the College was considered again in the March 1980. This had been prompted by a resolution from the Ministerial Synod of the Cornwall District 'expressing concern that for a period of 16 years Ministers appointed to the tutorial staff at Cliff had all been of a Conservative Evangelical background.'[41] This would seem to suggest that Meadley was the kind of person they liked and all others were less good. Arthur Skevington Wood had prepared a 'considered statement on the doctrinal position of Cliff College.'[42] It reiterated the statement of 1964, and the committee agreed with his assertion that 'no doctrinal test should be expected other than that to which all Methodist Ministers were subject, namely that they adhere to the historic creeds, the principles of the reformation, and the Forty-four sermons of John Wesley, embracing the doctrines of universal redemption, assurance and scriptural holiness.'[43] The Rev Dr A. Skevington Wood was on home ground in stating the Wesleyan doctrinal position and only the unwise would argue.

*The Rev Dr
Donald English*

The issue raised itself again in the autumn of 1981 when letters were received by the *Methodist Recorder* suggesting that following Arthur Wood a Principal who was not evangelical should be appointed. The matter was safely in the hands of the Home Mission Committee and the College had confidence in the General Secretary, Dr Donald English, to ensure a good appointment. I imagine this is why the matter was not mentioned in the College Committee, or at least recorded in the *Minutes*. In the end the Rev Dr Bill Davies was the person chosen, and because he was so well qualified and had wide experience of education, the issue disappeared. Moreover Bill brought the College much more 'stage centre' to the Church by his straight-forward manner, teaching, and honouring of other traditions. His significant contribution to Cliff and the whole Church was recognised by the Conference which made him President in 1988. Nevertheless not every part of the Church valued the work of Cliff.

The mistrust between the Division of Ministries and the College was brought to a head in the late 1980s. Students who had undertaken the Cliff Certificate and the second year Diploma course, which included a 10,000-word dissertation, and were candidates for the ministry were given no academic credit for this study. The Division of Ministries was contacted, but repeatedly refused to consider the two years' of study in lieu of any part of the requirement and insisted ministerial candidates had to have four GCSE qualifications. There were examples of students with two or three GCSE passes including English, and a good pass in the Cliff Diploma, but still having to take further GCSE exams at night school prior to candidating. The situation was ridiculous; it showed the narrowness of thinking in the Division at that time, and was typical of some parts of the Church which refused to believe Cliff was anything other than a basic training College. One of the curious features of liberal theology is that while it espouses a view which welcomes diversity of ideas, most liberal theologians have a closed mind to evangelical theology, and this was part of the agenda and the mistrust between the College and the Division of Ministries.

In more recent years and after detailed discussions in 1996 and 1997 the College was acknowledged as an essential part of the Methodist Church, a kind of wholly owned subsidiary, where the Methodist Council devolves its powers to the College Committee. The issue about theological narrowness was crushed when the University of Sheffield accepted Cliff and validated the programmes as being of a standard worthy of Higher Education. The academic worth and credibility of the College and its courses was then similarly understood and accepted, ecumenically and internationally. There is, however, still a view that within Methodism Cliff is not fairly considered, in the way that other Colleges are. For instance there was until just recently a list of 'Our Colleges' but it did not include Cliff College. The impression given is that the College is a kind of Cinderella in Methodism, though it receives considerable recognition from other denominations. Over the last ten years the College has grown and developed so that now it has eight full-time teaching staff, and over two hundred students registered on courses. At some point the Church will need to recognise the significant contribution Cliff is making in the development of mission practice, missiological thinking, and training.

In the prophetic tradition of Champness and Chadwick Cliff published a booklet, *A Gospel Call for Dynamic Change*, in the spring of 2003. In the booklet I gave an assessment of the present state of Methodism and the need to make difficult choices and considerable change to training, Circuit and District structure, terms and conditions for ministers, as well as to the purpose and focus of our work. I believed then that we had, under God, three to five years to make the necessary changes, or events would overtake the Church. My judgement is that the analysis in the booklet, and the suggested ways forward for the Church, remain crucially important for Methodism. All my opponents wrote to the *Methodist Recorder* though many wrote, called and e-mailed to me personally in support, in whole or in part, of the views expressed in the booklet. Dr Malcolm White who was a visiting speaker at the *Festival 2003*, noted sagely to me, 'For a man looking for an appointment next year it is the longest suicide note I have ever read'! Time will tell.

The key contribution made in the last ten years to this debate about the relationship between Cliff and the Methodist Church has been to state and restate the 'charisms' of the College. By charisms are meant those themes which make the College distinctive and form the heart of its life and ministry. These charisms were described at the Centenary Lecture and are referred to in the introduction of this book. They arise from a reading of the archive information about Champness, Cook and Chadwick, and reflection on the present ministry of the College. The charisms are not only a restatement of those themes which arise from past ministry but are guidelines which inform the College's present life and give direction for the future.

1   Champness is reported here by J.I. Brice, *Joyful News*, 28 May 1931.
2   *Joyful News,* 19 July 1888.
3   *Joyful News,* 19 July 1888.
4   *Joyful News,* 23 August 1922.
5   *Joyful News,* 1 September 1932.
6   *Joyful News,* 23 August 1922.
7   *Joyful News,* 23 August 1922.
8   *Joyful News,* 7 August 1930.
9   Letter to John Crowlesmith, 2 September 1930, reported in the *Joyful News,* 12 April 1945.
10 Paulus Scharff, p.305.
11 Paulus Scharff, pp.305-6.
12 *Minutes* of the Cliff College Committee, 15 November 1944.
13 *Minutes,* Home Mission Committee, 23 March 1945.
14 Letter, Broadbelt to Sir Robert Kay, 5 February 1945 in the College Archives.
15 *Joyful News,* 5 April 1945.
16 Deed, 31 December 1903.
17 Archive – Report from the Home Mission sub-committee, 8 February 1945, which reported on 23 March 1945 to the full committee.
18 Ibid.
19 Ibid.
20 Ibid.
21 'Metholay' in the *Joyful News,* 5 April 1945.
22 *Minutes* of the Cliff College Committee, 2 October 1953.
23 *Minutes* of the Cliff College Committee, 8 October 1964.
24 Ibid.
25 Ibid.
26 *Minutes* of the Cliff College Committee, 8 October 1964. Colin Roberts had been a student at the College for two terms, January to July 1905, and therefore his comments as Home Mission Secretary and past student had particular weight in this discussion.
27 *Joyful News,* 11 March 1909.
28 See the *Fundamentalist*, the Journal of the Wesley Bible Union. Vols 1-17 are in our Library. No publishing details.
29 *Journal of the Wesley Bible Union,* 1919, p.275.
30 *Joyful News,* 20 October 1932.
31 *Minutes* of the Cliff College Committee, 10 March 1966.
32 Undated paper, 'The Relation of the Home Mission Committee to the Cliff College Committee', paragraph 5.
33 *Constitution, Practice and Discipline of the Methodist Church* (Methodist Publishing House: London), S.O.341.
34 Report of the 'Ad Hoc sub-committee to the College General Committee' 6 March 1969.
35 Ibid.

cont.

36 Report of the 'Ad Hoc sub-committee to the College General Committee', 6 March 1969.

37 *Minutes,* Cliff College General Committee, 9 October 1969.

38 Tom Meadley, *'The Challenge of Cliff College Today',* Archives.

39 Report of the 'Ad Hoc sub-committee to the College General Committee' 6 March 1969

40 *Minutes,* Cliff College General Committee, 1 March 1973.

41 *Minutes,* Cliff College General Committee, 17 October 1980.

42 Ibid.

43 *Minutes,* Cliff College General Committee, 17 October 1980.

CHAPTER 18

Maybe One Day

Delving into the archives of the College is a wonderful privilege; it opens up worlds which which in effect go back over two hundred years. In this book I have attempted to set out the full details so that many more people can benefit from the joy of the story, and also learn from wise spiritual leaders who have contributed to the College's life. This chapter reveals that they also had feet of clay. Not everything happened easily, and some things still remain on the drawing board as visions. All these incidents show the depth, length and breadth the spiritual hope and enterprise of leaders of the College. Cook is a great example because he achieved so much in so short a time.

Chapter nine explained how Cook had an even greater vision than he achieved, though what he accomplished was in itself remarkable. His vision for an auditorium was eventually carried through by Broadbelt in 1939, but the development of housing for 'Ten Secular Tutors' was not even raised by Cook at the College committee. That may have been because there was a technical dispute with the architects Smith and Ensor about measurements following the building of Cliff Park. The house was actually built for Chadwick and it is clear from all the Committee minutes that Cook had an increasing vision for further building work at the College. Cliff Park was completed in the summer of 1907, and though the drawing of the houses for 'secular tutors' is not dated it would be reasonable to assume that the initial design was completed around that time. Cook was very happy with the way Cliff Park had been designed and built, but the dispute with the architects meant he could not proceed further.

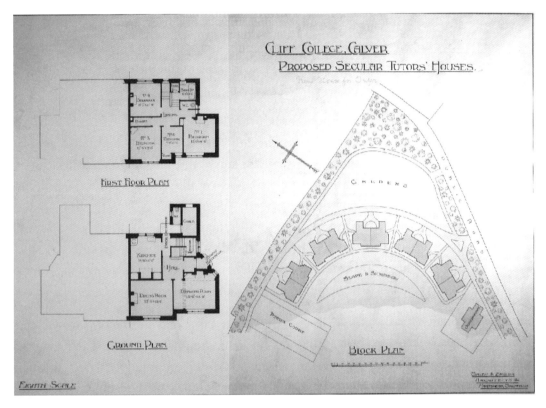

The Bridge Inn features in the history of the College. John Broadbelt described the situation as he saw it to Joseph Rank: 'You know there is a public house nearly opposite our main entrance. It is always a source of trouble to us. It attracts the rif-raf of the district and was always a trouble to Mr Chadwick'.[1] Apparently Chadwick, when he was buying land in the area, considered purchasing the Bridge Inn along with eight acres of land, but he 'missed it.'[2]

Pleading with Rank, Broadbelt wrote, 'O, if we could only buy it. We could close the public house and turn the house into a guest house and the land would be valuable. Will you give me permission to buy it? It would give Mr Chadwick great joy in Heaven and be of great value to us. I have prayed for two years that God would give it to us.'[3]

Broadbelt attempted to purchase the Bridge privately rather than at a public auction and had instructed the College's solicitor, Sir Robert Newbald Kay, to approach the auctioneers. They were unsuccessful, although the correspondence through the autumn suggests there was another purchaser who paid £2,000.[4] Broadbelt concluded that 'the matter had better be left for the moment'.[5]

This same question arose in 1944 when the Bridge Inn was again for sale and on this occasion the asking price was £10,000 to £12,000. Broadbelt considered the price 'exorbitant'[6] and Kay responded coolly to the suggestion it should be purchased: 'I do not think the Inn can do the College much harm, and it certainly is not worth entertaining at anything like the figure named.'[7] The Bridge Inn remains to this day.

Another attempted project came in Meadley's time. Though there is no mention in the College minutes, he made a planning application on the 1 January 1965 for permission to 'erect a Petrol Filling Station.'[8] The location for this proposed Filling Station was to be on the 'Main Road, Chapel to Baslow close to the entrance to Cliff College'. Apparently the proposed site was between Curbar Primary School and the College entrance.[9] Needless to say the Filling Station was not built but presumably Tom Meadley was attempting the laudable aim of seeking to establish a profitable enterprise to support the charitable work of the College.

NOTICE NO. 1

(To be given to owners and agricultural tenants as appropriate)

TOWN AND COUNTRY PLANNING ACT, 1962

Notice under Section 27 of application for planning permission

(a) insert address
or location
of proposed
development

Proposed development at (a) *Main Road., Chapel to Baslow close to entrance to Cliff College*

(b) Insert name
of Council

TAKE NOTICE that application is being made to the (b) *Bakewell Rural District*

(c) Insert name
of applicant

Council by (c) *Cliff College Training Home and Mission, Cliff College*

(d) Insert
description
and address
or location
of proposed
development

for planning permission to (d) *erect a Retail Filling Station*

If you should wish to make representations about the application, you should do so in writing within 21 days of the date of service of this notice to the * ~~Town Clerk~~

Clerk of the Council

(e) Insert address
of Council
(In the case of
the Yorkshire
Dales National
Park this will
be the County
Council)

at (e) *Bakewell*

Signed *JD Meadley*

*On behalf of *Cliff College Training Home and Mission*

Date *January 15th 1965*

Under Bill Davies we had the 'Serviette Vision' containing many items, most of which were undertaken when Eagles and Broadbelt buildings were opened in July 1990. One item which was firmly placed on the 'back burner' was the swimming pool. To be faithful to that vision I have always attempted to include the swimming pool as part of the developments which have been suggested, but without success. Maybe there will one day be a Mellor Memorial Swimming Pool!

484

Architect's drawing with the plans for Broadbelt and Eagles

In the last five years we have attempted what we now refer to as the 'Grand Scheme'. A £6.5million scheme which would have delivered a new dining room and worship hall, renovated and expanded the Stanton Centre, taken a tunnel under Cliff Lane for disabled access, and with lifts brought level access across the site. The cost, of course, was a great deal of money but in the year 2000 it seemed possible. The Methodist Church, at that time, raised and spent over £110 million per annum, most being raised and spent locally, so it did not seem unreasonable to believe that the Church would support the Connexional Appeal for the College with £3-4 million across six funding years. Cliff had really come centre stage over the previous twenty years and we believed Methodism would support and that Trusts and individual donations would follow. The stock market plunged after September 2001, however and the only

Trust to be supportive was the Laing Trust. The students, in a Christmas 2002 revue, prepared a visual presentation which referred to 'Mellor Towers' and superimposed the Empire State Building onto the College Orchard!

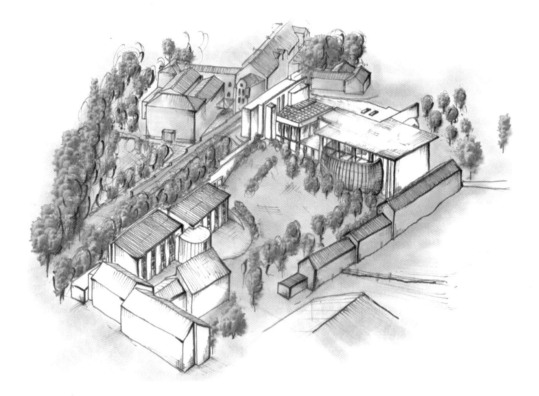

Financial and prayer support poured in from individuals and churches, some circuits donating from their advance funds, but not enough 'big hitters' donated funds to support a £6m project. The summer of 2002 was the time of reckoning. At this time John Steer became the Bursar, Andy Barnett had become the Estates Officer and we went back to the drawing board. What was our original purpose and vision which gave rise to this 'grand scheme'? We invited the

Rev Martin Turner, the Superintendent of the Westminster Central Hall and Mr Michael Sharp, who directs their Conference business, to come and looked at the options with us. That visit opened for us a new way of thinking about the buildings we had and the options for developing the site, and placed it within our financial reach.

The first phase is now completed, with the remarkable changes to be seen in Cliff Hall. The Stanton Centre renovation, the College library and research centre will be developed and a pathway for disabled access made between the College and the Conference Centres. Altogether almost £1m has been raised and because we have careful management of the project by Andy Barnett and John Steer we shall achieve around 80% of the original vision for only a fraction of the original price. There will be a new library, computer room, additional teaching spaces, a new 'hub' for the teaching and administrative staff based in what was the Principal's House, and a new entrance and reception area. There will also be enhanced Conference Centre facilities, with a new dining room and kitchen along with three new conference rooms, the Chatsworth Suite, Haddon Room, and the Derwent Room.

One particular area of academic interest relates to the College archives. The archives have been amassed over the years but they have been deliberately gathered and catalogued in the last twenty years. They contain all the main documentation which records the history of the Joyful News Mission, the *Joyful News*, the history of Cliff House and the College since 1904. The history of Cliff College is contained in minutes, accounts, correspondence, papers, books, magazines, photographs, film, video and slides. Altogether this makes it a considerable archive ranging over the whole history of the College and its antecedents from 1790 to today. One of the visions for the future of the College is to make this archive, already catalogued, available to research students.

The archives also contain material which is part of the history of wider Methodism. There are the letters and papers of one of John Wesley's contemporaries, Jonathan Fletcher, including in his own hand a *Proposal for a Union among Gospel Ministers* dated 19 April 1764, along with various letters, journals and sermons all belonging to or written by Fletcher. There is also a Dictionary belonging to his wife and signed Mary Bosanquet, Mrs Fletcher's maiden name. Among this collection is a very good specimen of an early Class Paper, of which Mary Fletcher was the leader and which sets out the names with remarks about their health and attendance.[10] The archives also contain John Wesley's Prayer Book signed by him, and dated 1770. It was presented to the College by the Rev J.A. Marchant[11] and originally given by Wesley to one of his preachers, Frederick Norman, in 1788. There is also a copy of the Geneva or Breeches Bible, where in the story of Adam and Eve, Genesis 3:7 is translated, 'Then the eyes of them were opened, and they knew that they were naked, and they sewed fig tree leaves together, and made themselves breeches.'[12]

This chapter could be described as the catalogue of failures, but that would be to miss the point. Those who have had both courage and vision for the College and its work have contributed substantially to its future. Charles Handy in his book *The New Alchemists*[13] calls for people who are pioneers, have initiative and will take risks. 'They sow seeds of the future; innovation and creativity, enterprise and entrepreneurship are the vogue words for the new millennium.'[14] What Handy had identified can be observed at Cliff over the last one hundred and twenty years, in the life and work of most of the Principals.

There is however another factor which is about prophetic vision. The ability under God, through prayer and reflection, to see over the horizon with sufficient clarity and to be able to relate that vision to others so that they can understand and contribute further to the development of that vision. Such people are 'seers in Israel' and we need them now in the British Church. This spiritual gift can be seen at work at work with most of the Cliff Principals. It is a gift to covet by all leaders, but to be used with wisdom and grace. Finally this chapter has nothing to do with failure, but about unfulfilled dreams and visions. With the support of committed colleagues, the Committee, and many supporters of the College, each Principal has carried out what they believed to be the work of God.

As for the unfulfilled dreams – "Maybe one day...."

1   *Letter*, to Joseph Rank, 20 May 1937.
2   *Letter*, to Joseph Rank, 20 May 1937.
3   *Letter*, to Joseph Rank, 20 May 1937.
4   *Letter*, to Robert Newbald Kay, 27 January 1944.
5   *Letter*, to Robert Newbald Kay, 4 January 1938.
6   *Letter*, to Robert Newbald Kay, 27 January 1944.
7   *Letter*, from Robert Newbald Kay, 28 January 1944.
8   Planning application Notice, 1 January 1965. The Notice was given to Mr Horace Dalton as an agricultural Tenant. His daughter Rosemary Thorpe passed it around 1995 to Maurice Houghton and to me for the archives.
9   According to Rosemary and Winston Thorpe.
10 The Class Papers are undated, but as Mary Fletcher is described as a widow it must date between 1785, the death of Jonathan Fletcher, and her own death in 1815.
11 *Joyful News,* 19 June 1958.
12 The Bible was presented to the College by Peter C. Todd at the opening of the New Conference Centre on 24 May 1969 and in memory of the ministry of the Rev Joe Blinco.
13 Charles Handy, *The New Alchemists*, (London: Hutchinson, 1999).
14 Handy, p.11.

Student Life at Cliff College

This chapter is by and about students. There are two main sources, one written and one photographic and in each case the information comes from the students themselves. The written recollections of past students are contained in letters, books and booklets, journals and *Minutes* of student meetings. Glimpses into the life of the College are also contained in seven magazines written and published by students from 1912 to 1992. There is also a massive photographic archive

which covers about 130 years, from James Hulme to Martyn Atkins, including whole albums, the earliest of which is a record of Thomas Cook's work at the College. The archives have been gathered and categorised over this last thirty years with the majority of the work done by two good friends of the College, Russell Houghton and Clive Taylor. Ex-students and friends have donated most of the items and these have added substantially to our picture of the College's life.

In the College archives there are two hand-written volumes of the *Cliff Collegian* published in monthly editions from October 1912 to February 1913. It is 'A Magazine by our students, for our students – Our magazine'.[1] Three duplicated magazines were produced, *Cosmorama*, published in February 1955; *Barkis '66* was of course in 1966 and *You've Got Room to Talk* in 1972. During 1968 in an attempt to raise money for the new Conference Centre, students published a printed magazine entitled *Cliff 1968* and priced at one shilling. The most recent magazine was a photocopied version produced in 1992 called *Cliff Toady*, a play on *Cliff Today*.

All the magazines contain a streak of sarcasm about the College and its life, as many of the quotes suggest. You would expect that to

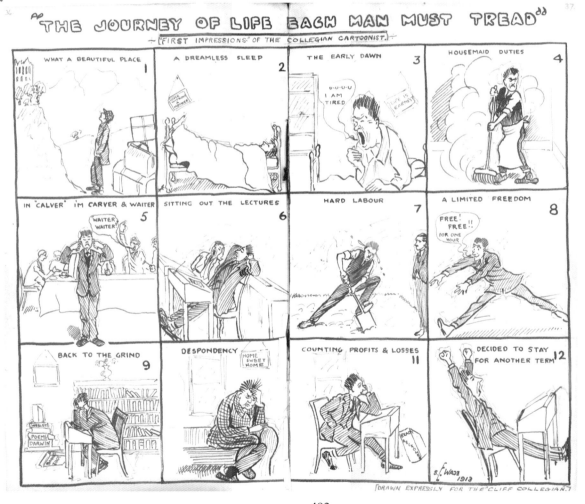

be the case in 1992 but there is an interesting and amusing cartoon in the January 1913 edition, giving the impressions of a new student, Stuart E. Wade who had previously been a litho-artist. The *Cliff Toady* has the sharpest comments with mocking humour on beloved people and practices, for instance: 'Mellor, G. Howard, Sort of Bibliography on legs. Seldom seen, but has been known to give occasional lectures in evangelism. Howard is gifted in his ability to write in tongues!'

The Principal wrote the Foreword for many of the magazines, though not in the *Cliff Collegian* or *Cliff Toady*. In *Barkis '66* Howard Belben boldly proclaimed this magazine to be the first such venture as he understood it, saying that if it were not so then 'some old Cliff man would put him right'. They obviously did for the next magazine *Cliff '68* is declared as the fourth one produced. Actually by my calculation it was the sixth if the two volumes of *Collegian* are counted separately.

The prevailing student view, which is repeated across the years, is one of a sense of privilege to be studying in such a place of peace and beauty. George Boak who was a student in 1924 recalls, 'When we step into the grounds of Cliff, it is like no other place. The College itself is built on rock, sustained by the prayers of thousands of people who have found faith and blessing there.'[2] Often students have written to the Principal after they have left the College and begin to realise the extent to which they have changed and the depth of what they learned. Typical of this is from Rosemary Besley (1968): 'I shall always thank the Lord for leading me to Cliff, and have happy and precious memories of my time there. It has been a year of wonderful Christian Fellowship, and one in which my Christian faith has been deepened and strengthened'.[3] Of course the College gives to students a love of evangelism; that is certainly my testimony and it is shared

Davies, William: Known affectionately as Doc, this is a sort of ministerial octopus. Aggressive hand-gestures may be used by Doc when backed into a corner.
Cliff Toady

'The Samuels' The Cliff College answer to the Oscars
Cliff Toady

by Adam H. Coe (1930): 'I am conscious always of my great debt to Cliff. All that I know of evangelism I owe to the College and the Fellowship'.[4]   Another is Paul Smith (1969): 'May I take this opportunity of expressing my increasing gratitude for all that God did for me through Cliff College. At the time I never realised just how valuable my time at Cliff really was; it is only now that I am beginning to appreciate all that Cliff did for me. At Cliff I first felt the longing to offer not a system of ethics or a basis of faith, but Christ.'[5]

From the beginning the student life was spartan and demanding. Champness commented in 1894 about the *Joyful News* training and work, 'When men wrote in response to the advertisements we put into *Joyful News*, I sent them a letter which shut some of them up at once. I told them they would get no wages but simply board and lodging. I would give them £1, and when they had spent it, they would have to give me an account of every halfpenny. They must do all I wanted them to do – clean their own shoes, dig the garden, and so forth. If I did not like them when they came, they would have to go back again. My means were very precarious, and when I had no money they would have to go home.'[6] He then added, 'When the men came to our house they wondered whether the letter I had sent had come from the same house, for my wife smiled on them and made them feel so much at home. I have twenty-three such men. They have done good service.'[7]

One of the profound experiences of Cliff is the sense of fellowship: 'We used that word "brother" because it was a Spiritual Brother-hood.'[8] It was in this context that students engaged with the daily routine. John Newbould (1906) recalls, 'The mornings were a bit of a bother to me at Cliff College for quite a while, as I had to stay in bed until the Call bell rang at half past six. For ten years, I had been

The Cliff Epicure.

[EDITORIAL: For the benefit of those who find delight in table delicacies, and as a standing witness to the liberality of Cliff fare – not to speak of its variety we append a carefully compiled list of the week's repasts!]

	BREAKFASTS.	DINNERS.		TEAS.	SUPPERS
	Porridge. Bread. Butter. Tea. Coffee &	VEGETABLES and		Bread & Butter Tea, and	Bread & Butter + Cheese
Sun.	Ham + Potted Meat	1. Roast Mutton	2. Milk Pudding	Cake	
Mon.	Ham & Potted Meat	1. Roast Beef	2. Jam roll	Buns	..
Tue.	Sausages	1. 'Irish' Stew	2. Currant Pudding	Jam	..
Wed.	Rissoles	1. Roast Mutton	2. Rice Pudding	Buns	..
Thur.	Polony	1. Roast Pork	2. Apple Pudding	Jam	..
Fri.	Ham or Fish	1. Fish or Roast Beef	2. Suet Pudding	Buns	..
Sat.	Ham	1. Cold Beef & Pickles	2. Jam Tart	Marmalade	and Corned Beef (Sundays)
	"The Glutton	Shall come to Poverty"…		Proverbs XXIII 21	

compelled to turn out every morning at five o'clock and be at work at six.'[9]   That is a very different response from the one most students make to the 'cow bell' rung for many years at 6:45a.m.

'The usual routine at Cliff in those days was, get up when the call bell rang at half past six … You had to make your bed. It was real fun to see the first attempts of some of the men at bed making … Then you had to sweep up the bed room and make things tidy. Nothing was to be left lying about. After that you got washed and shaved and had to be ready to answer the roll call at half past seven. After that you had a chance to get a blow of fresh air, if the morning was fine.   At five minutes to eight the first gong for breakfast sounded, to tell you to get ready. When it went again at eight o'clock you went to the Dining Room for breakfast.'[10]

495

The first Student Badge

Chadwick rose early and always had a cold bath, which he commended to the students. John Newbould tried it for a week and decided that 'what was good for Peter was not always good for Paul.'[11] However he did go for a swim in the river when there was snow on the ground. 'We were soon out again and it was quite a while before we were warm and comfortable again. Anyway, it gave us the chance of bragging that we had been for a swim in the river when there was snow and ice on the ground'.[12]

WESLEYAN METHODIST CHURCH.

Cliff College Training Home and Mission

(FORMERLY JOYFUL NEWS HOME AND MISSION).

PRINCIPAL - REV. S. CHADWICK.

RAILWAY STATION:
From the North—" GRINDLEFORD," L.M. & S.

TELEGRAMS } 41 BASLOW.
TELEPHONE

CLIFF COLLEGE,

CALVER, via Sheffield.

......Sept. 13th, 1930

COLLEGE TERM, October 3rd, to December 17th, 1930

My dear Brother,

The College term begins **Friday, October 3rd.** and we shall be glad to welcome you on that day, as soon after 3 p.m., as possible. The best Station is Grindleford, on the L. M. & S. Railway, and the Baslow 'Bus from the Station passes the College gates.

1. The Text Books required are to be had at the College. All told, they will not cost more than 30/-. If you have a good Atlas and a good Dictionary, bring them with you.

2. All linen and underclothing must be marked with your full name so as to avoid mistakes when sent to the Laundry. Only linen buttons on garments.

3. Every man must bring—
   (1) A Bible (Revised Version) of good clear type, and a Methodist Hymn Book.
   (2) A brush and comb.
   (3) Pyjamas.
   (4) A dark coat or jacket for meals and preaching appointments.
   (5) An old suit you can wear at manual labour.
   (6) A pair of strong boots and leggings if you have them.
   (7) A bicycle if you have one.
   (8) Soft Collars for everyday wear.
   (9) All mending materials, including buttons, etc.
   (10) Two table-napkins and a napkin ring.

Letters sent to students prior to joining the College

496

4. Do not bring Trunks, a large Suit-case should be sufficient.
   Do not bring a Library of your own. All the books you need besides Text Books will be found in the College Library.

5. Smoking is strictly prohibited at all times and places.

6. Contributions promised towards the cost of maintenance and education must be paid at the commencement of each term. Bring the money with you.

7. Each man must retain his Membership in his own Circuit. Class Meetings are held at the College, but payments of Class and Ticket-money must be made to the Leader in whose Class Book your name appears.

8. A little money will be needed for collections and incidental expenses.

Each man is expected to come for a course of strenuous study, to co-operate cheerfully in promoting the efficiency and well-being of the College, and to avoid whatever may be unseemly or unworthy.

With all good wishes and deepest interest in your welfare.

Yours very truly,

S. Chadwick.

P.S.—Kindly get your doctor to sign the enclosed health certificate, and return to us at once.

The devotional life with College morning prayers and student prayer meetings has been a key to the spiritual life of the College. Most students comment about the spiritual benefit of being at the College: 'I know I will always owe Cliff a great debt in all ways. Spiritually I am thankful that I have grown closer to our Lord Jesus Christ and am still, I feel, growing closer.'[13] Morning prayers were student led. 'After breakfast … morning prayers … were taken by the men in a kind of rota. Each morning one of the men would read the scripture and another would take the prayer.'[14] The Class Meeting seems to have been a significant feature instigated during the days of Chadwick and certainly after the First World War. Normally a tutor or evangelist preached and many students indicated the spiritual benefit of these times where the elements of Worship, Word and

497

Testimony are shared. Now there is normally a full range of instruments crowded at the front of the chapel. Formally there was just the organ and that was pumped by students on a rota which could be very demanding: 'Mr Stringer ... was very musical and played the chapel organ. We took turns at pumping the organ for him by hand. I can remember having to pump at great speed when he pulled out all the stops for the last verse of Charles Wesley's hymn, "And can it be" to the tune "Sagina"'.[15]

One issue which I had assumed was a contemporary problem, born of music centres and ghetto blasters, is the issue of noise created in the College. When interviewing students I always indicated that it is not great issues of theology that we fall out about, but noise. What is most interesting is that in the Autumn of 1912 in *The Cliff Collegian*, there is an 'Open Letter by G. Kettle' who makes 'A Plea for more Quietness'.[16] When Broadbelt was Principal the student representatives were called 'Captains' and they met weekly to discuss life at the College, often with a tutor, and crucially kept minutes of their meetings. Noise was often an issue then: 'The question of noise all over the College was again forwarded, and particular mention made to the shuffling of books, desks, etc before a lecture begins. Too much noise was also being made at the dining tables.'[17] Other unseemly behaviour was the occasion for censure: 'Several of the brethren had again been seen chewing in the lectures, and it was agreed this being most ungentlemanly, must stop. Notes too, most of them ridiculous had been passed around during 'prep' periods disturbing the work of most of the brethren.'[18]

There is within the received wisdom of the College a notion that early morning physical exercise was required of all students. There are in fact two occasions when we have evidence of this. In January 1936 one of the tutors, Mr Stringer, 'put forward various suggestions for periods of physical training.'[19] The next day it was agreed to have physical training on Wednesdays and Saturdays and at a subsequent meeting a precise timetable agreed: 'the timetable should be, Rising bell 6a.m.; Roll Call in P.T. dress 6:25a.m.; Private devotions 6:35-7:10. Physical Training 7:11-35a.m.'[20] It is not possible to determine whether J.H. Stringer led the students in their exercise. There is little further mention of this early exercise until 1939:[21] 'Owing to the fact that many of the brethren had been suffering from colds during the past fortnight it was decided that it would be a great benefit to have a half hour's Physical Training before morning devotions. It was finally agreed that every man should take part in this, every Tuesday, Thursday and Saturday, rising at 6 o'clock, answering roll-call at 6:20, and reporting for P.T. immediately afterwards. It was also agreed that the brethren must be in bed a half hour earlier on Monday, Wednesday, and Friday evenings, respectively.' This would be a sure way to cure all colds!

George Boak gives a detailed picture of the programme for the day as it had developed in the mid-1920s and when Chadwick's vision for the College as the home of the Methodist Friars was at its height. 'I think the boot men were about the first to rise. Each student was allowed to put outside his bedroom door one pair of shoes or boots to be taken to be cleaned and brought back. I think we had this duty once a week. The bellman went around at about 7 o'clock: "Rising Bell"; eight o'clock morning prayers in the Chapel; that left an hour to make the beds etc. I remember that one of the students was responsible for leading prayers. The Chapel at that time was over the back lane, and the building is now a dwelling house. Breakfast must have been 8:30. A chorus was sung before meals and after; any notices for the day were given out ... After breakfast, letters usually were laid out in the common room. News from home and friends was

College Officers specialise in their ability to totally transform the meaning of the notice you handed in before lunch
Cliff Toady

much looked for. Then at 9:30 the day's lectures began – two lectures per morning.'[22] 'Every lecture began with a chorus. Our precentor was John Bird, who eventually was minister of Duke Street Baptist Church, Richmond.' [23]

Student Manual c. 1922

Manual had begun at Castleton Hall in Rochdale and at Cliff it was organised under the watchful eye of Thomas Cook. After lunch, 'As soon as Thanks had been returned, as we still sat at table, Mr Cook would tell the men what their manual labour was for the afternoon. We were all pledged to do two hours manual labour each weekday, except Saturday ... Some men had regular work. One man would spend one hour in the early morning and another in the evening attending to the fowls and other jobs. Then one man and sometimes two, would have to help on the small farm ... men of various trades such as bricklayers, joiners, plumbers, etc., did repair work about the Estate. Others had their tasks allotted at the dinner table. Those tasks, or some of them, were to chop or saw up firewood, help dig in the garden or hoe or weed.'[24] Other students swept paths, cleaned cutlery, and some 'had to get up very early and clean all our boots, and have them at our bedroom doors before half past six in the morning.'[25]

> The Library has every book ever written – except the one you want
> *Cliff Toady*

George Boak recalls that his manual related to the building of the new library; 'I remember my job in "manual" sometimes was to transfer some of the rubble dug out of the foundations to where the path and the trees are now. The path leads to the tent field. This work with a barrow was more in my line than trying to get marks on examination papers. The papers could be a headache to me after spending nearly all my time in the open fields.'[26]

'We usually had lectures or classes in the mornings, and we all did some manual work in the afternoons, unless any of the students were qualified to help with the clerical work. My usual duty was to take wood and coal up to the Principal's study. He had an immense library, where he used to read new books and work his way through dictionaries year by year.'[27] Indeed the Principal had someone to wash his car and chauffeur him around in the old days!

Student Manual late 1920's

Attitudes toward manual varied greatly and still do. Some people take their allotted tasks with enthusiasm and enjoy the break in the routine of study. At other times it was possible to identify a 'Certain slackness in general behaviour is evident … arriving late at and returning early from Manual.'[28] One student came angrily to see me declaring the College to be a 'Christian Boot camp'! I assured him that six hours manual a week was not anything like a boot-camp, but the opportunity for the community to learn to share in the necessary tasks and to learn servant-hood. He returned to apologise much later in the year, having understood the purpose of manual. There have always been those who avoided hard work while 'they were very much out of sight … then one of them would spot the Rev Thomas Cook on his walk round to see how they were getting on. Then one man would say:

"Here's T.C." The brooms and shovels would soon be very busy so that when Mr Cook got up to them, one would think they were on "piece work".[29] That was 1905 and nothing changes!

Alan Wardlow leading prayers

Encouragement of students in preacher training has always been a significant part of the student experience. 'In the evenings students had private study but on Thursday evening different students conducted an evening service in the chapel and on the following morning we had a "clinic" about the service.'[30] George Boak recalls, 'Once a week a "Clinic Service" was held when a sermon was preached by one of the students. Then during the week the student who had preached the sermon had his efforts thoroughly criticised, just to put it together again in a way that might be to the benefit of all; but it was a trial to the one who had to stand the test.'[31] In more recent years the service was videoed and the preacher had to watch the service before a tutor and an evangelist helped the students reflect on the delivery and the content of the worship and preaching. The student suffered the critique but normally there was much encouragement for them as well. Clinics had a significant input to the teaching of the art of preaching and leading of worship until about 2000 when other methods were introduced.

Guidance has always been given not to smoke, something which almost has more prominence now than at any other stage. One incident is worth recording: 'With great enjoyment, Principal Rev Samuel Chadwick once told us the story of a student who had previously been a smoker before he went to Cliff College. He suffered in silence for some time, and then asked if he could see the Principal.

Cliff College Student badge

Then to the Principal he said, "I'll simply die if don't have a smoke". "Really", said the Principal, "Well then – just sit there and die".[32] Students were always urged not to drink at all and of course Champness and Chadwick were advocates of the Temperance movement. In recent years the rule has been applied that no drink is allowed on the premises.

A more ordered routine seems to have developed by the time that Ben Mackay was a student (1934-35). 'The routine of the College was all clear on a paper on my dressing table. A Bell rang at 6a.m., time to get up, pick up the mat from the floor, and downstairs for the roll call. After the roll call, outside to beat the mat's dust out and upstairs to clean and tidy the room and make the bed. Next wash and shave, downstairs in an ample wash place, washbasins, mirrors and toilets.'[33]

Speaking of Tea, every man is grateful to the authorities for their very generous provisions at every repast. The menu at Cliff will compare favourably with those of the other colleges. Day after day we hear men say, "My! We are well fed at Cliff". *Cliff Collegian, November 1912*

In those days students did not have access to the administrative corridors, nor should they have talked with the maids who were closely supervised by the matron. 'At prayers, the domestic staff marched in by a side door to the front of the chapel, led by the matron. The maids, young girls in white caps, blue dresses and white aprons, being as it were, ogled by the male audience.'[34] The matron was very much in charge of the daily life for students: 'Early in the term she had a bed brought into one of the lecture halls to demonstrate bed making. Many of the students could not even make a bed.'[35] The attempt by the matron to keep the students and maids apart was undermined by both parties. 'The maids had a sense of humour. One day they put Epsom salts, I think it was, into the students' porridge, then later in the morning enjoyed watching various students rushing out of lectures to the toilets.'[36]

There were some complaints by students which might be considered unreasonable: the pleas for a cooked breakfast every

Meeting Students'
inner needs 1950s

morning; the complaint that the tiny red light flashing on the fire-sensor in a bedroom kept one student awake; 'the fact that Matron was supplying morning cups of tea to two brethren who worked early in Mr Allen's study was commented on. It was considered advisable that the Chairman should see Matron, to stop the teas in case desire for early tea became general or suspicions of favouritism arose.'[37] Sometimes the rules were somewhat oppressive, chastising men who were spitting in the wash hand basins,[38] or refusing them leave to walk by the river or on the Edge after the evening meal.

Through the magazines some students revealed early their ability as writers and theologians. Leslie Weatherhead, a student in 1912-13, contributed to the *Cliff Collegian* with an article entitled the 'The Step Higher', which hints at his future writing skill and breadth of understanding:

> The common view of religion is that it necessitates a change from bad to good, from darkness to light from the power of Satan to God. That view is correct but incomplete … we must not only leave the bad for the good but we must leave the good for the better, the better for the best, and when Paul said he must leave the things of the past he meant not only the bad but the good that he might press on toward the goal, onto the prize of the <u>upward</u> calling of God in Christ.

> This principle is true in the animal world. Evolution is the working out of the law of ever mounting one step higher toward perfection. It

is true in the commercial world. A man invests in new machines not because his old ones are bad but because the new are better. Surely we must climb in the spiritual life – going from bad to good – from good to better – from better to best.'[39]

This is not the holiness theology of Cook or even Chadwick, but it does show Weatherhead's interest in a variety of scholarship, relating it to his theme. He also wrote other items for the magazine such as: 'War: Its Evils and Advantages', and 'Is Memory Eternal?', 'The Value of Dicken's Works', and 'Judges IV: Why Jael slew Sisera'.

There have always been those who came to the College with little or no educational background. It was Fiddian Moulton who first wrote of Cliff as the 'College of the Underprivileged'. I always quote Chadwick who said, 'the ploughboy from the field and the cobbler from his last, may come'. Unfortunately I cannot find the quote; maybe I dreamt it. A testimony from Reginald Courts, a farm worker from Bethany near Saltash, Cornwall illustrates the point. He came as a student in 1936 and responded to a call for workers in India, who would 'live as the Indian brethren'.[40] He writes of the beginning of his work, 'I commenced my work for the Lord in a small tent at Jabalpur, Central India and our Lord began to bless immediately'. By 1975 he was the National Supervisor responsible for the growth and development of the World Missionary Evangelism. When he wrote in 1975 W.M.E. was working in Nepal, Sikkim, Tibet, Bangladesh and Ceylon, as well as in India. His work was among destitute children and he led a team of 'Evangelists and Bible Women'. He was responsible for churches and 135 orphanages across India. Quite a work for a farm labourer with no education. Famously Samuel Chadwick remarked after the College examinations showed Herbert Silverwood had little academic prowess, 'If the Lord can use an ass, he can certainly use you!'[41]

> Mission – the modern equivalent of Trekking, but without shorts.
> *Cliff Toady*

505

Recently we had a student who came for two years and gained his Certificate in Biblical and Evangelistic Ministry. At the graduation he gave testimony, as many do, giving thanks to God because he had previously worked as a builder's labourer and when he came to Cliff he 'didn't have an 'O' level or an 'A' Level, the only level I had was a spirit-level'. Through the years the College has been a community of academics and non-academics, of out-and-out evangelists and caring pastors, of those who were beginning a journey of education and those who were returning to learning and finding a new vocation after many years. Many people came to the College 'to test a call' to ministry, and some were sent by Superintendent Ministers.[42] Some came because they felt the call of God and explored that call, going on to caring professions as did Jim Hall who became a nurse at a Psychiatric Hospital.[43] Others went into the ministry both in Britain and overseas.[44]

> Yes, we are already looking ahead to September 1966 and welcoming the new students to a mixed (very mixed!) Cliff.
>
> Frank Blackwell in *Barkis '66*

Cycles were provided for the students going preaching, but in the early days before the tarmac roads possession or loan of a bicycle was not always beneficial. 'The roads were all limestone. If you went out on a cycle on those roads when it was dry you were soon like a miller. If you went out on a wet day, you would find it very difficult to keep on your cycle. On wet limestone, it was like riding on grease. On a number of occasions, I have seen men return from their appointments in an awful mess. They have had a skid and come off their cycles. But they would gladly prefer that, than not be out preaching.'[45]

The student body is like the tide on a sandy beach, ebbing and flowing, with continuous waves having new energy to smooth the wrinkles, overcome the obstacles and offer the community a fresh start at least twice a day. Often that fellowship is most intense at times of concentrated activity such as in the missions or preparation for the major public events, the Anniversary, Celebration, Derwent, Festival. During the storms in the spring of 1968 when the reservoir of a quarry burst its banks and flooded Stoney Middleton, and students were called out in the early morning to help villagers rescue their belongings, the female students turned up with the minibus and urns of hot sweet tea – and the Derbyshire Times referred to them as the Women's Institute!

One article in *Cosmorama* reflects on the experience in the snow. 'Sunday, January 16th, most of the preaching appointments had been cancelled and so there were more students in the college than is usual. Bro G. Chapman had lit the Common Room fire, and nearly every student took advantage of the fact. In true Cliff tradition it was not long before the air was filled with singing and while the snow fell and the wind blew outside, the warmth of God's Holy Spirit quickened us and made the fellowship into a very wonderful experience of His presence. We sang choruses and hymns until we were almost hoarse, our concluding hymn being "Down in the valley with my Saviour I would go". As I sat and looked at each student in turn; there we were Bro ..... who had been disowned by his parents because he had owned Jesus, Bro..... who had travelled from Africa, to study and then go back and tell his own people of Jesus. Yes, there we were, a rather mixed 'bunch' and each with a story, yet all had found the Joy that comes through following Him.'[46] The sense of fellowship identified here continues to be found year on year at the College, though each year is so very different.

One of the concerns we had when the part-time courses began in 1995 was that either the sense of fellowship of the full-time students

would somehow diminish, or that the part-timers would not really cohere into a group because they would only be at the College for five, or ten days at a time, depending on the course. We need not have feared. The part-time courses have a sense of camaraderie, which is really quite intense, and the mix and interaction between the students of all courses is really very healthy and mutually beneficial.

People can idealise the College. It must be remembered it is full of fallen human beings, saved by grace, and sometimes there are issues to deal with. Occasionally students feel they ought to 'get to know' everyone at the same deep level. There is what I call the community formula. That is, the number of relationships in a group or community are R = N x (N – 1), where R is the number of relationships and N is the number of people. So in a College with 70 people the number of relationships are 70 x 69 = 4,830! Even on a mission team of six people the relationships total thirty. So it is not in any way surprising that levels of relationships vary.

Cliff is a fascinating and creative community with all its diverse life; an academic institution, a missionary organisation, with opportunity for the formation of future vocations, a place of pilgrimage and celebration, conferencing and consultation. It is also a place of prayer, worship, and contemplation.

The last word in this chapter is given over to Tom Meadley, for he articulates the feelings all staff have experienced at the end of a rewarding year:

> Another teaching year is over, and the men have dispersed. Once again, we go through the experience of sorrow as a particular temporary, though profoundly intimate, community disappears ... sooner or later, most of them enter into a profound experience of the reality and nearness of God in Christ through the Holy Spirit. By the time of the last meeting of Rejoicing and Rededication, one can sense that the Holy Spirit has become a personal power. The yearning to share the unspeakable riches of Christ has been born within. Latent powers have been released. A taste for the Word of God, the life of prayer, and practical service, has been created. One can only stammer utterly inadequate gratitude to God for the privilege of some slight share in the begetting process.[47]

Prize-giving (Graduation), the tears and emotion, the goodbye's, and that great sense of pride and achievement, moving on in God's service.

The Last 20 Years (83-84)

1 *Cliff Collegian,* October 1912, p.1.
2 George Boak, *Reflections,* p.4.
3 Letter to Howard Belben, 6 August 1968.
4 Letter to Howard Belben, 2 October 1969, forty years after he came to Cliff as a student.
5 Letter to Howard Belben, August 1973.
6 *Methodist Recorder,* 1894, p.50.
7 *Methodist Recorder,* 1894, p.50.
8 George Boak, *Reminiscences and Reflections,* p.4.
9 John Newbould, *The Roots and Early Growth of Cliff College* (Unpublished typed paper in the archives), p.17.
10 John Newbould, p.35.
11 John Newbould, p.32a.
12 John Newbould, p.32a.
13 Letter from Marilyn Holmes to Howard Belben, 15 October 1969.
14 John Newbould, p.35.
15 Ben Mackay, p.277.
16 G. Kettle, *The Cliff Collegian,* November 1912.
17 *Captain's Minute Book,* 25 January 1939.

cont.

18 *Captain's Minute Book,* 22 March 1939.
19 *Captain's Minute Book,* 15 January 1936.
20 *Captain's Minute Book,* 18 January 1936.
21 *Captain's Minute Book,* 7 October 1936, where a complaint is noted that students eager for P.T. were neglecting their private devotions.
22 George Boak, *Reminiscences and Reflections,* p.5.
23 Ben Mackay, p.277. The Rev John Bird was the minister at Duke Street Baptist when I was a student at Richmond College, 1969 – 72 and he baptised me by immersion in the summer of 1972.
24 John Newbould, p.36.
25 John Newbould, p.36.
26 George Boak, pp.4-5.
27 Stanley B. Smith, *Far to Go,* p.32.
28 *Captain's Minute Book,* 29 January 1935.
29 John Newbould, p.37.
30 Stanley B. Smith, p.32.
31 George Boak, *Reminiscences,* p.6.
32 Stanley B. Smith, *Far to Go,* p.32.
33 Stanley B. Smith, *Far to Go,* p.32.
34 Stanley B. Smith, *Far to Go,* p.32.
35 Ben Mackay, p.279.
36 Ben Mackay, p.279.
37 *Captain's Minute Book,* 28 January 1936.
38 *Captain's Minute Book,* 9 May 1935.
39 Leslie Weatherhead, 'The Step Higher', *Cliff Collegian,* February 1913. His biography *Doctor of Souls* acknowledges that Chadwick first taught him the art of preaching but concludes, 'Cliff did not suit him. Chadwick's stiff regime of classes in the morning and agricultural work in the kitchen gardens every afternoon he found heavy going', p.20.
40 Letter from Dr R Courts, 1975.
41 David Lazell, *Firebrand,* p.30, though I heard Herbert tell that tale many times.
42 See Eric Challoner, *It So Happened*, pp.73f.
43 Jim Hall, *A Cliff Man's Story* (Unpublished, 2003), p.1.
44 Raymond Rose (ed) *Forty Years on* and Ray Cummins (ed) *The Last 20 Years*, both published greetings from students in their respective years, 1962/3 and 1983/4. Most of the contributors are now in ordained or lay ministry.
45 John Newbould, p.54.
46 G.H. Lister, 'Snow Bound' in *Cosmorama,* p.6.
47 Tom Meadley, *Advance,* 22 August 1963.

CHAPTER 20

A Succession of Principals

John Arthur Broadbelt 1932–1948

C hadwick had died. The person who had built on Cook's remarkable legacy, gathered a group of excellent tutors, presided over the development of the Trekkers, acquired land and property for the College, had gone. On the day of his funeral the Committee met and confirmed the appointment of John Arthur Broadbelt. It had all the hallmarks of the passing of authority in the British Empire: the King is dead, long live the King!

It is also clear that the Conference of 1932 had appointed Broadbelt to be Chadwick's successor, something Dunning at least had hoped to be. Not surprisingly the next moves were delicate. It was a delicate matter presiding over the transition of a College in which the Principal had been ill for extended periods since 1922, and which Lambert, Dunning and Brice had not only run with great ability in Chadwick's enforced absences, but in which they had also deferred to Chadwick when he was well. Broadbelt had been a Central Hall superintendent, making the policy, raising funds and himself seeing it all through. Now he had colleagues, used to

running the College and supporting an ill Principal, one of whom had certainly hoped to become Chadwick's successor.

It was in the summer of 1933 when Dunning indicated he wished to move; he felt 'called to evangelistic service elsewhere.'[1] It is notable that the information about this came from Luke Wiseman, as head of the Home Mission Department, to the Committee and not Broadbelt as Principal of the College. The question of the vacancy was then considered, and the Rev George Allen was suggested as a tutor 'after a long and happy discussion.'[2] Luke Wiseman brought the news to the committee that David W. Lambert, who had been a tutor at the College for eight years was to be married. Lambert was still living in the College and the Committee decided to treat him 'as a Junior Minister would be treated in Circuit. That his house and furniture should be found and that the question of stipend should be left to the committee.'[3]

Dunning was thanked in his absence: 'That the Cliff College Committee desires to place on record its warmest thanks for the able and devoted service given to the training of Evangelists by the Rev N.G. Dunning for some 12 years. Mr Dunning came as an accepted candidate for the Ministry and was the assistant to the Rev Samuel Chadwick for some years. He did much to inaugurate the Team

Missions and led many of them himself with conspicuous success. After his visit to Australia, he was invited to be a tutor and succeeded the Rev Fiddian Moulton. For some years Mr Dunning had lectured on Theology and the content of the English Bible with much success and blessings. The committee prays that the Rev N.G. Dunning may be used greatly in his work in India and Australia.'[4] It is interesting that very warm comments were made by Broadbelt about all other staff, Allen, Lambert and Stringer at the same meeting.

Before his appointment Broadbelt's ministry had been very substantial. Years later the Rev Reg Walker, who became his son-in-law, wrote of Broadbelt that he was, 'known throughout Methodism and far beyond as the man who built, paid for, filled, and kept filled some of the greatest missions in Methodism. Dartford, Hull, Southall, Bristol, all speak of the unique power of organisation, his warmth of friendship, his abounding generosity, his mastery of the language the common man understands ... to "J.A.B.", the college owes a debt of gratitude it can never pay. His name will live on as one who not unworthily entered a great succession.'[5]

To this new post he brought and applied these gifts, building the Chadwick Memorial Chapel in 1932, and the three cottages and the house which today we call 'Lindum' in 1934. He introduced and encouraged donations to the 'Chadwick Evangelism Fund', and supported his colleagues in raising funding for a memorial gravestone at All Saints Parish Church, Curbar. Broadbelt was also instrumental

The Lilian Broadbelt memorial window in the Cliff College Chapel

in the extension of Calver Methodist Church, asking visitors to the Anniversary in 1936 to help by prayer and donations to build a Sunday School building. He 'gave a vigorous lead both in personal devotion and in the subsequent raising of monies from many sources'.[6] This they did and the Sunday School was opened free of debt in September of that year. Through his dashing style the Anniversary continued to develop, and the 1935 photograph of those who attended entered the bloodstream of evangelical Christians of all denominations, of Cliff being the place to be on 'Whit Monday'. He had seen the possibilities of the expansion of the Summer School by transforming it into the 'Derwent Convention'. In 1939 he built the huge Cliff Hall, with only the surety that it would be used one weekend and one week a year, and just the hope that it might have further use.

He faced personal tragedy when on Christmas morning in 1935 his wife Lilian Broadbelt died. A book was written in her memory and is a eulogy of her life, work and devotion to the work of her husband.[7] Wiseman paid tribute to her at the College Committee, 'He especially emphasised her insight into the hearts of the Evangelists. She had written an autograph letter each week to every man – 50 letters a week – and it was a labour of love.'[8] 'JAB', as he was affectionately known by friends and colleagues, did not contribute to the *Joyful News* again until 13 February 1936 when he explored the process of death and comfort for the bereaved. It is a very sensitive piece. By Easter his writing was full of confidence and forward planning.

Broadbelt was interested, with a kind of gentle and caring paternalism, in the welfare of staff and arranged for the provision of pensions through the Home Mission Department. To those who had given a life-time's service like Roberts, a house and pension was given. Lambert was promised a pension of £150 a year when he reached sixty-five, if he remained in the employment of the College.[9]

It was Broadbelt who with heartfelt comment reported with regret that Lambert had decided, after fourteen years service at Cliff, to go to the Faith Mission, 'in which Mrs Lambert was trained, and that he would be taking up work there at Christmas.'[10] The Rev J. Baines Atkinson had retired and he built what is known as 'Fir Tree Lodge' in Cliff Lane.

At the outbreak of war, as we have seen, the College was leased to the Sheffield High School for Girls. In fact the School evacuated to Cliff on Saturday 2 September 1939, a day before the outbreak of war was announced.[11] For his part, Broadbelt kept in touch with students and evangelists through a series of duplicated letters. The first edition is dated 26 January 1940, and Broadbelt used the letter to ensure that the students keep in touch with fellow students by hearing a summary of their news. He had hoped to make them monthly but they become more intermittent.[12]

Broadbelt was not really keen on the presence of the school. In another letter he described the situation with the girls. 'Some two hundred and fifty girls of all ages from five to eighteen are here, and a right happy lot of girls they are. You would hardly know the old place. If you could hear the noise you would wonder how I exist, for in the old days we did try to move the chairs as quietly as possible. And if a man was heard whistling he was courteously asked to send it home. There is no limit now to the noise. I often long for the return of the students and the opportunity of doing our own work.'[13]

The view from the school is written up in the *Calver Record* and it has interesting comment about the College buildings and grounds with the suggestion of limits placed on the school. 'The grounds are pretty, containing many fine trees, and a terraced rose-garden, but they were not really very suitable for children, as the trees must not be climbed, nor the banks used for slides ... the wide lawn was possible for ball games and admirable for quiet outdoor occupations.'[14] The College building was adapted easily enough for the purposes of a Girls' School. The small, plainly furnished study bedrooms of the students were used as dormitories for two or three girls, the lecture rooms, hall and library became form-rooms, and the dining room, besides serving its proper function, was a studio and form-room combined. The Laundry was changed into a laboratory, where, 'thanks to the ingenuity of the Chemistry mistress, an excellent standard in practical work was maintained. A very large hall built for special conferences in the grounds made a splendid place for indoor games and gymnastics.'[15]

Some of the older girls used the old Chapel, across Cliff Lane, as a dormitory and other girls and staff members were billeted in the local villages of Curbar, Calver and Baslow.[16] The upper Sixth had the privilege of using the flat above the Principal's House which must have been very intrusive to the Broadbelt family as there were in those days no doors on the stairs, nor incidentally into what we used to call the 'bookshop corridor'. The headmistress was also lodged in what we know today as the Principal's flat, wisely placed in a bedroom so she could hear any unnecessary noise.[17]

The proximity of the school, with 250 girls, to the Broadbelt family and the staff of the college must have brought its tensions. These are in part noted in the rules about climbing trees. Smokers among the school teaching staff were required to smoke in the lane, 'until our landlord lifted the smoking ban in the staff room.'[18] The school must also have taken responsibility for maintenance of the building, for a Miss Lucas the school secretary, is described as dealing with 'Plumbing, electrical repairs, air-raid warnings, billeting, the Milk Marketing Board, ration books, farming and finance.'[19]

Heavy snow falls came in the late January 1940. 'I wish you could see a photograph taken outside Cliff Park, with Mr Allen and myself standing in front of a snow drift that completely blocked the entrance at Cliff Park. The drifts were eight feet deep and we were a fortnight before we could get down the Lane.'[20] Each letter is full of cheery messages from Bro ---- who is always doing well. The letters are upbeat and positive.

The letters describe the devastation caused in the Sheffield air-raids. 'O Sheffield; you would hardly know much of it today. I think of the times some of you went to Barker's Pool for open-air meetings ... and of the marches through the streets singing choruses. Today Sheffield is badly wounded.'[21] The devastation comes over powerfully in his writing: 'It is a desolate place, but the people are wonderful. There is no defeatism among the folk. I had to go into Sheffield on the Friday after Hitler had done his worst. It was a sad experience and a glad one when one saw the people setting to work to put things right and to wipe up Hitler's mess. Happily the Victoria Hall was not hit but many of our churches are. We are safe at the College. I wish some of you could come and be 'roof spotters!' We shall have to watch for Incendiary bombs in the future.'[22] Some of the girls from the school had to remain at the College over Christmas. 'Many people regarded those of us left at Cliff with Pity, but I remember it as an outstanding enjoyable Christmas'.[23] Broadbelt's view was somewhat different, 'It has been a strange Christmas for us. Many – very many – of the girls of the High School have been in residence. It was not possible for them to go to their homes in Sheffield'.[24]

In May 1941 the tone was not quite so thoroughly positive about the war, as he recalled students who had died, in this country and as part of the British Expeditionary Force.[25] Throughout the circular letters there was a desire to return to the real work though he made the best of an unusual situation. 'The School remains in residence and though we long for the day when we can throw open the doors and welcome seventy men here, we are thankful to feel that at a time when so many of our cities are being raided, two hundred and fifty girls have found a place of refuge in the College.'[26]

JAB (as he was known) with his 'pride and joy'

He reported the work, triumphs and personal changes of the students. One student before the outbreak of war was the German, Adolf Gaidatsch who on 24 February 1940 was still at the College. In a later letter he remarks that, 'Bro. Gaidatsch…movements are, of course, restricted by the Police but he is happy to tell me he has work to do in a weaving mill'.[27]

The contact between the school and the College was not all fraught with difficulty. Mrs Chadwick at Stanton Ford House had staff members billeted with her, which clearly they enjoyed. 'Then in the morning, breakfast piping hot, and Mrs Chadwick beaming behind the teapot and urging us to make a good breakfast before setting out for the day's work.'[28] Her Christian faith must have shone out: 'the porch door of Mrs Chadwick's house at Stanton Ford was always wide open, true symbol of the generous hospitality to be found there … Yes Stanton Ford House was undoubtedly one of the good things of Calver.'[29] Jeanne Chapman, who was Broadbelt's step-daughter, later to be the wife of Howard Belben, attended the school and received an excellent education. She recalls happy years at the College at this time. The nature of the College as an evangelistic institution had a real impact on at least one pupil. Anne Greaves recalls, 'in May 1940 I managed to attend the Sun. evening service (of the) Anniversary Weekend. Joe Brice was the preacher (from Hosea I think), and I was converted. Jesus seemed so real to all the people around, and so I found Him to be'.[30] She indicates that the School 'authorities' were wary 'of the enthusiasm a few of us began to engender', though she found a quiet place along the 'prayer paths' where she could be alone, 'hence my affection for the paths along which I often walked, my New Testament in blazer pocket!'[31] The College staff were helpful to her and she, as a pupil, 'managed to establish friendships with several of the College staff who remained at Cliff during the war years.'[32]

Mr Allen was a Chaplain at Penhros College billeted during the war at Chatsworth House and preaching to two hundred girls every

Sunday.[33] Broadbelt was undertaking Cliff Weekends in Rugby, Huddersfield, Sheffield and other places, conducting weekend Services for the spread of Scriptural Holiness and Aggressive Evangelism, along with Correspondence courses and helping local circuits.[34] The plan of the weekend 'is to go on Saturday and conduct two or three meetings for the afternoon and the evening on the following lines: The Need of a Forward Movement; The Power of a Forward Movement (The Holy Spirit); The Expression of a Forward Movement (Evangelism). We then have follow up services on the Sunday.' [35] There was little in the way of a theological reflection on the War or the way it was progressing. To the students in ministry he simply said, 'I would like to suggest to all our old students who are in one or other of our Theological Colleges that they read and study the Methodist Doctrine of PERFECT LOVE and its relation to social conditions.'[36] He finished the final letter in our archives with the words, 'The School is still here, but one day we will welcome some of you as old students. There are about one hundred men waiting to come when the war is over.'[37]

It is difficult to read back into a text from November 1944, but when the Headmistress, Miss Macaulay, gave a speech at the Farewell party of November 1944 she mentioned by name the vicar, 'Mr Lister and the ministers and preachers at the chapel', and the farmer Mr Warren, but about Broadbelt she referred to 'our landlord, his family and household, for making it possible for us to live in this lovely place, and not only providing up-putting but also putting up with us and all our vagaries.'[38]

Though the Committee normally met annually an additional meeting was arranged during the Anniversary Weekend in May 1947. At that meeting Broadbelt asked to move from Cliff House to Cliff Park because of 'the heavy and varied responsibilities, increasing so greatly with the development of the College work'.[39] He and Eagles agreed to swap accommodation and whilst the teaching should remain the same, Mr Eagles would 'have pastoral oversight of the brethren'.[40] Broadbelt's energy and vitality was sapped, as were his creative ideas in the *Joyful News*. The arrangements, when made, were to the satisfaction of both.

In response to Broadbelt's request to retire a year earlier than intended on medical grounds, the President of Conference, Dr Farndale, summed up his contribution as 'deep spiritual concern - with splendid business acumen.'[41] Broadbelt was permitted to remain at Cliff Park and offered help in teaching as required. He had achieved a remarkable record in building works in the College, continued the great public events of the Anniversary, started the Derwent Convention, kept the college financially in a credit balance and added to the investments so that in 1943 there was £50,000 available. Broadbelt had managed to keep and develop the College at the height of his powers at Cliff, but the War intervened, and afterwards there was not the same energy nor spark.

It had been intended that Mr and Mrs Broadbelt should move to 'The Bungalow' the following year and the house was extended for that purpose. In fact they moved to Harrogate after one year. There is a sense of sadness about the last year, as though something were not quite right. The

John and "Ella" Broadbelt

committee made a decision to recognise in 'some worthy and appropriate way' the 'long and distinguished service' of John Broadbelt. It is important to note that both his predecessors had died in office; Broadbelt was the first to retire from the post of Principal. A sub-committee was set up but it never reported and no action was taken. As a result, the colossal contribution made by Broadbelt to Cliff College was never properly recognised. In this book I have attempted to rectify that, and to place on record the huge debt which Cliff owes to a deeply spiritual, wonderfully extrovert and gracious entrepreneur.

J. Edward Eagles MC 1948-1957

From the beginning of the new regime, there was established a very different approach to the governance of the College. Eagles asked the Committee to meet twice a year and to establish an Executive Committee.[42] After the first flurry of work, the pattern under Cook had been two committee meetings per year in March and November. Chadwick and Broadbelt had few committees, though in 1913 when Chadwick took over as Principal, there was a committee in April, June, July and October. No committees were recorded between November 1915 and May 1920, and afterwards they were normally annually. There were no meetings of the Committee in the years, 1924, 1925, 1927, a number of committees around Chadwick's death in 1932, and then annually but no committee was called in 1935, 1939 or 1942.

Immediately Eagles became Principal there was much more detail written into the minutes. This may suggest a more consultative style, or that in Eagles there was a person more nervous about making and taking key decisions: For instance, the request to purchase a wooden shed costing 'approximately £100, for the use of the Book Department',[43] or explaining the poor condition of a Shooting Brake used by the College for carrying things.[44] Chadwick did not call a Committee when he built the Library wing, and Broadbelt had the practice of identifying the project, raising the money and then

'Pop' Eagles

informing the Committee the project had been achieved.[45] The *Minutes* suggest that this practice of focussing on the minutiae of detail contributed to the loss of vision in the post-war period.

Edward (Ted) Eagles, who had been a chaplain in the First World War in which he gained the Military Cross, taught the classes on Christian Doctrine and produced his lectures in note form. The first edition was produced in 1948, not long after he became a tutor, but in 1950 an interleaved second edition of *Notes of Lectures on Christian Theology* was produced mainly for the use of students at Cliff. The preface sets out the purpose of the booklet as 'an initial and elementary view of theology ... a clear and simple statement of

Methodist Theology'.[46] Whilst teaching doctrine, he also focussed on Wesley's sermons and produced for students a summary of the teaching of Wesley's sermons. He was one of the few tutors of Cliff to make students read and therefore thoroughly engage with Wesley's text, rather than just read books about Wesley.

He adjusted some of the College facilities, ensuring a brick-built reservoir was erected, sufficient for the needs of the great public events. He also made 'adjustments to entrances, drives, kitchens, platforms, and bookstalls.'[47] He maintained the College but was not the entrepreneur his predecessors had been. He was also renowned for a collection of Staffordshire Pottery associated with Wesley which now resides in the Museum of World Methodism, in the Offices of the World Methodist Council at Lake Junalaska, North Carolina.

He was known affectionately by the students and throughout the Cliff community as 'Pop Eagles'.

James H. Goad wrote in his student year (1955-56): 'I owe a tremendous debt to Cliff ... (it) was invaluable to study God's word and for the practical side of the course, not to mention the wonderful fellowship, especially on the trek at Bridlington.[48]

James White (1954-55) entered the ministry of the United Methodist Church in the USA. He was a young student, 'not yet 18', and reflected; 'The evangelistic environment in which my young faith was nurtured by men like Eagles, Powell, Atkinson, Tom Butler and Ernie Steele has left an indelible mark on my ministry.[49]

It should never be overlooked, that the great genius of the Eagles years was his courage to be associated with the Billy Graham London Crusade and much more importantly for the College, the invitation to Billy Graham to attend the Anniversary of 1954. The detail of that is recorded elsewhere but Eagles should take much credit for that stance and decision. He also made the decision to expand the Anniversary meetings following the success of 1954 and established

the 'Top Tent' which Silverwood, Butler and others made so famous.

When his retirement was announced, Dr Sangster spoke of the sincere wishes of all the committee for the retirement of Mr Eagles. Warmest thanks were given for the excellent work he had done in preserving the essential ethos of the college, and greatly enhancing and preserving all that is truly good in its traditions.

Thomas D. Meadley BA,BD 1957-1965

Tom was the minister of Oxford Place, Leeds, immediately before his appointment as Principal, and in contrast to any Principal before or since had no contact with the College prior to that post. Amos Cresswell acknowledged that there was surprise expressed by the Cliff supporters that he was chosen but added that 'only those who did not know him wondered for long about the selection', which does recognise that there was some disquiet about him.

Tom Meadley had been profoundly influenced by the writing of P.T. Forsyth, and it was reading this remarkable theologian which convinced the young Tom to 'commit himself to the truth of the New Testament Christ'.[50] He trained for the ministry, worked for the Student Christian Movement and served in a number of circuits before becoming the Superintendent of Oxford Place, Leeds. It was from a successful ministry there that Sangster invited him to become the Principal of Cliff College.

It is curious that the *Minutes* of the College Committee do not mention Tom Meadley's arrival at the College. He was present in September 1957 bringing written and verbal reports[51] and though the names of the tutorial staff are listed in the *Minutes*, Dr Farndale, Len Sutch and Miss Hallam, there is no actual mention of Meadley's

name. This is remarkable and the only time it has happened. All other Principals have been welcomed, even when they have moved from Tutor to that elevated state. In fact he is mentioned only on 26 October 1961 regarding the appointment of an additional Treasurer, when he was named as the seconder of the motion,[52] and then again on 2 December 1963, when the decision was made to cease printing *Advance*, the successor to *Joyful News*, 'thanks are expressed to the Rev T.D. Meadley for all the help he had given to Mr Eagles and to Mr Cresswell during their periods as Editor.'

Tom Meadley came to the College at a difficult time. The post War period had meant difficulties with finance, there were fewer students because National Service continued, and there was a sense of depression in the Church. He brought a practical 'down-to-earth' approach to matters, and was a manly man. Sensibly, one of the first things he did was to gain some privacy for himself, Joan and their son John, by ensuring a door was placed at the college entrance to the Principal's flat. All future Principals have been grateful. Little renovation work had been done during the post-war period, the property needed repair and he saw to it. The library needed additional books for the new courses which he and his colleagues developed, and he made an appeal in the *Joyful News* for financial help and the gift of books, which was successful.

Meadley's time was not one of expansion; it was one of preparation and regrouping for the future. The *Minutes* suggest that this was indeed the case, with the College needing much repair, ceilings collapsing, as well as needed renovation and repainting of the

College and properties. The numbers of students were at their lowest ever in 1962 and 1963. Meadley did not, however, plan for closure, as was happening in other Methodist Colleges. Howard Belben often used to say, in relation to the developments of the College during his time as Principal, that he built on the foundation laid by Tom Meadley.

In many ways Meadley opened the College up to the local neighbourhood. At its best, that had always been the case but the archives reveal confidential documents from a medical advisor to the College Committee, suggesting the community was far too insular and inward looking.[53] Though not dated, it would appear to be around 1959. The report notes that most people lived, worked, worshipped, and for many, ate together every day in the term and during vacations. People were over-worked and rarely went out of the community. In the 1962 gale a long line of forty-foot conifers was blown over and Meadley welcomed the removal of 'these symbols of the harmful doctrine of separation'.[54] He was joined in these decisions by Amos Cresswell and Howard Belben, and together with other staff they prepared for the changes which would be beneficially introduced during the time Howard Belben was Principal.

Meadley taught doctrine, and to this he brought a great love of theology, especially P.T. Forsyth. Indeed, when I was appointed to the College, he wrote at great length encouraging me to commend the books of Forsyth, especially on the Cross. I did. He wrote most interesting articles for the *Joyful News*, giving a different slant to familiar topics. Maybe his finest contribution came in the doctrine of

Scriptural Holiness through his book *Top Level Talks* published after he left Cliff.[55] The book debunks false piety as surely as would Wesley, but carefully constructs a theology of sanctification based on scripture and with a real understanding of human experience.

The testimony of Michael Pederson (1962-63) is a typical response of students during Meadley's time. '... the great debt I owe to Cliff College. Not only was my own life greatly enriched by the fellowship I found there, but also, under the patience of a Principal and other tutors, I was introduced to intensive study for the first time in my life ... When I think that before I went to Cliff I had read no more than a dozen books in my life, I realise how much I owe to the College and its dedicated staff.'[56]

In 1965 he returned to circuit work becoming the Superintendent in Newton Abbot where he served before retirement. At the *Joyful News* Centenary he was asked to speak about 'Cliff Past'. He reflected that being asked to do so he felt like 'Marley's Ghost!'[57] In a nutshell he summarised the College; 'Essentially it is more than a Bible College, a creative mixture of the Benedictine Order while at College and the Franciscan Order while on mission out of College.'[58]

If he could he would invite us to 'Press On' and 'Keep Believing!'

Howard A.G. Belben MA,BD 1965 - 1977

H oward Belben was one of the, quite frankly few, quint essentially English gentlemen of the Methodist ministry. He typified all that Cliff College stood for, and for much of the latter half of the twentieth century he was the embodiment of its teaching and mission. His leadership, as Principal of the College, was combined with a vigorous family life, and the impact of the College was woven into their everyday lives for over twenty years. It was at Cliff that he met his wife Jeanne who was the step-daughter of John Broadbelt, and their children Ruth, Jane and Jim spent much of their early lives at the College. Howard Belben was leader of the Cliff community, eager for evangelistic mission, but also a respected leader in Methodism and British Church life.

More than half of Howard Belben's ministry was spent at Cliff. He was appointed as Tutor in 1947 after serving in the Guildford, Shepton Mallett, and Weston-super-Mare circuits. The scholarship, acquired as he read modern languages and theology at Emmanuel College, Cambridge, and his training in theology at Richmond College, along with his experience as Chaplain and Lecturer in Divinity at Southlands College, prepared him for his long association with Cliff. After assuming the superintendency of the Wolverhampton Darlington Street Circuit (1953-1957) and the Sheffield Mission (1957-1960), Howard returned to the College as Senior Tutor. He had already resumed his lectures in Old Testament Studies on a part-time basis during the illness of the Rev Dr W.E.

Farndale. When the Rev Tom Meadley left in 1965, Howard Belben proved to be a natural successor as Principal.

His gifts as a teacher enabled his students to realise the contemp-orary relevance of biblical revelation and the importance of the Old Testament. As a genuine educationalist he was always ready to introduce new methods of learning to the College. His courses on evangelism and counselling, represented by *The Mission of Jesus* (Epworth, 1970), were both stimulating and instructive, and students discovered their practical value when engaged in mission. Howard was himself eager to seize every opportunity to share in evangelistic outreach. His *Old Testament Notes* enlightened generations of students and opened up the Bible with characteristic clarity, attention to recent scholarship and an infectious enthusiasm for the testimony of God's dealings with his chosen people. Students from that generation will recall how at the end of each lecture he closed with suitable prayer, "O Lord we thank you for Malachi..." while at the same time closing his file and putting his spectacles in his top pocket. As a preacher he effectively combined clear biblical exposition with a down-to-earth realism which indicated that he never lost touch with the everyday demands of Christian living in the modern world.

Howard Belben was a man of deep integrity. What he said and preached, he lived. The man you met was the man he was, a characteristic which impressed itself on all who knew him. He showed himself to be a loyal and co-operative colleague to the tutorial staff, both before and after becoming Principal. Although firm in his convictions, he was always willing to listen patiently to the views of others and preferred to reach a unanimous consensus wherever possible. He had a great capacity to listen to people, to hear their grumbles and absorb their pain. He defused many situations by gentleness. On the Cliff estate he was regarded with affection as a true father in God, taking an interest in the overall welfare of each member of the community. Indeed all those who were students under him will recall the black filofax book in which he kept copious notes of all his students and their progress, something he continued throughout his retirement. In his relationships with the students, he constantly made himself available for pastoral counselling, regardless of the sacrifices involved in terms of time and energy. This, perhaps more than any other feature of his ministry at Cliff, represents his distinctive contribution and helped

Three successive Principals

to ensure that the College remained a Christian family rather than an impersonal institution.

Throughout his ministry Howard served on Connexional committees where his wisdom and attention to detail were greatly admired. He was part of the Methodist team who explored with the Anglicans the possibility of Union in the late 1960s, which was controversial for some of the supporters of Cliff. Howard was a founder member of both the Methodist Revival Fellowship and the Conservative Evangelicals in Methodism and played an important role as elder statesman in uniting them as Headway. His ministry was recognised ecumenically, and in particular by the many evangelistic organisations to which he lent his support. Not least of these was the Evangelical Alliance of which he was Vice-President for many years.

Howard was a man of tremendous energy, vision and drive. He was physically fit, running 'on the spot' every day until his retirement, and a man of deep devotion, commending to his students the practice of the devotional quiet time at morning, noon and night, which he himself diligently pursued. This personal, spiritual energy was reflected in the development of the College at this period. It was during his time as Principal that the enrolment of students at Cliff steadily increased and the doors of Cliff were opened to women as well as to men. Remembering the tradition of the past, he was particularly anxious to make room for the less privileged who could not afford the fees. The fulfilment of the College's decision to build a Conference Centre (now called The Stanton Centre) and renovate the Youth Camp, will continue to remind us of his commitment to the wider outreach of Cliff, and is a tribute to his vision and forward thinking. Both the Spring Bank Holiday Anniversary and the Derwent Convention maintained their numerical strength and spiritual impact under his leadership at a time when such events were not so popular. In these, and in the regular Cliff Conferences, there was an added element of therapeutic counselling, which arose directly from his own experience in this field.

In all of this, Jeanne supported her husband in the variety of the work of Cliff, and also fulfilled her own vocation both as a teacher and as a counsellor. Together they opened their home to staff, students and other visitors with characteristic generosity. Follow-ing his retirement in 1977, Howard and Jeanne first moved to

Nottingham and with Frank Lake pursued the ministry of counselling. They returned to Sheffield and made their home in the Sheffield Ecclesall Circuit, worshipping at Bents Green. Throughout his retirement he was welcomed as a preacher and Bible teacher in all parts of the country. He was also a wise counsellor to new Principals!

All those who knew him comment on Howard's steady and gentle way. He was so often a rock in a stormy sea. This inner strength flowed naturally out of his deeply rooted prayerful relationship with God and dutiful nature. He was rooted in the evangelical tradition to which he was unwaveringly loyal. He also found a proper pride in his family heritage, was a member of the Society of Genealogists and had meticulously traced his family tree to the seventeenth century. Born at Sherborne, in his beloved Dorset, he was devoted to his native county and was a member of the 'Old Dorsetmen's Association'. He had a deep love for poetry and could quote

substantial amounts from memory, a skill which was a great comfort to him when he could no longer see to read.

In the last few months of his life he became very frail and died on Tuesday 21 September 1999, aged 85. It was appropriately the feast of St Matthew, the teacher. He bore his illness with the quiet dignity that marked his entire life, always supported by Jeanne and his family.

CLIFF more than a COLLEGE

Dr Arthur Skevington Wood BA 1977-1983

D r Wood came to the College in 1970 with a very wide experience of thirty-four years in the ministry served in a variety of Circuits in Scotland and the north of England. He might have come earlier as revealed in correspondence between Eagles and Sangster, 'As far as the appointment of a successor to Mr Atkinson is concerned, there is a good deal in what you say respecting Skevington Wood'.[59] In those days the General Secretary of the Home Mission Department decided who should be appointed and informed the relevant committees. For whatever reason Arthur did not come at that time. Immediately before coming to Cliff, he travelled throughout the world as a representative for the Movement for World Evangelisation and was a regular speaker at the Filey Convention and one of the few Mehodists to speak at the Keswick Convention. While in Scotland he was awarded the PhD degree from the University of Edinburgh for his thesis on Thomas Haweis, and he maintained a lifelong interest in Church History and became a Fellow of the Royal Historical Society.

In his youth he was a keen sportsman and was both goalkeeper in the football team and wicket-keeper in the cricket team. He was also the opening bat at cricket and his role had been to keep his end while the other opener went for the runs. In sport and in theology he was an able Defender of the Faith.

Arthur Wood commenced his ministry in Glasgow and began there the fine ministry of expository preaching which was the hallmark of his sermons. We have some in the College archive and each one reads as he would have preached it. His sermons contained thorough exposition, full of Wesleyan theology, and were clear in outline and language, prepared with meticulous attention to detail. He always preached from a full script, though his sermons were no less powerful for being read. He had, according to Professor Howard Marshall, a 'remarkable combination of a faithful and effective preacher of the gospel and a meticulous scholar of the highest calibre.'[60] His work on Thomas Haweis was just the tip of an iceberg in relation to a wealth of scholarship on all matters biblical, theological and historical. From his pen came twenty books including *The Burning Heart*, about John Wesley, *And With Fire*; *Messages on Revival*; *Luther's Principles of Interpretation*, and *Evangelism: Its theology and Practice*. In addition he contributed to the three volume *History of Methodism*, and the *Dictionary of World Methodism*. He was also involved in the revision of *The International Standard Bible Encyclopeadia* as well as a regular contributor to many journals. Arthur Skevington Wood was a scholar evangelist, one of a rare breed.

It was during his first appointment that he met Mary Fearnley at a Christian Endeavour Holiday and they were married on 1 January

1943. She was to be at his side in his travels and supporting his ministry for nearly fifty years. He spoke at many conventions and pastors' conferences in Europe, Africa, the Caribbean and Asia, including India, Taiwan, South Korea and the Philippines. Mary supported him and took great interest in the student welfare when at Cliff. They had no children of their own, and the Cliff students were their 'family'.

With considerable ability Dr Wood taught Church History, Christian Doctrine, and Evangelistic Preaching during the time he was a member of the College staff. The courses, like his preaching, were characterized by a lucidity always produced by a mastery of his material. This combination of clarity and depth made his teaching invaluable to the generations of students who passed through Cliff during that time.

When Howard Belben retired in 1977, Dr Wood was the natural successor. The six years of his principalship saw important developments in the life of Cliff, particularly in the way the College became more firmly committed to making its contribution to the Methodist Connexion, and to the local churches of the Peak Methodist Circuit. Curiously he saw himself as a 'caretaker Principal' following Howard Belben. His insistence upon the appointment of a Director of Evangelism as an additional member of staff was a more characteristic monument to his influence than any new building might have been.

His gentle manner overlay a very firm disciplinary touch, and the serenity of personal relations during his time as Principal was a

Arthur and Mary in Israel

tribute to the unruffled way in which he was able to handle all those who were responsible to him whether students or staff. Arthur and Mary Wood together presided over the College community, seeing to the day to day needs of the students, and keeping them in order.

In spite of rising financial problems connected with the gradual diminution of local authority grants, the student enrolment figures were maintained virtually to the point of capacity. Regularly the student numbers were in the high seventies.

To those who knew him best, the most impressive thing was the way in which Dr Wood made room for so much in his life without ever appearing short of time. He continued to write books and exercise a wide-ranging preaching ministry while at the same time always being available to those who needed his counsel or help. The forward planning of College events was never allowed to be behind-hand, and the *Joyful News* Centenary year's celebrations in 1983 were digested without fuss.

This was all achieved in spite of health problems which made life difficult for both Dr and Mrs Wood. They were not allowed to obtrude, however, and the way in which they coped with their responsibilities was an inspiration to their colleagues and students alike. Arthur and Mary Wood retired to Sheffield and continued to retain links with the College until his death in January 1993. He gave to the College a considerable proportion of his extensive personal library when he retired, and returned to use the library when researching for articles and in particular for his contribution to the *Dictionary of Evangelical Biography*. When he died part of his legacy to the College was the remainder of his library, papers, sermons and the literary ownership of his works.

Arthur Skevington Wood was undoubtedly the greatest scholar amongst those who have been privileged to be Principal of Cliff. However, his most significant academic contribution is, in my view, his assessment of Wesley's doctrine of Christian Perfection entitled, 'Love Excluding Sin'.[61] The book is clarity itself, but the most compelling thing is that the author lived it out. 'We shall not see here on earth the like of Arthur Wood again, but his influence lives on both in his writings, and we are grateful for that legacy, and in our memories. We thank God for his life and witness.'[62]

Dr William R. Davies MA,BD 1983-1994

orn in Blackpool on 31 May 1932, William (Bill to all his many friends) Davies spent the first nineteen years of his life there and from childhood attended Lindale Methodist Church which was his spiritual home and from which he offered as a candidate for the Methodist ministry. He was educated at the Blackpool Grammar School and later at Hartley Victoria Theological College and the University of Manchester.

In 1949 he met Barbara at a Local Preachers' Class and they were married in 1955. They have two children, Michael and Helen, both of whom are married and have growing families.

Bill's first five years of ministry were on a large council overspill estate at Langley near Middleton in North Manchester. Beginning with two transferred members and an existing Sunday School of some 20-30 children, the work grew until there was an average attendance at worship of over 100, a Sunday School of over 300 and a Youth Club of some 80-100 members. A new church was built and opened in 1959.

Then came the ministry in Thornton where he inherited the churches at Fleetwood Road and Wignall. These continued to grow and five happy years were spent in the Fleetwood Circuit with many lovely memories. The churches were already well-filled on a Sunday, much due to the successful ministry of John Tudor, Bill's

predecessor, and on special occasions were packed to overflowing. Perhaps the main features of that period were the development of the mid-week fellowship and the Young Wives' groups. The fact that Bill and Barbara chose to return in their retirement to Thornton speaks for itself. Towards the end of that period Bill was awarded a PhD, in 1965, for a thesis on 'Fletcher of Madeley as Theologian'.

After this came a brief but happy one-year ministry amongst the warm-hearted folk of Stockton-on-Tees at Brunswick, a town centre church, and Newtown, a suburban church. Then Bill was appointed to Padgate College of Higher Education, a teacher-training college in Warrington where he served for thirteen years as Senior Lecturer in Religious Studies, teaching on the Certificate, BEd and PGCE courses. He was a College counsellor and introduced and developed pioneer courses in pastoral care and counselling. For many years he served on the Connexional Faith and Order Committee. At the same time he was a Sector Methodist minister in the Warrington Circuit, preaching regularly, but without pastoral charge. This period was for Bill and Barbara a time of spiritual renewal. This was especially through the influence of the charismatic movement.

Returning to the Stations in 1979, Bill became Superintendent Minister of Bradford Methodist Mission. This was a demanding job. Despite a very healthy congregation for a Central Hall, with some

544

wonderful people sharing in the ministry there, the work was demanding because of continuing building problems caused by dry-rot (someone said it had begun in the pulpit!). Bill had intended to stay at the Eastbrook Hall for a fairly long ministry, but after only four years, following a unanimous invitation from the Cliff College Committee backed by the Home Mission Division, he accepted the appointment of Principal at Cliff College and stayed there from 1983 until his retirement in 1994.

The reasoned statement for his appointment as Principal concluded with a sentence, with which I wholeheartedly agree: 'It is our firm conviction that Dr William Davies ... respected and trusted scholar, teacher, communicator, counsellor, pastor, advocate, leader, colleague, preacher, evangelist, Methodist Minister ... is the one who will best serve Christ and His Church as the next Principal of Cliff College.'[63]

Whilst at Cliff College, he presided over many changes, not least changing the name of the 'Anniversary' to Celebration Weekend in 1985. He raised the finance for the building of the Eagles and Broadbelt buildings, the refurbishment of Cliff Hall, and the development of the Marquee site. The Charismatic movement caused a growth of people seeking training for ministry and in the years 1986-1991 student numbers reached the high eighties. The largest number of full-time students in the College's history was in the years 1990-92 when there were ninety students. Dr Davies or

'Doc', as he was affectionately called by the students, could teach many subjects at short notice, though he taught Christian Doctrine, Church History and Preaching for most of his eleven years. To the great acclaim of the College and Cliff supporters he served as President of the Methodist Conference (1987-88) and Moderator of the Free Church Federal Council for England and Wales (1991-92). He still continues Connexional work by serving on a couple of Connexional committees, but this is now reducing.

Writing was and remains part of his ministry. He served as one of the editors of *Dunamis*, a magazine with a circulation of about 6,500 sharing teaching and testimony about charismatic renewal among the Methodist people, from 1973-1994. There were also numerous articles which appreared in a variety of papers, magazines and journals. This written work included three books: *Gathered into One*,[64] *Rocking the Boat*,[65] and *Spirit Without Measure*[66].

Since retiring in 1994 his preaching, speaking and teaching ministry has continued in Sunday Worship, Bible Weeks, Celebrations, Study Days and Conferences, most of which have taken him outside the Fleetwood Circuit. This ministry has been mainly in this country, not infrequently in Ireland, and very occasionally overseas. Because energy levels are not what they once were, this load is being gradually reduced.

Personal Reflections

This mission history is in many ways a personal journey. My whole life seems to have been affected in many ways by Cliff College. A remarkable Cliff Mission took place at Crosland Hill, Huddersfield when I was very young and from that time our family attended Cliff at least annually at the Anniversary. After schooling I became a student at Cliff College in 1967, fully intending at that time to follow a career in Housing Welfare. However, Howard Belben, then the Principal, suggested I should consider the ordained ministry. The rest, you might say, is history! Cliff College taught me a love of evangelism and a desire to minister. Howard Belben's love of scholarship, evangelism and life impressed me greatly. Following the year at Cliff I worked in a factory in Huddersfield as an 'unskilled machinist' which taught me much about life, and then went on to Richmond College, in south-west London, for ministerial training and the opportunity to think widely and deeply about the mission and ministry of the Church. The Principal, the Rev A. Raymond George, made a deep impression upon me during the four years of training. He showed me a breadth of churchmanship and a love of learning. After Richmond closed, the fourth year was at Wesley College, Bristol with Raymond George as my tutor. In Probationers studies I became a part-time student at Heythrop College with Dr Marcus Ward as tutor in New Testament studies.

In 1973 I was appointed to the S.E. London Mission working in Deptford and Greenwich and was the minister of St Mark's Greenwich, a URC Methodist Church. It was there I met Rosie, during her training at Goldsmith's College to be a Primary School Teacher. St. Mark's was a remarkable church, full of wonderful London characters, remarkably able people in the arts, health, teaching, civil service etc. It was an excellent appointment to commence ministry. We married in the Easter of 1975 and in 1976 moved to Addiscombe, Croydon to a vigorous church and ecumenical situation. Early in this appointment and because of my previous experience of ministering in church and community at Greenwich, I took the opportunity of training offered by AVEC, an agency working in Church and Community Development. Here I met the Rev Dr George Lovell who has been a mentor and friend since that time. This led to many kinds of different enterprises in the community and through the church, all the time seeking to marry both community care and action with mission and evangelism. That in turn led me to engage in a research project through the University of Durham, leading to an MA in Theology.[67]

Curiously, though it was not planned in that way, the research was ideal preparation for a new post at Cliff College. We had kept in touch with Cliff through this time and in 1980 and 1981 we came to the Derwent Week leading seminars on All Age Worship. When the post of Director of Evangelism for the Methodist Church was first talked about Rosie and I knew we should wait to apply. I came to Cliff College in 1983, though technically the appointment began in 1984. That was because we had arranged to leave Croydon that year

and our successor was already chosen. In effect I began work in the post early, and was able to engage in research and preparation for this newly formed post. It focussed on leading a team of Evangelists at Cliff, teaching present and new courses and developing policy, with others, for the church strategy in mission and evangelism. Our children Beth, Lydia and Tom were all born at Cliff, and though we lived in four separate houses, Cliff was our home for twenty-one years.

In 1994 I was appointed as the Principal of Cliff, an enormous privilege, and have seen through these years considerable development and change in the College. The initial conversations with the University of Sheffield began in April 1991 with the validating process taking place in the autumn of 1993. The first validated courses were offered from September 1994. It was immediately clear that the College could develop new programmes of study, and over the last ten years we moved from two courses to fourteen, and from seventy students to dealing with 250 students registered with the College (2003/4), many of them part-time. The College offers an Open Learning Centre, and though the numbers vary through the year about 200 are enrolled. In addition to all this we have formed an International Learning Centre which facilitates a course for one hundred students in Sierra Leone. It remains our hope that this course may be taken up in many other different countries.

Leaving a place which has given so much to me and my family is not easy, but there is a sense of this being the right time, leaving a platform upon which others can build. In the summer of 2004 we moved to Winchester to new beginnings. I have taken up the responsibility of the Superintendent of the Winchester Circuit and minister of the city centre United Church, both Methodist and United Reformed. We are beginning to settle into a new life in Winchester with some interesting possibilities in a lovely city.

The next few years at the College will form new chapters in a book yet to be written, but I have a confident hope about the future of the College under the direction and leadership of the Rev Dr Martyn Atkins. Martyn has already made a significant impact upon the academic work of the College being responsible since 1996 for the growing Postgraduate School which now has an International and Ecumenical reputation. He is widely acknowledged as one of the leading Missiologists of this country and with his leadership I pray and believe the College will go from strength to strength.

---

1 *Minutes* of the Cliff College Committee, 20 June 1933.
2 *Minutes* of the Cliff College Committee, 20 June 1933.
3 *Minutes* of the Cliff College Committee, 20 June 1933.
4 *Minutes* of the Cliff College Committee, 8 October 1934.
5 *The Christian,* 26 February 1954.
6 Richard Baggaley, *One hundred years of Methodism in Calver* (Calver Methodist Church, 1960), p.8.
7 Maldwyn Edwards, *Lilian Davis Broadbelt, A Memoir* (privately published from Cliff College).

cont.

8 *Minutes* of the Cliff College Committee, 1 October 1936.
9 *Minutes* of the Cliff College Committee, 1 October 1937.
10 *Minutes* of the Cliff College Committee, 30 September 1938.
11 W.M. Stopard and D.M. Taylor (eds), *Calver Record, Sheffield High School during Evacuation 1939 - 1944.* No date or publishing details. Written by two staff members, it reads as though published shortly after the war: cf. p.6.
12 Broadbelt, Letter 22 November 1940 explains his predicament. The first ones are dated 26 January, 24 February, 27 April, 19 July, as well as 22 November in 1940. In fact one is dated 2 January 1940 but it refers to the Christmas after the bombing of Sheffield which took place in December 1940 and therefore is probably 2 January 1941 with the date an administrative error. There are a number of slight errors in the minutes at this time suggesting careless typing. The other letters are dated 22 May, 22 August and 18 December 1941; 14 July and 25 November1942.
13 Broadbelt, letter 26 January 1940.
14 *Calver Record,* p.1.
15 *Calver Record,* p.1. The College Library was also the air-raid shelter being protected by the hillside. The hall was of course the newly built Cliff Hall.
16 *Calver Record,* p.3.
17 *Calver Record,* p.4.
18 *Calver Record,* p.5.
19 *Calver Record,* p.4.
20 Broadbelt, *Letter,* 24 February 1940.
21 Broadbelt, *Letter,* 2 January 1941.
22 Braodbelt, *Letter,* 2 January 1941.
23 *Calver Record,* p.8.
24 Broadbelt, *Letter,* 2 January 1941.
25 Broadbelt, *Letter,* 22 May 1941.
26 Broadbelt, *Letter,* 22 November 1940. In fact the *Calver Record,* indicates there were 270 girls altogether.
27 Broadbelt, *Letter,* 22 August 1941.
28 *Calver Record,* p.14.
29 *Calver Record,* p.14.
30 Letter from Anne Greaves, 8 December 2003, who was a pupil of the Sheffield High School, resident at Cliff from September 1939. Joe Brice preached from Hosea, 'How can I give thee up, O Ephraim?' and the *Joyful news* reports, 'There were several seekers after the appeal, and we parted praising God for His seal on a glorious day', 16 May 1940.
31 Ibid.
32 Ibid.
33 Broadbelt, *Letter,* 26 January 1940.
34 *Minutes* of the Cliff College Committee, 25 April 1941.
35 Broadbelt, *Letter,* 18 December 1941.
36 Broadbelt, *Letter,* 18 December 1941.
37 Broadbelt, *Letter,* 25 November 1942.
38 *Calver Record,* p.30.

cont.

39 *Minutes* of the Cliff College Committee, 12 May 1947.
40 Ibid.
41 *Minutes* of the Cliff College Committee, 18 May 1948. He served 44 years in the ministry even so.
42 *Minutes* of the Cliff College Committee, 22 September 1948.
43 *Minutes* of the Cliff College Executive Committee, 22 October 1951.
44 Ibid.
45 No committee was called between May 1923 and June 1926 during which period Chadwick built the Library Wing and Broadbelt had built the three Cottages in advance of the Committee in October 1934 and he had raised the money to build Lindum.
46 J.E. Eagles, *Notes of Lectures on Christian Theology* (Calver: Cliff College, 1950), both interleaved and ordinary, and a further third edition entitled *A Study Outline on Christian Theology,* containing much the same material, was published in 1959.
47 Amos Cresswell, *The Story of Cliff* (Calver: Joyful News Book Room, 1965), p.31.
48 James H. Goad, in a letter to Howard Belben, 22 November 1973.
49 W. James White, Letter to Howard Belpben, 7 December 1975.
50 Cresswell, *The story of Cliff,* p.34.
51 *Minutes* of the Cliff College Committee, 19 September 1957.
52 *Minutes* of the Cliff College Committee, 26 October 1961.
53 'Medical Comments on the Cliff College Situation', undated and anonymous.
54 Ibid.
55 Tom Meadley, *Top Level Talks: the Christian Summit Meeting* (London: Epworth Press, 1969).
56 Michael Pederson in a letter to the Rev Edward Sainsbury (secretary of the Cliff College Fellowship), 16 May 1968, Archives.
57 *Letter,* to Steven Wild, 27 April 1983, Archives.
58 *Letter,* to Steven Wild, 27 April 1983, Archives.
59 *Letter* to William Sangster, Archives.
60 Paul Taylor and Howard Mellor (eds), *Travelling Man* (Calver: Cliff College Publishing, 1994), p.28.
61 The text of this booklet is included in the book *Travelling Man.*
62 The Rev Dr William Davies, taken from the sermon preached at Arthur's funeral 5 February 1993.
63 *Agenda of the Methodist Conference,* 1982, p.109.
64 W.R. Davies (London: Faith Press, 1975).
65 W.R. Davies (London: Marshall Pickering, 1986).
66 W.R. Davies (London: Darton Longman and Todd, 1996).
67 A Theological Examination of the Non-Directive Approach to Church and Community Development with a Special Reference to the Nature of Evangelism. University of Durham, 1990.

Staff of Cliff College

1904 March - August

Rev Thomas Cook — *Principal*
Mr C.E. Oxenborow Rush, BA
Tutor in General Subjects
Rev Samuel Chadwick — *(p/t) Lecturer*
on the study of the English Bible
Mr William Jones Bsc — *asst in secular subs*
Rev J. Clapham Greaves — *(p/t) of*
Manchester giving lectures in theology
Miss Campion — *Matron*

1904

Rev Thomas Cook — *Principal*
Mr C.E. Oxenborow Rush, BA — *Tutor*
Rev Samuel Chadwick — *(p/t) Lecturer*
Rev Alfred Bingham — *Tutor in Homiletics*
Rev John Grimshaw — *Tutor in Theology*
Rev Marmaduke Riggall — *Tutor in Theology*
Mr Peter Williams, BA — *Assistant Tutor*
Mr John J. Studley — *Student-Tutor*
Miss Lilian Hovey — *Lecturer on Elocution*
Mr S. W. Thompsom BSc
Miss Campion — *Matron*

During the session 1906-7 the College was closed to students due to building work.

1907

Rev Thomas Cook — *Principal*
Rev Samuel Chadwick — *Tutor on the*
study of the English Bible and Homiletics
Rev John Grimshaw — *Tutor in Theology*
Mr C.E. Oxenborow Rush, BA — *Tutor*
Mr R.H. Hothersall, BA — *Assistant Tutor*
Mr E.M. Morley Bright — *Student-Tutor*
Miss Lilian Hovey — *Lecturer on Elocution*
Miss A. Douglas — *Eng Lit & Biblical Geog*
Miss Campion — *Matron*

1908

Rev Thomas Cook — *Principal*
Rev Samuel Chadwick — *Tutor*
Mr C.E. Oxenborow Rush, BA — *Tutor*
Rev John Grimshaw — *Tutor in Theology*
Mr E.M. Morley Bright — *Assistant Tutor*
Mr R.F. Priestley — *Student-Tutor*
Miss Lilian Hovey — *Lecturer on Elocution*
Miss A. Douglas — *As above*
Miss Campion — *Matron*

1909

Rev Thomas Cook — *Principal.*
Rev Samuel Chadwick — *Tutor*
Rev John Grimshaw — *Tutor in Theology*
Mr C.E. Oxenborow Rush, BA — *Tutor*
Mr R.F. Priestley — *Assistant Tutor*
Mr G.F. Lenton — *Student-Tutor*
Miss Lilian Hovey — *Lecturer on Elocution*
Miss A. Douglas — *As above*
Miss Campion — *Matron*

1910

Rev Thomas Cook — *Principal*
Rev Samuel Chadwick — *Tutor*
Rev John Grimshaw — *Tutor in Theology*
Rev W. Fiddian Moulton, MA
Church History, & c
Mr C.E. Oxenborow Rush, BA — *Tutor*
Mr L.S.S. Saunders — *Assistant Tutor*
Miss Lilian Hovey — *Lecturer on Elocution*
Miss A. Douglas — *As above*
Miss Campion — *Matron*

1911

Rev Thomas Cook — *Principal*
Rev Samuel Chadwick — *Tutor*
Rev W. Fiddian Moulton, MA
New Testament Literature & Ch History
Mr C.E. Oxenborow Rush, BA — *Tutor*
Mr L.S.S. Saunders — *Assistant Tutor*
Miss Lilian Hovey — *Lecturer on Elocution.*
Miss A. Douglas — *As above*
Miss Campion — *Matron*

1912

Rev Thomas Cook — *Principal (d Oct)*
Rev Samuel Chadwick
Appointed acting Principal Oct 1912
Rev Joseph Shrimpton — *Theol & Homiletics*
Rev W. Fiddian Moulton, MA — *Tutor*
Rev Thomas Kirkup — *Tutor in Theology*
Mr C.E. Oxenborow Rush, BA — *Tutor*
Mr K.D. East, BA — *Assistant Tutor*
Miss Lilian Hovey — *Lecturer on Elocution*

1913

Rev Samuel Chadwick — *Principal*
Rev W. Fiddian Moulton, MA — *Tutor*
Rev Thomas Kirkup. — *Tutor*

Mr C.E. Oxenborow Rush, BA   *Tutor*
Mr K.D. East, BA   *Tutor*
Miss Lilian Hovey   *Elocution*
Miss A. Douglas   *General superintendent*

1914
Rev Samuel Chadwick   *Principal*
Rev W. Fiddian Moulton, MA   *Tutor*
Rev Thomas Kirkup.   *Tutor*
Mr C.E. Oxenborow Rush, BA   *Tutor*
Mr W.N. Warren   *Tutor*
Miss Lilian Hovey   *Elocution*
Miss A. Douglas   *General superintendent*

1915 - 1918 the College was closed.

1919 (College reopened in the October)
Rev Samuel Chadwick   *Principal*
Rev W. Fiddian Moulton, MA   *Tutor*
Mr C.E. Oxenborow Rush, BA   *Tutor*
Rev Norman G Dunning BA   *Tutor*
Miss A. Douglas   *General superintendent*

1920 As 1919
1921 As 1919
1922 As 1919
1923
Rev Samuel Chadwick   *Principal*
Rev W. Fiddian Moulton, MA   *Tutor*
Mr C.E. Oxenborow Rush, BA   *Tutor*
    Rush left for Africa on 3 March 1924
Rev Norman Dunning MA, LLB   *Tutor*
Mr F. Noel Palmer   *Tutor*
Miss A. Douglas   *General superintendent*

1924
Rev Samuel Chadwick   *Principal*
Rev W. Fiddian Moulton, MA   *Tutor*
Mr D.W. Lambert, MA   *Tutor*
Mr W. Cameron Young   *Junior Tutor*
The Rev Dr J.G. Bickerton
    Visiting lecturer from Philadelphia
Miss A. Douglas   *General Superintendent*

1925
Rev Samuel Chadwick   *Principal*
Rev W. Fiddian Moulton, MA   *Tutor*
Mr D.W. Lambert, MA   *Tutor*
Mr W. Cameron Young   *Junior Tutor*
Miss A. Douglas   *General superintendent*

1926 As 1924

1927
Rev Samuel Chadwick   *Principal*
Rev W. Fiddian Moulton, MA   *Tutor*
    (ill for most of the year)
Mr D.W. Lambert, MA   *Tutor*
Rev J.I. Brice   *Tutor*
Mr R Hailwood   *Student Tutor*
Miss A Douglas *Biblical & English Literature*

1928
Rev Samuel Chadwick   *Principal*
Rev W. Fiddian Moulton, MA   *Tutor*
    (ill for most of the year)
Mr D.W. Lambert, MA   *Tutor*
Rev J.I. Brice   *Tutor*
Rev Norman Dunning MA, LLB   *Tutor*
Miss A Douglas *Biblical & English Literature*

1929
Rev Samuel Chadwick   *Principal*
Rev W. Fiddian Moulton, MA   *Tutor*
    died 17th Sept 1929
Mr D.W. Lambert, MA   *Tutor*
Rev J.I. Brice   *Tutor*
Rev Norman Dunning MA, LLB   *Tutor*
Miss A Douglas *Biblical & English Literature*

1930
As 1929 except Moulton

1931 Rev Samuel Chadwick   *Principal*
Mr D.W. Lambert MA   *Tutor*
Rev J.I. Brice   *Tutor*
Rev Norman Dunning MA, LLB   *Tutor*
Rev Dr J. G. Bickerton   *Visiting lecturer*
Miss A Douglas   *As above*

1932
Rev Samuel Chadwick (d. Oct)   *Principal*
Rev J.A. Broadbelt   *Principal*
    (appointed immediately, Oct 1932)
Mr D.W. Lambert MA   *Tutor*
Rev Norman Dunning MA, LLB   *Tutor*
Rev J Baines Atkinson   *Visiting Lecturer*
Miss Lilian Henderson   *Secretary*

1933 Rev J.A. Broadbelt   *Principal*
Rev Norman Dunning MA, LLB   *Tutor*
Mr D.W. Lambert MA   *Tutor*
Mr J. H. Stringer BA   *Tutor*
Rev J. Baines Atkinson BD *Visiting Lecturer*
Miss Lilian Henderson   *Secretary*

1934

Rev J.A. Broadbelt	*Principal*
Rev George Allen BA	}
Mr D.W. Lambert MA	} *Tutors*
Mr J. H. Stringer BA	}
Rev J. Baines Atkinson BD	*Visiting Lecturer*
Rev J.G. Bickerton DD	*Honorary Tutor*
Miss Lilian Henderson	*Secretary*
Miss Gladys Hall	*Matron*

1935 as 1934 plus

Mr H.H. Roberts	*Senior Evangelist*
Mr E.V. Haslock	*Secretary*
Sister Grace Crump	*Lady Superintendent*
Mrs Addyman	*Matron*

1936

Rev J.A. Broadbelt	*Principal*
Rev George Allen BA	}
Mr D.W. Lambert MA	} *Tutors*
Mr J.H. Stringer	}
Rev J. Baines Atkinson BD	*Visiting Lecturer*
Rev J.G. Bickerton DD	*Honorary Tutor*
Mr H.H. Roberts	*Hon. Senior Evangelist*
Mr Eric V. Haslock	*Secretary*
Mr J.A. Gray	*Assistant Secretary*
Miss Barraclough	*Lady Superintendent*
Sister Dulcie	*Matron*

1937 as 1936 minus Stringer

1938

Rev J.A. Broadbelt	*Principal*
Rev George Allen BA	}
Rev J.I. Brice MA	}*Tutors*
Mr D.W. Lambert MA	}
Mr T Fred Wilson	*Lay Tutor*
Rev J. Baines Atkinson BD	*Visiting Lecturer*
Rev J.G. Bickerton DD	*Honorary Tutor*
Mr H.H. Roberts	*Hon. Senior Evangelist*
Mr Eric V. Haslock	*Secretary*
Mr J.A. Gray	*Assistant Secretary*
Miss Barraclough	*Lady Superintendent*
Sister Dulcie	*Matron*

College reopened April 1945, Broadbelt and Allen undertook the teaching.

1945 Rev J.A. Broadbelt	*Principal*
Rev George Allen, BA	*Tutor*
Mr H. Clarke	*Assistant Tutor*
Rev J. Baines Atkinson BD	*Visiting Lecturer*

Mr Tom Butler	*Senior Evangelist*
Mr Eric V. Haslock	*Secretary*
Miss Catherine Murray	*Matron*

1946

Rev J.A. Broadbelt	*Principal*
Rev J.E. Eagles	} *Tutors*
Rev Maurice Barnett BA, BD	}
Rev J. Baines Atkinson BD	*Visiting Lecturer*
Mr Tom Butler	*Senior Evangelist*
Mr Eric V. Haslock	*Secretary*
Miss Catherine Murray	*Matron*

1947

Rev J.A. Broadbelt	*Principal*
Rev J.E. Eagles	} *Tutors*
Rev Howard Belben MA, BD	}
Rev J. Baines Atkinson BD	*Visiting Lecturer*
Mr Sainsbury	*Book Dept and Missions*
Mr Tom Butler	*Senior Evangelist*
Mr Eric V. Haslock	*Secretary*
Miss Catherine Murray	*Matron*

1948

Rev J.E. Eagles	*Principal*
Rev J. Baines Atkinson BD	} *Tutors*
Rev Howard Belben MA, BD	}
Rev J.A. Broadbelt	*p/t*
Mr Ted Budgell	*Book Steward*
Mr Tom Butler	*Senior Evangelist*
Mr Eric V. Haslock	*Secretary*
Mrs C Andrews (nee Murray)	*Matron*

1949 as 1948

1950 as 1948 minus Broadbelt

1951 as 1950 except

Miss Gwen Kettleborough	*Matron*

1952

Rev J.E. Eagles	*Principal*
Rev J. Baines Atkinson BD	} *Tutors*
Rev Howard Belben MA, BD	}
Rev Dr W.E. Farndale	*p/t*
Mr Ted Budgell	*Book Steward*
Mr Tom Butler	*Senior Evangelist*
Mr Eric V. Haslock	*Secretary*
Miss Gwen Kettleborough	*Matron*

1953

Rev J.E. Eagles	*Principal*
Rev J. Baines Atkinson BD	} *Tutors*
Rev Cyril H. Powell BA, MLitt	}

Rev Dr W.E. Farndale *p/t*
Mr Ted Budgell *Book Steward*
Mr Tom Butler *Senior Evangelist*
Mr Eric V. Haslock *Secretary*
Miss Gwen Kettleborough *Matron*
Mr George Chapman
Mr Syd Whymark *Gardener*

1954
Rev J.E. Eagles *Principal*
Rev J. Baines Atkinson BD } *Tutors*
Rev Cyril H. Powell BA, MLitt }
Rev Dr W.E. Farndale *p/t*
Miss Hallam p/t *English tuition*
Mr R Baggaley *Book Steward*
Mr Tom Butler *Senior Evangelist*
Mr Eric V. Haslock *Secretary*
Miss Gwen Kettleborough *Matron*
Mr Ted Budgell *Assistant Secretary*
Mr Syd Whymark *Gardener*

1955 as 1954

1956 Rev J.E. Eagles *Principal*
Rev J. Baines Atkinson, BD }
Rev Leonard E. Sutch } *Tutors*
Rev Dr W.E. Farndale }
Miss Hallam p/t *English tuition*
Mr R Baggaley *Book Steward*
Mr Tom Butler *Senior Evangelist*
Mr Eric V. Haslock *Secretary*
Miss Gwen Kettleborough *Matron*
Mr Ted Budgell *Assist Sec*
Mr Syd Whymark *Gardener*

1957
Rev Thomas D. Meadley BA,BD *Principal*
Rev Dr W.E. Farndale } *Tutors*
Rev Leonard E. Sutch }
Miss Hallam p/t *English tuition*
Mr R Baggaley *Book Steward*
Mr Ernest Steele *Senior Evangelist*
Mr Eric V. Haslock *Secretary*
Miss Gwen Kettleborough *Matron*
Mr Ted Budgell *Assist Sec*
Mr George Chapman *General Assistant*
Mr Syd Whymark *Gardener*

1958 as 1957 + Mr Frank Blackwell *Tutor*

1959
Rev Thomas Meadley *Principal*
Rev Leonard Sutch }
Rev David R. Hall MA } *Tutors*
Mr Frank Blackwell }
Dr W.E. Farndale *p/t*. During his illness
Howard A.G. Belben took the OT lectures,
travelling from Sheffield
Miss Hallam p/t *English tuition*
Mr R Baggaley *Book Steward*
Mr Ernest Steele *Senior Evangelist*
Mr Eric V. Haslock *Secretary*
Miss Gwen Kettleborough *Matron*
Miss June Hargreaves *Principal's Secretary*
Mr Ted Budgell *Estates Manager*
Mr George Chapman *General Assistant*
Mr Syd Whymark *Gardener*

1960 as 1959 except
Rev Howard A.G. Belben MA, BD
replaced Dr W.E. Farndale as *Tutor*

1961
Rev Thomas Meadley *Principal*
Rev Howard A.G. Belben MA,BD }
Rev Amos Cresswell MA } *Tutors*
Mr Frank Blackwell }
Miss Hallam p/t *English tuition*
Mr R Baggaley *Book Steward*
Mr Ernest Steele *Senior Evangelist*
Mr Eric V. Haslock *Secretary*
Miss Gwen Kettleborough *Matron*
Mr Ted Budgell *Estates Manager*
Mr George Chapman *General Assistant*
Mr Syd Whymark *Gardener*

1962 as 1961 plus
Mr Allan Stapleton *Finance Officer*
Miss Jean Hoyland *Matron*

1963 as 1962 except
Messrs Norman Smith & Malcolm Pears
Senior Evangelists
Miss Jean Digby *Matron*
Miss Margaret Bird *Principal's Sec*

1964 as 1963

1965
Rev Howard A.G. Belben MA,BD *Principal*
Rev Malcolm W. White BA, BSc }
Rev Amos Cresswell MA } *Tutors*

Mr Frank Blackwell   *Tutor*
Miss Hallam p/t   *English tuition*
Mr R Baggaley   *Book Steward*
Mr Norman Smith   *Senior Evangelist.*
Mr Allan Stapleton   *Finance Officer*
Mr Ted Budgell   *Estates Manager*
Mr George Chapman   *General Assistant*
Mr Syd Whymark   *Gardener*

1966 as 1965 except
Rev H.J. Royston Emms BSc, BD   *Tutor*
in place of Cresswell
Mr Denis Parkin   now   *Gardener*
Miss Margaret Bird   *Principal's Sec*

1967
Rev Howard Belben   *Principal*
Rev Malcolm White MA, BSc }
Rev H.J. Royston Emms BSc, BD } *Tutors*
Mr Frank Blackwell   }
Miss Hallam p/t   *English tuition*
Mr R Baggaley *Book Stwrd (died Nov 67)*
Mr Alec Passmore   *Senior Evangelist*
Mr Allan Stapleton   *Finance Officer*
Miss Gwen Kettleborough   *Matron*
Mr Ted Budgell   *Estates Manager*
Mr Roy Ingram   *Gardener*
Mr George Chapman   *General Assistant*
Miss Margaret Bird   *Principal's Sec*

1968
Rev Howard Belben   *Principal*
Rev Malcom White, MA, BSc   }
Rev H.J. Royston Emms BSc, BD} *Tutors*
Mr Frank Blackwell   }
Miss Mary Lambert MA   }
Miss Hallam p/t   *English tuition*
Miss Margaret Voaden   *Book Steward*
Alec Passmore   *Senior Evangelist*
Mr Allan Stapleton   *Finance Officer*
Mrs Budgell (nee Kettleborough)   *Matron*
Mr Ted Budgell   *Estates Manager*
Mr Roy Ingram   *Gardener*
Mr George Chapman   *General Assistant*
Miss Margaret Bird   *Principal's Sec*

1969
Rev Howard Belben   *Principal*
Rev Malcolm White MA, BSc   }
Rev David G. Sharp MA, BD   } *Tutors*
Mr Frank Blackwell   }

Miss Mary Lambert, MA   }
Miss Hallam p/t   *English tuition*
Mr Jack Henderson
    Administrative Officer (from April 1970)
Mrs Budgell   *Matron*
Mr George Chapman   *General Assistant*
Miss Margaret Voaden   *Book Steward*
Mr Alec Passmore   *Senior Evangelist*
Mr Ted Budgell   *Estates Manager*
Mr Roy Ingram   *Gardener*

1970
Rev Howard Belben   *Principal*
Rev Dr A Skevington Wood BA }
Rev David G. Sharp MA, BD   } *Tutors*
Miss Hallam p/t   *English tuition*
Mr Jack Henderson *Administrative Officer*
Mrs Budgell   *Matron*
Mr George Chapman   *General Assistant*
Miss Margaret Voaden   *Book Steward*
Mr Alec Passmore   *Senior Evangelist*
Mr Ted Budgell   *Estates Manager*
Mr Roy Ingram   *Gardener*

1971
Rev Howard Belben   *Principal*
Rev Dr A. Skevington Wood BA }
Rev David G. Sharp MA, BD   } *Tutors*
Mr Jack Henderson *Administrative Officer*
Mr George Chapman (rtd Dec)   *Gen Asst*
Miss Margaret Voaden   *Book Steward*
Mr Philip Bacon   *Senior Evangelist*
Mr Ted Budgell   *Estates Manager*
Mr Roy Ingram   *Gardener*

1972
Rev Howard Belben   *Principal*
Rev Dr A. Skevington Wood BA }
Rev David G. Sharp MA, BD   } *Tutors*
Dr Marjorie Sharp p/t   *English tuition*
Mr Jack Henderson *Administrative Officer*
Mr Frank Blackwell   *Book Steward*
Mr Philip Bacon   *Senior Evangelist*
Mr John Rands   *Maintenance Man*
Mr Roy Ingram   *Gardener*

1973 as 1972 except
Mrs Rands   *Book Steward*
Mr Sandy Roger   *Senior Evangelist*

1974 as 1973 plus
Mr Robert A. Mason BD, Cert Ed   *Tutor*
Mr Bert Andrew   *Conf Centre Warden*
1975
Rev Howard Belben   *Principal*
Rev Dr A. Skevington Wood BA }
Rev John B Job MA, BD   } *Tutors*
Mr Robert A. Mason BD, Cert Ed }
Mr Jack Henderson *Administrative Officer*
Mr Edward Wood   *Book Shop Manager*
Mr Sandy Roger   *Senior Evangelist*
Mr Albert Matthews   *Maintenance Man*
Mr Roy Ingram   *Gardener*
Mr Bert Andrew   *Conf Centre Warden*
1976 as 1975 except
Mr Paul Wells   *Senior Evangelist*
Mr Arad Forrest   *Gardener*
Mr Syd Bacon   *Conf Centre Warden*
Miss Alison Cowgill   *Secretary*
1977
Rev Dr A. Skevington Wood BA *Principal*
Rev John B. Job MA, BD   }
Rev Brian R. Hoare CertEd, BD   } *Tutors*
Mr Robert A. Mason BD, CertEd }
Mr Jack Henderson *Administrative Officer*
Mr Edward Wood   *Book Shop Manager*
Mr Paul Wells   *Senior Evangelist*
Mr Albert Matthews   *Maintenance Man*
Mr Arad Forrest   *Gardener*
Mr Syd Bacon *Conference Centre Warden*
Miss Alison Cowgill *Principal's Secretary*
1978 as 1977 except
Mr Tim Clarke   *Senior Evangelist*
Miss Edna Markwell   *Assist Matron*
1979 as 1978 except
Mr Desmond Curran   *Senior Evangelist*
Miss Edna Markwell   *Matron*
Mr Ken Morley   *Conference Centre Warden* (from January 1980)
1980 as 1979 except
Mr Stuart Crawford   *Senior Evangelist*
Mr Stuart Allen
1981 as 1980 except
Mr Andy Rich   *Senior Evangelist*
Miss Mary Pratt   *Assistant Matron*
Miss Kathy Lye   *Book Shop Mngr*

Mr Stuart Allen   *Gardener*
Mrs Charlotte Morley   *Conf Centre Warden*
1982 as 1981 except
Mr Ronald W. Abbott BSc, DipTh, CertEd
     replacing Mason as *Tutor*
Miss Hallam p/t   *English tuition*
Mr Maurice Houghton
     after Oct 1992 *Administrative Officer*
1983
Rev Dr William R. Davies MA, BD
     Principal
Rev John B. Job MA, BD   }
Rev Brian R. Hoare, Cert Ed, BD   } *Tutors*
Mr Ronald W. Abbott BSc, DipTh, }
Rev G. Howard Mellor BD
     Director of Evangelism
Mr Maurice Houghton   *Admin Officer*
Mr Paul Wakelam   *Senior Evangelist*
Miss Edna Markwell   *Matron*
Miss Mary Pratt   *Assistant Matron*
Mr Stuart Allen   *Gardener*
Miss Kathy Lye   *Bookshop Mngr* (to Dec)
Mr John Wilson   *Bookshop Manager* (from Feb 84)
Mr Albert Matthews   *Maintenance Officer*
Mrs Charlotte Morley *Conf Centre Warden*
Mr Brian Hall   *Assistant Warden*
Miss Alison Cowgill *Principal's Secretary* (until Easter 1984)
Mr Denis Haywood   *Janitor*
1984
Rev Dr William Davies   *Principal*
Rev Brian R. Hoare CertEd, BD   }
Mr Ronald W. Abbott   } *Tutor*
Rev Kathleen M. Bowe BEd, BA   }
Rev Howard Mellor BD   *Dir of Evanglm*
Mr Maurice Houghton   *Admin Officer*
Mr Paul Wakelam   *Senior Evangelist*
Miss Edna Markwell   *Matron*
Miss Glenda Holmes   *Assistant Matron*
Mr John Wilson   *Bookshop Manager*
Mr Albert Matthews   *Maintenance Officer*
Mr Stuart Allen   *Gardener*
Mrs Charlotte Morley   *Conf CentreWarden*
Mr Brian Hall *Conference Centre Warden* (from January 1985)
Miss Sharon Whittaker   *Principal's Sec*

Mr Denis Haywood   *Janitor*

1985 as 1984 except

Mr Philip Turner   *Assistant Warden*

1986 as 1985 except

Rev Dr Stephen Mosedale BSc, MA

  replaces Hoare as *Tutor*

Miss Jill Heeley   *Administrative Assistant*

Mr Alan Gillett   *Development Officer*

Mr Paul Trembling   *Janitor*

1987

Rev Dr William R. Davies MA,BD,

  Principal & Pres of Meth Conf

Mr Ronald W. Abbott   *Acting Principal*

Rev Kathleen M Bowe BEd, BA }

Rev Dr Stephen Mosedale BSc,MA} *Tutors*

Miss Mary Lambert MA   }

Rev Howard Mellor BD   *Dir of Evanglm*

Mr Maurice Houghton   *Admin Officer*

Miss Jill Heeley   *Administrative Assistant*

Mr Alan Gillett   *Development Officer*

Mr Paul Wakelam   *Senior Evangelist*

Miss Edna Markwell   *Matron*

Miss Glenda Holmes   *Assistant Matron*

Mr John Wilson   *Bookshop Manager*

Mr Albert Matthews   *Maintenance Officer*

  (died 4 October 1987)

Mr Vincent Cook   *Maintenance Officer*

Mr Stuart Allen   *Gardener*

Mr Philip Turner   *Conf Centre Warden*

Mr Roger Upfold   *Assistant Warden*

Miss Sharon Whittaker *Principal's Secretary*

Mr Paul Trembling   *Janitor*

1988 as 1987 except

Miss Kathryn Digby   *Admin Assistant*

Miss Elizabeth Timmins *Assistant Matron*

1989 as 1988 except

Miss Elizabeth Timmins   *Matron*

Miss Violet Bruce   *Assistant Matron*

Mr Ian Phipps   *Assistant Warden*

Miss Brenda Noble   *Chadwick's Bar*

Mr Denis Hayward   *Janitor*

1990

The Rev Dr William R. Davies, *Principal & Moderator of the Free Ch Federal Coun*

Mr Ronald W. Abbott   }

Rev Kathleen M. Bowe BEd, BA   } *Tutors*

Rev Dr Stephen Mosedale BSc, MA}

Rev Howard Mellor BD   *Dir of Evanglm*

Mr Maurice Houghton   *Admin Officer*

Miss Kathryn Digby   *Admin Assistant*

Mr Alan Gillett   *Development Officer*

  (until February 1991)

Miss Shirley Bradshaw MA *Snr Evangelist*

Miss Elizabeth Timmins   *Matron*

Miss Violet Bruce   *Assistant Matron*

Mr John Wilson   *Bookshop Manager*

Mr Vincent Cook   *Maintenance Officer*

Mr Stuart Allen   *Gardener*

Mr Philip Turner   *Conf Centre Warden*

Mr Ian Phipps   *Assistant Warden*

Miss Lea Pedrick   *Chadwick's Bar*

Miss Mary Culham   *Principal's Secretary*

Mr Paul Trembling   *Janitor*

1991 as 1990 except

Mr Clive Taylor *Advocacy and Resources*

1992 as 1991 except

Mr Richard J. Woolley BA   *Tutor*

  Replaces Abbott

Miss Susan Chambers *Bookshop Manager*

1993 as 1992 except

Rev Paul Ashby BSc, BA   *Tutor*

  replaces Bowe

Mr Alf Waite   *Senior Evangelist*

Mr Andrew Townsend   *Maintenance Asst*

Mrs Mary Goh (nee Culham)   *Prin's Sec*

1994

Rev Howard Mellor MA,BD   *Principal*

Rev Dr Stephen Mosedale BSc, MA}

Rev Paul Ashby BSc, BA   } *Tutors*

Mr Richard J. Woolley BA   }

Rev Philip Clarke BA,MA   *Dir of Evang*

Mr Maurice Houghton   *Admin Officer*

Miss Kathryn Digby   *Admin Assistant*

Mr Clive Taylor   *Advocacy & Resources*

Mr Alf Waite   *Senior Evangelist*

Miss Phyllis Walker   *Matron*

Miss Jennie Wallis   *Assistant Matron*

Miss Susan Chambers *Bookshop Manager*

Mr Vincent Cook   *Maintenance Officer*

Mr Andrew Townsend *Maintnce Assistant*

Mr Stuart Allen   *Gardener*

Mr Ian Phipps *Conference Centre Warden*

Mr Sean Worsley   *Assistant Warden*

Miss Lea Pedrick   *Chadwick's Bar*
Mrs Mary Goh   *Principal's Secretary*
Mr Denis Hayward   *Janitor*
1995 as 1994 except
Rev Peter Phillips DipTh, BA, MA
         replaces Mosedale as *Tutor*
Miss Helen Hollingsworth now *Admin Asst*
Mr Neil Offord   *Maintenance Assistant*
Mr Nick Cutts   *Asst Warden*
1996
Rev Howard Mellor   *Principal*
Mr Richard J. Woolley BA   }
Rev Paul Ashby BSc, BA   }*Tutors*
Rev Peter Phillips DipTh, BA, MA}
Rev Dr Martyn J. Atkins BA
      Director of Postgraduate Studies
Rev Philip Clarke BA,MA   *Dir of Evang*
Mr Maurice Houghton   *Admin Officer*
Miss Helen Hollingswort *Admin Assistant*
Mr Clive Taylor   *Advocacy and Resources*
Miss Elaine Jones   *Senior Evangelist*
Miss Phyllis Walker   *Matron*
Mrs Jennie Wallis   *Assistant Matron*
Mrs Eileen Bratt   *Bookshop Manager*
Mr Vincent Cook   *Maintenance Officer*
Mr Neil Offord   *Assistant Maintenance*
Mr Stuart Allen   *Gardener*
Mr Ian Phipps *Conference Centre Warden*
Mr Sean Worsley   *Assistant Warden*
Mr Nick Cutts   *Assistant Warden*

Mrs Mary Goh   *Principal's Secretary*
Mr Denis Hayward   *Janitor*
1997 as 1996 except
Mr Mark Chambers   *Senior Evangelist*
1998 as 1997 except
Mr Richard J. Woolley BA, MA   *Tutor*
      (left 31 December 1998)
Miss Helen Ashworth   *Assistant Matron*
Mr Kevin Waite   *Assistant Warden*
1999
Rev Howard Mellor   *Principal*
Rev Paul Ashby BSc, BA   }
Rev Peter Phillips DipTh,BA,MA }*Tutors*
Mrs Susanne Garnett MA, MEd   }
Rev Dr Martyn J. Atkins   *Dir Postgrad St*

Rev Philip Clarke BA,MA   *Dir of Evang*
Mr Maurice Houghton   *Admin Officer*
Miss Helen Hollingsworth *Admin Assistant*
Mr Clive Taylor   *Advocacy and Resources*
Mr Mark Chambers   *Senior Evangelist*
Miss Phyllis Walker   *Matron*
Miss Helen Ashworth   *Assistant Matron*
Mrs Eileen Bratt   *Bookshop Manager*
Mr Vincent Cook   *Maintenance Officer*
Mr Neil Offord   *Asst Maintenance Officer*
Mr Stuart Allen   *Gardener*
Mr Ian Phipps *Conference Centre Warden*
Mr Kevin Waite   *Assistant Warden*
Mrs Mary Goh   *Principal's Secretary*
Mr Denis Hayward   *Janitor*
2000 as 1999 except
Rev Richard Jackson BD, MA
         Postgraduate Tutor
Mr Nigel Brooke-Smith   *Finance Officer*
Miss Sue Peat   *Senior Evangelist*
Mrs Helen Osborne (nee Ashworth)
         Assistant Matron
Mr Vincent Cook
   Maintenance Officer (left October 2000)
Mr Andrew Barnett   *Maintenance Officer*
         (from Jan 2001)
Miss Helen Beech   *Conf Complex Asst*
2001
Rev Howard Mellor   *Principal*
Rev Peter Phillips DipTh,BA,MA   }
Rev Paul Ashby BSc, BA   }*Tutors*
Mrs Susanne Garnett MA,MEd   }
Mr Ian White, MA   }
Rev Dr Martyn J. Atkins   *Dir Postgrad St*
Rev Richard Jackson   *Postgraduate Tutor*
Rev Philip Clarke BA,MA   *Dir of Evang*
Mr Maurice Houghton   *Admin Officer*
Miss Helen Hollingsworth *Admin Assistant*
Mr Nigel Brooke-Smith   *Finance Officer*
Mr Clive Taylor   *Advocacy and Resources*
Miss Sue Peat   *Senior Evangelist*
Miss Phyllis Walker   *Matron*
Mrs Joyce Kimberlee   *Assistant Matron*
Mr Jim Shallow   *Bookshop Manager*
Mr Andrew Barnett   *Maintenance Officer*
Mr Neil Offord   *Asst Maintenance Officer*
Mr Stuart Allen   *Gardener*

Mr Ian Phipps *Conference Centre Warden*
Mr Kevin Waite *Asst Conference Warden*
Miss Helen Beech *Conf Complex Asst*
Mrs Tracey Harris *Principal's Secretary*
Mrs Theresa Phillips *Pg Admin*
Mr Denis Hayward *Janitor*

2002 as 2001 except
Rev Paul Dunstan BA, MA
Director of Evangelism
Mr John Steer LLB *Bursar*
Mrs Jan Thomas *Admin Assistant*
Mrs Wendy Addlington *Ug p/t Admin*

2003 as 2002 except
Rev Dr David Firth MA
replaces Ashby as *Tutor*
Ms Kate Wellington *Admin Assistant*
Mr Adam Hougham *Advocacy & Resources*
Miss Phyllis Walker (until Dec) *Matron*
Mr Chris Cole *Maintenance Assistant*
Mr Kevin Waite (until Oct) *Asst Warden*
Miss Helen Beech *Housekeeper*
Mrs Tracey Harris & Mrs Sue Smith
Principal's Secretary
Mr Denis Hayward (until Dec) *Janitor*
Mrs Bridget O'Shea *Asst Housekeeper*
Ms Lea Pedrick *Asst Housekeeper*
Miss Laura Gill *Asst Housekeeper*

2004
Rev Dr Martyn J Atkins BA *Principal*
Rev Dr Peter Phillips BA, MA }
Rev Dr David Firth MA } *Tutors*
Mr Ian White MA }
Rev Dr Philip Meadows BSc, MPhil,
Director of Postgraduate Studies
Rev Richard Jackson BD,MA *Pg Tutor*
Rev Steven Wild MA *Dir of Evangelism*
Mr John Steer LLB *Bursar*
Mr Nigel Brooke-Smith *Finance Officer*
Mr Adam Hougham *Advocacy & Resources*
Mrs Louise Mannheim *Librarian*
Miss Sue Peat *Senior Evangelist*
Mr John Hogarth *Bkshop & Recptn Mngr*
Mrs Debra Chalmers-Brown *Reception*
Mr Andrew Barnett *Maintenance Officer*
Mr Neil Offord *Asst Maintenance Officer*
Mr Chris Cole *Maintenance Assistant*
Mr Stuart Allen *Gardener*
Mr Ian Phipps *Conference Centre Mngr*
Mrs Tracey Harris & Mrs Sue Smith
Principal's Secretary
Mrs Theresa Phillips *Pg Admin*
Mrs Wendy Addlington *Ug p/t Admin*
Miss Helen Beech *Housekeeper*
Mrs Bridget O'Shea *Asst Housekeeper*
Ms Lea Pedrick *Asst Housekeeper*
Miss Emily Allen *Asst Housekeeper*

Some of the staff appointments are difficult to trace from the College records. I apologise unreservedly for any omissions and errors. The names of many staff in the early period of the College, such as gardeners, kitchen staff and maids, are simply not recorded. If you know of appointments made which are not recorded then please do send a letter to me addressed to the College. In more recent years there have been many temporary staff helping in the conference centres at busy times, and of course volunteers.

Of those who have worked part-time over a consistent period the following people are particularly worthy of note:

- Mrs Jackie Harvey, Secretary to Jack Henderson and correspondent secretary when Bill Davies was President.

- Joyce Hoare as part-time secretary to both Jack Henderson and Maurice Houghton.
- Maureen Houghton as a part-time Accounts Clerk since 1983.
- Gill Llewellyn who for 18 years was a part-time secretary first of all in the admin office and then as Secretary for the Director of Evangelism. Gill then for some further years continued as Minute Secretary for the Committee.